NATIONAL GEOGRAPHIC
Reach

Language • Literacy • Content

Program Authors

Nancy Frey

Lada Kratky

Nonie K. Lesaux

Sylvia Linan-Thompson

Deborah J. Short

Jennifer D. Turner

NATIONAL GEOGRAPHIC LEARNING | CENGAGE Learning

Literature Reviewers

Carmen Agra Deedy, Grace Lin, Jonda C. McNair, Anastasia Suen

Grade 6 Teacher Reviewers

Terrie Armstrong
Bilingual/ESL Program Team Leader
Houston Independent School District
Houston, TX

Irma Bravo Lawrence
*Director II, District and English Learner
Support Services*
Stanislaus County Office of Education
Turlock, CA

Julie Folkert
Language Arts Coordinator
Farmington Public Schools
Farmingto, MI

Norma Godina-Silva, Ph. D
*Bilingual Education/ESL/
Title III Consultant*
ESL-BilingualResources.com
El Paso, TX

Keely Krueger
Director of Bilingual Education
Woodstock Community Unit School 200
Woodstock, IL

Myra Junyk
Literacy Consultant
Toronto, ON, Canada

Lore Levene
Coordinator of Language Arts,
NBCTCommunity Consolidated School
District 59
Mt. Prospect, IL

Estee Lopez
*Professor of Literacy Education
and ELL Specialist*
College of New Rochelle
New Rochelle, NY

Christine Kay Williams
ESOL Teacher
Baltimore County Public Schools
Baltimore, MD

Acknowledgments
Grateful acknowledgment is given to the authors,
artists, photographers, museums, publishers, and
agents for permission to reprint copyrighted material.
Every effort has been made to secure the appropriate
permission. If any omissions have been made or if
corrections are required, please contact the Publisher.

Illustrator Credits:
Front Cover: Joel Sotelo

Acknowledgments and credits continue on page 665.

For product information and technology assistance, contact us at
Customer & Sales Support, 888-915-3276

For permission to use material from this text or product, submit
all requests online at **www.cengage.com/permissions**
Further permissions questions can be emailed to
permissionrequest@cengage.com

National Geographic Learning | Cengage Learning
1 Lower Ragsdale Drive
Building 1, Suite 200
Monterey, CA 93940

Cengage Learning is a leading provider of customized learning solutions
with office locations around the globe, including Singapore, the United
Kingdom, Australia, Mexico, Brazil, and Japan. Locate your local office at
www.cengage.com/global.

Cengage Learning products are represented in Canada by Nelson Education, Ltd.

Visit National Geographic Learning online at **NGL.Cengage.com**
Visit our corporate website at **www.cengage.com**

Printed in the USA.
RR Donnelley, Willard, OH, USA

ISBN: 978-13051-13602

Printed in the United States of America
16 17 18 19 20 21 22 23
13 12 11 10 9 8 7 6 5 4 3 2

Contents at a Glance

Table of Contents

The Power of Choice

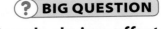
How do choices affect who you are?

SOCIAL STUDIES
▸ Society and Choices
▸ Identity and Choices

Table of Contents

Survival

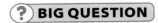
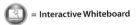

Unit 2

SCIENCE
▸ **Understanding Adaptations**
▸ **Survival**

Table of Contents

Digging Up the Past

(?) BIG QUESTION

How can we bring the past to life?

  = Comprehension Coach   = Interactive Whiteboard   = NGReach.com

SOCIAL STUDIES

- ▸ Ancient Egypt
- ▸ Ancient Perspectives

Table of Contents

Our Diverse Earth

? BIG QUESTION

Is diversity valuable?

 = Comprehension Coach   = Interactive Whiteboard = NGReach.com

x

Unit 4

SCIENCE
- ▸ Ecosystems
- ▸ Conservation

Table of Contents

A Time to Act

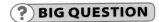 **BIG QUESTION**

Why do people take a stand?

Unit 5

SOCIAL STUDIES
▸ Standing Up for Civil Rights
▸ Making a Difference

Table of Contents

Food for Thought

(?) **BIG QUESTION**

How can we feed a growing planet?

 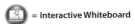
 = Comprehension Coach   = Interactive Whiteboard   = NGReach.com

SOCIAL STUDIES

▸ Agriculture Past and Present
▸ Rethinking Agriculture

Table of Contents

Ancient China

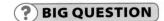 **BIG QUESTION**

Why should we study ancient cultures?

Unit 7

SOCIAL STUDIES
▸ Change and Continuity
▸ Diverse Lives

Table of Contents

Earth and Beyond

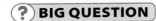? **BIG QUESTION**

How does studying Earth tell us about other planets?

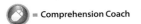 

Unit 8

SCIENCE
▸ Exploring Earth and Space
▸ Inspiring Exploration

Genres at a Glance

THE POWER OF CHOICE

BIG Question

How do choices affect who you are?

Unit at a Glance
▶ **Language**: Give Information, Ask and Answer Questions, Social Studies Words
▶ **Literacy**: Preview and Predict, Monitor
▶ **Content**: Choices

Unit
1

Share What You Know

❶ **Read** this quotation: "It is our choices . . . that show what we truly are, far more than our abilities." - J.K. Rowling

❷ **Think** about choices.

❸ **Discuss** how choices make a difference.

Build Background: Watch a video about making choices.
Ⓝ NGReach.com

Give Information

Listen to the information given in the poem. Then use
Language Frames to give information about lions.

The Hunt ((MP3))

The lion male is called king of the beasts,
but it's lion queens who perform great feats.
While lion males wait far, far away,
the females use darkness to stalk their prey.
They crouch in the dark, using grasses to hide.
Then they move as a team to attack from all sides.
They return with their meal—a prize from the fight.
Then they rest through the day . . . and wait for the night.

Social Studies Vocabulary

Key Words

capable

encounter

figure

reputation

resistance

Key Words

Study the photos and captions. Use **Key Words** and other words to talk about the choices some Maasai people in Kenya must make about lions.

◀ In Kenya, lions have a well-known **reputation** as fierce beasts. Their great strength and ability make them **capable** of killing many animals, including the cows in a herd. But lions are endangered and disappearing from the grasslands.

▶ Many Maasai people herd cows. Some of the herders think they should kill any lions they see or **encounter**. Others disagree and show **resistance** to that idea. They want to **figure** out a solution that will protect both their cows and the lions.

Talk Together

What problem do some of the Maasai people have with lions? How could the choices the Maasai make about the lions shape and affect their lives? Use **Language Frames** from page 4 and **Key Words** to discuss these questions and give information about the topic.

Main Idea

As you read about a topic, identify important details that the author repeats or explains. Then put the details together to help you figure out the **main idea**, or most important idea, of the text.

Look Into the Text

> Where I live in northern Kenya, the lion is a symbol of bravery and pride. Lions have a special presence. **If you kill a lion, you are respected by everyone.** Other warriors even make up songs about how brave you are. **So it is every warrior's dream to kill a lion at one point or another.** Growing up, . . . I'd never come face-to-face with a lion, ever.

"Both of these **details** from the text tell about killing lions."

Map and Talk

A main idea diagram can help you keep track of important details as you read. After you finish reading, use the details to determine the main idea of the entire selection.

Main Idea Diagram

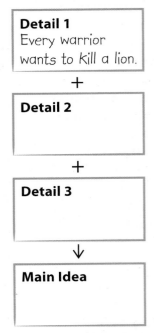

Detail 1
Every warrior wants to kill a lion.

+

Detail 2

+

Detail 3

↓

Main Idea

Talk Together

Interview a partner about an important choice he or she has made. Use a main idea diagram to keep track of the main idea and the supporting details.

Academic Vocabulary

More Key Words

Use these words to talk about *Facing the Lion* and "A Work in Progress."

assumption
(u-**sump**-shun) *noun*

An **assumption** is something that is believed to be true. When the dog wagged its tail, the boy made the **assumption** that the dog was friendly.

diverge
(du-**vurj**) *verb*

When two things or ideas **diverge**, they differ or move away from each other. This hiking trail has two paths that **diverge** in different directions.

exclude
(iks-**klüd**) *verb*

When you **exclude** something, you leave it out. I **exclude** nuts from the recipe because I am allergic to them.

optional
(**ahp**-shu-nul) *adjective*

Something that is **optional** is not needed or required. At our school, learning to play an instrument is an **optional** activity that you can choose.

potential
(pu-**ten**-shul) *noun*

Potential is the ability to change or improve in the future. The kids have **potential** to become great basketball players one day.

Talk Together

Work with a partner. Make a Word Web of examples for each **Key Word**.

weekend
sports

dessert

optional

extra credit
assignments

vacation
trips

Add words to My Vocabulary Notebook.
NGReach.com

7

Learn to Preview and Predict

Do you look through a book to see what it is like before you read it? If you do, you use the first step of a good reading strategy. Active readers **preview** a text before they read. As they read, they **predict**, or guess, what will happen next in the text.

How to Preview and Predict

 1. Preview the text. Read the title. Then look at the pictures, text, and graphic features. Skim the first few paragraphs. What do you think this text is about?

 2. As you read, use details to predict, or guess, what will come next in the text.

 3. Read on to confirm, or check, your prediction. As you learn more details, you may need to revise a prediction or make a new one.

> The text is about
> _____ .
>
> I read _____ , and so I
> predict that _____ .
>
> My prediction was
> _____ . Now, I
> predict _____ .

Here's how one student made a prediction.

Look Into the Text

In order to get them away from ticks, **the cattle had been taken down to the lowlands**. There's good grass there, though it's drier than in the high country, with some rocks here and there. There are no ticks, so you don't have to worry about the health of the cattle, but **the area is known for its fierce lions. They roam freely there, as if they own the land**.

"The text is about the **topic** of moving cattle."

"I read **details** about fierce lions in the area, and so I predict that lions will attack the cows. I will read on to check or change my prediction."

Previewing a text and making predictions about what will happen next can make your reading more fun. It can also help you better understand and remember what you read.

Language Frames

The text is about _____.

I read _____, and so
I predict that _____.

My prediction was _____.
Now, I predict _____.

Read the biographical profile and sample notes. Use
Language Frames to tell a partner about your predictions.

Profile

Living in
TWO WORLDS

Joseph Lemasolai Lekuton was born in a cow-dung hut in rural Kenya, which is a country in Africa. The son of often-moving cow herders, the **assumption** was that Lekuton also would grow up to be a cow herder and a Maasai warrior. Lekuton did not plan to attend school. In fact, no one in his village had gone to school. Schooling was **optional**, and fees **excluded** many children from getting an education.

When Lekuton was about six years old, his older brother was chosen to attend a school 50 miles away. His brother's **resistance** to go became an opportunity for Lekuton—he went instead. Lekuton lived at the school, but his personal path never **diverged** too far from his family's. When Lekuton came home for vacations, he herded cattle and took part in traditional tribal ceremonies. ◄

Lekuton showed great **potential** as a student. A sponsor made it possible for him to attend high school. Then Lekuton earned a scholarship to St. Lawrence University in New York.

After college, Lekuton taught social studies in Virginia. During that time, he earned a degree from Harvard University and published a book about his life, including exciting **encounters** with wildlife in Kenya. He developed a **reputation** as a talented, **capable** Kenyan writer. Lekuton also continued to **figure** out ways to be a part of his two different worlds—the new world where he lived and taught and the cow-herding Maasai life back in Kenya. ◄

Lekuton led groups of his students and their families to Kenya to help build water systems for schools and villages. He organized a program to give cows to families who needed help. Lekuton also raised money to provide educational opportunities for children. For his service to the country, Lekuton became the youngest recipient of Kenya's Order of the Grand Warrior in June of 2001. He is now a member of Kenya's Parliament, which is similar to Congress in the United States. ◄

The text is about a man named Joseph Lemasolai Lekuton.

I read the title, and so I predict that the text will tell about how he lives in two different places.

My prediction was correct because the profile tells how Lekuton lived at school and at home. Now, I predict that he will move to another city.

◄ = a good place to stop and make a prediction

9

Read an Autobiography

Genre

An **autobiography** is nonfiction. It is the story of a person's life, written by that person. The author of an autobiography shares about important life experiences from his or her unique viewpoint. *Facing the Lion* was written by Joseph Lekuton about his own life with help from another writer named Herman Viola.

Point of View

Point of view describes how a story is told. The author of an autobiography writes in the **first-person point of view** and uses words such as *I, me, we*, or *us* to tell the personal story.

> Everyone was in a trance. **I** felt that something inside **me** was about to burst, that **my** heart was about to come out. **I** was ready. Then **we** came face-to-face with the lions.

FROM **FACING THE LION**

by Joseph Lemasolai Lekuton
with Herman Viola

Comprehension Coach

▶ **Set a Purpose**
Learn about Lekuton's first
encounter with lions.

I'M GOING TO TELL YOU the lion story.

Where I live in northern Kenya, the lion is a symbol of bravery and pride. Lions have a special presence. If you kill a lion, you are respected by everyone. Other **warriors** even make up songs about how brave you are. So it is every warrior's dream to kill a lion **at one point or another**. Growing up, I'd had a lot of interaction with wild animals—elephants, rhinos, cape buffalo, hyenas. But at the time of this story—when I was about 14—I'd never **come face-to-face with** a lion, ever. I'd heard stories from all the young warriors who told me, "Wow, you know yesterday we chased this lion—" bragging about it. And I always said, **"Big deal."** What's the big deal about a lion? It's just an animal. If I can defend myself against elephants or rhinos, I thought, why not a lion?

I was just back from school for vacation. It was December, and there was enough rain. It was green and beautiful everywhere. The cows were giving plenty of milk. In order to get them away from ticks, the cattle had been taken down to the lowlands. There's good grass there, though it's drier than in the high country, with some rocks here and there. There are no ticks, so you don't have to worry about the health of the cattle, but the area is known for its fierce lions. They roam freely there, as if they own the land.

In Other Words
warriors brave fighters
at one point or another sometime
come face-to-face with seen; been close to
"Big deal." "That is not very special."

Giraffes, impalas,
zebras, and gazelles
near Lake Nakuru
National Park, Kenya

I spent two days in the village with my mom, then my brother Ngoliong came home to have his hair braided and asked me to go to the cattle camp along with an **elder** who was on his way there. I'd say the cattle camp was 18 to 24 miles away, depending on the route, through some rocky areas and a lot of shrubs. My spear was broken, so I left it at home. I carried a small stick and a small club. I wore my *nanga*, which is a red cloth, tied around my waist.

It took us all day to get there, but at sunset we were walking through the gap in the **acacia-branch fence** that surrounded our camp. There were several cattle camps scattered over a five-mile **radius**. At night we could see fires in the distance, so we knew that we were not alone. As soon as we got there my brother Lmatarion told us that two lions had been terrorizing the camps. But lions are smart. Like thieves, they go somewhere, they look, they take, but they don't go back to the same place again.

Well, that was our unlucky day. That evening when the cows got back from grazing, we had a lot of milk to drink, so we were well fed. We sat together around the fire and sang songs—songs about our girlfriends, bravery songs. We **swapped** stories, and I told stories about school. The others were always curious to understand school. There were four families in the camp, but most of the older warriors were back at the village seeing their girlfriends and getting their hair braided. So there were only three experienced warriors who could fight a lion, plus the one elder who had come down with me. The rest of us were younger.

We went to bed around 11:30 or 12. We all slept out under the stars in the cattle camp—no bed, just a **cowhide** spread on bare soil. And at night it gets cold in those desert areas. For a cover I used the *nanga* that I had worn during the day. The piece of cloth barely covered my body, and I kept trying to make it longer and pull it close around me, but it wouldn't stretch. I curled myself underneath it trying to stay warm.

Everything was silent. The sky was clear. There was no sign of clouds. The fire was just out. The stars were like millions of diamonds in the sky. One by one everybody fell asleep. Although I was tired, I was the last to sleep. I was so excited about taking the cows out the following morning.

In Other Words
elder older, important leader of the group
◄ **acacia-branch fence** fence made of branches
radius area
swapped shared; told
cowhide cow skin

Maasai men and boys watching their cattle

During the middle of the night, I woke to this huge sound—like rain, but not really like rain. I looked up. The starlight was gone, clouds were everywhere, and there was a drizzle falling. But that wasn't the sound. The sound was all of the cows starting to pee. All of them, in every direction. And that is the sign of a lion. A hyena doesn't make them do that. An elephant doesn't make them do that. A person doesn't. Only the lion. We knew right away that a lion was about to attack us.

The other warriors started making a lot of noise, and I got up with them, but I couldn't find my shoes. I'd taken them off before I went to sleep, and now it was pitch black. Some warriors, when they know there's danger, sleep with their shoes in their hands and their spears right next to them. But I couldn't find my shoes, and I didn't even have a spear. Then the lion made just one noise: *bhwuuuu!* One huge roar. We started running toward the noise. Right then we heard a cow making a **rasping, guttural** sound, and we knew that the lion had her by the throat.

Cows were everywhere. They ran into one another and into us, too. We could hear noises from all directions—people shouting, cows running—but we couldn't see a thing. My brother heard the lion right next to him and threw his spear. He missed the lion—and lucky for the rest of us, he missed us, too. Eventually, we began to get used to the darkness, but it was still difficult to tell a lion from a cow. My brother was the first to arrive where the cow had been killed.

The way we figured it was this: Two lions had attacked the camp. Lions are very intelligent. They had split up. One had stayed at the southern end of the camp where we were sleeping, while the other had gone to the northern end. The wind was blowing from south to north. The cows smelled the lion at the southern end and **stampeded** to the north—toward the other waiting lion.

When I asked my brother, "Hey, what's going on?" he said, "The lion killed Ngoneya." Ngoneya was my mother's favorite cow and Ngoneya's family was the best one in the herd. My mother depended on her to produce more milk than any other cow. She loved Ngoneya, really. At night she would get up to pet her.

I was very angry. I said, "I wish to see this lion right now. He's going to see a man he's never seen before."

16

Just as we were talking, a second death cry came from the other end of the camp. Again we ran, but as we got closer, I told everyone to stop. "He's going to kill all the cows!" I told my brother. And I think this is where school thinking comes in. I told him, "Look. If we keep on chasing this lion, he's going to kill more and more. So why don't we let him eat what he has now, and tomorrow morning we will go hunting for him."

My brother said, "Yes, that's a good idea," and it was agreed. For the first time I felt like I was part of the brotherhood of warriors. I had just made a decision I was proud of.

▶ **Before You Move On**

1. **Details** Ngoneya's death was a serious loss for Lekuton's family. Which details from the text support this idea?

2. **Make Inferences** How did attending school make Lekuton more **capable** of stopping the lions?

17

It was muddy, it was dark, we were in the middle of nowhere, and right then we had cows that were miles away. They had stampeded in every direction, and we could not protect them. So we came back to camp and made a big fire. I looked for my shoes and I found them. By that time I was bruised all over from the cows banging into me, and my legs were bloody from the scratches I got from the acacia thorns. I hurt all over.

We started talking about how we were going to hunt the lion the next day. I could tell my brother was worried and wanted to get me out of danger. He said, "Listen, you're fast, you can run. Run and tell the people at the other camps to come and help. We only have three real warriors here; the rest of you are younger."

"No way," I said. "Are you kidding me? I'm a warrior. I'm just as brave as you, and I'm not going anywhere." At this point, I hadn't actually seen the lion, and I absolutely refused to leave.

My brother said, "I'm going to ask you one more time, please go. Go get help. Go to the other camp and tell the warriors that we've found the two lions that have been terrorizing everyone, and we need to kill them today."

And I said, "No, I'm not going."

So he said, "Fine," and sent the youngest boy, who was only about eight.

When daylight came, I took the little boy's spear and walked out from the camp with the others. Barely 200 yards away were the two lions. One had its head right in the cow, eating from the inside. And one was just lying around: She was full. As we approached them, we sang a lion song: "We're going to get the lion, it's going to be a great day for all of us, all the warriors will be happy, we'll save all our cows."

As we got closer, the older man who was with us kept telling us to be careful. We should wait for help, he said. "This is dangerous. You have no idea what lions can do." But no one would listen to him.

The other guys were saying, "We can do it. Be brave, everyone." We were encouraging each other, **hyping ourselves up**.

My brother was so angry, so upset about our mother's favorite cow that he was crying. "You killed Ngoneya," he was saying. "You are going to **pay for it**."

Everyone was **in a trance**. I felt that something inside me was about to burst, that my heart was about to come out. I was ready. Then we came face-to-face with the lions. The female lion walked away, but the male stayed. We formed a little semicircle around the male, with our long spears raised. We didn't move. The lion had stopped eating and was now looking at us. It felt like he was looking right at me. He was big, really big. His tail was thumping the ground.

In Other Words
hyping ourselves up building up our courage
pay for it be punished
in a trance focused

He gave one loud roar to warn us. Everything shook. The ground where I was standing started to tremble. I could see right into his throat, that's how close we were. His mouth was huge and full of **gore from** the cow. I could count his teeth. His face and mane were red with blood. Blood was everywhere.

The lion slowly got up so he could show us his full presence. He roared again. The second roar almost broke my eardrums. The lion was now pacing up and down, walking in small circles. He was looking at our feet and then at our eyes. They say a lion can figure out who will be the first person to spear it.

I edged closer to my brother, being careful not to give any sign of lifting or throwing my spear, and I said, "Where's that other camp?"

My brother said to me, "Oh, you're going now?" He gave me a look—a look that seemed to say, You watch out because someone might think you are afraid.

But I said, "Just tell me where to go." He told me. I gave him my spear. "It will help you," I said, and then I **took off** in the direction of the other cattle camp. No warrior looked back to see where I was going. They were all concentrating on the lion.

As I ran toward the next camp, I saw that the little boy had done his job well. Warriors were coming, lots of them, chanting songs, asking our warriors to wait for them. The lion **stood his ground** until he saw so many men coming down, warriors in red clothes. It must have seemed to him that the whole hillside was red in color. The lion then started to look for a way out.

The warriors reasoned that the lion had eaten too much to run fast and that the muddy ground would slow him up. They thought they could run after him and kill him. They were wrong. As soon as they took their positions, the lion surged forward and took off running. The warriors were left behind. There was nothing they could do except pray that they would meet this lion again.

From that time on, I knew **the word in the village was** that I had run away from the lion. There was no way I could prevent it.

"You know the young Lekuton warrior?"

"Yeah."

"He was afraid of the lion."

In Other Words

gore from blood and parts of
took off ran
stood his ground was ready to fight
the word in the village was people were saying

My brother tried to support me, but in our society, once **word like that gets out**, that's it. So I knew that I'd have to prove myself, to prove that I'm not **a coward**. So from then on, every time I came home for vacation, I went to the cattle camp on my own. I'd get my spear, I'd get my shoes. Even if it was 30 miles from the village, I'd go on my own, through **thick and thin**, through the forest and deserts. When I got there I'd take the cattle out on my own. Always I hoped something would attack our cattle so I could protect them. ❖

In Other Words

word like that gets out people believe something about you

a coward someone who is afraid

thick and thin easy and difficult areas

▶ **Before You Move On**

1. **Confirm Prediction** How does the lion hunt affect Lekuton? Cite evidence to support your answer.

2. **Summarize** What **assumptions** does Lekuton's village make about him before and after this experience?

Think and Respond

Key Words

assumption	figure
capable	optional
diverge	potential
encounter	reputation
exclude	resistance

Talk About It 💬

1. *Facing the Lion* is an autobiography. How does Lekuton help you understand his experiences from his own viewpoint?

2. Imagine that you are Lekuton. Give information about the lions to the warriors in the other cattle camp based on facts and details from the autobiography.

3. Based on what you have read, do you think Lekuton is prepared or unprepared to face another lion at the end of the story?

4. What things does Lekuton value, or care about, the most in this selection? Cite evidence from the text to support your answer.

5. Does Lekuton deserve the **reputation** of being called a coward by his village? Support your judgment with evidence from the text.

6. Lekuton **encounters** real lions. Identify another challenge or danger that he describes in the selection. How does this compare to facing a lion?

Learn test-taking strategies and answer more questions.
🖉 NGReach.com

Write About It ✏️

Imagine you are Lekuton's brother. Write an autobiographical account that describes their **encounter** with the lions from his point of view. Use techniques such as pacing, dialogue, and descriptive words to write about the event. Include at least three **Key Words**, and include evidence and examples from the text.

> My brother Joseph spent many months each year at school, so many people in our village made the **assumption** that he did not care about our way of life.

Main Idea

Use a main idea diagram to record the important details of *Facing the Lion*. Then use the details to determine the main idea of the selection.

Main Idea Diagram

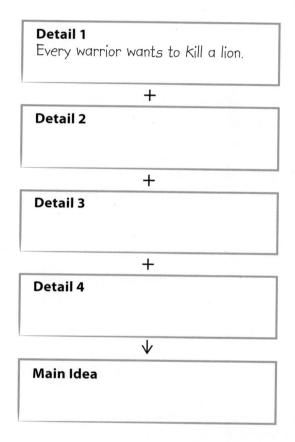

> **Detail 1**
> Every warrior wants to kill a lion.
>
> +
>
> **Detail 2**
>
> +
>
> **Detail 3**
>
> +
>
> **Detail 4**
>
> ↓
>
> **Main Idea**

Use your main idea diagram to retell the main idea of the autobiography to a partner. Explain how the details helped you figure out the main idea.

Fluency  Comprehension Coach

Use the Comprehension Coach to practice reading with intonation. Rate your reading.

 **Talk Together**

Think about the choices Lekuton had to make. How can difficult choices affect your life and **reputation**? Discuss your ideas with a partner. Include **Key Words** and evidence from the text.

Use a Dictionary

When you read a word that has multiple meanings, try using context clues, or the nearby words and phrases, to figure out the right meaning. You may also use a print or digital **dictionary** to find all of the word's meanings and parts of speech. Then decide which meaning makes the most sense in the text you read.

EXAMPLES

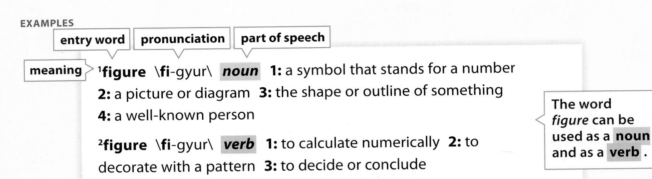

entry word | pronunciation | part of speech

meaning >

¹**figure** \fi-gyur\ *noun* **1:** a symbol that stands for a number **2:** a picture or diagram **3:** the shape or outline of something **4:** a well-known person

²**figure** \fi-gyur\ *verb* **1:** to calculate numerically **2:** to decorate with a pattern **3:** to decide or conclude

The word *figure* can be used as a **noun** and as a **verb**.

Which definition of *figure* above best describes a famous actor or singer?

Try It

Read the sentences. Use the dictionary entries to answer the questions.

The hunters follow the lions' trails until they diverge into two separate directions. Then the hunters figure out which path to follow.

1. **Which dictionary feature helps you understand how to say figure?**

   A pronunciation

   B part of speech

   C meaning

   D example sentence

2. **Which entry gives the best meaning of figure as it is used in the sentence?**

   A ¹**figure:** definition 1

   B ¹**figure:** definition 4

   C ²**figure:** definition 2

   D ²**figure:** definition 3

A Work in Progress

Connect Across Texts You read about Joseph Lekuton's choices. Now read about how Aimee Mullins's choices changed her life.

Genre A **speech** is a message about a specific topic that is spoken before an audience.

by Aimee Mullins
as told on *The Moth Radio Hour*

*Aimee Mullins has built a career as an athlete, model, actor, and **advocate for** women, sports, and the next generation of **prosthetics**. Mullins was born without fibular bones and had both of her legs **amputated** below the knee when she was an infant. She learned to walk on prosthetics, then to run— competing at national and international levels as a champion **sprinter**, setting world records at the 1996 Paralympics in Atlanta. In 1999, Aimee made her runway debut as a model in London. She's a passionate voice heralding a new kind of thinking about bodies and identities. Aimee also has received **accolades** for her work as an actor on stage and film.*

In Other Words
advocate for *person who supports*
prosthetics *artificial body parts*
amputated *removed*
sprinter *runner*
accolades *praise; positive comments*

▶ **Before You Move On**

1. **Predict** Preview the photos and text. What do you predict the speech will be about? Read on to confirm your prediction.

2. **Draw Conclusions** What issues does Mullins care about? What makes her an effective advocate for these issues?

When I was fourteen it was Easter Sunday, and I was gonna be wearing a dress that I had purchased with my own money—the first thing I ever bought that wasn't on sale. Momentous event; you never forget it. I'd had a **paper route** since I was twelve, and I went to The Limited, and I bought this dress that I thought was the height of sophistication—sleeveless safari dress, belted, hits at the knee.

Coming downstairs into the living room, I see my father waiting to take us to church. He takes one look at me, and he says, "That doesn't look right. Go upstairs and change."

I was like, "What? My super-classy dress? What are you talking about? It's the best thing I own."

He said, "No, you can see the knee joint when you walk. It doesn't look right. It's inappropriate to go out like that. Go change."

And I think something snapped in me. I refused to change. And it was the first time I **defied** my father. I refused to hide something about myself that was true, and I refused to be embarrassed about something so that other people could feel more comfortable.

I was **grounded** for that defiance.

So after church the extended family convenes at my grandmother's house and everybody's complimenting me on how nice I look in this dress and I'm like, "Really? You think I look nice? Because my parents think I look inappropriate."

I **outed them** (kinda mean, really).

But I think **the public utterance of** this idea that I should somehow hide myself was so shocking to hear that it changed their mind about why they were doing it.

And I had always managed to get through life with somewhat of a positive attitude, but I think this was the start of me being able to accept myself. You know, okay, I'm not normal. I have strengths. I've got weaknesses. It is what it is.

And I had always been athletic, but it wasn't until college that I started this adventure in Track and Field. I had gone through a lifetime of being given legs that just barely got me by. And I thought, Well, maybe I'm just having the wrong conversations with the wrong people. Maybe I need to go find people who say, "Yes, we can create anything for you in the space between where your leg ends and the ground."

▶ **Before You Move On**

1. **Confirm Prediction** What is the main focus of Mullins's speech so far? Revise your prediction or form a new one.

2. **Explain** Why was Mullins's decision about the dress an important event for her and her parents? How did they each respond?

And so I started working with engineers, fashion designers, sculptors, Hollywood prosthetic makeup artists, and wax museum designers to build legs for me.

I decided I wanted to be the fastest woman in the world on prosthetic legs and I was lucky enough to **arrive in track** at just the right time to be the first person to get these radical sprinting legs modeled after the hind leg of a cheetah, the fastest thing that runs—woven carbon fiber. I was able to set three world records with those legs. And they made no attempt at **approximating humanness**.

Then I get these incredibly lifelike silicon legs—hand-painted, capillaries, veins. And, hey, I can be as tall as I wanna be, so I get different legs for different heights. I don't have to shave. I can wear open-toed shoes in the winter. And most importantly, I can **opt out of the cankles** I most certainly would've inherited genetically.

And then I get these legs made for me by **the late, great Alexander McQueen**, and they were hand-carved of solid ash with grapevines and magnolias all over them and a six-inch heel. And I was able to walk the runways of the world with supermodels. I was suddenly in this whirlwind of adventure and excitement. I was being invited to go around the world and speak about these adventures, and how I had legs that looked like glass, legs covered in feathers, porcelain legs, jellyfish legs—all wearable sculpture.

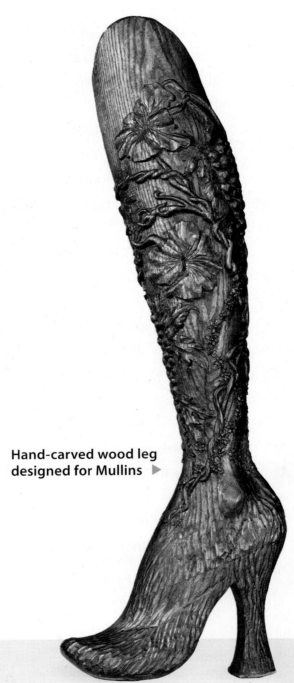

Hand-carved wood leg designed for Mullins ▶

In Other Words

arrive in track start competing in Track and Field
approximating humanness pretending to look like normal legs
opt out of the cankles avoid getting the unattractive ankles
the late, great Alexander McQueen a famous clothing designer

Mullins competing in the women's long jump event at the Paralympics

▶ **Before You Move On**

1. **Cause/Effect** How did Mullins's new legs affect her life? Cite evidence from the speech to support your response.

2. **Author's Viewpoint** What is Mullins's opinion about having legs made from unusual materials?

A prosthetic limb doesn't represent the need to replace loss anymore. It can stand as a symbol that the wearer has the power to create whatever it is they want to create.

—Aimee Mullins

And I get this call from a guy who had seen me speak years ago, when I was at the beginning of my track career, and he says, "We loved it. We want you to come back." And it was clear to me he didn't know all these amazing things that had happened to me since my sports career.

So as I'm telling him, he says, "Whoa, whoa, whoa. Hold on, Aimee. The reason everybody liked you all those years ago was because you were this sweet, **vulnerable**, **naïve** girl, and if you walk onstage today, and you are this **polished** young woman with too many accomplishments, I'm afraid they won't like you."

For real, he said that. Wow.

He apparently didn't think I was vulnerable enough now. He was asking me to be less than, a little more **downtrodden**. He was asking me to disable myself for him and his audience.

And what was so shocking to me about that was that I realized I had moved past mere acceptance of my difference. I was having fun with my difference. Thank God I'm not normal. I get to be extraordinary. And I'll decide what is a weakness and what is a strength.

And so I refused his request.

In Other Words
vulnerable helpless
naïve innocent
polished confident and successful
downtrodden hopeless and needy

And a few days later, I'm walking in downtown Manhattan at a street fair, and I get this tug on my shirt, and I look down. It's this little girl I met a year earlier when she was at a **pivotal** moment in her life. She had been born with a brittle bone disease that resulted in her left leg being seven centimeters shorter than her right. She wore **a brace and orthopedic shoes** and they **got her by**, but she wanted to do more.

And like all **Internet-savvy** kindergarteners, she gets on the computer and Googles "new leg," and she comes up with dozens of images of prosthetics, many of them mine.

And she prints them out, goes to school, **does show-and-tell on it**, comes home, and makes a startling pronouncement to her parents: "I wanna get rid of my bad leg," she says. "When can I get a new leg?"

And ultimately that was the decision her parents and doctors made for her. So here she was, six months after the amputation, and right there in the middle of the street fair, she hikes up her jeans leg to show me her cool new leg. And it's pink, and it's tattooed with the characters of *High School Musical 3*, replete with red, sequined Mary Janes on her feet.

And she was proud of it. She was proud of herself. And the marvelous thing was that this six-year-old understood something that it took me twenty-something years to get, but that we both did discover—that when we can celebrate and truly own what it is that makes us different, we're able to find the source of our greatest creative power.

Thank you. ❖

In Other Words

pivotal very important

a brace and orthopedic shoes equipment on her legs

got her by helped her walk

Internet-savvy computer-using

does a show-and-tell on it tells her class about it

▶ **Before You Move On**

1. **Author's Viewpoint** How does Mullins feel about being "different"? What details support your answer?

2. **Make Inferences** What advice would Mullins give to someone who is facing challenges in life?

Compare Main Ideas

Facing the Lion and "A Work in Progress" both include choices. Use a comparison chart to compare the main ideas and important details from these texts. Then synthesize, or put together, the ideas in the chart to tell what they show about Lekuton and Mullins.

Comparison Chart

	Facing the Lion	"A Work in Progress"
genre	autobiography	
main idea		
author's choice		

Talk Together

How do the two selections help you understand the ways that choices can affect people's lives? Use text evidence and **Key Words** to talk about your ideas with a small group.

Complete Sentences

A sentence expresses a complete thought. A **complete sentence** has two parts: a subject and a predicate. The **subject** is who or what the sentence is about. The **predicate** is what the subject is, does, or has.

Grammar Rules Complete Sentences

The **complete subject** includes all the words that tell about the subject. The **simple subject** is the most important noun or nouns in the subject.	**A bright, young girl** spoke to Aimee Mullins.
The **complete predicate** includes the verb and all the other words in the predicate. The **simple predicate** is the main verb in the predicate.	A bright, young girl **spoke** to Aimee **Mullins**

Read Complete Sentences

Writers and speakers use complete subjects and predicates to expand their ideas and provide more details about the subject and verb. Read this passage based on "A Work in Progress." Find the complete and simple subject and the complete and simple predicate in each sentence.

Model and athlete Aimee Mullins speaks about her prosthetic legs. The large audience listens to her story. Her prosthetic legs fascinate them. Mullins's amazing courage is inspiring as well.

Write Complete Sentences

Reread page 33. Write three complete sentences to explain how you would change the way people think about disabilities. Then trade sentences with a partner, and find the complete and simple subjects and the complete and simple predicates in each other's sentences.

Language Frames

- Why/What _____ ?
- This is _____ .
- Can you explain more about _____ ?
- _____ because _____ .

Ask and Answer Questions

Listen to the interview. Then use the **Language Frames** to interview a partner. Ask and answer questions about each other, making sure to elaborate and give details in your responses.

Who Are You? (((MP3)))

Eva: Malika, I noticed that you always wear a beautiful headscarf. Why do you wear it every day?

Malika: This is my hijab. I choose to wear it every day because it is one way that I can express my Muslim faith.

Eva: Can you explain more about why you wear it?

Malika: Sure! I cover my hair and neck because I want to dress modestly. Some women wear the hijab when leaving the house, but I wear it all the time. I see it as an important part of my culture and faith.

Eva: What other parts of your culture are important to you?

Malika: Every year, my parents practice zakat. That means that they give to people who are in need. My whole family tries to volunteer at the community shelter, too. It feels good to help people.

Key Words
associate
confront
preservation
sensitive
tolerance

Key Words

Look at the photograph and read the opinion. Use **Key Words** and other words to talk about the choices people make about culture.

Our world is filled with people from many cultures. Because we are not all the same, it is important to be aware of and **sensitive** to people's feelings. We should never angrily try to **confront** people who are different. Instead, we should treat people with respect, acceptance, and **tolerance** because this is a world that we all share.

Many people make choices based on their cultures or beliefs. For example, the hijab is a headscarf that people **associate** with, or connect to, the Muslim faith. Many people want to keep their traditions the same because the **preservation** of their customs is important to them. They want to keep their cultures alive for many future generations.

Talk Together

What choices do people make about their cultures and traditions? What choices do you make to understand the cultures and traditions of others? Use **Language Frames** from page 36 and **Key Words** to pose and respond to questions with a partner. Remember to elaborate on your ideas and include comments that contribute to your discussion of the topic.

Characters and Plot

In fiction, the **characters** are the people that the story is about. The **plot** is the series of episodes, or events, that make up the story. In many stories, the way that characters respond to events may change and influence what happens next.

In the following passage, a girl named Amal has made a choice that becomes an important plot event in the story. Look for ways that the school secretary responds and changes because of this event.

Look Into the Text

"I need to see Ms. Walsh."

"Can't it wait until recess? Ms. Walsh might not be too happy about you skipping homeroom."

I grin at her and whisper conspiratorially. "She doesn't know I'm wearing the veil."

She looks at me with wide eyes and tells me to take a seat.

I'm buzzed in soon afterward and enter a large room . . .

"After learning about Amal's **choice**, the secretary **responds**. She looks surprised and changes what she was going to do."

Map and Talk

You can use a character-and-plot chart to record information about how characters respond and change as the plot moves from the beginning to the end of the story.

Character-and-Plot Chart

Character	Plot Event	Response
school secretary	sees Amal's veil	

Talk Together

Tell a partner about a time that someone you know made an important decision. How did you respond? What did you do? Your partner completes a character-and-plot chart and uses it to retell your story.

More Key Words

Use these words to talk about *Does My Head Look Big in This?* and "The Jacket."

awareness
(u-**wair**-nes) *noun*

When you have **awareness** of something, you see or understand it. They used their **awareness** of traffic and safety rules to cross the street.

conform
(kun-**form**) *verb*

When you **conform**, you follow a rule or way of doing things. In some schools, all students must **conform** to a dress code by wearing a uniform.

intent
(in-**tent**) *noun*

An **intent** is a plan to do something. The student studies hard with the **intent** of passing a difficult test.

interaction
(in-tur-**ak**-shun) *noun*

An **interaction** is when people talk or do activities with one another. This is an **interaction** between three friends.

involve
(in-**vawlv**) *verb*

To **involve** means to include. Winning a baseball game may **involve** speed, strength, and teamwork.

Talk Together

Make a Word Map for each **Key Word**. Then compare your maps with a partner's.

Definition: follow a rule	Characteristics: being like others
Example: go to school on time	Non-example: go to school late

conform

Add words to My Vocabulary Notebook.
 NGReach.com

Learn to Monitor

As you read, make sure you understand the text. If there is something you do not understand, you can stop to **monitor**, or check, your progress.

How to Monitor

？	1. When you do not understand part of the text, stop reading. Think about what the text means.
👁	2. If you still do not understand, reread the text or read on. Use context clues or vocabulary resources to understand unknown words. If the text is still unclear, ask for help.
💭	3. Think about how doing these things helps you better understand the text.

I'm confused about
_____ .

I _____ to help me
_____ .

Now I understand
_____ .

Here's how one student monitored her reading.

Look Into the Text

"Amal . . . Did you speak to anyone about wearing . . . about abandoning our school uniforms?"

"I wouldn't exactly call it abandoning."

Her eyes narrow. One thing about teachers and principals. They hate to be **contradicted** .

"I'm confused about the **word** contradicted. I find **evidence** to help me see what Ms. Walsh hates. Now I understand that being contradicted means 'being told you're wrong.'"

As you read, pause to monitor your understanding of the text. Try to clarify each misunderstanding as you encounter it.

Talk Together

Read the interview and sample notes. Use **Language Frames** to monitor as you read. Then talk with a partner about how you monitored your reading.

Interview

A NEW LOOK *FOR*
DANVIR KAPOOR

Marcos: We met in the first grade. I asked why your hair was so long. Do you remember what you told me?

Danvir: [*laughing*] Yes, I told you that I was a Sikh and that we don't cut our hair—ever—and that all my long hair was twisted into a knot on top of my head. Then you said, "You're sick?" And I had to explain that "Sikh" was the name for people in my religion. ◀

Marcos: Well, now that we're in sixth grade, I'm still curious. Why don't Sikhs cut their hair?

Danvir: The **intent** is to keep our hair in its natural state. We don't cut our hair, and we don't **conform** to fashion by styling our hair or shaving our facial hair. It's part of the **preservation** of our beliefs.

Marcos: You recently had your Dastar Bandi ceremony. Can you tell me more about that? ◀

Danvir: A Dastar Bandi is a turban-tying ceremony that **involves** making a lifetime commitment to Sikhism. When Sikhism began in India, only royalty wore the turbans, or dastars. Sikhs now believe that all people are created equal, and the dastar, which means "turban" in Punjab, is a symbol of faith and equality. ◀

Marcos: How will wearing a dastar affect your **interactions** with others?

Danvir: My parents say that many people **associate** turbans with negative things, so they are worried that others will **confront** me for being different. Questions like yours, however, help raise **awareness**. I won't have trouble at our school because my friends always show me **tolerance** and respect. I know that they are **sensitive** to people of different cultures.

Marcos: Thank you for speaking with me, Danvir. I think your new dastar looks great!

> I'm confused about why Sikhs don't cut their hair.
>
> I read on to help me find an answer.
>
> Now I understand that Sihks want to keep their hair in its natural state.

◀ = a good place to stop and monitor your reading

41

Read Realistic Fiction

Genre

A **realistic fiction** story tells about events that could happen in real life. It includes realistic characters, settings, and plot events.

Narrator

In fiction, the **narrator** is the person who tells the story. The narrator can be a character who is describing the events or someone who isn't directly involved in the story. In *Does My Head Look Big in This?*, the narrator is a female character named Amal. She uses words like *I*, *me*, and *my* to tell the story.

Ms. Walsh is seated at her desk, her head down as she continues writing. She motions at **me** to take a seat on the plain pine chair beside her desk. She does this without looking up. **I** tiptoe across to the chair, then sit down on the edge.

FROM
DOES my HEAD
LOOK BIG IN THIS?

by
Randa Abdel-Fattah
illustrated by Kali Ciesemier

Comprehension Coach

▶ **Set a Purpose**
Find out what happens when Amal
makes an important choice.

"I need to see Ms. Walsh."

"Can't it wait until recess? Ms. Walsh might not be too happy
about you skipping homeroom."

I grin at her and whisper conspiratorially. "She doesn't know I'm
wearing the veil."

She looks at me with wide eyes and tells me to take a seat.

I'm **buzzed in** soon afterward and enter a large room filled with
beautiful mahogany furnishings and plush armchairs. The burgundy
walls are decorated with massive portraits of earlier principals and
framed photographs of past graduating classes. Trophies and plaques
line the floor-to-ceiling shelves.

Ms. Walsh is seated at her desk, her head down as she continues
writing. She motions at me to take a seat on the plain pine chair beside her
desk. She does this without looking up. I tiptoe across to the chair, then sit
down on the edge.

*Please God. Please God. Please God. Don't let her **freak out on** me.*

After half a minute she stops writing. The countdown in my
head begins.

Three.

"So, Amal, what is so important that—"

Two.

" . . . you had to see me first thing—"

One.

She looks at me.

" . . . today . . ."

In Other Words
buzzed in let into Ms. Walsh's office
freak out on *get upset with*

44

I think songs. I think "Take My Breath Away" and "It's In Your Eyes."

And then she coughs. Ahh, the comforting sound of an awkward *ahem*. When in doubt as to how to react, **buy some time and roll that phlegm**.

Twice if you must.

"Ahem . . . er . . . "

"Hi, Ms. Walsh. Sorry to barge in on you without an appointment but because it was winter break I couldn't make one and I thought I should see you first thing this morning, before I go to school, you know what I'm saying? I . . . I've . . . I've decided to wear the hijab. You know how I'm Muslim and all? Well, it's part of my religion to wear the hijab and I'm sorry if I've kind of shocked you like this but it was almost like an overnight decision . . . kind of thing . . . " I stop rambling and look down at my hands nervously, saying a silent prayer that she won't have a fit.

She sounds like she needs **a ventilator**. She draws in a huge breath of air, leans back in her chair, and gazes intently at me: "Well now, Amal Mohamed Nas—Nas—Nasru—" I cut her off. It's too painful to watch. She never fails to stutter like the Rain Man when she **takes a shot at** my last name.

In Other Words

buy some time and roll that phlegm take time
    to think and clear your throat

a ventilator help breathing

takes a shot at tries to say

45

"Mohamed Nasrullah Abdel-Hakim," I complete for her. I smile, trying to send off a million happy vibes with every spasmodic twitch of my facial muscles. **I'm under no delusions** that she's going to take this easily. After all, she has a reputation for popping a painkiller from the trauma of seeing a student wearing the wrong socks. No pharmacist will have sufficient supplies for her now.

Instead, she half smiles, half winces and runs her fingers through her hair. I momentarily feel sorry for her because I'm not about to pretend that this is the **equivalent of** mismatched socks or the wrong-colored hair clip. There seems to be something almost X-Men-like about this piece of material on my head. Too many people look at it as though it has bizarre powers sewn into its microfibers. Powers that transform Muslim girls into UCOs (Unidentified Covered Objects), which turn Muslim girls from an "us" into a "them." Ms. Walsh probably wants to deal with detentions, board meetings, curriculum changes, teachers' pay raises. Figuring out how to deal with a Muslim kid wearing the veil at her stuffy old prep school is probably the last thing she expected to pop up in her job description. But although I understand her viewpoint, I've got to stand up for myself. As much as I would like to live in a comic-book character's life, I really would rather not be treated like a UCO.

"Amal . . . hmm . . . I don't want to—I mean, I want to **tread delicately on** this . . . sensitive issue . . . hmm . . . Did you speak to anyone about wearing . . . about abandoning our school uniforms?"

"I wouldn't exactly call it abandoning."

Her eyes narrow. One thing about teachers and principals. They hate to be contradicted.

In Other Words
I'm under no delusions I do not believe
equivalent of same as
tread delicately on be careful about

I bite my lip, worried she'll erupt, and then quickly say something before she has a chance to. "I would have spoken to you earlier except today is my first school day wearing it. I made the decision during the holidays."

"Hmm . . . now let me see." She presses her fingers down on her temples. "So your parents have made you wear the veil permanently now? Starting from today? Your *first* day of the second semester. Couldn't it wait until tomorrow? After they'd spoken to me?"

I stare at her in shock. "My parents? Who mentioned my parents?"

"The veil, dear." Her voice is annoyingly phony. "So you've been made to wear it from today?"

"Nobody has *made* me wear it, Ms. Walsh. It's my decision." I shift in the chair, my butt numb from the hard wood.

"*Your* decision to cover yourself up?" she asks with the faintest hint of skepticism.

I look at her with a bewildered expression. "Yes, it was my decision."

She gives me another *ahem*. "Well, Amal. I'm not sure what to do here. I hope you appreciate that this isn't Hid—Hida—your old *Coburg* school. This is a **reputable educational establishment**. We have more than one hundred years of proud history. A history of tradition, Amal. Of conformity with the rules and policies of this institution. We have a strict uniform policy. And you have walked in, on your first day back from the holidays, and have been so **presumptuous** as to alter it without **authorization**."

In Other Words
reputable educational establishment respected school
presumptuous rude; bold
authorization permission

"But Ms. Walsh, it's not like I've put in an eyebrow ring or grown a mohawk or dyed my uniform pink. I'm still in school uniform. I know it's the first time a student has worn it, but couldn't you make an exception? I'm not doing this because I'm trying to rebel against the rules."

She looks uncomfortable and leans back in her leather chair. "But you've made no effort to seek the school's permission. This certainly wasn't raised at your enrollment interview. I recall your parents. They seemed like very decent, straightforward people. I'm rather disappointed they never mentioned this. I saw your mother wearing the veil, but I never suspected you would be wearing it too."

"But my enrollment interview was more than six months ago! I didn't *seriously* start to contemplate going ahead with this until last week. And even *then* I was still unsure. I only made my final decision four days ago!"

"Why didn't you at least approach me when you were thinking about it? You should have consulted me first."

It takes me a solid minute to realize my jaw is hanging down.

"Er . . . it was personal . . . "

"Well, obviously not. It's rather public, don't you think? Personal is something tucked under your shirt. Personal is rosary beads in your pocket. I would suggest, Amal, that your veil is not, of all things, personal. Now don't get me wrong; I respect your religion. We live in a multicultural society, and we should accept and tolerate people no matter what their creed, race, or color. But you must understand that I have an educational institution to run, and there are certain guidelines. I'm sure your parents will appreciate that."

"I'm not going around preaching or anything. It's something . . . for myself."

She looks at me incredulously.

"My parents had nothing to do with it. They found out last week.

They were even concerned for me—"

"Concerned?"

"Yes, they were worried I wasn't ready. Actually, they were freaking out more about how I'd **be able to cope**. Being the only one in the school with it on."

"Let me get this right." She sits up straight in her chair. "They were actually opposed to this decision to cover up?"

"Well, not *opposed*. Just, I don't know, cautious. Worried for me. Because of the reaction I might get." I look at her, but she ignores my tone and is suddenly shuffling papers on her desk and flashing me a large, friendly smile.

"Well, Amal. Let's discuss this later, shall we? You've got class to attend." She scribbles out a late note and hands it to me. "Here you go. Now have a wonderful first day back, and I will speak to you soon."

She gives me a fake smile and resumes writing, an invitation for me to leave **pronto**. I nod back, careful not to slam the door behind me as I leave.

In Other Words
be able to cope act if people were rude to me
pronto quickly

▶ **Before You Move On**

1. **Clarify** What does Amal mean when she says her choice is *personal*?

2. **Make Inferences** Why does Ms. Walsh's attitude change? Cite evidence from the text.

▶ **Predict**

What will Amal's **interactions** with
other students be like?

It's Wednesday. The only people who haven't freaked
out about my hijab have been Simone and Eileen. Oh, and
Josh Goldberg. Josh's Jewish. He's got orthodox Jewish
cousins, but from what I can tell, he's a secular Jew. I don't
think my hijab's really strange to him, though. Orthodox
Jewish women also cover their hair, and there are tons more
things that are similar with our faiths. We kind of **hit it off**
from my first week at **McCleans**.

As for the rest of my class, it's been two whole days
since the start of the grading period, and there's still an
uncomfortable *politeness* between me and everybody else.
Well, I wouldn't call it politeness with Tia, Claire, and Rita,
who are still into **their sniggering routine**, which is fine.
That I can handle. At least they're acknowledging I exist.
But everyone else is acting way too **civil with** me.

When it comes to the guys, well, some of them are
kind of acting almost scared of me. As though they're
not allowed to talk to me, or I'll bark at them if they say
something. One of the guys, Tim Manne, accidentally
bumped into me while we were walking out of class and
then fumbled and *apologized* and moved on quickly, like he
didn't want me to think he'd given me an invitation to talk.
Since my first day here, I've *never* heard a guy apologize to a
girl for bumping into her. I was about to make a joke about
it, to **ease the tension**, but he was already halfway down
the hallway.

In Other Words
hit it off were friends immediately
McCleans our school
their sniggering routine laughing at me
civil with polite to
ease the tension show that I was not upset

And then there's Adam. He hasn't spoken a word to me since the start of the new semester. He just smiles awkwardly if our eyes meet and quickly turns his head away. It's gruesome. When he ignores me like this, it feels as though somebody has a potato peeler and is torturously peeling away the layers of my skin. This morning I'm in the hallway when I overhear some girls talking about me next to the lockers. One of them says the word *oppressed*, and the other one is saying something about me looking like a slob. I can't go up to them, because then they'll know I've been eavesdropping. So I walk slowly away, feeling like a boiling kettle of water about to whistle and screech.

I'd like to say that I walked back to the lockers and planted myself in front of those girls. I'd like to say that I looked them in the eye and gave them a **pulverizing comeback line** that left them shocked and speechless. But don't you just hate yourself when you always think of the killer line when it's too late?

Anyway, by the time I've got the **guts** to even think about turning back, the bell has rung, and the moment has passed.

So I just keep walking. Monday morning. And my class has finally decided to **confront** me about my hijab. I almost want to jump up and down with relief. I can handle an insult or **an interrogation**. I can't handle going from getting along with everybody (**with the obvious exception of** Tia and her **Mini-Mes**) to being a social **outcast**.

In Other Words

pulverizing comeback line strong response
guts courage
an interrogation a lot of questions
with the obvious exception of except for

Mini-Mes followers
outcast outsider

Somehow, in between classes after lunch on Monday everybody suddenly finds the guts to approach me, wanting to know what's going on with my new look.

"Did your parents force you?" Kristy asks, all wide-eyed and **appalled**.

"My dad told me if I don't wear it he'll marry me off to a sixty-five-year-old camel owner in Egypt."

"No!" She's actually horrified.

"I was invited to the wedding," Eileen adds.

"*Really?*" This is definitely a case of **dropped-from-the-cradle**.

"Hey! Amal!" Tim Manne calls out. "What's the deal with that thing on your head?"

"I've gone bald."

"Get out!"

"I'm on the Advanced Hair Program."

For a second his eyes flicker with shock. Then Josh punches him on the shoulder. "Punked!"

"Like I believed her," Tim says, looking sheepish.

"Doesn't it get hot?" someone asks.

"Can I touch it?"

"Can you swim?"

"Do you wear it in the shower?"

"So is it like nuns? Are you married to Jesus now?"

It's unreal. Everybody's asking me about my decision and seems genuinely interested in hearing what I have to say. They're all huddled around me, and I'm having the best time explaining to them how I put it on and when I have to wear it. Then Adam plants himself in front of me and starts joining in with the rest of them, and I want to plant a massive kiss on his face except that really would be defeating the purpose of my entire **spiritual road trip** now, wouldn't it?

"So it's your choice then?" he asks.

In Other Words
appalled upset
dropped-from-the-cradle not understanding
"Get out!" "You must be joking!"
spiritual road trip choice to change

"Oh yeah!" I answer. "One hundred percent."

"Wow . . . so how come it looks different on you?"

"What do you mean?"

"Like you see some women covering their faces and other women wearing really bright material with that red paint on their hand. Are they all Islamic too?"

"You mean Muslim."

"Huh?"

"What she means," Josh says, "is that the religion is Islam, and the followers are Muslim. Like you can't say to somebody you're a Judaism or a Catholicism. Get it?"

"Yup." Adam nods his head. "So are they *Muslim*, like you?"

"Yeah, they are. But, every girl is going to interpret the hijab differently. It depends on their culture or their fashion sense, you know? There's no uniform for it."

"I get you," Adam says.

"A lot of Africans wear those really colorful wraparound dresses and veils," I continue. "Um, stricter women cover their face, but it's not required in Islam. It's their choice to **go to that extent**."

"Will you ever cover yours?" Adam asks.

"Nah! No way."

"OK . . . cool."

We all keep talking until our Chemistry teacher, Ms. Samuels, walks in and announces she's going to test us to see if we studied over the holidays. We get stuck with an impromptu quiz, and Kristy passes me a note with exclamation marks and smiley faces all over it.

I'm really glad your dad didn't go through with the wedding!!!

Sweet of her. But **cradle theory confirmed**. ❖

In Other Words
go to that extent do so much
cradle theory confirmed she didn't understand

▶ **Before You Move On**
1. **Make Comparisons** How do people at Amal's school respond to her decision?
2. **Point of View** How does Amal's point of view as the narrator affect the story? Cite examples from the text.

Key Words

associate	interaction
awareness	involve
conform	preservation
confront	sensitive
intent	tolerance

Talk About It

1. *Does My Head Look Big in This?* is realistic fiction. What are some details in Amal's story that remind you of real **interactions** between people in your school?

2. Compare Amal and Ms. Walsh's viewpoints, or opinions, about Amal's choice to wear the veil. Use evidence from the text to support the comparison.

3. What questions do you still have about Amal, her experiences, or her hijab at the end of the story? Look back into the text to ask and answer questions you are still thinking about.

4. Using examples from the text, analyze how Amal's sense of humor helps her **confront** tough situations.

5. Many people feel that they need to **conform** to the rules and ideas of people around them. How do you think Amal would respond to this attitude? Explain your opinion using evidence from the text.

6. What is an important theme, or message, of the story? How do the characters and plot events support this theme?

Learn test-taking strategies and answer more questions.
 NGReach.com

Write About It

Write an e-mail from Amal to a friend at her old school to explain her decision. Use at least three **Key Words** and support your ideas with evidence from the text.

● ● ● ✉   RE: a big decision

Hi, Elise!
I have to tell you about a huge decision I just made. During the holidays, I decided to start wearing the hijab. Well, all the people I **associate** with at school started treating me like an outcast.

Characters and Plot

Use a character-and-plot chart to record how different characters respond to the events in *Does My Head Look Big in This?*

Character-and-Plot Chart

Character	Plot Event	Response
school secretary	sees Amal's veil	

Use your character-and-plot chart to retell the story to a partner. Describe Amal's choice and how characters respond and change in response to the plot events. Use **Key Words**.

Fluency  Comprehension Coach

Use the Comprehension Coach to practice reading with expression. Rate your reading.

Talk Together

Amal's choices affect her relationships with others. What are some ways that choices affect your life? Discuss your ideas with a partner. Use **Key Words**.

Use a Thesaurus

A **thesaurus** is a reference that lists synonyms and antonyms. Synonyms are words with similar meanings, like *intent* and *plan*. Antonyms are words with opposite meanings, like *conform* and *rebel*. When you write, you can use a thesaurus to find the best words to express your ideas.

EXAMPLES

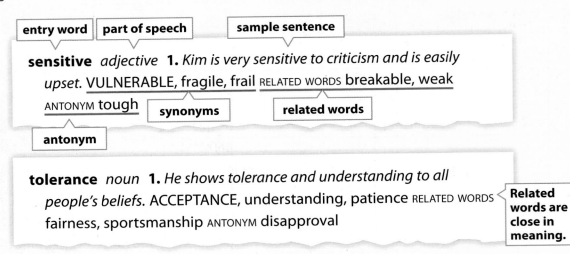

| entry word | part of speech | | sample sentence |

sensitive *adjective* **1.** *Kim is very sensitive to criticism and is easily upset.* VULNERABLE, fragile, frail RELATED WORDS breakable, weak ANTONYM tough

| synonyms | related words |
| antonym |

tolerance *noun* **1.** *He shows tolerance and understanding to all people's beliefs.* ACCEPTANCE, understanding, patience RELATED WORDS fairness, sportsmanship ANTONYM disapproval

> Related words are close in meaning.

Try It

Read the sentences. Then use the thesaurus entries above to answer the questions.

Amal was <u>sensitive</u> about how people would react to her decision to wear the veil. Most of her friends showed <u>tolerance</u> and respected her choice.

1. **You want to replace the word <u>sensitive</u>. Which word is the best synonym to replace it?**

   A breakable

   B tough

   C frail

   D vulnerable

2. **You want to replace the word <u>tolerance</u>. Which is the best synonym to replace it?**

   A acceptance

   B fairness

   C disapproval

   D sportsmanship

Connect Across Texts You read about Amal's choice and how it affected others. Now read about a boy named Francisco and a choice he must make.

Genre An **autobiography** is the story of a person's life written by that person.

THE JACKET
from THE CIRCUIT

by Francisco Jiménez | illustrated by Claire Cotts

My favorite time in school was when we did art, which was every afternoon, after the teacher had read to us. Since I did not understand Miss Scalapino when she explained the art lessons, she let me do whatever I wanted. I drew all kinds of animals but mostly birds and butterflies. I sketched them in pencil and then colored them using every color in my crayon box. Miss Scalapino even tacked one of my drawings up on the board for everyone to see. After of couple of weeks it disappeared, and I did not know how to ask where it had gone.

One cold Thursday morning, during recess, I was the only kid on the playground without a jacket. Mr. Sims must have noticed I was shivering because that afternoon, after school, he took me to his office and pulled out a green jacket from a large cardboard box that was full of used clothes and toys.

▶ Before You Move On

1. **Point of View** Which specific words and ideas in the text indicate that the story is told from the author's point of view?
2. **Predict** Based on what you have read, what problem do you think Francisco will face?

57

He handed it to me and gestured for me to try it on. It smelled like graham crackers. I put it on, but it was too big, so he rolled up the sleeves about two inches to make it fit. I took it home and **showed it off** to my parents. They smiled. I liked it because it was green, and it hid my **suspenders**.

The next day I was on the playground wearing my new jacket and waiting for the first bell to ring when I saw Curtis coming at me like an angry bull. Aiming his head directly at me, and pulling his arms straight back with his hands clenched, he stomped up to me and started yelling. I did not understand him, but I knew it had

something to do with the jacket because he began to pull on it, trying to take it off me. Next thing I knew, he and I were on the ground wrestling. Kids circled around us. I could hear them yelling Curtis's name and something else. I knew I **had no chance**, but I stubbornly held on to my jacket. He pulled on one of the sleeves so hard that it ripped at the shoulder. He pulled on the right pocket, and it ripped. Then Miss Scalapino's face appeared above. She pushed Curtis off of me and grabbed me by the back of the collar and picked me up off the ground. It took all the power I had not to cry.

In Other Words
showed it off proudly showed it
suspenders straps that held up my pants
had no chance could not win the fight

On the way to the classroom Arthur told me that Curtis claimed the jacket was his, that he had lost it at the beginning of the year. He also said that the teacher told Curtis and me that we were being punished. We had to sit on the bench during recess for the rest of the week. I did not see the jacket again. Curtis got it, but I never saw him wear it.

For the rest of the day, I could not even pretend I was paying attention to Miss Scalapino, I was so embarrassed. I laid my head on top of my desk and closed my eyes. I kept thinking about what had happened that morning. I wanted to fall asleep and wake up to find it was only a dream. The teacher called my name, but I did not answer. I heard her walk up to me. I did not know what to expect. She gently shook me by the shoulders. Again, I did not respond. Miss Scalapino must have thought I was asleep because she left me alone, even when it was time for recess and everyone left the room.

Once the room was quiet, I slowly opened my eyes. I had had them closed for so long that the sunlight coming through the windows blinded me. I rubbed my eyes with the back of my hands and then looked to my left at the jar. I looked for the caterpillar but could not see it. Thinking it might be hidden, I put my hand in the jar and lightly stirred the leaves. To my surprise, the caterpillar had spun itself into a cocoon and had attached itself to a small twig. It looked like a tiny, cotton bulb, just like Roberto had said it would. I gently stroked it with my index finger, picturing it asleep and peaceful.

▶ Before You Move On

1. **Plot** What is Francisco's problem at school? Confirm or change your prediction.
2. **Make Inferences** Why does Curtis get so angry about the jacket? Cite evidence from the text to support your inference.

At the end of the school day, Miss Scalapino gave me a note to take home to my parents. Papá and Mamá did not know how to read, but they did not have to. As soon as they saw my swollen upper lip and the scratches on my left cheek, they knew what the note said. When I told them what happened, they were very upset but relieved that I did not disrespect the teacher.

For the next several days, going to school and facing Miss Scalapino was harder than ever. However, I slowly began to get over what happened that Friday. Once I got used to the routine in school and I picked up some English words, I felt more comfortable in class.

On Wednesday, May 23, a few days before the end of the school year, Miss Scalapino took me by surprise. After we were all sitting down and she had **taken roll**, she called for everyone's attention. I did not understand what she said, but I heard her say my name as she held up a blue ribbon. She then picked up my drawing of the butterfly that had disappeared weeks before and held it up for everyone to see. She walked up to me and handed me the drawing and the silk blue ribbon that had a number one printed on it in gold. I knew then I had received first prize for my

drawing. I was so proud, I felt **like bursting out of my skin**. My classmates, including Curtis, stretched their necks to see the ribbon.

That afternoon, during our free period, I went over to check on the caterpillar. I turned the jar around, trying to see the cocoon. It was beginning to crack open. I excitedly cried out, "Look, look," pointing to it. The whole class, like a swarm of bees, rushed over to the counter. Miss Scalapino took the jar and placed it on top of a desk in the middle of the classroom so everyone could see it. For the next several minutes we all stood there watching the butterfly emerge from its cocoon, **in slow motion**.

In Other Words

taken roll made sure everyone was there
like bursting out of my skin very happy and excited
in slow motion very slowly

At the end of the day, just before the last bell, Miss Scalapino picked up the jar and took the class outside to the playground. She placed the jar on the ground, and we all circled around her. I had a hard time seeing over the other kids so Miss Scalapino called me and motioned for me to open the jar. I broke through the circle, knelt on the ground, and unscrewed the top. Like magic, the butterfly flew into the air, fluttering its wings up and down.

After school I waited in line for my bus in front of the playground. I proudly carried the blue ribbon in my right hand and the drawing in the other. Arthur and Curtis came up and stood behind me to wait for their bus. Curtis motioned for me to show him the drawing again. I held it up so he could see it.

"He really likes it, Francisco," Arthur said to me in Spanish.

"*¿Cómo se dice 'es tuyo' en inglés?*" I asked.

"It's yours," answered Arthur.

"It's yours," I repeated, handing the drawing to Curtis. ❖

In Other Words

¿Como se dice 'es tuyo' en inglés? *How do you say 'it's yours' in English?* (Spanish)

▶ **Before You Move On**

1. **Plot** How is Francisco's problem solved?
2. **Make Inferences** How do Francisco's teachers feel about him? Cite evidence from the text to support your ideas.

Respond and Extend

Key Words

associate	interaction
awareness	involve
conform	preservation
confront	sensitive
intent	tolerance

Compare Characters

Does My Head Look Big in This? and "The Jacket" both
involve choices that people make. Use a chart to compare
the characters' responses to their problems. Then analyze the
information and explain what it shows about the two characters.

Narrator/Character Chart

	Does My Head Look Big in This?	"The Jacket"
Narrator or Main Character	Amal	Francisco Jiménez
Problem		
Thoughts and Feelings		
Choices		
Actions and Responses		

Talk **Together**

How do both of the selections show ways that choices can affect the way
people respond to you? Use **Key Words** and text evidence to discuss your
ideas with a small group.

Subject-Verb Agreement

The subject and verb of a sentence must agree in number.

Grammar Rules Subject-Verb Agreement

The verb you use depends on the noun in the subject. Choose the right **verb** for singular or plural **subjects**.	**Francisco needs** help at school. **His teachers want** to help him.
If the **nouns** in a **compound subject** are connected by **and**, use a **verb** that goes with plural nouns.	**Curtis and Francisco fight** over the jacket.
If the nouns in a **compound subject** are connected by **or** or **nor**, look at the **last noun**. Determine whether the noun is singular or plural. Use the **verb** that matches the noun.	Either **the teachers or Arthur explains** the problem. Neither **Arthur nor the teachers understand** what Francisco needs.

Read Sentences with Correct Subject-Verb Agreement

To keep their writing clear, good writers make sure their subjects and verbs agree. Read this passage based on "The Jacket." Identify the subject and verb in each sentence. Explain how you know why the subjects and verbs agree.

> Miss Scalapino shows Francisco's drawing to the class. Francisco and his classmates admire his prize. Arthur or Curtis asks to see the drawing again.

Write Sentences with Correct Subject-Verb Agreement

Reread pages 58–59 of "The Jacket." Write a short paragraph that describes the problem that Francisco and Curtis have about the jacket. Include one sentence with a singular subject, one with a plural subject, and one with a compound subject. Make sure each verb agrees with its subject. Then compare your sentences with a partner's.

Write About Yourself

Write a Personal Narrative

Write about a time when you had to make a choice. Then add your story to a class book about choices.

Study a Model

A personal narrative is a true story about something that happened to you. You are the narrator telling about the events. Read Li's story about a choice she made.

The Audition
by Li Stewart

When I grow up, I want to be a choreographer. Nothing would be more fun than making up dances for a living! When the dance studio announced auditions for a student-choreographed dance show, I felt both excited and scared. How could I get the job?

With the auditions only a month away, I had to choose music and create my dance steps. First, I picked my favorite song. Next, I tried out dance moves. For the **soft, trilling** part of the music, I waved my arms **like a bird**. For the **loud, rhythmic** part, I moved with **sharp, jagged** steps. Then, I looked at dance videos for more ideas. At last, I was ready!

Two weeks later, I stepped onto the stage. The first part went fine, but then I missed a jump. I was so upset that I wanted to give up right there. But then I made a choice: I would do my best and never give up! I took a deep breath and let the music and all my rehearsing take over. After the last chord, I bowed to the judges and smiled to myself. I had done it!

The beginning introduces the problem.

Li tells how she responded to the events.

She organizes the events in sequence and uses transitions to make the sequence clear.

She uses vivid language to help readers picture the events.

The ending tells whether Li's problem is solved.

Prewrite

1. **Choose a Topic** What experience will you write about? Talk with a partner to choose a time in your life when you had to make a choice.

Language Frames	
Tell Your Ideas	**Respond to Ideas**
• An important choice I made recently was _____ .	• Why was _____ an important choice for you?
• I remember when I _____ .	• How did you _____ ?
• One thing that happened to me was _____ .	• What happened when _____ ?

> Use sentences and questions like these to help you decide about a topic.

2. **Gather Information** Collect precise words and descriptive details that tell about your experience and the order of events. Write your feelings, and tell what happened because of your choice.

3. **Get Organized** Use a sequence chain to help organize your ideas.

Sequence Chain

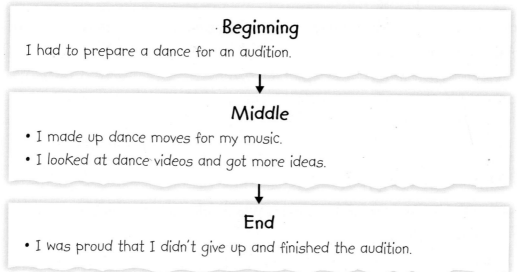

Beginning

I had to prepare a dance for an audition.

⬇

Middle

• I made up dance moves for my music.
• I looked at dance videos and got more ideas.

⬇

End

• I was proud that I didn't give up and finished the audition.

Draft

Use your sequence chain and the details you collected to write your draft. Tell what happened and how you responded to the events. Give descriptive details to develop the experience. Use transition words as you describe the events.

Revise

1. **Read, Retell, Respond** Read your draft aloud to a partner. Your partner listens and then retells the story. Then talk about ways to improve your writing.

Language Frames	
Retell	**Make Suggestions**
• The choice you made was _____ . • In the beginning, you _____ . After that, you _____ . At the end, you _____ . • The details you included are _____ . • You felt _____ about _____ .	• The sequence of events isn't clear. Could you add a transition, such as _____ ? • I really like the part about _____ . Can you add more descriptive details to help me picture it? • I'm not sure how you felt about _____ . Maybe you could include _____ .

Use sentences like these to respond to your partner's writing.

2. **Make Changes** Think about your draft and your partner's suggestions. Use the Revising Marks on page 617 to mark your changes.

   • Make sure you have sequenced story events logically and used transition words to make the sequence clear.

   > Next,
   > I tried out dance moves.
   > First,
   > I chose my favorite song.

   • Do you have enough descriptive details? Would adding details help convey events more clearly?

   > the soft, trilling   like a bird
   > For part of the music, I waved my arms.

Edit and Proofread

Work with a partner to edit and proofread your personal narrative. Pay special attention to using complete sentences and correct subject-verb agreement. Use the marks on page 618 to show your changes.

Publish

1. **On Your Own** Make a final copy of your personal narrative. Think about how to share it with your classmates. You can read your personal narrative aloud or retell it as though you were telling it to a younger brother or sister.

Spelling Tip

Some nouns change in spelling when they are plural. Use the correct spelling when there is more than one.

person → people

scarf → scarves

hero → heroes

Presentation Tips	
If you are the speaker . . .	**If you are the listener . . .**
Change your voice to express your feelings and to emphasize your responses to events in the story.	Listen for details that help you picture what the speaker is describing.
Use gestures if they feel natural.	Make connections to similar experiences in your own life.

2. **In a Group** Gather all the personal narratives from your class. Bind them into a class book, and work together to decide on a good title. To add interest to your own story, add computer art or scan in a photo.

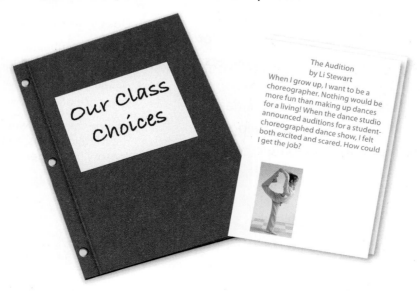

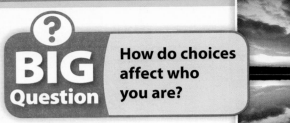 **BIG Question**

 **How do choices affect who you are?**

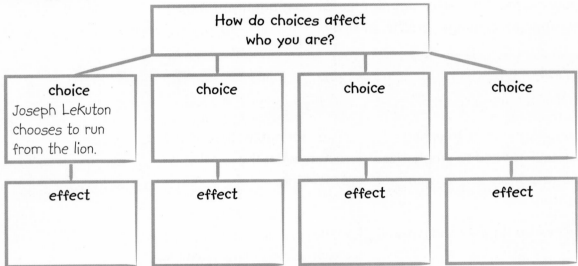

Talk Together

In this unit you found many answers to the **Big Question**. Now use your concept map to discuss it with the class. Think about the different choices the people and characters in the selections made. How did these choices affect their lives?

Concept Map

```
                How do choices affect
                     who you are?

   choice          choice          choice          choice
Joseph Lekuton
chooses to run
from the lion.

   effect          effect          effect          effect
```

Performance Task: Narrative

Consider the choices people made in the selections you've read, including the **Small Group Reading** books. Write a short story that includes two people or characters from two of the selections. The characters meet and have to make a choice. Use what you know about the characters' traits and personalities to describe what this choice might be. Use dialogue to show how the characters discuss the choice with one another.

Checklist

Does your short story

- ✓ clearly describe the characters and setting?
- ✓ clearly develop the sequence of events?
- ✓ include transition words, descriptive details, and sensory language?

Share Your Ideas

Choose one of these ways to share your ideas about the **Big Question**.

Write It!

Write a Letter

Write a letter to thank a friend for something he or she did recently. Explain how the choices your friend made affected you personally. Include specific details about your friend's action that you appreciated.

Talk About It!

Conduct an Interview

Choose students to role-play the real people in this unit. Then prepare questions for an interview. Ask about the different choices they made and how their decisions affected their lives in positive and negative ways.

Do It!

Perform a Skit

As a class, brainstorm a list of scenarios in which a choice needs to be made. For example, *You've been secretly getting tutoring. Your best friend wants to know where you go every afternoon. Do you tell the truth?* Work with a partner to choose one scenario and prepare a skit to perform for the class.

Write It!

Write an Adventure Story

Working with a partner, use presentation software to write a short "choose your own adventure" story. Whenever your main character has to make a choice, give the readers two options. The reader clicks to make a choice for the character and then reads the effect of that choice. Remember to write an outcome for each choice you offer.

Survival

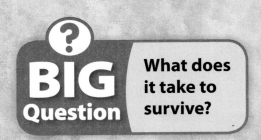

BIG Question What does it take to survive?

Unit at a Glance
▶ **Language**: Describe, Elaborate, Science Words
▶ **Literacy**: Visualize
▶ **Content**: Survival

Unit 2

Share What You Know

❶ **List** some things that help humans and animals survive.

❷ **Write** one survival method. Tape it to your partner's back.

❸ **Ask** questions. Try to guess each other's survival methods.

Build Background: Watch a video about survival.
NGReach.com

Describe

Look at the photo and listen to the description of the scene. Then use **Language Frames** to describe something else you notice in the photo.

Hidden Animals ((MP3))

I notice brown leaves scattered on a forest floor. They look dirty and ragged.

The photo shows a hidden leaf-litter toad. Its brownish skin color and ragged body shape make it look a lot like a leaf.

The toad has a stripe down its back. The stripe looks similar to the spine that goes down the center of a leaf.

These amazing adaptations hide the leaf-litter toad from predators.

Science Vocabulary

Key Words

| camouflage |
| deception |
| duplicate |
| mimic |
| parasite |
| variation |

Key Words

Look at the photos and read the descriptions. Use **Key Words** and other words to talk about **variations**, or different types, of adaptations that help some animals and insects survive.

How do some organisms survive?

DECEPTION

Their adaptations use a form of **deception** to make them appear like other creatures. The eye-like spots on this butterfly make predators think it is a dangerous owl.

DUPLICATION

Their colors or patterns **duplicate**, or look very similar to, other creatures. This king snake has a pattern that looks much like the pattern of a poisonous coral snake.

king snake

MIMICRY

Their appearance or behavior can **mimic**, or look or act like, another creature. A robber fly looks and sounds like a bumblebee.

robber fly

CAMOUFLAGE

Because of **camouflage**, they can blend into their surroundings. This owl's colors, patterns, and markings help it hide in a tree.

PARASITISM

They are **parasites** who live by feeding on other creatures. This tick feeds on the blood of other animals.

Talk Together

Talk with a partner about ways that animals and insects adapt to survive. Then use the **Language Frames** from page 72 and **Key Words** to describe one of the organisms in the photos above.

Main Idea and Details

Nonfiction authors often organize their writing into sections. Each section has a **main idea** and **details** that support it. When you put the main ideas of each section together, you can figure out the author's main idea for the entire selection.

MASTERS OF DISGUISE

What seems to be one thing in nature is often an imposter in disguise. Looking through the viewfinder of my camera, I have seen **plants that look like rocks, shrimp that resemble blades of grass, and flowers that up and fly away. A fly passes as a wasp; a caterpillar is disguised as a twig.** Deceptions such as these allow organisms to hide from predators . . .

"The **heading** and the **details** are both about disguises."

"The **main idea** is about how living things have adaptations that help them hide."

Map and Talk

You can use a main idea chart to record important information from each section of a text. After you finish reading, analyze the main ideas of each section in order to figure out the main idea of the entire selection.

Main Idea Chart

Section Head	Important Details	Main Idea of Section
Masters of Disguise (page 80)	1. Plants look like rocks. 2. 3.	Living things have adaptations that help them hide.

Talk Together

Tell a partner about two animals that have amazing abilities. Your partner creates a main idea chart that uses the animals' names as section heads and then records your details and main ideas about each animal. Then work together to determine a main idea that is true about both animals.

Academic Vocabulary

More Key Words

Use these words to talk about "Deception: Formula for Survival" and "Living Nightmares."

asset

(**a**-set) *noun*

An **asset** is something valuable and useful. When you are hiking, a compass is a helpful **asset** that shows direction.

convince

(kun-**vints**) *verb*

To **convince** means to make someone believe something is true. The kids will **convince** their mother to agree with their idea.

emerge

(i-**murj**) *verb*

To **emerge** is to appear from somewhere hidden. The sun will soon **emerge** from behind the dark clouds.

ensure

(in-**shoor**) *verb*

To **ensure** means to make certain. This girl uses a watch to **ensure** that she meets her friend on time.

resemblance

(ri-**zem**-blunts) *noun*

When things share a **resemblance**, they look alike. The twins share a strong **resemblance** because their features are very similar.

Talk Together

Work with a partner. Write a question using a **Key Word**. Answer the question using a different **Key Word**, if possible. Use all of the words twice.

Question: When will the animal <u>emerge</u> from hiding?

Answer: when it can <u>ensure</u> that it is safe

Add words to My Vocabulary Notebook.
NGReach.com

75

Learn to Visualize

When you read, do you picture how the people or scenes look? Do you imagine how things sound or smell? Sensory images are details that can help you visualize a text through all five senses: sight, sound, smell, taste, and touch.

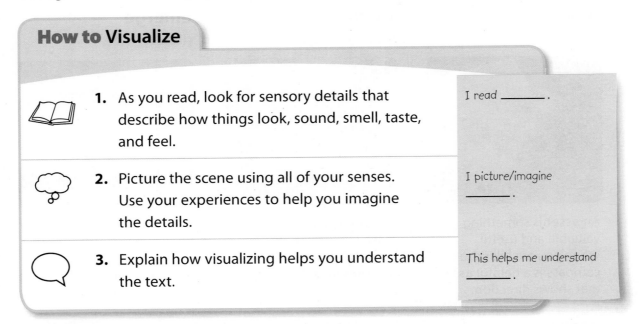

How to Visualize

1. As you read, look for sensory details that describe how things look, sound, smell, taste, and feel.

   I read _____.

2. Picture the scene using all of your senses. Use your experiences to help you imagine the details.

   I picture/imagine _____.

3. Explain how visualizing helps you understand the text.

   This helps me understand _____.

Here's how one student visualized a text about a kind of caterpillar called a looper.

Look Into the Text

When I bumped this branch inadvertently, the looper quickly became rigid in a vertical position, and **when I touched it, I found that the normally soft caterpillar had become as stiff as the adjacent twig.**

"I read **details** about a looper."

"I saw a moth that looks like an owl. I imagine a looper that looks and feels like a twig."

"This helps me understand how the looper hides."

Picturing a scene by using your senses and experiences can help you visualize what the author is describing. It can also help you better understand and remember what you read.

Talk Together

Read the scientific notebook entries and sample notes. Use **Language Frames** to visualize details as you read. Then talk with a partner about how you visualized the text.

Scientific Notebook

RAINFOREST OBSERVATIONS

Monday, May 28th

On my first day in the rainforest, I encountered a sloth resting high up in a leafy, green tree. The large, hairy mammal was hanging upside-down from its long arms and gripping a branch with its long, curved claws.

Sloths' slow speed hardly seems like a helpful **asset**, but it plays a key role in their ability to **camouflage** themselves in their surroundings. Because sloths move so slowly, small algae grow on their fur. The algae turns their grayish brown hair to a silvery green color that **ensures** they will be hidden in the rainforest canopy. ◀

I read that sloths have "long, curved claws."

I imagine claws that look like hooks!

This helps me understand how sloths hold on to trees when they are hanging upside-down.

Tuesday, May 29th

At night, when the katydids **emerge**, the rainforest becomes a choir of chirping insects. Katydids are masters of **deception**. Their ability to **mimic** their surroundings can fool even a careful observer. One kind I spotted on the forest floor was a dry, dusty brown. I was **convinced** that it was another one of the leaves that crackled and crunched beneath my feet. Another **variation** had a remarkable **resemblance** to a leaf that had been eaten by insects. Its markings even **duplicated** the long, narrow veins exactly the way they look on a real leaf! ◀

Thursday, May 31st

Leafcutter ants are small but mighty creatures that work together. Larger workers use their jaws to cut pieces of leaf. Then they carry the leaves back to the nest. Smaller ants ride on the leaf pieces to keep harmful **parasites** from laying eggs on the larger workers. ◀

Today was my last day in the rainforest, but I will bring home a new appreciation for the diversity and adaptability of the amazing creatures that call the rainforest home.

◀ = a good place to visualize a detail

Read a Science Article

Genre

A **science article** is nonfiction. It gives facts and information about a topic related to the natural world.

Text Features

Science articles can include **photographs** that show readers what the author is explaining within the text. Photos can also present new information in a visual way. As you read, analyze the different types of information provided in the text and photos. Then combine the information in order to understand the author's ideas.

. . . the normally soft caterpillar had become as stiff as the adjacent twig.

NATIONAL
GEOGRAPHIC

DECEPTION

FORMULA
FOR
SURVIVAL

by Robert Sisson

Comprehension Coach

▶ **Set a Purpose**

Learn how some creatures have different kinds of adaptations that help them survive.

MASTERS OF
DISGUISE

What seems to be one thing in nature is often **an imposter in an intriguing disguise**. Concentrating through the viewfinder of my camera, I have seen plants that look like rocks, shrimp resembling blades of grass, and flowers that up and fly away. A fly passes as a wasp; a caterpillar is disguised as a twig. **Deceptions** such as these allow organisms to hide from predators or potential victims and to increase chances of **procreation**.

Consider the two insects in the photo *(below)*. The one on the left is a species of ant that tastes bad to predatory birds. The "ant" on the right is actually a tasty plant bug whose body shape, coloring, and food sources resemble those of its unsavory neighbor. To strengthen the mirror image, it also **mimics** the ant's posture and movements.

In Other Words

an imposter in an intriguing disguise
    something that looks like something else
procreation producing children

80

CAMOUFLAGE TO HUNT OR HIDE

At desert's edge, I was observing a crab spider on a flower of the same color, when a bee buzzed over. Failing to see the spider, the bee ended up as breakfast. Then I spotted a looper, or inchworm, under the blossom, chewing bits of petal and sticking them on its back *(left)*. As I watched, the looper inched its way up onto the center of the blossom.

The spider, alerted by the movement, climbed over the edge of the flower to look for the intruder and froze. And so did the looper and I—for the predator was standing on the camouflaged insect *(below)*. The spider finally **withdrew**, and I could breathe again.

On that one blossom I had seen two **aspects** of deception—**camouflage** to help catch prey and camouflage to escape capture.

In Other Words
withdrew went away
aspects variations

▶ Before You Move On

1. **Visualize** Use text details to imagine an organism described on page 80. How does visualizing help you understand the text?
2. **Make Comparisons** How do the looper and crab spider both have adaptations that use **deception**?

HIDING IN PLAIN SIGHT

Loopers usually hunch their way along with the **gait** of an **inverted U** that opens and closes. When I bumped this branch inadvertently, the looper quickly **became rigid in a vertical position** (below), and when I touched it, I found that the normally soft caterpillar had become as stiff as the **adjacent** twig.

Another looper, crawling from one twig to another, sensed a threat. It froze in a horizontal position, so realistically that a predator ant strolled across it—and even stopped **en route** to **preen** (below).

Scientists have given many names to such deceptions: mimicry, cryptic coloration, camouflage, protective resemblance . They theorize that at some point **a mutant** individual is born with, for example, coloring closer to that of the leaves **on which its species browses**.

In Other Words

gait movement

inverted U upside-down letter *U*

became rigid in a vertical position made itself look hard and tall

adjacent nearby

en route on the way

preen clean itself

a mutant an unusual

on which its species browses that the species eats

82

Hungry birds, feeding on **its kin**, are likely to overlook it. And so it lives to breed and pass on the **protective adaptation**. Continuing adaptation allows the species to become a deceiver, often with more than one mode of disguise.

A successful mimic may not only look, feel, smell, and move like **its model**, but it even may **gear** its life to the same seasons in which its model operates. As mimics change to resemble their models, the models themselves are also changing. Too many good-tasting mimics in a population of untasty models would be unfortunate for both, for if predators were as likely to have a good meal as a bad one, they would begin to dine on mimic and model alike. So it is in the best interest of the model to look as unlike the mimic as possible. Call it anti-mimicry, if you wish.

In Other Words

its kin other insects
protective adaptation trait that keeps it safe
its model the organism it copies
gear match

▶ **Before You Move On**

1. **Summarize** Explain why a model that is copied by too many mimics might need to adapt to change its appearance.

2. **Main Idea/Details** What is the main idea of this section? What details support the main idea?

DEADLY DECEPTION

At first, it seems a common sight, a fly prowling along a twig *(top, left)*. Suddenly the twig comes alive *(top, right)*—lashing out with clawed forelegs to **pinion** the hapless fly. My electronic flash **froze the strike**—it all took less than a tenth of a second—to show for the first time what had always before been a blur.

Discovered by Steve Montgomery of the University of Hawaii, this caterpillar of a geometrid moth strikes when tactile hairs on its body are touched. After capturing its prey, it holds the fly so the legs cannot **get purchase** in an attempt to escape.

In Other Words

pinion trap

froze the strike took a picture of the event

get purchase find a good grip

CHANGING DISGUISES

As a butterfly-to-be changes from an egg on a leaf to an adult, it adopts a series of disguises. After hatching, the tiger swallowtail larva survives by resembling a bird dropping *(below, lower right)*.

Three molts later, it has turned green to match the leaves on which it feeds *(below, left)*. The **false eyespots** on the caterpillar's head give it a snakelike look that may frighten away predators. In **the pupal stage** it seems just another broken twig on a tree trunk *(below, upper right)*.

In Other Words

Three molts later After the larva's skin has changed three times

false eyespots colors that look like eyes

the pupal stage this young form

▶ **Before You Move On**

1. **Explain** How does the caterpillar of a geometrid moth catch its prey? Include text evidence in your answer.

2. **Clarify** How do the tiger swallowtail's adaptations demonstrate **variation**?

EXPERIMENTING WITH MIMICRY

Although mimicry was first scientifically described in the middle of the 19th century by Henry Walter Bates, an English **naturalist**, only recently has it been experimentally **duplicated** under natural conditions by **entomologists** Gilbert Waldbauer, Michael Jeffords, and James Sternburg of the University of Illinois.

"Other scientists have shown that the process indeed works in the laboratory," Waldbauer told me, "but demonstrating it in **the field** is a different matter. In our tests we use the day-flying male of the dark promethean moth—a natural mimic of the bad-tasting pipe-vine swallowtail butterfly.

"The promethean is shaped much like a butterfly and flies like one too. And the male is relatively easy to recapture in a trap **baited with** a female of the species.

"We paint some of the moths orange and leave dark wing markings to resemble the **unpalatable** monarch butterfly. Others we paint yellow, leaving wing markings that make them look like the tiger swallowtail, which is tastier to birds. A third batch is marked with black paint, so that their weight matches that of the other groups without altering their appearance to predators.

"We release equal numbers of all three groups in the center of a one-mile-wide circle of baited traps *(above, left)*. As we had expected, more of our mimics painted to look like unsavory models are caught in the traps undamaged, whereas the yellow ones may have beak-shaped bites taken out of their wings *(above, center, right)*.

"**Survivors** are 37 percent 'monarchs' and 39 percent 'pipe-vine swallowtails,' but only 24 percent 'tiger swallowtails.' **Batesian mimicry** does seem to be effective."

In Other Words

naturalist scientist who studied plants, animals, and insects
entomologists scientists who study insects
the field a natural setting
baited with holding

unpalatable bad-tasting
Survivors The moths that live
Batesian mimicry The kind of mimicry Bates described

As factory smoke blackened tree trunks in England during **the Industrial Revolution**, some insects adapted to the color change. E.B. Ford of Oxford University notes that the change in moths has been **striking**.

"More than a hundred species have become **predominantly** black in England," he told me. "It is known as 'industrial melanism,' and it has also occurred in the United States."

He mentioned a study done by an associate, H.B.D. Kettlewell, using the peppered moth, which flies at night and rests exposed on tree trunks during the day. Kettlewell released equal numbers of pale and black moths in an unpolluted forest *(top, left)*. Birds took more than six times as many black moths as pale ones. But in **an industrial area**, blacks survived pale moths by four to one *(center, left)*.

The black moths are spreading for reasons other than camouflage. Genetically, most of them have become hardier—more tolerant of pollution—than the pale forms and have increased in industrial regions.

More than a century of industrialization has passed, and the British have made progress against air pollution. A sign of that success is the increase of pale moths in some industrial districts *(bottom, left)*.

In Other Words

the Industrial Revolution a historical time when many machines and factories were built

striking impressive

predominantly mostly

an industrial area a place with many factories

▶ **Before You Move On**

1. **Details** How does the experiment described on page 86 show that mimicry is effective? Use evidence from the text for support.

2. **Make Inferences** Why was it important for moths to adapt and change color during the Industrial Revolution?

UNDERWATER DISAPPEARING ACTS

Each time I count, I come up with a different number of grass, or phantom, shrimp in this picture *(facing page)*. Their body colors are so perfect that they seem to come and go before my eyes. There are at least 17 of them in and around the turtle grass—I think. Note that the dark green ones rest on dark green grass; brown and black ones choose dead or dying grass.

Sometimes a dark shrimp **masquerades as** a shadow under a leaf, which supports a **lighter-hued** shrimp on top.

Witness another victory at sea. A dwarf sea horse sways in the current, **festooned with appendages** that make them seem like the **plumes of hydroids** on the turtle grass to which it is anchored *(top, left)*.

In Other Words

masquerades as pretends to be
lighter-hued lighter-colored
festooned with appendages covered with parts
plumes of hydroids body parts of other sea creatures

▶ **Before You Move On**

1. **Main Idea/Details** Review the details in this section. What is the main idea that they support?

2. **Use Text Features** How do the photos provide information that helps you better understand the text?

EXPERTS OF
DECEIT

Living stones are plants that survive by looking like rocks in southern Africa's deserts *(below)*. Veined wings hide a leaf katydid on a forest floor *(top, right)*.

Treehoppers march up a branch *(center, right)*, usually **aslant** like the real thorns. Some do stray onto thornless branches or face the wrong direction, but birds quickly scanning the branches usually do not spot them.

The blooms *(bottom, right)* are **larval** plant hoppers, members of a group of insects that deceive **en masse** rather than individually. **Botanists** in East Africa have picked plants adorned with the adult insects—and have been startled to see the "flowers" fly away.

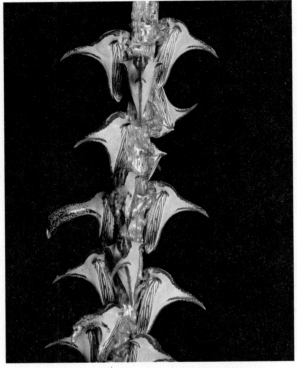

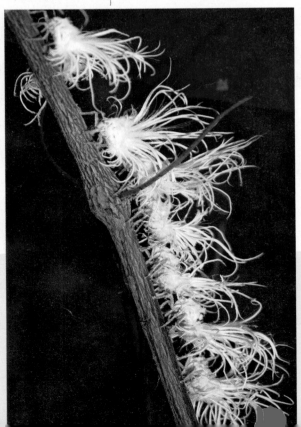

In Other Words

aslant shaped and placed
larval young
en masse in groups
Botanists Scientists who study plants

The feisty wasp is especially popular as a model for other insects.

An insect I photographed in Costa Rica, a mantispid, occurs there in five different color forms, and each of the five mimics a different species of paper wasp.

Study the two face-to-face insects *(below)*, and select the real wasp. Answer: the one on the right. Its companion is a hover fly, a striking mimic of the wasp.

At least one hover fly species not only looks like a wasp but also sounds like one. The **frequency of its wingbeats** is 147 a second, very close to its model's 150. Scientists call this **audio** mimicry—another adaptation in the effort to survive by deception. ❖

In Other Words

frequency of its wingbeats number of times it moves its wings

audio sound

▶ **Before You Move On**

1. **Make Judgments** Based on the photos and text, which organisms on page 90 have the most effective adaptations?

2. **Visualize** Based on what you know about hover flies and the description in the text, how do you imagine they sound?

Key Words

asset	ensure
camouflage	mimic
convince	parasite
deception	resemblance
duplicate	variation
emerge	

Talk About It

1. How do photos and text provide information in different ways? Choose a specific combination of photos and text from the science article, and explain how it helps you understand information.

2. Describe how both predators and prey have adaptations that **mimic** others as a way to survive. Include evidence from the text to support your description.

3. Review the section headings and evaluate whether they are helpful in determining the main idea in each section. Cite specific examples.

4. Why is **camouflage** an important **asset** to some animals in nature? Combine specific evidence from the text to form a generalization.

5. Which two organisms from the selection have adaptations that are the most similar? Which two organisms have adaptations that are the most different? Use evidence from the text to support your judgment.

6. The science article is written from the author's first-person point of view. Analyze how this affects your understanding of the information.

Learn test-taking strategies and answer more questions.
⊘ NGReach.com

Write About It

Imagine that you are an organism in this selection. Write a paragraph that describes how your adaptations help you survive. Use at least three **Key Words** and sensory details to help your reader visualize your description.

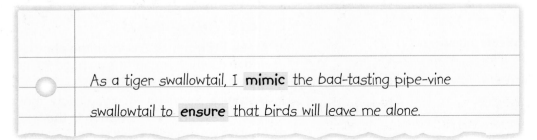

As a tiger swallowtail, I **mimic** the bad-tasting pipe-vine swallowtail to **ensure** that birds will leave me alone.

Main Idea and Details

Use a main idea chart to keep track of the main idea and supporting details in each section of "Deception: A Formula for Survival." Then analyze the chart to figure out the main idea of the entire science article.

Main Idea Chart

Section Head	Important Details	Main Idea of Section
Masters of Disguise (page 80)	1. Plants look like rocks. 2. 3.	Living things have adaptations that help them hide.
	1.	

Use your main idea chart to summarize the main idea of each section to a partner. Then use **Key Words** as you explain how you used the information to determine the author's main idea for the entire selection.

Fluency  Comprehension Coach

Use the Comprehension Coach to practice reading with phrasing. Rate your reading.

Talk Together

Which of the insects and animals described in the article have the most effective methods of **deception** to help them survive? Use **Key Words** and cite text evidence in your discussion.

Relate Words

When you read a new word, ask yourself, "Does this new word look like a word I already know?" Some words belong in the same **word family** because they look similar and have related meanings. You can use what you know about a familiar word to help you figure out the meaning of the new word.

Word	Definition	Related Words
deception *(noun)*	the act of tricking	deceive *(verb)*, deceiver *(noun)*
duplicate *(verb)*	to copy	duplication *(noun)*
emerge *(verb)*	to appear	emerging *(adjective)*, emergence *(noun)*
mimic *(verb)*	to imitate	mimicry *(noun)*
resemblance *(noun)*	the state of being alike	resemble *(verb)*
variation *(noun)*	different type	vary *(verb)*, variety *(noun)*, variable *(noun)*

The chart above shows some related words. You already know the meaning of the verb **mimic**. What do you think the noun *mimicry* may be about?

Try It

Read the sentences. Then answer the questions.

There are many different types of butterflies in the woods. Because of this large **variety** of butterflies, it is common to find two species that **resemble** each other with similar colors and markings.

1. **What is the best definition for variety in the text?**

   A number of different things

   B collection of the same things

   C similarity between things

   D different names for things

2. **What is the best definition for resemble in the text?**

   A to identify

   B to differ from

   C to look or seem like

   D to model after

NATIONAL GEOGRAPHIC

Connect Across Texts You learned about adaptations organisms use for **deception**. Now learn about more adaptations organisms use for survival.

Genre A **science feature** is a short, nonfiction text that focuses on a specific science topic.

Living Nightmares
by Lynn Brunelle

GHOSTS

These see-through animals are masters of deception.

SPOOKFISH Deep in the ocean, you see two green dots **bobbing** in the water. The dots are eyes, but they don't seem attached to a body at all. This weird animal is called a spookfish, and it has a distinctive, ghostly, see-through head. Even though this may look scary, this see-through head is actually an adaptation, and it helps the fish survive.

A spookfish lives 800 meters (about half a mile) under the surface of the ocean, and here, its clear head and dark gray body blend into the dark water. In fact, it's hard to **spot** the fish as it floats almost motionless.

Since this fish's clear skin is like a window, the spookfish can see through it. Its round, green eyes are tucked under its skin, and they move around under its skin as it searches for prey. The fish can point its eyes forward so it can see in front of its face, and it can rotate its eyes upward to look out of the top of its head.

Since the spookfish has these unique eyes, it can spot a jellyfish floating above. Small, silver fish are trapped in the jellyfish's stinging tentacles, and the spookfish **darts** up to steal one. It swims headfirst into the tentacles, and since its eyes are safely covered by skin, they won't get stung.

In Other Words
bobbing bouncing up and down
spot see
darts quickly swims

▶ **Before You Move On**
1. **Main Idea/Details** What special features make the spookfish different from most other fish? Use evidence from the text to support your answer.
2. **Visualize** Which details from the text help you picture the spookfish and its habitat?

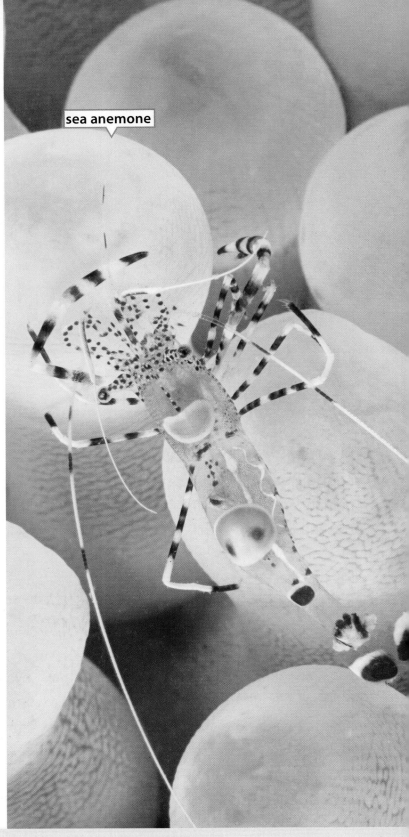

sea anemone

GHOST SHRIMP A spookfish isn't the only ghostly sea **critter**. We spot our next one on a sea anemone. It's hard to see it, because a ghost shrimp's body is mostly clear.

The shrimp uses its body as **camouflage**, so it can blend in wherever it goes. Other critters see only the surface on which the shrimp is standing, so the shrimp remains safely hidden from predators.

Being clear only works as long as the ghost shrimp doesn't eat. When the shrimp **nibbles algae**, its food shows through its transparent body.

In Other Words
critter animal; creature
nibbles algae eats small plants

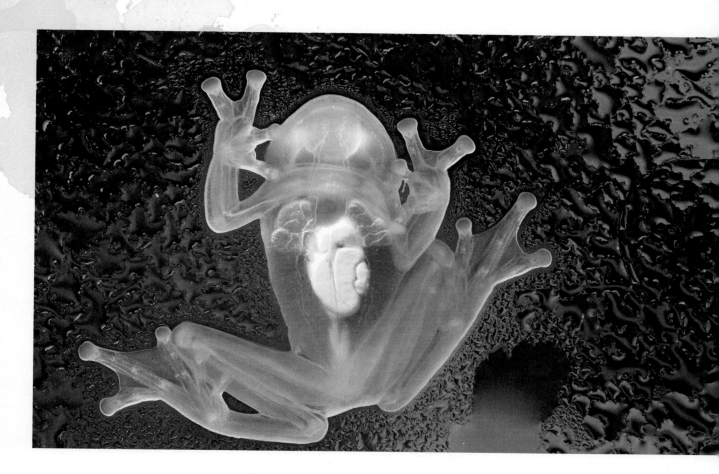

GLASS FROG Another ghostly creature lives in a rain forest; it makes a squeaky "peep" sound. The sound seems like it's coming from a pale, green leaf, but it looks as if there is no critter on the leaf.

Suddenly, a bump on the leaf wiggles, and it's a frog. Like the other ghostly creatures you've read about, this frog is a master of disguise. Because it blends in with the leaf, it is almost invisible until it moves. It's not the same color as the leaf, however. Like the shrimp, a glass frog blends in because it has almost no color at all.

The skin on its belly is clear, and its back is pale green. The bright green of the leaf shines right through this frog; it makes the frog look like part of the leaf. This **resemblance** helps the glass frog hide from its predators.

Most of the time, this frog blends in. Flip the frog over, however, and you can see its insides. You can see its heart pumping blood and watch food squeeze through its guts.

▶ **Before You Move On**

1. **Make Inferences** What might happen if a ghost shrimp is eating when a predator swims by? Why?

2. **Explain** Why is the adaptation of **camouflage** so important to the ghost shrimp and the glass frog?

ZOMBIES

Some organisms use mind control to get ahead.

ZOMBIE ANT A line of ants marches through a rain forest. One by one, the ants climb a tree trunk to head up to their warm, dry nest. Suddenly, one ant stumbles out of line, twitches a little, and then drops to the ground. Something is wrong because these ants usually never step out of line.

Near the ground, the ant finds a leaf. It crawls under the leaf where it's damp and shady, and then it bites into the leaf. Suddenly, the ant's jaws lock, and it can't let go or even move. The ant hangs from the leaf, slowly dying. This ant is acting odd for a scary reason—because it's a zombie. You can't see it, but a killer now controls the ant.

The ant was fine days earlier, until it picked up a tiny **hitchhiker** smaller than a grain of sand. The hitchhiker was a **fungus spore**, and it dug its way into the ant's body. Even though the ant doesn't feel a thing, the **parasite** goes to work inside the ant's body. It reproduces and spreads, and it eventually takes over the ant's brain. The fungus inside of it makes the ant find a damp, shady place, because that's where a fungus grows best.

The fungus sprouts from the ant's head, and this makes the ant look like it is growing antennae. By now, the ant is dead, but the fungus keeps growing until it explodes. These new splattered spores will attach themselves to other ants to make new zombies.

In Other Words
get ahead get what they need
hitchhiker traveler
fungus spore tiny intruder

ZOMBIE SNAIL Fungi aren't the only zombie masters. A kind of flatworm **hijacks** a snail, and the results aren't pretty. Like the fungus, the worm is a parasite. As the snail slowly crawls across the ground looking for bird droppings to eat, it has no idea that flatworm eggs are in the droppings.

When the snail eats the droppings, the flatworm eggs hatch inside the snail. When the young flatworms start to grow, they move into the snail's eyestalks, which are the long stems that hold the snail's eyes. The snail's eyestalks start to grow bigger and more colorful.

Because its body has been taken over, the snail starts acting very odd. Usually, it hides in the shadows to avoid predators. Now, the flatworms have taken over its brain, and they make the snail crawl into wide-open spaces.

The snail wriggles its swollen eyestalks; they look like juicy caterpillars. A bird sees the moving eyestalks, swoops in, and rips the eyestalks off the snail. The doomed snail crawls away, but inside the bird's gut, the flatworms finish growing. They lay eggs, and these eggs may become food for more snails.

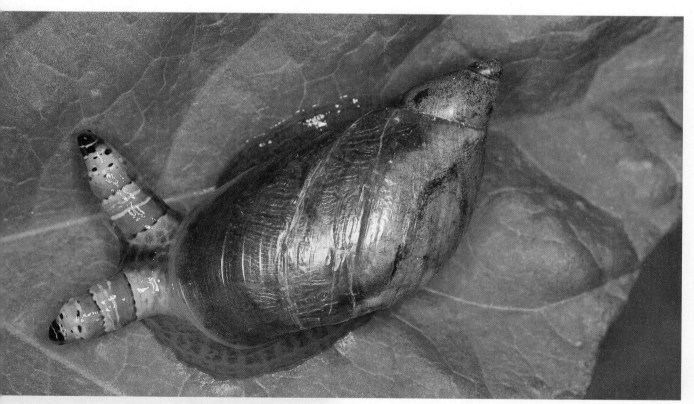

In Other Words
hijacks takes over

▶ **Before You Move On**

1. **Compare** How do the fungus spore and flatworm's adaptations help them survive?
2. **Author's Viewpoint** How does the author view the **parasites** in this section? Cite evidence to support your response.

DEVILS

These critters use scary looks and sounds to survive.

TASMANIAN DEVIL Just after midnight, a howl rises from a forest in Australia. A fearsome growl answers it, and then there's a scream. Sharp teeth **flash**, and fur flies. This forest sounds haunted, but these sounds are just caused by two Tasmanian devils fighting over a dead animal.

These scavengers eat dead animals, and it's best to stay out of their way. They may weigh only about 8 kg (about 17 pounds), but they have one of the most powerful bites of any mammal. Their teeth crush bones and rip apart fur and guts.

These devils fight over food, they **brawl** over space, they battle for mates, and they attack predators. When Tasmanian devils fight, their ears turn bright red. Then they spray a stinky smell, **gnash** their teeth, and scream. They act devilish in order to survive.

THORNY DEVIL A second kind of devil lives in a desert in Australia. Spikes stick out from its body, and they look like sharp thorns. Meet the thorny devil lizard. Its prickly outside makes it look dangerous, but its looks are an interesting adaptation.

At dawn, the lizard rubs against a bush that is covered in dew. Dew runs down its spikes and into tiny grooves on its skin. The grooves lead to the lizard's mouth, allowing the lizard to drink the dew. Now it can survive another **devilishly** hot day in the desert.

Despite its looks, only ants should fear the thorny devil. It licks them up with its tongue and crunches them with its teeth. In fact, it can eat as many as 3,000 ants in a meal.

In Other Words
flash bite and tear
brawl fight
gnash grind
devilishly horribly

HICKORY HORNED DEVIL Our last creepy critter, the hickory horned devil, crawls along a branch high in a tree. This devil is a caterpillar, and it can grow up to 15 cm long. When it **rears up**, nearly a dozen spiky red and black horns stick out of its head. It shakes its head and buzzes. This creepy critter looks and acts devilish in order to scare away predators and get back to what it does best—munching tree leaves.

From devils to zombie masters to ghosts, these critters may seem like living nightmares. Some seem to vanish, and others howl horribly or force victims to grow freaky body parts. Their adaptations may make them look and act scary, but each adaptation helps them survive. ❖

In Other Words
rears up stands up straight

▶ **Before You Move On**

1. **Use Text Features** How do the photographs present information in a different way than the text? Cite specific examples.

2. **Interpret** Why does this science feature describe these creatures as "living nightmares"?

Respond and Extend

Compare Texts

The selections, "Deception: Formula for Survival" and
"Living Nightmares" both tell about ways that animals
survive. Think about the main idea of each text and the details the authors include.
Then work with a partner to complete the chart below. Use the information to evaluate
how the two selections present information about the same scientific topic.

Comparison Chart

	"Deception: Formula for Survival"	"Living Nightmares"
Main Idea of Selection	Some species _____ .	Some species _____ .
Details That Support the Main Idea	1. 2. 3.	1. 2. 3.
Text Features		

Talk Together

How do the authors of "Deception: Formula for Survival" and "Living
Nightmares" help you understand how species are adapted for survival?
Use **Key Words** and text evidence to talk about your ideas.

Subject and Object Pronouns

A **pronoun** is a word that takes the place of a noun. The type of pronoun to use depends on how it is used in a sentence.

Grammar Rules Subject and Object Pronouns	
Use a **subject pronoun** in place of a **noun** as the subject of a sentence.	The **jellyfish** floats by. **It** does not see the transparent spookfish.
The subject pronouns are *I, you, he, she, it, we,* and *they*.	The **eyes** of a spookfish are odd. **They** are tucked under the skin.
Use an **object pronoun** in place of a **noun** after an <u>action verb</u>.	Small, silver **fish** are trapped. The spookfish <u>eats</u> **them**.
Also use an **object pronoun** in place of a **noun** after a <u>preposition</u>. The object pronouns are *me, you, him, her, it, us,* and *them*.	The **tentacles** sting, but the spookfish swims <u>through</u> **them**.

Read Subject and Object Pronouns

Writers want to avoid repeating the same words too many times, so they use subject and object pronouns to take the place of some repeated nouns. Read this passage from "Living Nightmares." Identify the subject and object pronouns. How do they make the writing smooth and easy to read?

> Despite its looks, only ants should fear the thorny devil. It licks them up with its tongue and crunches them with its teeth. In fact, it can eat as many as 3,000 ants in a meal.

Write Subject and Object Pronouns

Write a short paragraph about one of the creatures in "Living Nightmares." Include at least two subject and object pronouns. Then compare your work with a partner's.

Language Frames

- For example, _____ .
- In addition _____ .
- Not only _____ , but _____ .

Elaborate

Look at the photo and listen to the presentation. Then use **Language Frames** to elaborate on an important detail about survival from the presentation.

Survival Basics ((MP3))

When it comes to survival, humans and animals share many similarities. For example, all living creatures require food and water in order to survive. Without these two basic things, most living things would die within days. In addition to essential nutrients, humans and animals also require shelter to keep them safe from different kinds of danger, such as severe weather and predators. Not only do humans build their own homes, but many animals build complicated shelters, too, such as birds that build nests and beavers that construct dams. All living things share the same basic needs, and all have found amazing ways to adapt and survive.

Science Vocabulary

Key Words

Key Words

exhaust

necessity

overcome

reliance

resourceful

Look at the illustration and read the text. Use **Key Words** and other words to talk about how you can **overcome**, or conquer, the challenges in nature.

Tips for Hiking

When you are hiking, the most important **necessity** that you must have is water. Take small sips so that you do not **exhaust**, or use up, your water supply too quickly.

TIP 1

If you have to camp overnight, you can be creative and **resourceful** by making a shelter out of the materials around you.

TIP 2

TIP 3

Most hikers wear sturdy boots or shoes. Some also have a **reliance** on tools, such as walking sticks. They need these tools to stay safe on the trail.

Talk Together

Talk with a partner about the three safety tips above. Then give another safety tip. Use the **Language Frames** from page 104 and **Key Words** to elaborate on your idea with more information and details.

Character

Most stories focus on a main **character** who has a problem or goal. To understand the character, think about the person's:

- **motives:** reasons why the character does or says something.

- **actions:** what the character says and does.

As you read the story, look for text evidence that helps you understand the main character.

Look Into the Text

Here I am and that is nowhere. With his mind opened and thoughts happening, it all tried to come in with a rush, all of what had occurred and he could not take it. The whole thing turned into a confused jumble that made no sense. So he fought it down and tried to take one thing at a time . . .

My name is Brian Robeson and I am thirteen years old and I am alone in the north woods of Canada.

All right, he thought, that's simple enough.

"Brian's **motive** is that he is confused and scared. He needs to figure out what is happening."

"His **actions** are to calm down and think clearly."

Map and Talk

A character chart can help you analyze details about a character's motives and actions to help you learn more about the character.

Character Chart

Character: Brian Robeson	
Motives	**Actions**
wants to figure out what is happening	

Talk Together

Tell a partner about a time you had to do something important. What motivated you? What actions did you take? Describe the experience while a partner completes a character chart about the experience and explains something that it shows about you.

Academic Vocabulary

More Key Words

Use these words to talk about *Hatchet* and "Survival Stories: The Girl Who Fell from the Sky."

concentrate
(**kon**-sun-trāt) *verb*

When you **concentrate**, you give all of your attention to something. The boy must **concentrate** when he glues the tiny pieces together.

intense
(in-**tens**) *adjective*

Something that is **intense** is very strong. The **intense** wind made the tree tops bend over.

motivation
(mō-tu-**vā**-shun) *noun*

Motivation is the reason for doing something. My **motivation** for studying is to get good grades.

resilience
(ri-**zil**-yunts) *noun*

When you show **resilience**, you can recover from or adapt to difficult situations. Plants show **resilience** by growing in places with little or no soil.

resolve
(ri-**zolv**) *verb*

When you **resolve** to do something, you reach a decision about it. After seeing the litter, the kids **resolve** to pick up trash once a week.

Talk Together

With a partner, make an Expanded Meaning Map for each **Key Word**.

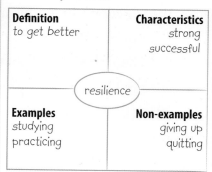

Definition	Characteristics
to get better	strong
	successful
resilience	
Examples	Non-examples
studying	giving up
practicing	quitting

Add words to My Vocabulary Notebook.
NGReach.com

Learn to Visualize

As you read, use details in the text to create mental images, or pictures in your mind. When you combine these images with your own experience, you react to what you read. These reactions, or emotional responses, can deepen your understanding of the text.

How to Visualize

1. As you read, notice words and phrases that create images in your mind.

2. Describe what you "see" and "hear" in your mind.

3. Combine these mental images of the text with your own experience to identify how you feel. Consider how identifying your emotional responses helps you understand text.

I read _____.

I see/hear _____.

I feel _____.
I understand _____.

Here's how one student visualized a text and responded.

Look Into the Text

"I'm hungry." He said it aloud. In normal tones at first, then louder and louder until he was yelling it. "I'm hungry, I'm hungry, I'm hungry!"

When he stopped there was sudden silence, not just from him but the clicks and blurps and bird sounds of the forest as well. The noise of his voice had startled everything and it was quiet. He looked around, listened with his mouth open, and realized that in all his life he had never heard silence before. Complete silence. There had always been some sound, some kind of sound.

"I read **details** about the silence."

"I hear the total silence in the forest."

"I remember feeling silence like that, so I feel worried about Brian. I understand how scared and lonely he must feel."

Visualizing and forming emotional responses to the text can help you relate to the story and gain a deeper understanding of what you've read.

Talk Together

Read the journal entry and sample notes. Use **Language Frames** to visualize and form emotional responses as you read. Then talk with a partner about how you responded to the text.

Journal Entry

A Backcountry Adventure

Sunday, July 10th

We are back from our three-day camping trip to the Shenandoah Valley. Mom and Dad had *been* concerned about our family's **reliance** on computers, cell phones, and video games for entertainment. So they decided a camping trip would help us **overcome** our dependence on electronic devices. I knew we'd have to be **resilient** in order to find a way to survive without the comforts of home.

When you camp in the backcountry, you have to carry all of your supplies with you. We could only bring **necessities** that we needed to survive, such as food, clothes, a camp stove, fuel, rope, a map, and a water container. At first, I was surprised that we weren't bringing bottled water with us. Then my heavy, overstuffed backpack made me realize we'd soon **exhaust** any supply we could carry. Instead, we'd have to be **resourceful** and boil or filter water from nearby streams. ◄

Our first day in the wilderness was incredible. We scrabbled up rocky paths and waded in an ice-cold stream that made my feet tingle. Fragrant wildflowers waved their colorful petals at us. I felt like I had stepped into a dreamy landscape painting. After all that exercise, an **intense** hunger burned in the pit of my stomach. Mom's homemade trail mix had never tasted so good. ◄

At night, the darkness seemed like a black curtain had *been* dropped over us. I tried to read with a flashlight, but I couldn't **concentrate**. I finally fell asleep to a chorus of chirping crickets.

By our last day, I had blistered feet and bug-bitten arms. I was ready to go home. I couldn't wait to play video games. But a funny thing happened. Soon after I started my favorite game, I lost the **motivation** to continue. I headed outside to get some fresh air. Mom and Dad's plan had worked after all. Right then I **resolved** to spend more time in the great outdoors. ◄

I read about the supplies the family needs to carry.

I *see* big, heavy packs bulging with food and equipment.

I *feel* sympathy for the family because each person has to carry a heavy load.

I understand why the family could only pack necessities.

◄ = a good place to form mental images

Read an Adventure Story

Genre

An **adventure story** tells about events that are dangerous or exciting. In this fictional adventure story, the author describes how a character reacts to his experiences and **overcomes** obstacles.

Point of View

Point of view describes how a story is told. In **third-person point of view**, a narrator who is not a character tells the story. When the third-person point of view is **omniscient**, the narrator knows everything about the story's events, including all of the character's thoughts and feelings.

The narrator describes the character's actions and thoughts.

> Brian rubbed his stomach. The hunger had been there but something else—fear, pain—had held it down. Now, with the thought of the burger, the emptiness roared at him.

from HATCHET
by Gary Paulsen
ILLUSTRATED BY JULIANA KOLESOVA

▶ **Set a Purpose**
Find out about a challenge
that a 13-year-old boy
must **overcome** in the forest.

Here I am and that is nowhere. With his mind **opened** and thoughts happening, it all tried to come in with a rush, all of what had occurred and he could not **take it**. The whole thing turned into a confused jumble that made no sense. So he **fought it down** and tried to take one thing at a time.

He had been flying north to visit his father for a couple of months in the summer, and the pilot had had a heart attack and had died, and the plane had crashed somewhere in the Canadian north woods but he did not know how far they had flown or in what direction or where he was . . .

In Other Words
opened able to think
take it understand it all
fought it down made himself calm down

112

Slow down, he thought. Slow down more.

My name is Brian Robeson and I am thirteen years old and I am alone in the north woods of Canada.

All right, he thought, that's simple enough.

I was flying to visit my father and the plane crashed and sank in a lake.

There, keep it that way. Short thoughts.

I do not know where I am.

Which doesn't mean much. More to the point, *they* do not know where I am—*they* meaning anybody who might be wanting to look for me. The searchers.

They would look for him, look for the plane. His father and mother would be **frantic**. They would tear the world apart to find him. Brian had seen searches on the news, seen movies about lost planes. When a plane went down they **mounted extensive searches** and almost always they found the plane within a day or two. Pilots all filed flight plans—a detailed plan for where and when they were going to fly, with all the courses explained. They would come, they would look for him. The searchers would get government planes and cover both sides of the flight plan filed by the pilot and search until they found him.

Maybe even today. They might come today. This was the second day after the crash. No. Brian frowned. Was it the first day or the second day? They had gone down in the afternoon and he had spent the whole night **out cold**. So this was the first real day. But they could still come today. They would have started the search immediately when Brian's plane did not arrive.

In Other Words

frantic very afraid and worried

mounted extensive searches sent many people to help

out cold unconscious

Yeah, they would probably come today.

Probably come in here with amphibious planes, small bushplanes with floats that could land right here on the lake and pick him up and take him home.

Which home? The father home or the mother home. He stopped the thinking. It didn't matter. Either on to his dad or back to his mother. Either way he would probably be home by late night or early morning, home where he could sit down and eat a large, cheesy, juicy burger with tomatoes and double fries with ketchup and a thick chocolate shake.

And there came hunger.

Brian rubbed his stomach. The hunger had been there but something else—fear, pain—had held it down. Now, with the thought of the burger, the emptiness **roared at him**. He could not believe the hunger, had never felt it this way. The lake water had filled his stomach but left it hungry, and now it demanded food, screamed for food.

And there was, he thought, absolutely nothing to eat.

Nothing.

What did they do in the movies when they got stranded like this? Oh, yes, the hero usually found some kind of plant that he knew was good to eat and that took care of it. Just ate the plant until he was full or used some kind of cute trap to catch an animal and cook it over a **slick** little fire and pretty soon he had a full eight-course meal.

The trouble, Brian thought, looking around, was that all he could see was grass and brush. There was nothing obvious to eat and aside from about a million birds and the beaver he hadn't seen animals to trap and cook, and even if he got one somehow he didn't have any matches so he couldn't have a fire . . .

In Other Words
roared at him was **intense**
slick perfect

Nothing.

It kept coming back to that. He had nothing.

Well, almost nothing. As a matter of fact, he thought, I don't know what I've got or haven't got. Maybe I should try and figure out just how I **stand**. It will give me something to do—keep me from thinking of food. Until they come to find me.

Brian had once had an English teacher, a guy named Perpich, who was always talking about being positive, thinking positive, **staying on top of things**. That's how Perpich had put it—stay positive and stay on top of things. Brian thought of him now—wondered how to stay positive and stay on top of this. All Perpich would say is that I have to get motivated. He was always telling kids to get motivated.

Brian changed position so he was sitting on his knees. He reached into his pockets and took out everything he had and laid it on the grass in front of him.

It was **pitiful** enough. A quarter, three dimes, a nickel, and two pennies. A fingernail clipper. A billfold with a twenty dollar bill— "In case you get stranded at the airport in some small town and have to buy food," his mother had said—and **some odd** pieces of paper.

In Other Words

stand am doing

staying on top of things keeping focused on what you need to do

pitiful sad

some odd a few

And on his belt, somehow still there, the hatchet his mother had given him. He had forgotten it and now reached around and took it out and put it in the grass. There was a touch of rust already forming on the cutting edge of the blade and he rubbed it off with his thumb.

That was it.

He frowned. No, wait—if he was going to **play the game, might as well play it right**. Perpich would tell him to quit messing around. Get motivated. Look at *all* of it, Robeson.

He had on a pair of good tennis shoes, now almost dry. And socks. And jeans and underwear and a thin leather belt and a T-shirt with a windbreaker so torn it hung on him in tatters.

And a watch. He had a digital watch still on his wrist but it was broken from the crash—the little screen blank—and he took it off and almost threw it away but stopped the hand motion and lay the watch on the grass with the rest of it.

There. That was it.

No, wait. One other thing. Those were all the things he had, but he also had himself. Perpich used to **drum that into them**—"You are your most valuable asset. Don't forget that. *You* are the best thing you have."

In Other Words

play the game, might as well play it right survive, he had to do his best

drum that into them always remind them

▶ **Before You Move On**

1. **Paraphrase** What lessons has Brian learned from Perpich?

2. **Point of View** Identify examples in which the narrator includes Brian's thoughts. How does this help you understand the story?

▶ **Predict**
Will Brian have the **resilience** he
needs to survive?

Brian looked around again. *I wish you were here, Perpich. I'm hungry and I'd trade everything I have for a hamburger.*

"I'm hungry." He said it aloud. In normal tones at first, then louder and louder until he was yelling it. "I'm hungry, I'm hungry, I'm hungry!"

When he stopped there was sudden silence, not just from him but the clicks and blurps and bird sounds of the forest as well. The noise of his voice had startled everything and it was quiet. He looked around, listened with his mouth open, and realized that in all his life he had never heard silence before. Complete silence. There had always been some sound, some kind of sound.

It lasted only a few seconds, but it was so **intense** that it seemed to become part of him. Nothing. There was no sound. Then the bird started again, and some kind of buzzing insect, and then a chattering and a cawing, and soon there was the same background of sound.

Which left him still hungry.

Of course, he thought, putting the coins and the rest back in his pocket and the hatchet in his belt—*of course if they come tonight or even if they take as long as tomorrow the hunger is no big thing. People have gone for many days without food as long as they've got water. Even if they don't come until late tomorrow I'll be all right. Lose a little weight, maybe, but the first hamburger and a malt and fries will bring it right back.*

A mental picture of a hamburger, the way they showed it in the television commercials, thundered into his thoughts. Rich colors, the meat juicy and hot . . .

He pushed the picture away. *So even if they didn't find him until tomorrow,* he thought, *he would be all right.* He had plenty of water, although he wasn't sure if it was good and clean or not.

He sat again by the tree, his back against it. There was a thing bothering him. He wasn't quite sure what it was but it kept chewing at the edge of his thoughts. Something about the plane and the pilot that would change things . . .

Ahh, there it was—the moment when the pilot had his heart attack his right foot had jerked down on the rudder pedal and the plane had **slewed** sideways. What did that mean? Why did that keep coming into his thinking that way, nudging and pushing?

It means, a voice in his thoughts said, that they might not be coming for you tonight or even tomorrow. When the pilot pushed the rudder pedal the plane had jerked to the side and **assumed** a new course. Brian could not remember how much it had pulled around, but it wouldn't have had to be much because after that, with the pilot dead, Brian had flown for hour after hour on the new course.

Well away from the flight plan the pilot had filed. Many hours, at maybe 160 miles an hour. Even if it was only a little off course, with that speed and time Brian might now be sitting several hundred miles off to the side of the recorded flight plan.

And they would probably search most heavily at first along the flight plan course. They might go out to the side a little, but he could easily be three, four hundred miles to the side. He could not know, could not think of how far he might have flown wrong because he didn't know the original course and didn't know how much they had pulled sideways.

Quite a bit—that's how he remembered it. Quite a jerk to the side. It pulled his head over sharply when the plane had swung around.

They might not find him for two or three days. He felt his heartbeat increase as the fear started. The thought was there but he fought it down for a time, pushed it away, then it exploded out.

They might not find him for a long time.

In Other Words
slewed turned
assumed taken

And the next thought was there as well, that they might never find him, but that was panic and he fought it down and tried to stay positive. They searched hard when a plane went down, they used many men and planes and they would go to the side, they would know he was off from the flight path, he had talked to the man on the radio, they would somehow know . . .

It would be all right.

They would find him. Maybe not tomorrow, but soon. Soon. Soon. They would find him soon.

Gradually, like sloshing oil his thoughts settled back and the panic was gone. Say they didn't come for two days—no, say they didn't come for three days, even push that to four days—he could live with that. He would have to live with that. He didn't want to think of them taking longer. But say four days. He had to do something. He couldn't just sit at the bottom of this tree and stare down at the lake for four days.

And nights. He was in deep woods and didn't have any matches, couldn't make a fire. There were large things in the woods. There were wolves, he thought, and bears—other things. In the dark he would be in the open here, just sitting at the bottom of a tree.

He looked around suddenly, felt the hair on the back of his neck go up. Things might be looking at him right now, waiting for him—waiting for dark so they could move in and take him.

He fingered the hatchet at his belt. It was the only weapon he had, but it was something.

He had to have some kind of shelter. No, make that more: He had to have some kind of shelter and he had to have something to eat.

He pulled himself to his feet and jerked the back of his shirt down before the mosquitos could get at it. He had to do something to help himself.

I have to get motivated, he thought, remembering Perpich. Right now I'm all I've got. I have to do something. ❖

▶ **Before You Move On**

1. **Character** What motivates Brian to stop panicking and take action?

2. **Visualize** Which details help you picture Brian's actions and feelings? How do they help you understand the story?

GARY PAULSEN

AWARD WINNER

Much of Gary Paulsen's work is inspired by his real-life adventures. When he was just 14, he traveled with the circus. He spent summers working on ranches and ships. Becoming independent at a young age became a major theme in many of his novels, including *Hatchet* and its four sequels. Paulsen also competed twice in the Iditarod, a brutal 1,180-mile Alaskan dog sled race that inspired him to write an award-winning novel called *Dogsong*.

Thanks to Paulsen's writing, his readers are invited to join in his experiences, too.

Paulsen says that writers should write something every day. "Even if you wind up deleting everything you've written, at least keep your hand moving and the words flowing." With luck—and hard work—his readers could go on to write about their own real-life adventures.

Writer's Craft

In *Hatchet*, the author uses a combination of long and short sentences to convey Brian's sense of helplessness and fear: "I was flying to visit my father and the plane crashed and sank in a lake. There, keep it that way. Short thoughts."

Write a brief description of a scary situation. Use a variety of sentence lengths to convey your mood. Think about how you can share your personal thoughts in your description like Brian in the novel.

Think and Respond

Key Words

concentrate	overcome
exhaust	reliance
intense	resilience
motivation	resolve
necessity	resourceful

Talk About It

1. *Hatchet* is an adventure story. Use specific examples from the text to describe Brian's situation and the obstacles he must **overcome**.

2. Identify the **necessities** that Brian needs in order to survive in the wilderness. Elaborate on the dangers Brian faces and how he should deal with them.

3. What causes Brian to change his attitude about waiting for rescue? Use evidence from the text to explain the change and what this shows about Brian.

4. How does Brian show **resilience** during his ordeal? Cite evidence from the text to support your answer.

5. Review Brian's actions. Based on what you have read and what you know about survival, which of Brian's decisions is the best example of being **resourceful**? Why?

6. How would Brian's story be different if it were told from Brian's viewpoint instead of a third-person narrator? Choose a specific scene from the selection and analyze how the point of view affects the story.

Learn test-taking strategies and answer more questions.
 NGReach.com

Write About It

Imagine that Brian has been rescued. Write a speech in which Brian describes and elaborates on his experiences. Use at least three **Key Words**.

Well, at first I was **overcome** *with panic. I couldn't believe all the things that had happened to me in such a short time.*

Analyze Character

Use a character chart to organize your thoughts about Brian. Look back at the story to see what Brian does and why he does it.

Character Chart

Character: Brian Robeson	
Motives	**Actions**
wants to figure out what is happening	stops panicking and tries to think clearly

Use your character chart to describe Brian to a partner. Explain what his actions and **motivations** show you about his character. Use **Key Words**.

Fluency  Comprehension Coach

Use the Comprehension Coach to practice reading with expression. Rate your reading.

Talk Together

What qualities are the key to survival in the wilderness? Include **Key Words** and examples from Brian's experiences in *Hatchet* as you discuss your ideas with a small group.

Shades of Meaning

Good writers choose words that say exactly what they mean. Many words have **synonyms**, or words that have similar meanings. You can consult a thesaurus for synonyms. Then arrange the words on a synonym scale to show how they relate.

EXAMPLES

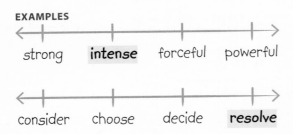

According to the synonym scale above, the word *consider* is not as strong a word as *resolve*. What is another word you could add to the scale?

Try It

Read the sentence. Then answer the two-part question. First, answer part A.
Then answer part B.

> That night, the storm completely destroyed Brian's shelter, ruined his supplies, and threatened his life.

PART A

1. **What is most likely the author's reason for describing the shelter as "completely destroyed"?**

   A   to give details about Brian's shelter

   B   to show the strength of the storm

   C   to show how to survive a storm

   D   to explain why Brian has a shelter

PART B

2. **Which synonym best describes the storm in part A?**

   A   strong

   B   intense

   C   forceful

   D   powerful

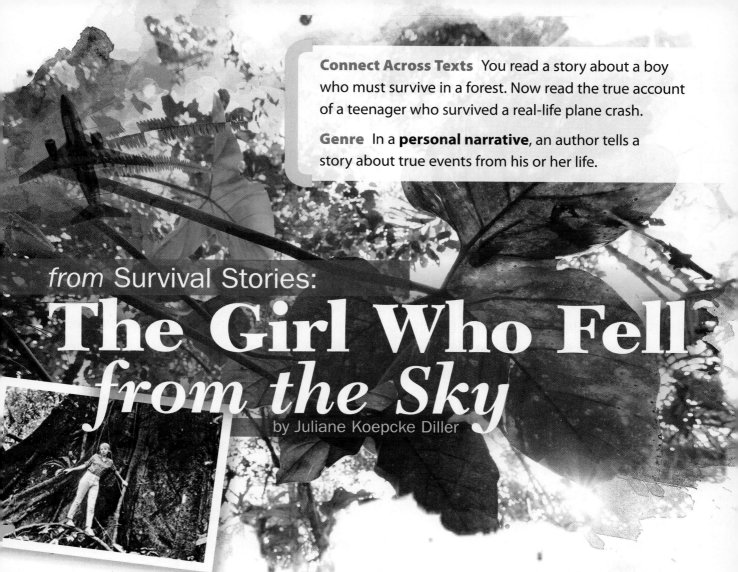

Connect Across Texts You read a story about a boy who must survive in a forest. Now read the true account of a teenager who survived a real-life plane crash.

Genre In a **personal narrative**, an author tells a story about true events from his or her life.

from Survival Stories:

The Girl Who Fell from the Sky

by Juliane Koepcke Diller

▲ **Juliane Koepcke Diller in the Peruvian rain forest**

The first half of the hour-long flight from Lima to Pucallpa is uneventful. We're served a sandwich and a drink for breakfast. Ten minutes later, as the **flight attendants** begin to clean up, we fly into a huge thunderstorm.

Suddenly, daylight turns to night and lightning flashes from all directions. People gasp as the plane shakes violently. Bags, wrapped gifts, and clothing fall from overhead lockers. Sandwich trays soar through the air, and half-finished drinks spill onto passengers' heads. People scream and cry.

"Hopefully this goes all right," my mother says nervously.

In Other Words
flight attendants workers on the airplane

▶ **Before You Move On**
1. **Setting** How does the setting of the narrative drastically change? Use evidence from the text to support your answer.
2. **Make Connections** What is a connection that helps you understand Diller's feelings about this experience?

125

I see a blinding white light over the right wing. I don't know whether it's a flash of lightning or an explosion. I lose all sense of time. The airplane begins to **nosedive**. From my seat in the back, I can see down the aisle into the cockpit.

My ears, my head, my whole body are filled with the deep roar of the plane. Over everything, I hear my mother say calmly, "Now it's all over."

We're falling fast. People's shouts and the roar of the turbines suddenly go silent.

My mother is no longer at my side, and I'm no longer in the plane. I'm still strapped into my seat on the bench, at an altitude of about 10,000 feet. I'm alone. And I'm falling.

My free fall is quiet. I see nothing around me. The seat belt squeezes my belly so tight that I can't breathe. Before I feel fear, I lose consciousness.

When I **come to**, I'm upside down, still falling, the Peruvian rain forest spinning slowly toward me. The densely packed treetops remind me of broccoli. I see everything as if through a fog before I pass out again.

When I regain consciousness, I've landed in the middle of the jungle. My seat belt is unfastened, so I must have woken up at some point. I've crawled deeper into the sheltering back of the three-seat bench that

was fastened to me when I fell from the sky. Wet and muddy, I lie there for the rest of the day and night.

I will never forget the image I see when I open my eyes the next morning: The crowns of the giant trees above me are **suffused** with golden light, bathing everything in a green glow. I feel abandoned, helpless, and utterly alone. My mother's seat beside me is empty.

I can't stand up. I hear the soft ticking of my watch but can't read the time. I can't see straight. I realize that my left eye is swollen shut; I can see only through a narrow slit in my right eye. My glasses have disappeared, but I finally manage to read the time.

It's 9 a.m. I feel dizzy again and lie exhausted on the rain forest floor. After a while, I manage to rise to my knees, but I feel so dizzy that I immediately lie back down. I try again, and eventually I'm able to hold myself in that position. I touch my right collarbone; it's clearly broken. I find a deep gash on my left **calf**, which looks as if it has been cut by a rough metal edge. Strangely, it's not bleeding.

I get down on all fours and crawl around, searching for my mother. I call her name, but only the voices of the jungle answer me.

In Other Words
nosedive fall toward the ground
come to wake up
suffused filled
calf lower leg

◄ katydid

For someone who has never been in the rain forest, it can seem threatening. Huge trees cast mysterious shadows. Water drips constantly. The rain forest often has a musty smell from the plants that intertwine and ramble, grow and decay.

Insects rule the jungle, and I encounter them all: ants, beetles, butterflies, grasshoppers, mosquitoes. A certain type of fly will lay eggs under the skin or in wounds. Stingless wild bees like to cling to hair.

Luckily, I'd lived in the jungle long enough as a child to be acquainted with the bugs and other creatures that scurry, rustle, whistle, and snarl. There was almost nothing my parents hadn't taught me about the jungle. I only had to find this knowledge in my **concussion-fogged** head.

Suddenly I'm seized by an **intense** thirst. Thick drops of water sparkle on the leaves around me, and I lick them up. I walk in small circles around my seat, aware of how quickly you can lose your **orientation** in the jungle. I memorize the location and markings of one tree to **keep my bearings**.

In Other Words

concussion-fogged injured and confused
orientation sense of direction
keep my bearings remember where I am

▶ **Before You Move On**

1. **Visualize** What words does the author use to help you picture the forest? How does this make you feel about her situation?

2. **Point of View** How does the author's first-person point of view help you understand the story?

127

I find no trace of the crash. No wreckage, no people. But I do discover a bag of candy and eat a piece.

I hear the hum of airplane engines overhead. I look up, but the trees are too dense: There's no way I can make myself noticeable here. A feeling of powerlessness **overcomes** me. I have to get out of the thick of the forest so that rescuers can see me. Soon the engines' hum fades away.

I hear the dripping, tinkling, gurgle of water that I hadn't noticed before. Nearby I find a spring, feeding a tiny **rivulet**. This fills me with hope. Not only have I found water to drink, but I'm convinced that this little stream will lead the way to my rescue.

I try to follow the rivulet closely, but there are often tree trunks lying across it, or dense **undergrowth** blocks my way. Little by little, the rivulet grows wider and turns into a stream, which is partly dry, so that I can easily walk beside the water. Around six o'clock it gets dark, and I look in the streambed for a protected spot where I can spend the night. I eat another candy.

In Other Words
rivulet stream of running water
undergrowth plant life

December 28, my watch, a gift from my grandmother, stops for good, so I try to count the days as I go. The stream turns into a larger stream, then finally into a small river. Since it's the rainy season, there's barely any fruit to pick, and I've sucked on my last candy. I don't have a knife to use to **hack palm hearts** out of the stems of the palm trees. Nor can I catch fish or cook roots. I don't dare eat anything else. Much of what grows in the jungle is poisonous, so I keep my hands off what I don't recognize. But I do drink a great deal of water from the stream.

Despite counting, I mix up the days. On December 29 or 30, the fifth or sixth day of my trek, I hear a buzzing, groaning sound that immediately turns my **apathetic** mood into **euphoria**. It's the unmistakable call of a hoatzin, a subtropical bird that nests exclusively near open stretches of water—where people settle! At home in Panguana, I heard this call often.

With new impetus, I walk faster, following the sound. Finally, I'm standing on the bank of a large river, but there's **not a soul** in sight. I hear planes in the distance, but as time passes, the noise fades. I believe that they've given up, having rescued all the passengers except me.

Intense anger overcomes me. How can the pilots turn around, now that I've finally reached an open stretch of water after all these days? Soon, my anger gives way to a terrible **despair**.

But I don't give up. Where there is a river, people cannot be far away.

The riverbank is much too densely overgrown for me to carry on hiking along it. I know stingrays rest in the riverbanks, so I walk carefully. Progress is so slow that I decide to swim in the middle of the river instead—stingrays won't venture into the deep water. I have to look out for piranhas, but I've learned that fish are dangerous only in standing water. I also expect to encounter caimans, alligator-like reptiles, but they generally don't attack people.

▼ hoatzin

In Other Words
hack palm hearts cut vegetables
apathetic hopeless
euphoria great happiness
not a soul no one
despair feeling of sadness

▶ **Before You Move On**

1. **Make Connections** How is the author's attitude different from Brian's attitude in *Hatchet*? How does reading Brian's story help you understand this text?

2. **Clarify** Use context clues to figure out the meaning of the phrase *new impetus*.

Each night when the sun sets, I search for a reasonably safe spot on the bank where I can try to sleep. Mosquitoes and small flies called midges buzz around my head and try to crawl into my ears and nose. Even worse are the nights when it rains. Ice-cold drops pelt me, soaking my thin summer dress. The wind makes me **shiver to the core**. On those bleak nights, as I cower under a tree or in a bush, I feel **utterly abandoned**.

By day, I go on swimming, but I'm getting weaker. I drink a lot of river water, which fills my stomach, but I know I should eat something.

One morning, I feel a sharp pain in my upper back. When I touch it, my hand comes away bloody. The sun has burned my skin as I swim. I will learn later that I have **second-degree** burns.

As the days wear on, my eyes and ears fool me. Often I'm convinced I see the roof of a house on the riverbank or hear chickens clucking. I am so horribly tired.

I fantasize about food, from elaborate feasts to simple meals. Each morning it gets harder to stand up and get into the cold water. Is there any **sense in going on**? Yes, I tell myself. I have to keep going.

I spend the tenth day drifting in the water. I'm constantly bumping into logs, and it requires a great deal of strength to climb over them and not break any bones

Amazon River

in these collisions. In the evening, I find a gravel bank that looks like a good place to sleep. I doze off for a few minutes. When I wake up, I see something that doesn't belong here: a boat. I rub my eyes, look three times, and it's still there. A boat!

I swim over and touch it. Only then can I really believe it. I notice a **beaten trail** leading up the bank from the river. I'm sure I'll find people there, but I'm so weak that it takes me hours to make it up the hill.

When I get to the top, I see a small shelter, but no people. A path leads from the shack into the forest. I'm certain that the owner of the boat will emerge at any moment, but no one comes. It gets dark, and I spend the night there.

The next morning, I wake and still no one has **shown up**. It begins to rain, and I crawl into the shelter and wrap a **tarp** around my shoulders.

The rain stops in the afternoon. I no longer have the strength to struggle to my feet. I tell myself that I'll rest at the hut one more day, then keep moving.

At twilight I hear voices. I'm imagining them, I think. But the voices get closer. When three men come out of the forest and see me, they stop in shock.

"I'm a girl who was in the LANSA crash," I say in Spanish. "My name is Juliane." ❖

In Other Words
beaten trail path that has been used often
shown up come; appeared
tarp plastic sheet

▶ **Before You Move On**

1. **Draw Conclusions** What will happen to Diller now that she has found people? How do you know?

2. **Use Text Evidence** What examples and evidence from the story illustrate what Diller is like?

131

Key Words

concentrate	overcome
exhaust	reliance
intense	resilience
motivation	resolve
necessity	resourceful

Compare Choices

The main characters in the selections *Hatchet* and "Survival Stories: The Girl Who Fell from the Sky" both face many obstacles. Use a comparison chart to compare how the characters respond to their situations. Then use the information to draw a conclusion about the choices the characters make in order to survive.

Comparison Chart

	Hatchet	"Survival Stories: The Girl Who Fell from the Sky"
Person / Character	Brian Robeson	Juliane Koepcke Diller
Problem		
Goal or Motive		
Choices Made to Achieve Goal	1. 2. 3.	1. 2. 3.

Talk Together

What qualities do Juliane and Brian share that help them in a survival situation? How do these qualities affect the choices they make? Use **Key Words** and cite text evidence to talk with a partner about your ideas.

Possessive Adjectives and Pronouns

Use possessives to show ownership. A **possessive adjective** identifies who owns something or has something. A **possessive pronoun** refers to the thing owned and who owns or has it.

Grammar Rules Possessive Adjectives and Pronouns	
Use a **possessive adjective** before a **noun**. The possessive adjectives are *my, your, his, her, its, our,* and *their.*	The plane adjusted **its wings**. Passengers were upset when **their bags** fell.
A **possessive pronoun** is used in place of one or more **nouns**. The possessive pronouns are *mine, yours, his, hers, ours* and *theirs.*	Both **Juliane Koepcke Diller** and **Brian Robeson** have adventures. **Theirs** are both tales of bravery. **Hers** is a true story. **His** is fiction.

Read Possessive Adjectives and Pronouns

Writers use possessive adjectives and possessive pronouns to make their writing clearer and easier to understand. Read this passage based on *Hatchet*. Identify the possessive adjectives and possessive pronouns.

> Brian Robeson was scared. His plane had crashed. Its pilot was gone. "My parents will begin searching," Brian thought. "But for now, all of the life-saving decisions are mine."

Write Possessive Adjectives and Pronouns

Reread the first two pages of "Survival Stories: The Girl Who Fell from the Sky." Write sentences about what happens to Juliane Koepcke Diller. Be sure to include at least two sentences with possessive adjectives and two with possessive pronouns. Then trade sentences with a partner. Find the possessive adjectives and possessive pronouns in each other's sentences.

133

Write to Inform

Write an Expository Report

Write an expository report on the topic of animal survival.
Then add it to a class magazine about how animals survive.

Study a Model

In an expository report, you present information about a topic. You start by
introducing a main idea about the topic. Then you illustrate and elaborate on
the topic with supporting details and examples. Read an expository report by
Gabriel Ponce.

Survival in the Dark
By Gabriel Ponce

Humans need night-vision goggles—or at least
flashlights—to see in the dark, but not every
creature has trouble at night. Many animals have
developed amazing adaptations that allow them to
survive in the dark.

The first sentence introduces the topic in an interesting way.

The main idea is the most important idea about the topic.

Some animals rely on senses other than sight
to survive in dark habitats. For example, bats
use sounds and their echoes to locate food and
sense predators in the dark. This ability is called
echolocation, and it allows bats to thrive in caves.
Other animals, such as mole rats, are almost blind
but use their sharp sense of smell to detect predators
in the dark.

Each paragraph includes details and examples that support the main idea.

Other animals adapt to the dark by emitting their
own light. This is called bioluminescence. Fireflies
use this ability to communicate. Bioluminescence is
also useful for creatures that live deep in the ocean
where light from the surface does not reach. Two
of these "living lights" are appropriately named the
lanternfish and flashlight fish.

Domain-specific vocabulary helps explain the topic.

From bats to fireflies to fish, nature has created
many fascinating ways for animals to thrive and
survive in the dark.

The conclusion repeats the main idea of the report.

Prewrite

1. **Choose a Topic to Write About** Think about the science articles you have read on animal survival. Talk with a partner to choose a topic to write about.

<table>
<tr><td colspan="2" align="center">**Language Frames**</td></tr>
<tr>
<td>

Tell Your Ideas

• One interesting thing about this topic is _____ .

• I would like people to know _____ .

• Writing about _____ will help me _____ .

</td>
<td>

Respond to Ideas

• I don't know much about _____ . Can you tell me more?

• I'm not sure why you want to write about _____ . Can you clarify?

• I don't think I agree with your choice because _____ .

</td>
</tr>
</table>

> Use sentences and questions like these to choose a topic.

2. **Gather Information** Use self-stick notes to mark important information in books, or take notes and then underline or highlight ideas. You may also use a computer to record and organize the information you find. Always note the sources where you found the information, such as Web sites, books, or magazines.

3. **Get Organized** Use a main idea chart to help you organize your ideas.

Main Idea Chart

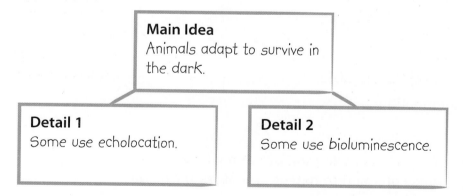

Draft

Use the main idea chart and the ideas you collected to write a draft that includes a main idea and supporting details. Be sure to write the ideas in your own words with a style that is appropriate for an expository report.

Revise

1. **Read, Retell, Respond** Read your draft aloud to a partner. Your partner listens and then retells your main points. Then talk about ways to support your main ideas and improve your writing.

Language Frames	
Retell	**Make Suggestions**
• You wrote about _____ . • The main idea of your report is _____ . • The important details are _____ .	• Your main idea needs to be developed more. Add _____ . • Could you clarify the detail about _____ ? • I like that you included _____ . Can you give another example of _____ ?

2. **Make Changes** Think about your draft and your partner's suggestions. Use the Revising Marks on page 617 to mark your changes.

   • Did you introduce your topic in an interesting way?

   > Humans may need night-vision goggles—or at least flashlights—to see in the dark, but not every creature has trouble at night.
   > ~~In the dark, no one can see.~~

   • Did you include only details related to your main idea? Do you need to delete unnecessary information?

   > Other animals, such as mole rats, are almost blind but use their sharp sense of smell to detect predators in the dark. ~~They are born to serve their queen.~~

Edit and Proofread

Work with a partner to edit and proofread your report. Pay special attention to using pronouns and possessives correctly. Use the marks on page 618 to show your changes.

Use the marks on page 618 to show your changes.

Publish

1. **On Your Own** Make a final copy of your report. Read it to a group of your classmates.

Presentation Tips	
If you are the speaker . . .	**If you are the listener . . .**
Work on pronouncing words correctly. Practice saying any scientific or technical terms.	Listen for the main idea and supporting details.
Adjust your volume, pitch, and tone to keep your report interesting.	Afterward, share your own knowledge and ideas about the topic.

2. **With a Group** Combine your reports into a class magazine. Design a cover and think of a great title. Add graphics to the reports and format them in various ways. Add section heads and use different fonts and colors.

STAYING ALIVE

A Magazine About How Animals Survive

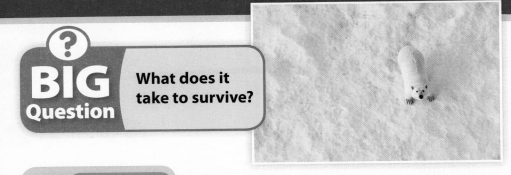

BIG Question

What does it take to survive?

In this unit you found many answers to the **Big Question**. Now use your concept map to discuss it with the class. Think about some things that people and animals need in order to survive.

Concept Map

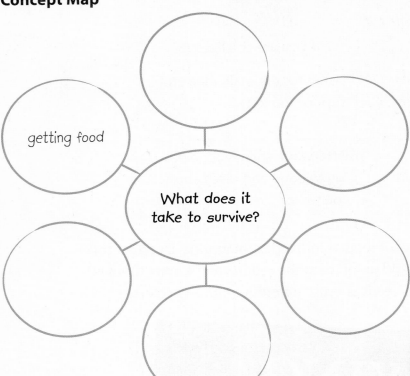

getting food

What does it take to survive?

Performance Task: Explanatory

Consider what you learned from the selections and the **Small Group Reading** books about survival. Write an article for a children's science magazine that explains what living things need in order to survive.

Checklist

Does your article

☑ use text evidence from the selections about survival?

☑ clearly introduce the topic?

☑ include facts, definitions, details, or other information and examples from the sources?

☑ include precise language and transition words?

Share Your Ideas

Choose one of these ways to share your ideas about the **Big Question**.

Write It!

Write an Ode

An ode is a short poem written to praise its subject. Write an ode about your favorite animal. Describe how it uses survival skills to get food or to defend itself from predators. Read your ode to the class.

Talk About It!

Do a Mock News Report

Use your knowledge from the unit and pretend that you are a news reporter informing your viewers about a real or imaginary event that includes the topic of survival. Write down some key points that you would like to talk about during your mock news report. Report your story to the class.

Do It!

Make a Presentation

Use the Internet to research a person who had to survive in the wild alone. Use presentation software to describe how the person came to be stranded in the wild and what he or she did to survive. Include pictures, maps, or other visuals in your presentation.

SURVIVAL STORY

Carlos Torres survived at sea for 15 days.

Write It!

Write a Brochure

Imagine that you run a survival camp for people who like the great outdoors. What skills would you teach? What activities would you plan to help campers practice their skills? Use ideas from the selections and from the Internet to plan your camp brochure.

8 WEEK
Survival Camp Training

• build fires
• make shelters
• find food

Digging Up the Past

BIG Question

How can we bring the past to life?

Unit at a Glance
► **Language**: Define and Explain, Engage in Discussion, Social Studies Words
► **Literacy**: Ask Questions
► **Content**: Ancient Egypt

Unit
3

Share What You Know

❶ **Think** about objects that can teach us about life in the past.

❷ **Draw** one object and label it.

❸ **Share** your drawing. Explain what it shows about the past.

Build Background: Watch a video about ancient Egypt.
Ⓝ NGReach.com

Define and Explain

Language Frames

- _____ means _____ .
- For example, _____ .
- _____ because _____ .

Look at the photos and listen to the explanation. Listen for definitions of unfamiliar words. Then use **Language Frames** to define or explain something else in the photos.

archaeologist

excavation site

skull

hand tool

hand tool

An Archaeologist at Work ((MP3))

Archaeologists are scientists who study life in the past. To do this, they often need to excavate historical sites. To _excavate_ means to uncover objects that have been buried in the earth. The objects are buried because layers of debris, or dirt and sand, build up over time. As a result, archaeologists may have to dig deep in order to excavate old buildings, pots, and even bones. They must work slowly and carefully. For example, when excavating delicate objects, they often use hand tools like small shovels and brushes to keep the precious items safe.

Social Studies Vocabulary

Key Words

Key Words

archaeological

artifact

chronological

civilization

dynasty

pharaoh

tomb

Look at the time line and images. Read the captions. Then use **Key Words** and other words to talk about how **archaeological** research, such as digging up objects, can teach us about an ancient **civilization**, or life in a specific country or area.

| Middle Kingdom Dynasties 1975–1640 B.C.E. | New Kingdom Dynasties 1539–1075 B.C.E. | Late Period Dynasties 715–332 B.C.E. |

▲ Archaeologists search for clues about how people lived in the past. They may study certain **dynasties**, or periods of time when a specific person or family ruled. Then they can organize the dynasties on a **chronological** time line to show the exact order that the historical periods occurred.

◄ The archaeologists explore a **tomb** where one or more people are buried. This tomb contains the body of someone who died long ago.

pharaoh

governors and nobles

common people

▲ **Artifacts**, or historical objects like carvings, give the scientists clues that someone important is buried here.

▲ The tomb was built for an ancient **pharaoh**. He was a great leader who ruled as king.

Talk Together

Talk with a partner about how archaeologists uncover information that brings the past to life. Use **Language Frames** from page 142 and **Key Words** to define and explain information that contributes to the topic of archaeology.

Chronological Order

History articles are usually written in **chronological order**, or the exact order in which events happened. But sometimes the author starts with a present-day discovery and then tells what that discovery teaches us about another series of events that occurred in the past. As you read, look for time-order words and phrases to help you determine the sequence of events.

Look Into the Text

In 1827, John Gardner Wilkinson was one of the founders of Egyptology. He designated the tomb KV 5. This meant that it was the fifth tomb beyond the entrance to the King's Valley. Then **for more than 150 years**, KV 5 was all but forgotten.

In 1989, I was directing a mapping project in the Valley of the Kings. I wanted to relocate KV 5 . . .

"These **time-order words** give clues to the order of events. **Some dates** tell about events that happened more than 150 years ago. **Other dates** tell about a more recent time."

Map and Talk

You can use a double time line to keep track of events that take place in two different time periods.

Double Time Line

Historical Events

| 1827: Wilkinson named the tomb KV 5. | | |

More Recent Events

| 1989: The author was looking for KV 5. | | |

Talk Together

Tell a partner about a time you looked at an old family photo or heard a story about something that happened to your family in the past. Write the events you learned about your family on one time line and the present-day events on a second time line.

More Key Words

Use these words to talk about "Valley of the Kings" and "Animals Everlasting."

analytical
(a-na-**li**-ti-kul) *adjective*

When you study something in an **analytical** way, you break the information into parts so that it is easier to understand. A scientist does an **analytical** study of the liquid by separating it and studying each part.

depict
(di-**pikt**) *verb*

When you **depict** something, you show it in a picture or with words. The artist's drawing **depicts** the girl.

powerful
(**pou**-ur-ful) *adjective*

A **powerful** person has the ability to control other people or things. The **powerful** judge makes important decisions in a courtroom.

representation
(rep-ri-zen-**tā**-shun) *noun*

A **representation** is a picture or other image that stands for a person or thing. This statue is a **representation** of an ancient Egyptian king.

reveal
(ri-**vēl**) *verb*

When you **reveal** something, you show or explain it to others. The magician **reveals** the rabbit that was in his hat.

Talk Together

Work with a partner. Make an Expanded Meaning Map for each **Key Word**.

What the Word Means
an image that stands for a person or thing

Word
representation

Examples
painting, statue, drawing

What It Is Like
looks like the person

Add words to My Vocabulary Notebook.
NGReach.com

Learn to Ask Questions

Do you ever wonder about something you have read? Do you ever get confused by a text? Ask yourself a question and then try to find the answer in the text.

How to Ask Questions

1. As you read, pay attention to each question that comes to your mind.

2. Think about where you might find an answer to the question. You can go back and reread the text or keep your question in mind and read on.

3. Think about how the answer helps you understand more about the text.

As I read about _____,
I wonder _____.

I can _____.

Now I understand _____.

Here's how one student asked questions and looked for answers in the text.

Look Into the Text

The tomb has turned out to be **the largest ever found** in the Valley of the Kings. **It was a family mausoleum**—the burial place of many of the sons of Ramses II. **It contains at least 110 chambers**, and its artifacts and hieroglyphs promise to change what we know about **Ramses II, one of antiquity's most powerful rulers**.

"As I read **information** about the tomb, I wonder why the tomb is so large."

"I can read on to find more **details** about the tomb."

"Now I understand that the tomb is large because it contains many chambers for the members of a powerful family."

Asking questions helps you learn and clarify new information as you read. It can also help you figure out what is happening in the text and what is important.

Talk Together

Read the news article and sample notes. Use **Language Frames** to ask and answer questions as you read. Talk with a partner about the questions you asked and how you answered them.

News Article

Hunt for a Hidden Tomb

EGYPT, 1989 — Archaeologist Kent Weeks and his team are on the hunt for an Egyptian **tomb** that has been neglected for more than a century. Weeks isn't looking for a major **archaeological** discovery. He is more concerned about plans for construction near the entrance of the Valley of the Kings, the burial site for many of ancient Egypt's most **powerful pharaohs**. Worried that the road construction might damage underground tombs, the team will begin by excavating a tomb known as KV 5, which is considered unimportant by most archaeologists today. ◄

If they do locate KV 5, Weeks and his team are prepared for a great deal of work ahead. Unlike archaeologists who are **depicted** in action movies, these real-life scientists and historians seldom stumble into huge chambers filled with glittering treasures. Instead, their work involves breaking through layers of sand and silt that have washed into the underground tombs over the centuries. In many places, the debris may be like a solid wall of concrete, but there is no way to blast through the barriers without damaging precious, delicate **artifacts**. As a result, it can take

days of hard work to **reveal** just a few inches at a time. ◄

If they are lucky, their work will lead to more decades of research and study. Scientists will conduct tests and **analytical** research on any remains found within the tomb. Egyptologists will analyze artwork, such as statues and other **representations** of rulers and gods. By putting the clues together piece by piece, they are often able to reconstruct a **chronological** order of events for important **dynasties** that once ruled over one of the world's most glorious **civilizations**. ◄

> As I read about the archaeologists, I wonder why they are looking for such an unimportant tomb.
>
> I can reread the text. It says that Weeks is worried that construction will damage the tomb.
>
> Now I understand that he wants to explore the tomb before it is damaged.

◄ = a good place to stop and ask or answer questions

147

ANCIENT EGYPT

Read a Magazine Article

Genre

Most **magazine articles** are nonfiction. "Valley of the Kings" gives facts and information from the point of view of an archaeologist as he studies ancient Egypt.

Text Features

A **diagram** shows the parts of an object, how a location or building is structured, or how something works. A diagram can include descriptive labels, symbols, or locator numbers that correspond to the information. It can also include a key that tells what the symbols or locator numbers represent.

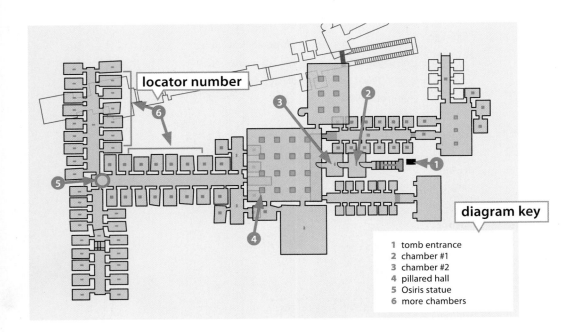

locator number

diagram key

1 tomb entrance
2 chamber #1
3 chamber #2
4 pillared hall
5 Osiris statue
6 more chambers

Valley
of the
Kings

by Dr. Kent R. Weeks

Valley of the Kings,
Luxor, Egypt

Comprehension Coach

STEPPING INTO THE PAST

No one had ventured inside the ancient Egyptian **tomb** since 1825, when a British traveler and **draftsman** named James Burton sketched its first few chambers. The tomb lay somewhere near the entrance to the Valley of the Kings— burial place of New Kingdom **pharaohs** who ruled Egypt at the peak of its military power, between 1539 and 1078 B.C.E.

In 1827, John Gardner Wilkinson was one of the **founders of Egyptology**. He designated the tomb KV 5. This meant that it was the fifth tomb beyond the entrance to the King's Valley. Then for more than 150 years, KV 5 was all but forgotten.

In 1989, I was directing a **mapping project** in the Valley of the Kings. I wanted to relocate KV 5, not because it held treasures—it didn't—but because the roadway at the valley's entrance was being widened. The roadwork seemed likely to damage any tomb in its path. That path, I believed, lay right above KV 5.

The tomb has turned out to be the largest ever found in the Valley of the Kings. It was a family mausoleum—the burial place of many of the sons of Ramses II. It contains at least 110 chambers, and its **artifacts** and **hieroglyphs** promise to change what we know about Ramses II, one of **antiquity's** most **powerful** rulers. During his long reign, ancient Egypt controlled lands from present-day Sudan northeast into Syria. Of all the pharaohs, he was the most prolific builder. To glorify his name, Ramses erected dozens of imposing temples and monuments along the Nile.

In Other Words

draftsman person who makes blueprints and other technical drawings

founders of Egyptology first archaeologists to study ancient Egypt

mapping project team to locate and map **tombs**

hieroglyphs ancient Egyptian writing

antiquity's the ancient past's

150

RAMSES II FAMILY TREE

Ramses II was a powerful pharaoh who had a long, successful rule during Egypt's nineteenth **dynasty**. Egyptologists are still investigating how many children Ramses II had with his wives, but Dr. Kent Weeks estimates that up to 20 of his sons are buried in KV 5. Below is a family tree that includes Ramses II's known children with Queen Isetnofret.

Because archaeologists are still uncovering clues about ancient Egyptian history, many of the dates and details are approximate.

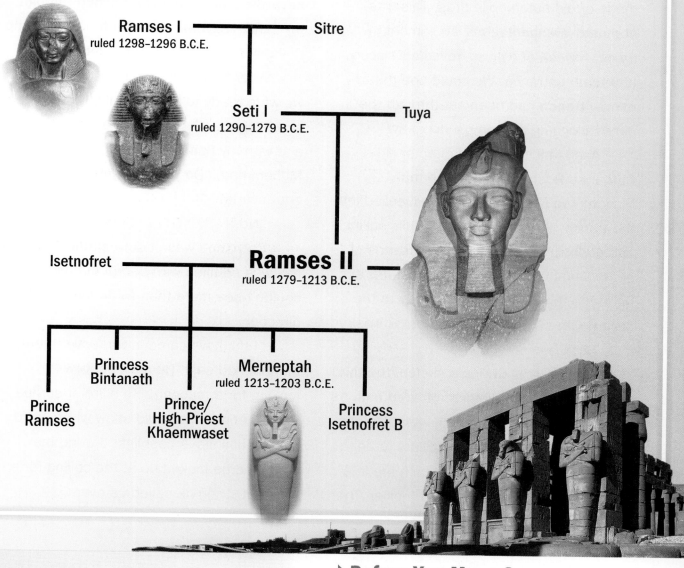

Ramses I
ruled 1298–1296 B.C.E.

Sitre

Seti I
ruled 1290–1279 B.C.E.

Tuya

Isetnofret

Ramses II
ruled 1279–1213 B.C.E.

Prince
Ramses

Princess
Bintanath

Prince/
High-Priest
Khaemwaset

Merneptah
ruled 1213–1203 B.C.E.

Princess
Isetnofret B

▶ Before You Move On

1. **Cause/Effect** Why did Weeks try to relocate **tomb** KV 5?

2. **Use Text Features** What important information does the family tree show about the **dynasty** of Ramses II?

On a hot Tuesday morning in July 1989, our workmen began digging just east of the roadway. With crude homemade hoes, they scraped away debris. This they carted off in baskets made of old automobile tires. This was standard **archaeological** equipment in Egypt. A week of digging **revealed** traces of a tomb entrance. We could see that a narrow **trench** had been cut through the debris clogging the tomb's doorway.

Assistant excavation director Catharine Roehrig, senior workman Muhammad Mahmoud, and I squeezed into the trench. Soon, we were painfully pulling and pushing ourselves over thousands of sharp limestone fragments. To our left and right, the tomb was packed nearly to the ceiling with silt and limestone chips washed in by flash floods.

According to Burton's sketch, the third **chamber** was a **cavernous, pillared hall**. As we crawled along the trench, we could see the broken tops of massive pillars jutting up through the debris. The trench made a sharp turn to the right to avoid a pillar. Then it began weaving between two- and three-ton slabs of limestone that had fallen from the ceiling. No part of the ceiling appeared to have collapsed since Burton's visit in 1825, but the fallen blocks **were unnerving nevertheless**. A headline flashed through my mind: "Egyptologists Flattened as Tomb Collapses. Pharaoh's Curse Returns."

After 20 minutes in the stifling heat, we were ready to leave. Soaking wet, sweat streaking my glasses, covered in mud, and with my flashlight fading, I turned to Muhammad. "Do you remember where the entrance is?"

"No."

Catharine wasn't sure either. The hall was so filled with debris that we couldn't see more than a few inches in any direction.

"I think we came in from over there," Muhammad said. He crawled forward, looking for a recognizable pillar or scrape in the debris that would show where we'd been. Shining his flashlight around the chamber, he looked up at the ceiling for a moment. Then he called us over.

In Other Words
trench ditch
chamber room
cavernous, pillared hall large hallway with tall columns
were unnerving nevertheless still worried me

152

Dr. Kent Weeks (in white hat) and excavation foreman Ahmed Mahmoud Hassan examine a tomb that is being cleared in KV 5.

"Look," he said. Directly above him, we could see crude black letters written with the smoke of a candle: BURTON 1825.

After a few more wrong turns, we clambered out of the tomb. Catharine scraped mud from her clothes. She wondered aloud about the **tomb's original occupants**. "Remember Elizabeth Thomas? She thought this might be a tomb for children of Ramses II. Thomas didn't have any proof. But she knew more about the Valley of the Kings than any other Egyptologist in this century. Her theory should be checked out."

In Other Words
tomb's original occupants people who were buried there

▶ **Before You Move On**

1. **Ask Questions** Why was Weeks worried while his team explored the **tomb**? Reread the text to find the answer.

2. **Explain** What evidence did the team find to prove that they had relocated KV 5?

Between 1539 and 1078 B.C.E., almost every pharaoh was buried in the Valley of the Kings.

EXPLORING THE VALLEY

I decided to become an Egyptologist when I was eight, my interest in an ancient **civilization** winning out over dreams of **intergalactic** travel. Although my parents never tried to **dissuade** me from so unlikely a career, one aunt regularly pointed out that an interest in ancient Egypt couldn't possibly lead to a decent job. My friends, **on the other hand**, agreed that cutting open mummies and searching gold-filled tombs were worthy goals.

In Other Words
intergalactic space
dissuade stop
on the other hand however

Not long after I **took my Ph.D.** in Egyptology from Yale, the Oriental Institute at the University of Chicago made me director of its field headquarters in Luxor. This is the modern town built atop ancient Thebes. Surrounded by so many tombs and temples, I had a wonderful opportunity to delve into the archaeology of the New Kingdom—Egypt's golden imperial age.

The warrior pharaohs of the New Kingdom conquered Palestine and Syria with horse-drawn chariots and other advanced military techniques. For three centuries, Egypt was the strongest nation in the world. At Thebes, the pharaohs built larger and grander temples. They wanted to proclaim the might and wealth that made their religious capital "the queen of cities . . . greater than any other city." The city proper stood on the east bank of the Nile. The **necropolis**, with its royal temples and rock-cut tombs, lay on the west.

Now, seated on a rock outcropping with my back to the Valley of the Kings, I peer down on a series of stony hills. They are pockmarked with the entrances to hundreds, perhaps thousands, of private tombs from the New Kingdom. Most have been **plundered** but not excavated.

At first glance, the Valley of the Kings seems little different from hundreds of other valleys at the desert's edge. Shaped like a human hand with fingers splayed, the Valley of the Kings covers only about seven acres—smaller than nearby valleys. Towering over it is el-Qurn, a 1,500-foot peak shaped like a pyramid. Some Egyptologists believe that this natural symbol of the sun god Re led to the selection of the Valley of the Kings as the site of royal tombs. Another reason was security. There's only one narrow **gorge** leading into the valley.

Centuries ago, Roman travelers scratched their names on tomb walls. Ancient robbers **despoiled** most of the royal mummies. Then they carted away the treasures buried with the mummies so that the deceased could live as they had on Earth—furniture, papyrus scrolls, amulets, jewelry, ritual objects, statues. Napoleon Bonaparte brought a team of scholars to record Egyptian antiquities when his army invaded in 1798. Adventurers and archaeologists in the 19th and 20th centuries entered tomb after tomb. Now our team was ready to uncover what time, weather, and careless humans had left behind.

In Other Words

took my Ph.D. got my top academic degree
necropolis ancient cemetery
plundered robbed
gorge passage of land
despoiled stole or destroyed

▶ Before You Move On

1. **Chronological Order** What important events happened to KV 5 before Weeks began his work in 1989?

2. **Use Text Evidence** Why was the Valley of the Kings a good location for the **tombs** of Egyptian **pharaohs**?

First, University of Michigan Egyptology student Marjorie Aronow, Ahmed Mahmoud, and I cleared the doorway in the rear wall of the pillared hall. Then we began digging in the chamber beyond, which we assumed would be small. I struggled through the narrow crawl space into the chamber.

"Look," Ahmed said. He was pointing to a gap in the wall of debris that lay ahead.

I shone my flashlight into the gap. There was nothing but blackness. Strange, I thought. The light should reflect off a wall. Crawling forward, we found the **corridor**. It was about nine feet wide and continued a hundred feet into the hillside. There was one door on the left, another on the right, then two more, then four. We counted doors as we crawled forward: 10, 12, 16, 18. Other tomb corridors in the Valley of the Kings have at most one or two doorways cut into their walls. I had never seen a corridor like this one in any Egyptian tomb.

Ahmed pointed his flashlight down the corridor. "What's that?" he asked suddenly.

Marjorie gasped. As we turned our flashlights that way, a human form took shape. Ahmed began whispering a prayer from the Koran.

The figure stood ghostlike at the end of the corridor. As we **inched** closer, the form became clearer. It was a five-foot carving. Even though the face was missing, we recognized it as the god of the afterlife, Osiris.

It was a strange feeling. There we sat, 200 feet underground in utter silence, our light focused on an image of the god of the afterlife. For an instant, it was 1275 B.C.E. again, and this was ancient Thebes. I could imagine priests chanting prayers and shaking tambourines. I could feel the floor tremble as great **sarcophagi** were dragged down the corridor. I could smell incense and feel priestly robes brush my arm as the **funeral procession** moved slowly past.

In Other Words
corridor passageway
inched moved slowly
sarcophagi decorated coffins
funeral procession line of people going to the burial

Weeks's team discovered this statue of Osiris at the end of a corridor in KV 5. Osiris was the Egyptian god of the afterlife, the underworld, and the dead.

▶ **Before You Move On**

1. **Visualize** Which details from Weeks's description best help you imagine an Egyptian funeral procession?

2. **Make Inferences** How does Weeks feel about the discoveries that were **revealed** in KV 5? Support your inference with details.

157

Finally I aimed my **beam** at the doorways to the left and right of the statue. More surprises. These doors didn't lead to small side chambers, as the other doorways in the corridor did. Instead, they led into yet other corridors that extended even deeper into the bedrock. And there were yet more doorways cut into *their* walls.

"I can't believe it," Marjorie kept repeating.

Suddenly KV 5 had gone from a small, unimportant tomb to . . . to what? We crawled back down the corridor, re-counting the doors.

Dr. Kent Weeks and his wife, Susan, examine a hundred-foot hallway in KV 5 that is lined with doors and chambers. At the end of the corridor is the statue of Osiris.

In Other Words
beam flashlight

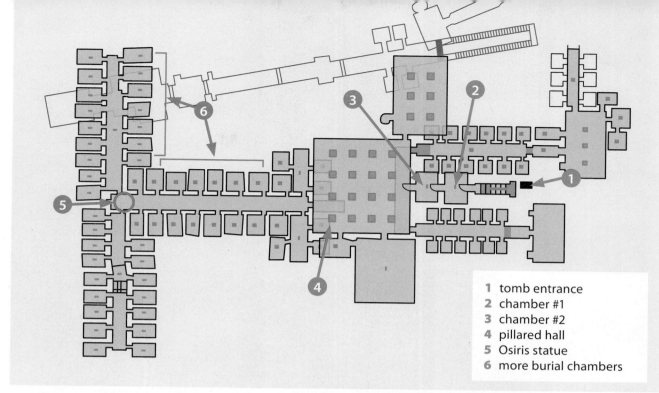

▲ **a diagram of KV 5 based on decades of work from Weeks's Theban Mapping Project**

1 tomb entrance
2 chamber #1
3 chamber #2
4 pillared hall
5 Osiris statue
6 more burial chambers

"There have to be over 65 chambers in the tomb," I said. I was **underestimating**, as we later discovered. No tomb in the Valley of the Kings has more than 30 chambers. Most have only six or eight.

And there was something else. **Inscriptions** in Chambers 1 and 2 indicated that KV 5 was the burial place of several sons of Ramses II. Of the 30-plus sons, we knew that Merneptah was buried in his own tomb in the Valley of the Kings. Two others may also have had separate tombs. Could the rest be here in KV 5? Could the corridors slope downward to a lower level of rooms? Or might other corridors descend to a cluster of burial chambers?

Marjorie, Muhammad, and I were the first people in **millennia** to see these corridors, to touch these carvings, to breathe this stale air. What a humbling experience to sit where Ramses II had come on sad occasions to bury his sons. None of us said a word.

Twenty minutes later, we crawled out of the tomb. We were sweating and filthy and smiling. As the **magnitude** of our discovery began to sink in, I thought to myself: "I know how we're going to be spending the next 20 years."

In Other Words
underestimating guessing too low
Inscriptions Carvings
millennia thousands of years
magnitude size and importance

▶ **Before You Move On**

1. **Details** What evidence supports the idea that KV 5 was an important discovery for the archaeologists?

2. **Use Text Features** How does the diagram on page 159 give information that supports the author's text description of KV 5?

▲ The burial chambers in KV 5 include human remains and fragments of canopic jars, which once held the organs of the deceased. This complete set was used for a young pharaoh named King Tutankhamun, whose tomb was discovered in KV 62.

STUDYING THE PHARAOHS

Outliving at least 12 of his sons, Ramses II ruled for an impressive 66 years. During his long reign, Ramses expanded and secured Egypt's borders. He built grandiose temples and colossal statues of himself up and down the Nile Valley.

Ramses II died in August 1213 B.C.E., when he was about 90 years old. His tomb lies less than 200 feet from KV 5. It remains one of the great unknowns in the Valley of the Kings. Though the entrance corridor is accessible, thick layers of flood debris still fill most of the tomb. That makes our knowledge of its art and architecture **sketchy**. At some places, the debris was so deep, we were often unsure whether we were walking down sloping corridors or silt-covered stairways.

Ramses was worshiped as a **deity** in his own time. Since he was a living god, his sons attended to many of his **secular** duties. They worked in their father's place, settling legal **disputes** and **conducting foreign relations**. They also oversaw Egypt's

In Other Words

sketchy incomplete
deity god
secular non-religious
disputes disagreements

conducting foreign relations communicating with rulers or governments from other nations

agriculture, irrigation, and economy. This may explain why a tomb as unusual as KV 5 came into existence. His sons held positions of greater responsibility than crown princes had in the past. So, when they died before he did, each was given a tomb more elaborate than that of an ordinary prince. Each may have had not only a burial chamber but also several beautifully decorated rooms filled with offerings and funerary goods.

This past year, we unearthed an adult male skeleton from a pit in Chamber 2. Was he a son of Ramses II? Toward the center of the pit, we uncovered the mummified leg of a young cow. This must have been one of the food offerings that had been brought to the tomb to **sustain the deceased** in the afterlife. Another day, we found three human skulls.

Excavating the skeleton proved extremely difficult. The bones were soft. The fragments were embedded in mud and limestone chips. We had to work with dental picks and artists' brushes to loosen the debris and gently brush it away. Some bones were in bad shape. We had to apply a thin solution of **adhesive** every few minutes to keep them from disintegrating.

I squatted in a space only 30 inches wide, braced against the wall with one hand to keep from falling over while I cleaned the skeleton with the other. It often took 10 or 15 minutes to clean and **stabilize** a single square inch. Every half hour, one of the workmen had to help me out of the pit. I needed time to **hobble about** and restore my blocked circulation.

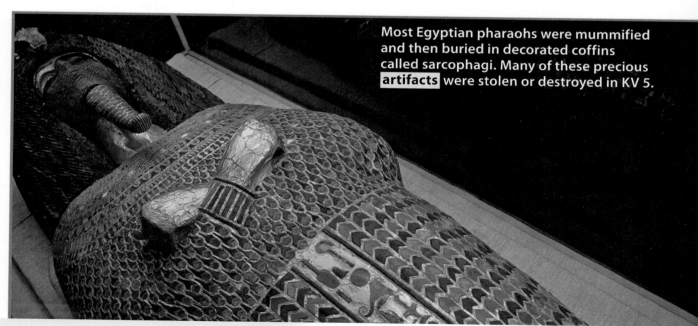

Most Egyptian pharaohs were mummified and then buried in decorated coffins called sarcophagi. Many of these precious artifacts were stolen or destroyed in KV 5.

In Other Words

sustain the deceased feed the dead
adhesive glue
stabilize prepare
hobble about stretch and move

▶ **Before You Move On**

1. **Use Text Evidence** What evidence supports the idea that the sons of Ramses II were well respected?

2. **Explain** What are some of the challenges that archaeologists face when excavating **tombs** like KV 5?

Dr. Kent Weeks and his wife, Susan, stand by the statue of Osiris in KV 5. Their team analyzes decorations and pieces together fragments to learn about the lives and beliefs of ancient Egyptians.

To find out if the skulls and skeleton belong to Ramses's sons, we'll need to run **DNA analyses**. X-rays and other tests will tell us their age at death, cause of death, **ailments**, and injuries. These are the parts of life no hieroglyphic texts ever discuss.

We have collected so much material from KV 5 that it will take us years to analyze it all. There are fragments of **plaster reliefs** to compare with decorations in other tombs. There is pottery to reconstruct and date. We also have bones to identify and test. As a general rule, one day's work in the field **generates** three or four days' work in the laboratory, library, computer room, and office.

Just before shutting down our work for the season, we removed the three skulls from the pit. We left the skeleton in place. At some point we'll have him x-rayed. But for now, as our excavation foreman said, "We can let him sleep." ❖

In Other Words

DNA analyses **analytical** tests on cells in the bones
ailments illnesses
plaster reliefs carvings and statues
generates leads to

THE WORK CONTINUES

The temples, monuments, and tombs of ancient Egypt have been uncovered and studied for centuries. But when Dr. Kent Weeks first went to Egypt in 1978, he had difficulty finding many of the archaeological sites he had traveled so far to see.

"The need for a **comprehensive** map of Thebes struck me as urgent," Weeks said. "I decided to do something about it."

Weeks created a specialized team whose goal was to record significant archaeological, geographic, and **ethnographic** features in the ancient Egyptian capital of Thebes. The team focused on the Valley of the Kings, where it rediscovered the forgotten entrance to KV 5 in 1989.

Two and a half decades later, Weeks's organization, now known as the Theban Mapping Project (TMP), still has a great deal of work to do. Centuries of **looters**, careless researchers, and an increase in tourism have threatened precious Egyptian sites. As a result, the team has expanded its work to several different areas:

- The TMP continues to excavate KV 5. It is producing 3-D models of the tombs.
- In 2000, it published the *Atlas of the Valley of the Kings*. This is updated annually on the TMP Web site as new discoveries are made.
- In 2004, it created a management plan that would preserve archaeological sites in the Valley of the Kings.
- In 2011, the TMP opened a public library with texts in Arabic and English. Its goal is to educate researchers, government planners, and even children about Egypt's rich history.

By continuing this work, Weeks and the TMP hope to protect and preserve the wonders of ancient Egypt for generations to come.

In Other Words
comprehensive full and complete
ethnographic cultural
looters people stealing treasures

▶ **Before You Move On**

1. **Ask Questions** What work still needs to be done in KV 5? Look for evidence in the text to find an answer.

2. **Summarize** In your own words, describe the goals of the Theban Mapping Project.

Key Words

analytical	dynasty
archaeological	pharaoh
artifact	powerful
chronological	representation
civilization	reveal
depict	tomb

Talk About It

1. How do text features like diagrams and photos present information in different ways? How does a specific example from the magazine article add to your understanding of the topic?

2. Imagine that you are Dr. Kent Weeks. Explain the significance of your team's rediscovery of **tomb** KV 5 based on evidence from the text.

3. Why is understanding **chronological** order important when reading this magazine article? Use examples from the text to support your answer.

4. What questions do you still have about the **archaeological** process used by Weeks and his team? How can you find answers to your questions?

5. Analyze how Weeks used details from the **artifacts** he found to make inferences about Ramses II and his sons.

6. What can you generalize about Egyptian burial practices based on what you read about KV 5? Use text evidence to support your generalization.

Learn test-taking strategies and answer more questions.
 NGReach.com

Write About It

When he was young, Dr. Weeks's aunt discouraged him from becoming an archaeologist. Write an e-mail from Dr. Weeks to his aunt to explain why he became an Egyptologist and why his work is important. Use at least three **Key Words**.

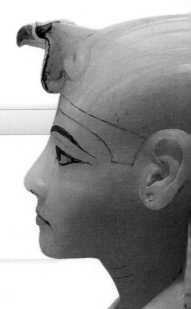

○ ○ ○ ✉   My Amazing Job

Dear Aunt Janice,

Do you remember a conversation we had when I was eight? You thought it was a horrible idea for me to dream of an **archaeological** career. I wanted to write to you now to tell you what I have learned about this amazing job.

Chronological Order

Use the double time line to record events from "Valley of the Kings." In your own words, write about the events that happened to different archaeologists and the events that occurred in ancient Egypt.

Double Time Line

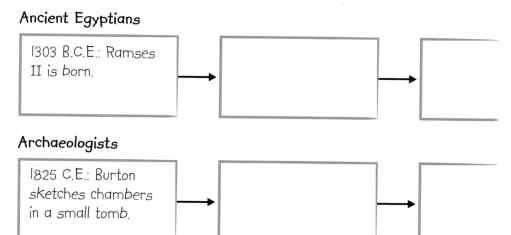

Ancient Egyptians

| 1303 B.C.E.: Ramses II is born. | → | | → | |

Archaeologists

| 1825 C.E.: Burton sketches chambers in a small tomb. | → | | → | |

Summarize the important events from the first time line to a partner. Tell the events in **chronological** order, and explain how the events are related. Your partner summarizes events from the second chain. Use **Key Words**.

Fluency  Comprehension Coach

Use the Comprehension Coach to practice reading with phrasing. Rate your reading.

Talk Together

Which specific details from "Valley of the Kings" brought the ancient past to life for you? Discuss your ideas with a partner. Use **Key Words** and text evidence to share your ideas.

Suffixes and Base Words

A **base word** is a complete word that makes sense by itself. You can add a **suffix** to the end of a base word to change its meaning or how it is used in a sentence. Sometimes, the spelling of the base word changes when you add a suffix.

EXAMPLES

The suffix -*ful* means "full of."

power + -ful = powerful

The suffix -*ion* means "the action of."

excavate + -ion = excavation

Base Word	Suffix	New Word	Meaning
govern	-or	governor	a person who governs
ornament	-al	ornamental	having the characteristics of an ornament
examine	-ation	examination	the result of examining

The chart above shows some other common suffixes. The suffix -*al* means "having the characteristics of." What do you think *archaeological* and *chronological* mean?

Try It

Read the sentences. Then answer the questions. Use the chart to help you.

The <u>excavator</u> carefully uncovered several clay pots. The pots were covered with paintings, carvings, and other <u>representations</u> of pharaohs.

1. **Look at the suffix -*or*. What is the best meaning for the word <u>excavator</u>?**

   A   an area where people excavate

   B   an object that has been excavated

   C   a room to store excavated items

   D   a person who excavates

2. **Look for the suffix -*ation*. What is the best meaning for the word <u>representations</u>?**

   A   pots that represent

   B   images that represent

   C   areas that represent

   D   people who represent

Connect Across Texts You read about how an Egyptologist **revealed** facts about a **powerful** **pharaoh**. Now read about how another archaeologist reveals facts about everyday people in ancient Egypt.

Genre A **magazine article** is usually nonfiction text that gives facts and information about a topic.

ANIMALS EVERLASTING

by A. R. Williams

For many decades, archaeologists and treasure seekers led expeditions through the Egyptian desert. Their **quest** was to find royal **tombs** and splendid gold and painted masks and coffins. These would be sent to adorn the estates and museums of Europe and America. Lying among the ancient **artifacts** lay many thousands of mummified animals that turned up at **sacred** sites throughout Egypt. To those early explorers, the carefully preserved remains were just things to be cleared away to get at the good stuff. Few people studied them, and their importance was generally unrecognized.

◀ **cat mummy from Abydos, Egypt**

In Other Words
quest goal
sacred religious

▶ **Before You Move On**

1. **Author's Viewpoint** What evidence from the text shows the author's opinion about the early treasure seekers?

2. **Ask Questions** Where were the animal mummies found? Reread or read on to find the answer.

▲ Ikram studies the mummy of an ibis—a bird once worshipped in ancient Egypt.

In the past century, archaeology has become less of a trophy hunt and more of a science. Excavators now realize that much of their sites' wealth lies in the multitude of details about ordinary folks. Archaeologists want to know what they did, what they thought, how they prayed. Animal mummies are a big part of that **pay dirt**.

"They're really **manifestations of** daily life," says Egyptologist Salima Ikram. "Pets, food, death, religion. They cover everything the Egyptians were concerned with." Ikram specializes in zooarchaeology—the study of ancient animal remains. She has helped launch a new line of research into cats and other creatures that were preserved with great skill and care. As a professor at the American University in Cairo, she adopted the Egyptian Museum's **languishing** collection of animal mummies as a research project. She spent time taking precise measurements, peering beneath linen bandages with x-rays, and **cataloging** her findings. Then she created a gallery for the collection. The result was a bridge between people today and those of long ago. "You look at these animals, and suddenly you say, Oh, King So-and-So had

In Other Words
pay dirt reward they want
manifestations of information about
languishing forgotten; ignored
cataloging recording

a pet. I have a pet. And instead of being at a distance of 5,000-plus years, the ancient Egyptians become people."

Today the animal mummies are one of the most popular exhibits in the whole treasure-filled museum. Visitors of all ages, Egyptians and foreigners, press in shoulder to shoulder to get a look. Behind glass panels lie cats wrapped in strips of linen that form diamonds, stripes, squares, and crisscrosses. Shrews in boxes of carved limestone. Rams covered with gilded and beaded casings. A gazelle wrapped in a tattered mat of papyrus, so thoroughly flattened by mummification that Ikram named it Roadkill. A 17-foot, knobby-backed crocodile, buried with baby croc mummies in its mouth. Ibises in bundles with intricate **appliqués**. Hawks. Fish. Even tiny scarab beetles and the dung balls they ate.

Some animal mummies were preserved so that the deceased would have companionship in eternity. Ancient Egyptians who could afford it prepared their tombs lavishly. They hoped that their assembled personal items would magically be available to them after death. Beginning in about 2950 B.C.E., kings of the 1st **dynasty** were buried at Abydos with dogs,

lions, and donkeys. More than 2,500 years later, during the 30th dynasty, a commoner at Abydos named Hapi-men was laid to rest with his small dog curled at his feet.

Other mummies were **provisions** for the dead. The best cuts of beef, succulent ducks, geese, and pigeons were salted, dried, and wrapped in linen. "Victual mummies" is what Ikram calls this gourmet jerky for the **hereafter**. "Whether or not you got it regularly in life didn't matter because you got it for eternity."

And some animals were mummified because they were sacred animals. They were worshipped at their own **cult** centers—bulls at Armant and Heliopolis, fish at Esna, rams at Elephantine Island, crocodiles at Kom Ombo. Ikram believes the idea of such divine creatures was born at the dawn of Egyptian **civilization**. It was a time when heavier rainfall than today made the land green and bountiful. Surrounded by animals, people began to connect them with specific gods according to their habits.

Take crocodiles, symbols of Sobek, a water god. Captive crocodiles led an **indulged** life and were buried with due ceremony after death.

In Other Words
appliqués decorations
provisions food and supplies
hereafter afterlife
cult religious
indulged easy; protected

▶ **Before You Move On**
1. **Explain** Why does Ikram believe it is important to study animal mummies?
2. **Draw Conclusions** What do animal mummies show about how ancient Egyptians viewed the afterlife?

The most numerous mummies, buried by the millions as at the site of Istabl Antar, were votive objects. These were offered up during yearly festivals at the temples of animal cults. Like county fairs, these great gatherings enlivened religious centers up and down the Nile. **Pilgrims** arrived by the hundreds of thousands and set up camp. Music and dancing filled the **processional route**. Merchants sold food, drink, and souvenirs. Priests became salesmen, offering simply wrapped mummies. They also provided more elaborate ones for people who could spend more—or thought they should. With incense swirling all around, the faithful ended their journey by delivering their chosen mummy to the temple with a prayer.

Some places were associated with just one god and its symbolic animal. But old, **venerated** sites, such as Abydos, have yielded whole **menageries** of votive mummies, each species a link to a particular god. At Abydos, the burial ground of Egypt's first rulers, excavations have uncovered ibis mummies. These likely represented Thoth, the god of wisdom and writing. Falcons probably evoked the sky-god Horus, protector of the living king. And

dogs had ties to the jackal-headed Anubis, the guardian of the dead. By donating one of these mummies to the temple, a pilgrim could win favor with its god. "The creature was always whispering in the god's ear. It said, 'Here he is, here comes your **devotee**, be nice,'" explains Ikram.

Part of Ikram's work is to find out how the ancient **embalmers** worked—a subject on which the ancient texts are silent or

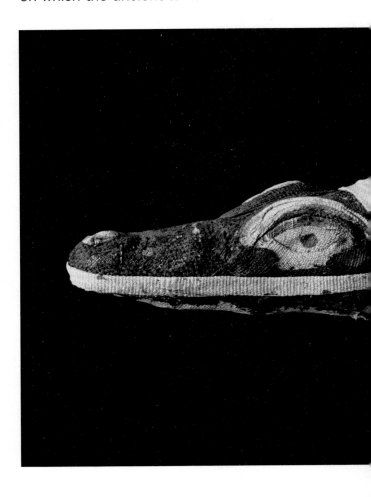

ambiguous. Therefore, she conducts experiments in mummification. Using rabbits purchased from local butchers, she studies different processes and materials that ancient embalmers may have used.

Like the animals mummified more than 3,000 years ago, Ikram's test subjects went to a happy afterlife. Once the lab work was done, she and her students followed **protocol** and wrapped each body in bandages printed with magical spells. Reciting prayers and burning incense, they laid the mummies to rest in a classroom cabinet, where they **draw** visitors—including me. As an offering, I sketch plump carrots and symbols to multiply the bunch by a thousand. Ikram assures me that the pictures have instantly become real in the hereafter, and her rabbits are twitching their noses with joy. ❖

crocodile mummy from the 1st century B.C.E.

▶ **Before You Move On**

1. **Summarize** Why did ancient Egyptians create animal mummies? Cite specific examples from the text.

2. **Make Inferences** How do Ikram and her students treat their mummy experiments? Why do they do this?

ANIMAL MUMMIES

This map shows various sites in Egypt where animal mummies have been discovered.

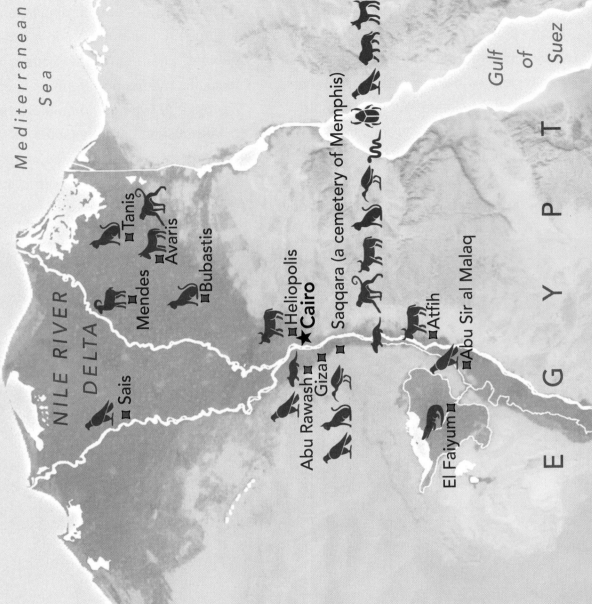

Mediterranean Sea

Tanis

Avaris

Mendes

Bubastis

Sais

NILE RIVER DELTA

Heliopolis
Cairo

Saqqara (a cemetery of Memphis)

Abu Rawash
Giza

Atfih

Abu Sir al Malaq

El Faiyum

E G Y P T

Gulf of Suez

ANIMAL MUMMIES
Species buried in select areas

- Site
- Cat
- Cow/Bull
- Crocodile
- Dog
- Donkey
- Elephant
- Fish
- Gazelle
- Horse

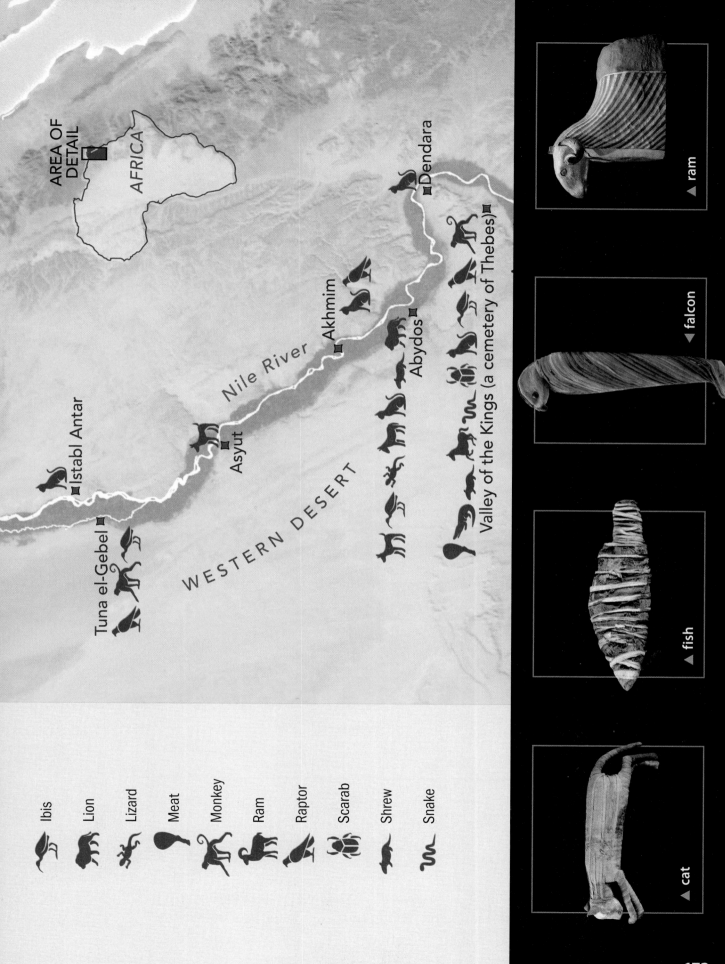

AREA OF
DETAIL

AFRICA

Istabl Antar

Tuna el-Gebel

Nile River

Asyut

WESTERN DESERT

Akhmim

Abydos

Dendara

Valley of the Kings (a cemetery of Thebes)

Ibis

Lion

Lizard

Meat

Monkey

Ram

Raptor

Scarab

Shrew

Snake

▲ ram

▲ falcon

▲ fish

▲ cat

173

Respond and Extend

Key Words

analytical	dynasty
archaeological	pharaoh
artifact	powerful
chronological	representation
civilization	reveal
depict	tomb

Compare Information

Both "Valley of the Kings" and "Animals Everlasting" describe **archaeological** discoveries from ancient Egypt. Work with a partner to compare the way information is presented in the two selections. Record examples in the comparison chart and then discuss how reading both selections helped you synthesize, or put together, information about the ancient **civilization** of Egypt.

Comparison Chart

	"Valley of the Kings"	"Animals Everlasting"
Topic		An Egyptologist studies animal mummies.
Text	details about the structure, art, remains, and chambers in the tomb	
Main Ideas		
Text Features		

Talk Together

How do Weeks's and Ikram's discoveries add to our knowledge of the ancient past? How does that information help bring the past to life? Use **Key Words** and cite evidence from the text to talk about your ideas.

Progressive Tenses

The **progressive tense** tells about an action that occurs over a period of time. The main verb always ends in **–ing**.

Grammar Rules Progressive Tenses

• A **present progressive verb** tells about an action as it is happening. It uses the auxiliary verb **am**, **is**, or **are**.	Dr. Weeks **is working** in KV 5.
• A **past progressive verb** tells about an action that was happening over a period of time in the past. It uses the auxiliary verb **was** or **were**.	He **was searching** for clues about Ramses II for many years.
• A **future progressive verb** tells about an action that will be happening over a period of time in the future. It uses the auxiliary verbs **will be**.	Future archaeologists **will be using** new analytical tools for many years.

Read Progressive Tenses

Some writers use progressive tenses to clarify whether actions happen in the past, present, or future. Read this passage based on "Valley of the Kings." How do auxiliary verbs show when each action takes place?

> For months in 1989, Dr. Kent Weeks and his team were investigating a small tomb in the Valley of the Kings. Their work revealed a huge tomb complex. Today, the archaeologists are excavating dozens of chambers in the tomb. Their discoveries are changing what we know about life in ancient Egypt. They will be studying these treasures for decades to come.

Write Progressive Tenses

Reread page 150 of "Valley of the Kings," and write a short paragraph to summarize the information. Include at least one sentence for each progressive tense. Then compare your sentences with a partner's.

Language Frames

- I agree with _____ because _____ .
- What can you learn about _____ from _____ ?
- I think you said _____ . Is that right?
- I'd like to add on. I think _____ .

Engage in Discussion

Listen to Oscar and Emre's discussion with their teacher.
Then use **Language Frames** to engage in a discussion about
historical stories.

Stories of the Past ((MP3))

Oscar: My family went to the museum on Saturday. We've been reading about ancient Egypt in class, but after seeing the exhibit there, I've decided that museums are the best way to learn about history.

Emre: I agree with Oscar about museums because I saw the same exhibit last summer. Watching documentaries and reading nonfiction books are helpful, but there's something really fascinating about seeing an actual mummy.

Teacher: I understand what you mean. It's different seeing the real thing. If you prefer seeing real artifacts, what is your opinion about historical fiction? What can you learn about an historical time or place from reading a made-up story?

Emre: I still like reading novels about the past. Even if the characters and events aren't real, the stories make me care about the people who lived in those times.

Teacher: Oscar, I think you said that you learn the most at museums. Is that right?

Oscar: That's right, but I understand Emre's viewpoint about fiction, too. I'd like to add on to that idea. I think that historical fiction is a great way to find out whether you're interested in a topic. Then you can look for other ways to learn about the facts.

Key Words

chamber

command

hieroglyphics

peer

plunder

procession

Key Words

Study the illustration and descriptions. Use **Key Words** and other words to discuss what we learn when we **peer** into ancient tombs.

Death in Ancient Egypt

1 When an important person died in ancient Egypt, people walked together in a funeral **procession** that followed the body as it was carried to the tomb.

2 The dead were buried with food and belongings they would need in the afterlife.

3 Wealthy Egyptians **commanded**, or ordered, that treasures be buried with them. Over the years, robbers **plundered**, or stole, many precious objects.

4 An Egyptian tomb had **chambers**, or special rooms, that were often decorated.

5 **Hieroglyphics**, a form of symbol writing, covered the walls with messages.

Talk Together

How does studying Egyptian tombs bring the past to life? Use **Language Frames** from page 176 and **Key Words** to discuss this question with a group.

Plot

Plot is the series of events that happens in a story. It usually begins when a main character encounters a conflict, or problem. Throughout the story, the character responds to major plot events, including the turning point, or climax, of the story. All of the events lead to the final resolution at the end of the story.

Look Into the Text

After what seemed like hours, the wind died down. I could smell smoke and saw that flickering flames lit up the painted walls of the tomb where we were sheltering. Four men stood around a ladder that led down to the underground burial chambers. They were gathering up beautiful jewelry and golden decorations broken off from furniture. I heard one hiss, "Hurry! We have been too long. The moon is high. It is near the time we told the guards to come."

"The **conflict** occurs when the narrator sees four men rob a tomb. I can read on to learn about the character's response and the next plot events."

Map and Talk

A plot diagram can help you keep track of story events. Analyzing how characters respond to the conflict, events, turning point, and resolution can help you better understand the story.

Plot Diagram

Turning point

Resolution

Events   3.   3.
           2.   2.   Character's
        1.   1.   Responses

Conflict Men are robbing the tomb.

Talk Together

Talk with a partner about a story you have recently read. Create a plot diagram that identifies how the main character responds to important story events and how the events lead to the resolution of the story.

More Key Words

Use these words to talk about *The Journal of Nakht* and *The Golden Goblet*.

consider
(kun-**si**-dur) *verb*

When you **consider** something, you think about it carefully. The boy **considers** which snack to choose.

contribute
(kun-**tri**-byūt) *verb*

To **contribute** means to give an object or an idea to others. Each student will **contribute** one dollar to help people in need.

impact
(**im**-pakt) *noun*

An **impact** is the effect one thing has on another. The creative science teacher had a positive **impact** on her students.

perspective
(pur-**spek**-tiv) *noun*

A **perspective** is a point of view. The students discussed their different **perspectives** about the issues.

significant
(sig-**ni**-fi-kunt) *adjective*

Something **significant** is important. Finding King Tut's tomb was a **significant** discovery for archaeologists.

Talk Together

Use a **Key Word** to ask a question. Your partner answers using another **Key Word**, if possible. Use each word twice.

> Will the rain have an impact on the game?

> Yes, rain will have a significant impact on whether we can play today..

Add words to My Vocabulary Notebook.
 NGReach.com

Learn to Ask Questions

When you read, you can **ask questions** to help you understand a story and its characters. Sometimes, a question is answered directly in a text. At other times, you have to combine story details with what you already know to infer an answer.

How to Ask Questions

1. As you read, ask yourself questions to understand something confusing, to track what is happening, or to understand the author's viewpoint.

   As I read, I wonder _____ .

2. Reread the text or read on to find any answers that are right there.

   I find details about _____ in the text. Now I know _____ .

3. If the exact answers are not there, think about the details. Think about what you already know. Put them together to come up with answers for your questions.

   I link _____ and _____ to figure out that _____ .

Here's how one student asked a question and found an answer.

Look Into the Text

Tamyt and I scurried to the darkest corner so they would not see us. When the men slunk past our hiding place, Tamyt shrank back, and I saw why when I followed her eyes. A torch lit up the hand of the man carrying it, and he had only three fingers! On one finger was a gold ring engraved with signs.

"As I read **details** about the kids' actions, I wonder why they are hiding."

"I find **details** about the men and Tamyt's response to them in the text. Now I know that Tamyt is afraid of one of the men."

Asking yourself questions as you read can help you figure out what is happening and what the author is trying to say.

Language Frames

As I read, I wonder
_____ .

I find details about _____
in the text. Now I know
_____ .

I link _____ and _____
to figure out that _____ .

Talk Together

Read the historical fiction story and sample notes. Use
Language Frames to ask and answer questions with a partner.

Historical Fiction

A Day IN THE Life of a Scribe

Khu worked quickly but carefully as he transcribed the historical text onto a papyrus scroll. The writing teachers **commanded** excellence, and the smallest of mistakes could mean a strike on the back or—worse—starting over. Khu dipped his reed brush into the ink and, with a few swift strokes, was finished. ◄

"Well done, Khu," said a voice at his shoulder. Khu stood at the writing teacher's words. He hadn't heard the teacher approach, and the kind words had a more powerful **impact** on the boy than the punishing sting of a stick.

"I thank you, Teacher," he answered, bowing slightly to hide his pride. To receive such praise was indeed **significant**. ◄

As the teacher departed, Khu surveyed the room. Here and there, younger boys leaned over pottery shards, pieces of wood, or smooth stones, learning to write by copying short sayings and myths. With more than 700 symbols—and many more combinations for layers of meaning—there was much to learn. The older boys, like Khu, used papyrus scrolls, demonstrating their knowledge by copying official documents and histories. ◄

On this night, Khu thought to himself, *Father will take one of these boys as an apprentice.* He **considered** the possibilities. From his **perspective**, Yaferu was the best choice. He was the eldest, and his **hieroglyphics** were sharp and precise. He was quick, honest, and excelled at math. A scribe who could do accounting had much to **contribute** when it was time to tally the harvest or collect taxes.

Khu gathered his tools, packed them into his scribal kit, and headed for the door.

"Khu, wait," Yaferu called out. "I'll come with you. Your father has summoned me to your house, though I know not why."

Khu smiled knowingly as he linked arms with his friend and began to walk home. ◄

As I read, I wonder
where Khu is.

I find details about
transcribing, texts,
writing teachers, and
ink in the text. Now I
know that Khu is in a
writing school.

I link Khu's actions
and what I know about
ancient Egypt to figure
out that he is a student
learning to be a scribe.

◄ = a good place to stop and ask or answer a question

Read a Diary

Genre

A **diary** is a record of a person's thoughts, feelings, and experiences. *The Journal of Nakht* is a fictional account of a young scribe in ancient Egypt. While the events and most of the characters were created by the author, the setting and descriptions of life in ancient Egypt are based on historical facts.

Setting

The setting of a story is **where** and **when** it takes place. This story is set in ancient Egypt during the rule of the real King Hatshepsut. Look for dates, locations, and other details that can tell you more about the setting.

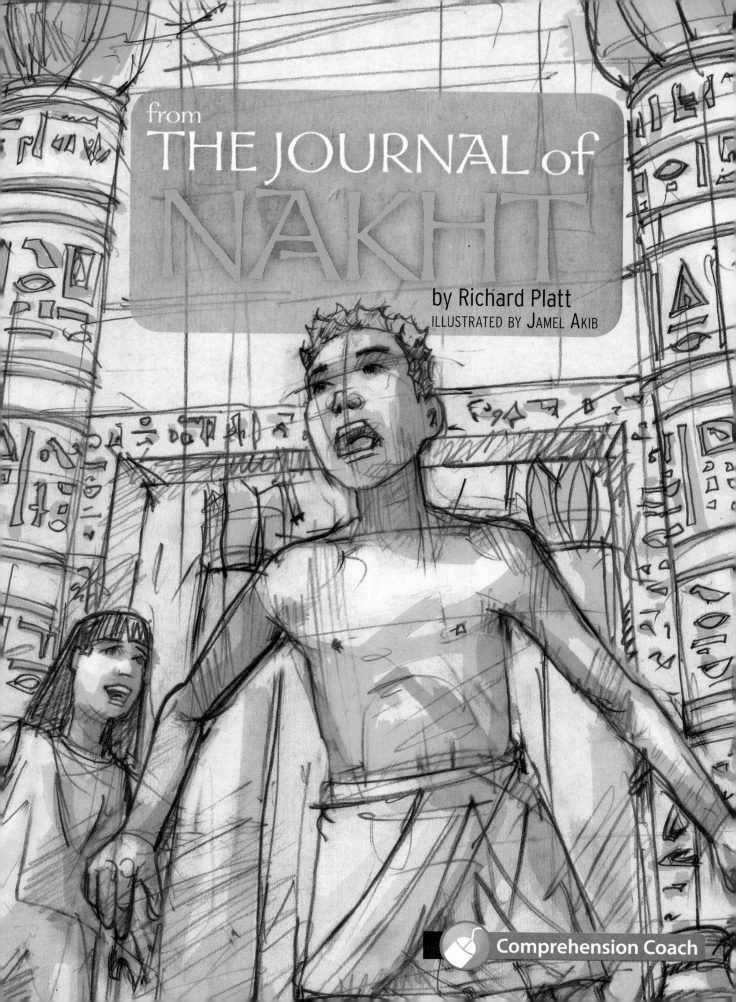

from
THE JOURNAL of
NAKHT

by Richard Platt
ILLUSTRATED BY Jamel Akib

Comprehension Coach

▶ **Set a Purpose**
Find out what happens to Nakht
and his sister in the City of the Dead.

THE CITY OF THE DEAD

First day of the second month of planting

Our trip to Saqqara nearly landed Tamyt and me in jail! And it is only now—three days later—that I dare write down what happened.

When we reached the City of the Dead, I was disappointed. Though the biggest pyramid (Djoser's) is tall and impressive, the other three are small and dull. We passed by quickly because a strong breeze from the desert was **whipping up the sand** and stinging our legs. There was shelter among the other tombs, which surround the bigger pyramids like buildings in a town.

All the robbed tombs seemed alike, so after we had seen the first few with Father, Tamyt and I began to chase each other through the narrow alleys between them. We enjoyed this game so much that we did not notice the breeze becoming a storm. By then, all we could do was find better shelter. Sand choked and half blinded us and matted our hair. We crept through a doorway and huddled together.

After what seemed like hours, the wind **died down**. I could smell smoke and saw that **flickering** flames lit up the painted walls of the tomb where we were sheltering. Four men stood around a ladder that led down to the underground burial **chambers** . They were gathering up beautiful jewelry and golden decorations broken off from furniture. I heard one hiss, "Hurry! We have been too long. The moon is high. It is near the time we told the guards to come."

In Other Words
whipping up the sand making the sand blow
died down became calm
flickering moving

Tamyt and I scurried to the darkest corner so they would not see us. When the men **slunk** past our hiding place, Tamyt shrank back, and I saw why when I followed her eyes. A torch lit up the hand of the man carrying it, and he had only three fingers! On one finger was a gold ring engraved with signs.

I glimpsed the ring for just a moment before they hurried off into the night. When they had gone, I ran to the ladder and started to climb down. Tamyt called, "Nakht! No!" but then she climbed down after me. A sweet smell filled the tunnel, and the glow from tiny lamps led away to where **it forked**. Tamyt grabbed me and whispered that we should turn back, but I broke free and followed the lamps down the left tunnel.

Where the narrow corridor grew wider, the scent was overpowering. Tamyt's whispers rose to a shriek: "*Look!*" The burial chamber was **in chaos**, and the brightly painted coffin lid was split in two. I lit a splinter and held it up. It blazed just long enough for us to glimpse into the coffin at a shiny black face. The tomb robbers had ripped off the mummy's linen strips to get at jewelry bound between them. It was the sweet smell of the **funeral ointments** that filled the tunnels.

In Other Words

slunk moved slowly

it forked the tunnel turned into two different tunnels

in chaos disturbed and messy

funeral ointments liquids and pastes used to make mummies

There was another **horror to follow**: we heard footsteps on the ladder! I grabbed Tamyt, and we scarcely had time to slip into the shadow of another dark chamber before bright torches lit up the tunnel. It was not the robbers returning but the cemetery guards. Tamyt and I thought the guards would search everywhere and find us, but instead the two men merely glanced around, then climbed out. It was as if they had *expected* to discover the robbery.

As soon as they had left, we rushed to the **foot of the shaft**, but the ladder had gone. We could see its end high above us—far out of reach.

Father came after daybreak. His voice calling our names woke us, and when we replied, he lowered the ladder. We climbed out, and I was sure this time I would get a beating, but instead he just looked tired and **relieved**.

I sat in front of him as we rode home in our second-best chariot.

"When the wind dropped last night, it was too dark to find you on my own," he told us. "I could not ask the guards for help because I should not have been there myself."

I remember no more of what he said, for I fell asleep. Both Tamyt and I had been too afraid to get much sleep as uninvited guests in the underground tomb.

Fourth day

Today I did not go to school. I stayed home with Tamyt, for Father wanted to know what we had seen at Saqqara.

We told him everything we could remember. When he heard about the three-fingered man and his ring, he urged us to tell him what the ring looked like. I could remember there was an owl carved on it, and a grain store. But there were other signs as well, and no matter how hard I tried, I could not remember what they were. Worse than this, Father asked, "Which finger was missing?" and neither of us knew. Of course, losing a finger is not unusual: few **quarrymen** have all eight.

Father thanked us for our help, but I could tell that he wished we had noticed more.

In Other Words
horror to follow scary event after that
foot of the shaft entrance
relieved thankful
quarrymen men who break apart rocks for work

Tenth day

These past days I have been unable to write, for my left arm has been quite useless. Returning from school a few days ago, May and I stopped by the river, where there is a rope hanging from a tree. May swung on the rope and landed **nimbly** on his feet. Then he challenged me to do the same. I leaped and clung to the rope as he had, and it carried me high into the air. But as I swung back, I lost my grip, and the ground rushed up toward me. I put out my arm, but the ground was stronger and my arm snapped like a twig.

May laughed at first, but when he realized how badly I was hurt, his eyes filled with fear. He helped me home, and as soon as Mother saw me, she sent **Ahmose for the Sunu**.

Though he does not usually see patients in the afternoon, the Sunu came immediately, for Ahmose made my injuries sound far worse than they really were. Once he had examined me, however, he sighed with relief, saying, "The boy has only a broken arm." Then he **commanded** Ahmose to cut down a tree branch about one cubit long and a hand thick.

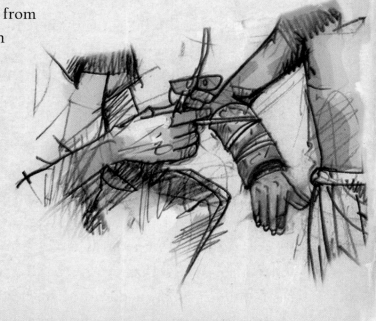

When Ahmose returned, the Sunu took the stick and, with a knife, cut the bark from it. Then he poured honey where my skin was broken and wrapped the bark around it. Finally he tied the bark up so I could not move my arm. While doing all this, he **recited** a magic spell to heal me.

Finally the Sunu brought out a tiny jar shaped like the head of a poppy. He mixed the powder in it with water and made me sip it. This bitter medicine slowly made the pain in my head and arm go away and then sent me to sleep.

In Other Words

nimbly easily

Ahmose for the Sunu our servant, Ahmose, to find the doctor

recited performed

▶ **Before You Move On**

1. **Plot** What is the main conflict, or problem, for Nakht and Tamyt?

2. **Setting** What details in the text tell you about life in ancient Egypt?

First day of the second month of heat

Something so incredible has happened that I cannot make my brush shape the letters fast enough! But I know I must not hurry. Unless I write down everything from the beginning, I will spoil the end of the tale—just as a roast duck spoils if the fire is too hot.

Yesterday began normally enough, but we knew that in the evening the **Controller of Granaries** would be coming to eat with us. So from the moment the sun rose, Father was asking nervously about the food and other arrangements. After a hundred questions, Tamyt and Mother refused to answer any more, and they **bustled** off to organize the meal.

This took all day (and indeed, the fussing had begun a week ago). There was more food than I have ever seen. Besides a delicious ox head, there were birds' eggs and both fresh and pickled fish. Ahmose strangled and plucked some of the ducks in the garden, where they have been fattening ever since we finally trapped them in the Delta.

The Controller of Granaries came an hour late. He arrived in a **procession** fit for a priest. Though Father was furious at his lateness, we all bowed low to him anyway. When we gathered to eat, Father said I had to sit next to him. I thought this was very odd, for I normally sit with Tamyt, but Father stared hard at me, as he does only when he is about to be cross, so I sat down.

At dinner, we talked about the tomb robberies. The Controller said that the robbers had killed a man who discovered them at work. When Tamyt heard this, her eyes grew wide with **alarm at** *our* narrow escape. The conversation ended with Father saying, "Don't worry, sir. I feel we are close to solving the mystery." The Controller simply nodded with his head down, but he looked up suddenly when Father continued, "The answer has been staring me in the face all the time."

In Other Words
Controller of Granaries official in charge of grain
bustled hurried
alarm at fear at the thought of

When we were ready to eat fruit, the Controller of Granaries picked
up a fig and held it in his left hand to peel it. The light from the lamp fell
on his ring, and I saw that it was just like the ring the tomb robber had
worn at Saqqara! I jumped up and pointed. "The ring!" I gasped. "It's carved
with the same symbols!" The cup I had been holding fell to the floor and
smashed, and Mother came and slapped my hand. She pushed me to sit
down, hissing, "Now apologize!" in my ear.

I made an excuse, and the meal went on, but after this slip, I thought
the Controller of Granaries looked at me very strangely: never directly but
out of the corner of his eye.

But there was another shock to come. When it was time for the
Controller to go, I watched his servants help him down the steps. I gazed at
their muscular arms, down to where their big hands gripped their master's
arms to assist him. It was then that I noticed that one of them had a finger
missing, like the tomb robber we saw at the City of the Dead!

I might have been mistaken about the ring, but this time I was sure. I jumped forward and grabbed the servant's arm, shouting, "It's him! He's a tomb robber!"

Tamyt ran forward to help me, but the robber was quicker. He let go of the Controller of Granaries—who lost his balance and **sprawled** down the steps—and pushed us roughly away. In a few long **bounds**, he had reached the garden wall. Without looking to see what lay beyond,

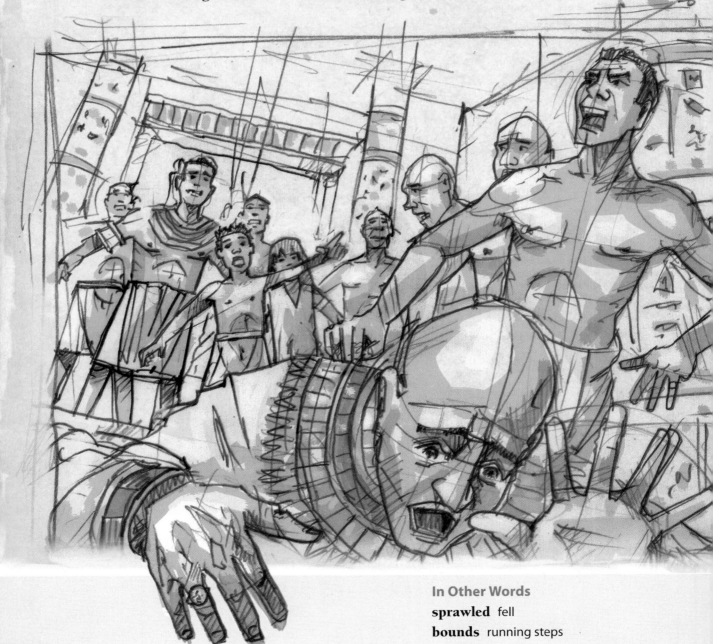

In Other Words
sprawled fell
bounds running steps

he vaulted straight over it and escaped into the street. I ran after him, but his long legs had taken him out of sight even before I heard the gate slam shut behind me.

By the time I got back to the house, everyone was inside again. The Controller sat **defiantly** on a chair, but his servants stood roped together in a sulky row. To get the city guard to take them away and lock them up, Father had to agree to take the blame for any trouble the Controller might cause *and* promise each guard a fat goose and two **cubits of linen**. And so it was that Tamyt and I caught the tomb robbers—in our own house!

Fourth day of the second month of heat

Since the arrest of the Controller of Granaries, everyone in Memphis seems to know us. People I have never seen before greet me by name in the street. Strangers stand and point at our house.

Eighth day

The Vizier, the king's most important official, arrived in Memphis today to question the Controller of Granaries.

Father said that the Controller denied everything at first and angrily demanded to be released. However, he seemed less sure of himself when the Vizier suggested they go to visit his house, which has been **sealed** since his arrest.

It took a whole day's searching to find the stolen treasures. Indeed they might never have been found if the Vizier had not asked for a drink of water. The sharp-eyed guard who went to the well noticed a scraping of gold on a stone at its edge. Lowering himself on the well rope, he discovered, halfway down, a hidden chamber filled with tomb ornaments.

In Other Words
defiantly angrily
cubits of linen lengths of cloth
sealed locked

▶ **Before You Move On**

1. **Confirm Predictions/Explain** What evidence causes the guilty men to be caught?

2. **Ask Questions** What is Nakht like? Combine details from the text to find the answer.

▶ **Predict**

What will happen to Nakht and his family because of their actions?

Eleventh day

Today I went with Father into the fields to escape the crowds and heat in town. He wanted to see a machine that a farmer had built by the river to bring water to his crops. The name of this machine is *shaduf*, but a better name would be "stork," for it looks just like that bird drinking from the river.

The action of the machine was very simple. The farmer pulled down on the rope to lower the bucket into the water. When it was full, the weight of the lump of clay on the other end lifted the heavy bucket out of the water as if it weighed nothing! Finally the farmer tipped the water into a **trough** that slopes toward his field.

Our curiosity was soon satisfied, and we sat down in the shade of a tree and discussed the tomb robberies and the Controller of Granaries.

"The robbers broke into only the richest tombs," Father explained, "and when the officials hurried me around Saqqara, I began to suspect they were protecting someone important. When you told me about the short time the guards spent at the tomb, it convinced me that these were not ordinary tomb robbers."

I asked him how he guessed the Controller of Granaries was involved, and he scratched his head thoughtfully. "Well, you said that there were hieroglyphs of an owl and a granary on the tomb robber's ring. Those are the symbols for a controller of granaries. Members of the household might wear them too. Of course, only one of them recently bought a *very* large house, much larger than you would expect for a man of his importance. I knew he wouldn't rob tombs himself, so I guessed he sent his servants. I thought you or Tamyt might recognize the **scoundrels** again if you could get close enough. So I needed an occasion at which the Controller could show off. **I threw a banquet**, and sure enough, he brought his whole entourage."

I didn't know what an entourage was, but I didn't want to interrupt.

"I wasn't sure how the evening would unfold," he continued, "but we caught them—even the three-fingered man did not escape the guards for long."

When I asked him what would happen to the Controller, he did not reply but got up and said, "Come. It's cooler now. Let's go home."

In Other Words
trough large container for water
scoundrels criminals; robbers
I threw a banquet I invited people to a big meal

Twelfth day of the third month of heat

I hardly slept last night, and had to rise TWO HOURS before dawn to wash and dress for our trip to the palace this morning. Though it is only a short walk away, Father was concerned that we would get our new clothes dusty on the way, so he sent for chairs to **collect us** just after sunrise. Father went in one, and Tamyt and I shared the other. This ride made me feel like a prince, for it was the first time I have ever been carried anywhere in a chair.

Alas, there was hardly time to enjoy it, for we were soon at the palace gates, and then inside. The palace is a little like a temple—but as a temple courtyard is big and airy, so the palace is bigger and airier. Great trees grow in the palace garden, but the walls are so high that the trees are almost invisible from the outside. There is water everywhere—in pools and in trickling streams. The ceilings are so high that you must **crane your neck** to look up at them, and gold and brilliant colors cover everything. But what surprised me most of all was that—like us—the king lives in a house of mud! I had

In Other Words
collect us pick us up
crane your neck tilt your head back

expected that the palace would be built of stone, like a tomb, but it is not. As we rode in, we saw a new wall being built, and it was made of mud bricks.

Once we were inside the palace, we stood for *hours* in a long line waiting to see the king, but we stayed cool under brightly colored linen tents.

While we waited, **a courtier** told us how to behave before the king. Nobody is allowed to speak directly to his face. Even his closest advisers must look away and talk as if he is not there at all. For instance, they do not say, "Do you want me to do this or that?" but, "Does the king wish me to do this or that?"

We learned all this as we moved slowly across an inner courtyard toward the throne. I could see little because there were so many people, but as we drew closer, I **spied** King Hatshepsut sitting in the shade between two great towering columns.

The first thing I noticed was how thin and small he was. Because he is all-powerful, I had expected to see a bigger man. The king's small size made the crown he wore seem enormous, and his broad gold collar looked especially large below such a slim face.

In Other Words
a courtier someone who worked in the king's palace
spied saw

The long line moved slower than a snail up a reed, but eventually we were close enough to see the king clearly. It was Tamyt who noticed first . . . Her eyes **grew as round as lotus pads**. She turned to me and gasped, "The king is a WOMAN!"

I looked carefully, and Tamyt was right. Underneath the false beard and great crown, King Hatshepsut really is a woman!

Father whispered, "Of course! Didn't you realize?" But before I could reply, it was our turn, and we bowed low. A servant **read out** what we had done, but so quickly I could hardly understand it. Then another official **nudged** me and **muttered**, "Move along now." But as he did, the king looked straight at us and held up his—her—hand.

"Wait a minute!" she said to the official, and then to us, "You two have been very clever and brave." She smiled. "Thank you." She nodded and we were hurried away.

It was all over in less time than it takes an ibis to pluck a fish from the water, but the king had *spoken* to us, as if we were viziers, or gods! ❖

In Other Words

grew as round as lotus pads widened in surprise

read out read a report about

nudged pushed

muttered said quietly

▶ **Before You Move On**

1. **Plot** What important event does Nakht record in this diary entry? How does his family respond to the event?

2. **Ask Questions** What did you discover about the king? Connect details that give clues about who the king really is.

Meet the Author

RICHARD PLATT

Richard Platt didn't always want to be a writer. At first, he wanted to be a photographer. Then he started writing about photography in magazine articles and books. After Platt got a job editing children's books, he started writing stories for children. One of the things Platt loves most about writing is that he gets to research "strange, wacky, and obscure subjects."

Along with creating exciting tales about pirates, castles, and ancient Egypt, Platt has written television scripts, information for museums, and restaurant reviews. He says, "I will—and do—write about almost anything because it's the variety of my work that I enjoy." What types of books would you enjoy writing?

Writer's Craft

In *The Journal of Nakht*, the author uses vivid words to help readers imagine the setting of the story. For instance, "a strong breeze from the desert was whipping up the sand," and "flickering flames lit up the painted walls." Write a description of a place using vivid words to bring the scene to life. Think about how vivid verbs, adjectives, and adverbs can create more dimension in your description.

Key Words

chamber	peer
command	perspective
consider	plunder
contribute	procession
hieroglyphics	significant
impact	

Talk About It 🗨

1. *The Journal of Nakht* is a fictional diary. How would the story have changed if it had been written as a regular fiction story?

2. Reread the scene on page 186 in which the cemetery guards come to check on the tomb. How does this scene **contribute** to the overall development of the plot?

3. How does going to the palace to meet King Hatshepsut change Nakht's **perspective** about his life and world?

4. Explain how Nakht changes from the beginning to the end of the diary. Use text evidence to support your conclusion.

5. Compare your life with details of Nakht's life. How does making connections help you answer questions or understand more about the story?

6. How do the illustrations and details about the setting contribute to your understanding of ancient Egyptian life? Cite at least three examples from the diary entries to support your ideas.

Learn test-taking strategies and answer more questions.
🌐 **NGReach.com**

Write About It 🖊

Think about Tamyt's response to the events in the tomb. Write a personal letter from Tamyt to a friend to describe the events from her **perspective**. Use at least three **Key Words**.

> Dear Friend,
>
>   Nakht and I ended up in an underground tomb **chamber** after a storm. I thought we were safe, but I was wrong!

Plot

Use a plot diagram to record the main events in *The Journal of Nakht* and how the characters respond to these events. Include the turning point and the resolution.

Plot Diagram

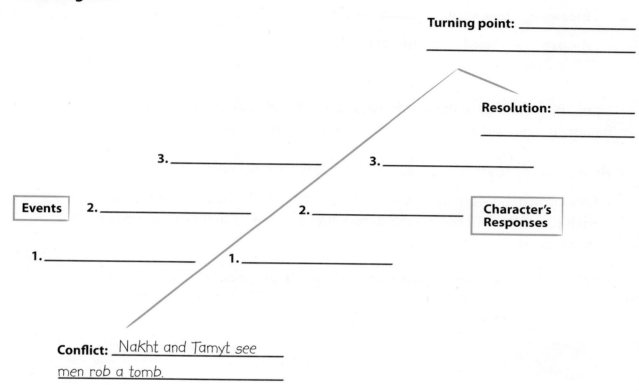

Turning point: _____

_____

Resolution: _____

_____

3. _____   3. _____

Events   2. _____   2. _____   Character's Responses

1. _____   1. _____

Conflict: <u>Nakht and Tamyt see</u>
<u>men rob a tomb.</u>

Use your plot diagram to retell the story events to a partner. Explain how the characters' responses to different events help move the plot forward.

Fluency Comprehension Coach

Use the Comprehension Coach to practice reading with expression. Rate your reading.

Talk Together

How does *The Journal of Nakht* bring the past to life through its entries? Discuss your ideas with a partner. Use **Key Words**.

Compound Words

A **compound word** is made up of two or more base words. Sometimes you can define a compound word if you know the meanings of the smaller words.

EXAMPLE

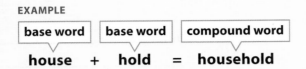

base word	base word	compound word

house + hold = household

Using the meanings of the words *house* and *hold*, you can figure out that *household* means "things held in a house" or "things related to a house."

Here are some strategies to figure out the meanings of compound words:

- Break down the word into its smaller parts, and think about the meaning of each part. Then put the meanings together and see if the new word makes more sense.

- Look for nearby context clues that might give hints about the word's meaning.

Try It

Read the sentences. Then answer the questions. Use the strategies above.

> We arrived at the tomb just after <u>sunrise</u>. It was evident that tomb robbers had recently plundered the <u>underground</u> chamber. A large wooden chest had been forced open and emptied.

1. **What is the best meaning for the compound word <u>sunrise</u>?**

   A the time when the sun is overhead

   B the time when the sun comes up

   C the time when people see the sun

   D the time when the sun sets

2. **What is the best meaning for the compound word <u>underground</u>?**

   A under a chamber

   B along the ground

   C below the ground

   D above a chamber

Connect Across Texts You read how Nakht encountered tomb robbers in ancient Egypt. Now read how another boy faces tomb robbers who include his brother, Gebu.

Genre Historical fiction is based in a real time and place, but many of the characters, events, and details are created by the author.

from The Golden Goblet

BY
Eloise Jarvis McGraw
ILLUSTRATED BY JOEL SPECTOR

*T*here was a silence that seemed as long as time itself to Ranofer, who lay in a tight ball, dizzy with fright, on the floor of the passage. Then he heard Gebu's voice in the second room, sounding unconcerned as ever.

"It was nothing. You're afraid of **your own shadow**."

"I tell you I heard a sound," the voice of Wenamon insisted.

"There is no one here but us and the dead. **Make haste** with those boxes, now."

Slowly, uncertainly, Ranofer rose to his knees, then stood. No one here? But what was that face he had seen? Trembling, he **peered** again through the opening, and met the same pair of eyes. This time, though he shrank back involuntarily, he realized that they did not move, did not live. They were the inlaid glass eyes of a life-sized wooden statue, and he saw now that they had been partially smashed, as if from **the blow of a dagger hilt**. Gebu and Wenamon had wanted no gaze upon them as they went about their evil work, especially the gaze of this watchful *ushabti* placed here as servant and **guardian** of the dead.

In Other Words
your own shadow everything
Make haste Hurry
the blow of a dagger hilt being hit with the handle of a large knife
guardian guard; protector

▶ **Before You Move On**

1. **Explain** Why is Ranofer frightened? List at least two reasons from the text.
2. **Ask Questions** What question do you have about the *ushabti*? Combine details or read on to find an answer.

201

Nervously Ranofer examined the **figure** more closely, and his fear of its **vengeance** changed to an unexpected pity. It was the statue of a slim and lovely servant girl, wearing a painted white dress and a painted gilt necklace, steadying a box on one shoulder and carrying a painted wooden duck by its feet in her other hand. Her expression was one of **serenity** and joy, and the sculptor who carved her had been a master. Now her clear, wide eyes were cloudy and blinded by the blow that had splintered them; her beauty was marred and her usefulness as a watchful guardian ended. It was like seeing some innocent, happy creature lying murdered, victim of Gebu's **callous** greed.

Ranofer's gaze turned from her to move in wonder about the rest of the **chamber**, which was dimly illumined by the glow of the torch from the next room. As he looked a strange emotion took possession of him. Beyond and around the graceful statue were articles of household furniture, arranged as in a beautiful home. There were armchairs and beds of carved wood decorated with gold, there were alabaster honey jars, painted boxes resting on delicately wrought ivory legs. There was a wicker trunk ventilated by little slatted openings, through which the fragrance of the perfumed garments within escaped into the room. There were winecups arranged on shelves, there were scent jars and jeweled collars and arm bands. Everywhere was the gleam of gold.

In Other Words
figure statue
vengeance revenge; anger
serenity peacefulness
callous selfish

It was not the gold, however, that held Ranofer's gaze and drew him slowly through the jagged entrance to stand, silent and awed, within the Precious Habitation. It was the garlands of flowers, only a little withered, as if placed here in love and grief only yesterday, and the sight of a worn oaken staff leaning against the wall, of two pairs of sandals, a new and an old, of favorite joints of meat placed neatly in boxes as if for a journey. Whatever he had expected, it was not this intimate look of home, of a well-loved room to which its owner might at any moment return. Whatever horrors haunted the passage, they were not here, in this quiet **sanctuary**.

Who was the owner? Ranofer's eyes searched farther, and halted in surprise. There were two owners. Slowly, soundlessly, he crossed the chamber to the pair of silver-inlaid coffins, on the lids of which were sculptured in gold the figures of their occupants, a man and a woman. They lay as if sleeping, side by side, their folded hands **eloquent of** the same defenseless trust that had caused them to order a sweet-faced servant girl as their only guardian. As Ranofer looked into their quiet golden faces the stealthy sounds of **plundering** in the next room became horrible to him. For the first time he fully understood this crime.

He straightened, all his fear gone and in its place hot fury. Those merciless and wicked ones!—to break into this sacred place and steal the treasures meant to comfort this old couple through their Three Thousand Years! Whether rich gold or worn-out sandals, these things belonged to them, no living human had a right to set foot in this chamber, not even the son of Thutra, who meant no harm. Almost, he could hear the helpless fluttering of these Old Ones' frightened **bas**. So strong was the sensation that he dropped to his knees in profound apology for his own **intrusion**. As he did so he saw something else, a stack of wine jars just beyond one of the coffins. They were capped with linen and sealed with clay, and pressed into the clay was a mark as well known to Ranofer as it was to everyone else in Egypt. It was the personal seal of the great noble, Huaa, only two years dead, the beloved father of Queen Tiy.

In Other Words
sanctuary place of rest
eloquent of showing
bas souls; spirits
intrusion entry

▶ **Before You Move On**

1. **Setting** Describe the tomb. What does this setting show about life in ancient Egypt?

2. **Ask Questions** Why do Ranofer's feelings change as he examines the tomb? Combine details to figure out the answer.

Shocked to his very toes, Ranofer scrambled up and retreated a few respectful steps, involuntarily stretching out his hands toward the coffins **in the gesture of homage**. Here lay Huaa and his cherished wife Tuaa, the parents of the queen of Egypt. And here he stood, an insignificant nobody, daring to gaze into their faces! He was acutely, desperately embarrassed; he felt like a **dusty urchin** trespassing in a palace, which he was. Worse, at any moment those thieves would be in here to wreck and **pillage**, to tear the gold trim from chairs and chests, to snatch the jewel boxes, to break open the beautiful coffins and even strip the wrappings from the royal mummies themselves in search of golden amulets. It must not happen. These Old Ones should have someone grand and fierce to protect them.

They have only me, Ranofer thought. I must do something—anything—go fetch help—

204

He turned and started swiftly toward the entrance hole, too swiftly, for his elbow grazed a little inlaid table and tilted the alabaster vase upon it. He clutched at it wildly but it fell, shattering on the stone floor with a crash that echoed like the very sound of doom.

The small noises in the chamber beyond ceased instantly. Ranofer breathed a prayer to Osiris and flung himself behind the coffins, which was all he had time to do before the torch and Gebu's murderous face appeared in the doorway.

"*Ast!*" came Wenamon's hiss. "I told you we were not alone!"

"We will be soon," Gebu answered in tones that **turned Ranofer cold**. He could see their two shadows on the wall, black and clear-cut: Gebu's bulky one, Wenamon's, thin and vulture-shaped, behind it. The shadows moved, rippled in deadly silence along the wall, leaped crazily to the rough ceiling and down again as the two began methodically to search the room. The dancing black shapes advanced relentlessly toward the coffins, looming huge as giants as they came nearer. Ranofer's hand groped out blindly and closed on a small heavy object that felt like a jewel box. At that instant Gebu's **rage-distorted** face was thrust over the coffin.

Ranofer lunged to his feet and hurled the box with all his strength.

There was a glittering shower of gems as the box struck Gebu full in the eyes, **jarring** the torch from his hand. He gave a hoarse cry and staggered backward into Wenamon, who began to scream and curse as he fought the flame that was licking upwards into his cloak. In that one instant of confusion Ranofer saw his chance. He seized the nearest wine jar and aimed it straight at the blaze. There was a splattering crash and the torch hissed out, plunging the chamber into darkness. With the reek of wine and scorched cloth rising strong about him, Ranofer leaped for the far wall, feeling frantically along it for the entrance hole. Behind him the dark was **hideous with** yells and curses, with the sounds of splintering wood and jewelry crushed under foot as the two thieves plunged this way and that over the wine-slippery floor in search of him.

In Other Words
turned Ranofer cold scared Ranofer
rage-distorted angry; furious
jarring knocking
hideous with filled with angry

▶ **Before You Move On**

1. **Plot** What important decision does Ranofer make in the tomb? How does this affect his actions?

2. **Summarize** In your own words, explain how Ranofer defends himself.

Where, in the name of all the gods, was the hole?

His fingers met a jagged bit of plaster and, beside it, empty space. In an instant he was through the hole and stumbling along the black passage, bent double under its crowding roof, banging and bumping into its **roughhewn** walls, but running, flying away from the death behind him. The sounds of rage faded as he ran, grew fainter with every bend, then suddenly grew louder. The thieves had found the wall opening, too, and were after him, in the passage. He scrambled around a curve, almost fell, dashed on again and **brought up with** a stunning impact against solid wall. Walls on three sides of him? Was he trapped? He wasted precious moments seeking a way around the obstruction; then his hand touched a rough shelf of stone. A step! He had reached the bottom of the entrance shaft much sooner than he had expected, for his **headlong flight** back had **consumed** far less time than his first cautious, crawling journey.

He clawed at the wall, found step after narrow step and hoisted his trembling body up them one by one. As he put his weight on the last one it crumbled under him. In a panic he flung both arms over the top of the shaft and for a terrible moment hung there, then wriggling, straining, pushing, he was over the top and through the crevice in the rocks.

The sunlight hit him like a blow. Half blind and shaking all over, he could think only of that last crumbled step and what it could mean to him. The thieves might climb past by jumping and then wriggling as he had done, but they could not get out if the top of the shaft were solidly blocked. They would have nothing to stand on to shove away the stones. He could hear stumbling, rapid footsteps approaching the bottom of the shaft, and Gebu's enraged voice bellowing his name; but already he was grabbing up rocks as fast as he could move, his eyes squinted

In Other Words
roughhewn unfinished
brought up with was stopped suddenly by
headlong flight run
consumed taken

tight against the glare of day. He hurled a few into the shaft and felt a fierce joy at the roar of pain below, and the thud of someone falling. Quickly he wedged some larger stones into the crevice, then began to shove and strain at the biggest, a boulder three times the size of his head, which had originally blocked the entrance.

It would not budge. He put his shoulder to it, dug his toes into the hot sands, and shoved with all his strength. It **stirred** a little, tilted. He heard more scrambling sounds below and gave one last desperate thrust. The boulder tipped and rolled across the opening.

For a moment he could do nothing but lean upon the boulder and gasp for breath. There was still space behind it, but he could push it no closer. **Amon willing**, it would delay them a little while, but that was all.

He turned and started running across the red wasteland of the Valley in the direction of the Nile. After the closeness of the tomb the hot, free wind of the desert poured over him like the breath of life itself, but he could take no joy in it. If only the stone had rolled closer, there would be time to plan, to act in safety; but there was no time, there was nothing but more and more danger. Gebu was strong as **Set himself**. Sooner or later the stone would be tilting, moving, rolling free. ❖

In Other Words
stirred moved
Amon willing If the god Amon helped him
Set himself the Egyptian god Set

▶ **Before You Move On**
1. **Figurative Language** What does "The sunlight hit him like a blow" mean? Use context clues to figure out an answer.
2. **Character** Describe some of Ranofer's traits based on his actions and decisions in the tomb.

207

Key Words

chamber	peer
command	perspective
consider	plunder
contribute	procession
hieroglyphics	significant
impact	

Compare Details

The authors of *The Journal of Nakht* and *The Golden Goblet* both use historical facts and fictional details to write about similar topics and themes. Work with a partner to complete a comparison chart with details from both texts. Then use the information to synthesize, or put together, a general idea about ancient Egyptian life.

Comparison Chart

	The Journal of Nakht	*The Golden Goblet*
Genre		Historical fiction
Narrator's Point of View	First-person: Nakht writes about his own thoughts and feelings.	
Historical Facts		
Fictional Details		
Theme		

Talk Together

How do the historical fiction story and the fictional diary bring the past to life? What **perspective** do they give you that informational texts like "The Valley of the Kings" and "Animals Everlasting" do not? Use **Key Words** and evidence from the selections to talk about your ideas with a partner.

Grammar and Spelling

Modals

A **modal** works together with another verb. The **main verb** tells the action. The modal supports the main verb's meaning.

Grammar Rules Modals

Some **modals** change the meaning of the **main verb**.

• Use **can** to tell what someone or something is able to do.	We **can learn** about the ancient Egyptians.
• Use **could**, **may**, or **might** to tell what is possible or permitted.	Experts **may discover** the person's name. They **might tell** us about the mummy.
• Use **should** to tell what is good for someone to do.	We **should care** for ancient artifacts.
• Use **must** to tell what someone has to or needs to do.	We **must do** all we can to protect the tombs.
• Use **would** to tell what someone is willing to do.	I **would like** to visit an ancient tomb.

Read Modals

Writers often use helping verbs to give advice or guidance. Read this passage based on *The Journal of Nakht*. What modals can you find?

> When you are in King Hatshepsut's presence, you must be respectful. The pharaoh might speak to you. You may respond, but you may not address the pharaoh directly. Instead you must speak as if the pharaoh is not there.

Write Modals

Reread pages 203–204 of *The Golden Goblet* to find Ranofer's thoughts about plundering tombs. Write a paragraph that explains why plundering a tomb is wrong. Include at least two sentences that use modals. Then compare your sentences with a partner's.

Write as a Researcher

Write a Research Report

Write a report that brings to life some aspect of ancient Egypt. Place your reports in a class book called *Bringing Ancient Egypt to Life*.

Study a Model

A research report is a nonfiction report that gives information about a topic. But it is more than a collection of facts. It is also a way of sharing the conclusions you make based on those facts. You gather information, think about what you've learned, and describe what it all means.

Read Julia's report about the pharaoh Hatshepsut.

Hatshepsut: The Woman Pharaoh of Egypt
by Julia Nguyen

An ancient Egyptian statue depicts a pharaoh. All the usual signs are there: the figure wears a pharaoh's striped headdress and traditional false beard. But it has the body of a woman! It is the pharaoh Hatshepsut. **Hatshepsut, who lived about 3,500 years ago, was an unusual woman who became a powerful ruler.**

The path Hatshepsut took to become pharaoh was unheard of for a woman in ancient Egypt. She was the daughter of the pharaoh Thutmose I and the wife of his successor, Thutmose II. **When her husband died**, his son, Thutmose III, was supposed to inherit the throne. But Thutmose III was still a child, so Hatshepsut stepped in as temporary ruler. **After seven successful years**, Hatshepsut seized power for herself. She was crowned king of all of Egypt, and Thutmose III was pushed aside.

The title and introduction capture the reader's interest and tell what the report is about.

The introduction also presents the **central idea**.

Each paragraph has a **topic sentence** that supports the central idea.

The report has a clear organization. Events are presented in the **chronological sequence** in which they happened.

The Egyptians seemed to accept Hatshepsut as their king, and she enjoyed a peaceful and successful 21-year reign. She expanded trade into parts of Africa and the Middle East. This brought riches to her country and her people. Hatshepsut also built many temples throughout Egypt. One of her most magnificent temples still stands at Deir el Bahri.

No one knows how Hatshepsut's reign ended, but when it did, Thutmose III came to power. At some point during Thutmose III's reign, there was an effort to destroy statues and images of Hatshepsut. Her name was removed from official records. According to author Chip Brown, the work to remove Hatshepsut from history "was careful and precise."

Not all evidence of Hatshepsut was erased, however. In the nineteenth century, Egyptologists succeeded in deciphering hieroglyphics that told about Hatshepsut. Today people are able to marvel at the achievements of this amazing woman pharaoh.

The writer supports her ideas with **facts and details**.

Bibliography

Brown, C. (2009, April). The King Herself. *National Geographic Magazine, 88–111.*

Hatshepsut. (2014). In *Encyclopædia Britannica*. Retrieved from http://www.britannica.com/EBchecked/topic/256896/Hatshepsut

History.com Staff (2009). *Hatshepsut*. Retrieved from http://www.history.com/topics/ancient-history/Hatshepsut

The bibliography on the final page lists the sources Julia used. Julia conducted her research by reading these sources to gather the information she used for her report.

Prewrite

1. **Choose a Central Idea** Think about what you have learned about ancient Egypt. What aspect of ancient Egyptian civilization is most interesting to you? Work with a partner to brainstorm and discuss ideas. Narrow your topic to one that you can cover well in a short report.

2. **List Your Research Questions** What do you already know about your topic? What do you want to find out? With your partner, think of questions you could use to guide your research. You can add to this list as you learn more.

> ## Research Questions
>
> - Who was Hatshepsut?
> - How did she come to power?
> - What are some achievements of her reign?
> - How do we know about her today?

3. **Create a Research Plan** A research report must contain information from several different sources. Your research plan contains your questions and your ideas about the sources you can use to answer them. Your sources may include both print and digital texts and visual information. Determine the search terms and methods you will use for online research.

Topic: Hatshepsut

Text Sources	Visual Sources
• magazine article about Hatshepsut and her legacy • online encyclopedia entry about Hatshepsut	• photos of statues, temples, and other artifacts related to Hatshepsut • video about unsolved mysteries about Hatshepsut • a visit to a museum

Text sources are materials that you read online or in print. They include **primary sources**, such as letters and diaries, and **secondary sources**, such as nonfiction books, periodicals, Web sites, and reference books.

Visual information may be found online, in print, or in person. You can get visual information from viewing videos, photographs, charts, graphs, diagrams, and so on. A museum visit also provides visual information.

Gather Information

1. **Identify Credible Sources** Credible, or valid, sources are up to date and written or created by a group or person who is an expert on the topic. Be sure to assess the credibility of each source you find.

   Evaluate the accuracy and reliability of each source. The facts you find should match from source to source. Try to find each fact in two different sources.

   Review each source to locate information. Skim the tables of contents, headings, and pictures. On a Web site, check the menus and links.

2. **Record Sources** Use numbered index cards or create a searchable document or matrix on a computer to record important information about each source.

   Source Card

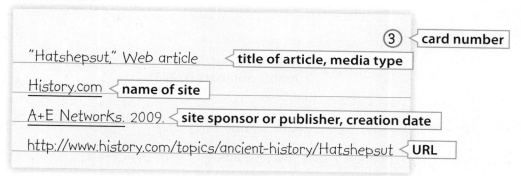

3. **Take Notes** Record important words, phrases, and ideas from your research in your own words. This is called *paraphrasing*. If you quote from your source or pick up anything word for word, use quotation marks and name the source.

   Include visuals in your report. Keep a separate file for any pictures, maps, or charts you may want to use. Be sure to record their sources.

   Note Card

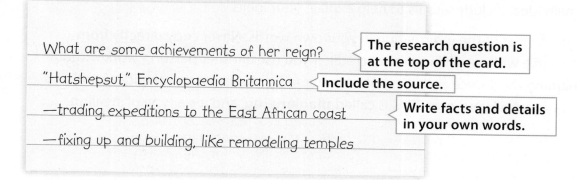

Get Organized

1. **Sort the Information** Use the research questions to sort your notes into categories. If you have a lot of information, create subcategories based on your main ideas. Group all of your information in a logical order.

2. **Organize Your Details** Use an outline or another graphic organizer to organize how you will present the information. Each category from your cards becomes a main idea. The details from each card support the main ideas.

Outline

Use Roman numerals for main ideas.

Use capital letters for supporting points. There must always be at least an A and a B.

I. Hatshepsut's path to power was unheard of.
   A. Daughter and wife of pharaoh
   B. Husband died, the son was supposed to rule
      1. The son was a child
      2. Hatshepsut became temporary ruler
   C. After 7 years, she seized power and became King
II. Hatshepsut had a peaceful and successful reign
   A. Expanded trade
   B. Built many temples

Add more details using Arabic numbers (1, 2, 3).

Draft

1. Use your outline or graphic organizer to guide you as you write. Begin with an introduction that tells what the report is about. Then write a paragraph for each main idea. Include visuals to help explain your ideas.

2. Put the rest of the information in your own words. Never copy directly from a source without giving proper credit. If you use another person's work without naming the source and using quotation marks, you claim that the ideas and words are all your own. This is called **plagiarizing**, and it's a type of stealing.

Revise

1. **Read, Retell, Respond** Read the draft of your report to a partner. Your partner listens and summarizes the main points of the report. Then discuss specific ways that you can improve your writing.

2. **Make Changes** Think about your draft and your partner's suggestions. Use the Revising Marks on page 617 to mark your changes.

   - Are your facts presented in a logical order that your readers can follow? Move any that seem out of place.

   > She was crowned king of all of Egypt. ~~That was because~~ after seven years, Hatshepsut seized power for herself and Thutmose III was pushed aside.

   - Did you use your own words in each sentence? If not, make the sentence into a quote and name the source. Or rewrite the sentence in your own words.

   > She expanded trade into parts of Africa and the Middle East. ~~During her reign, she was responsible for the extension of trade into Eastern Africa and across the Sinai peninsula.~~

Edit and Proofread

Work with a partner to edit and proofread your research report. Carefully check all your facts as well as names, dates, and numbers. Make sure direct quotes are in quotation marks. Also check to be sure you have used formal language throughout your report. Use the marks on page 618 to show your changes.

Publish

1. **Make a Final Copy** Finalize your research report. Ask your teacher if there is a special format, or way of presenting your report, that you should use. At the end, add a bibliography to cite all of your sources.

2. **Share with Others** Present your paper as an oral report or multimedia slideshow. Include images you used. Then, with your classmates, collect your reports and publish them in a book called *Bringing Ancient Egypt to Life*.

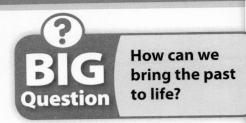

BIG Question

How can we bring the past to life?

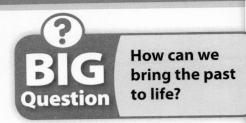

Talk Together

In this unit you found many answers to the **Big Question**. Now use your concept map to discuss it with the class. List what this unit taught you about ancient Egypt.

KWL Chart

How can we bring the past to life?		
What I Know Already	**What I Want to Know**	**What I Learned**
People study Egyptian pyramids and mummies.	How can mummies help us learn about the past?	

Performance Task: Explanatory

Remember what you learned about ancient Egypt from reading the selections, including the **Small Group Reading** books. Choose something about ancient Egypt that interests you, such as an archaeological site, an unusual custom, or a pharaoh. Write a blog entry that explains what you learned about this topic or person.

Checklist

Does your blog entry

- ✓ use text evidence from the selections about Egypt?
- ✓ clearly introduce the topic?
- ✓ include facts, definitions, details, or other information and examples from the sources?
- ✓ include precise language and transition words?

216

Share Your Ideas

Choose one of these ways to share your ideas about the **Big Question**.

Write It!

Write a Story

Pretend that you are an archaeologist. Write about discovering your first mummy. Where did you find the tomb and how did you find it? Describe what you see in the tomb including artifacts, artwork, and other clues about ancient Egyptian life. Include as many details as possible. Why is this discovery important?

Talk About It!

Conduct an Interview

In groups of three, conduct an interview with one character from *The Journal of Nakht* and one character from *The Golden Goblet*. Decide who will be the interviewer and who will play the characters. Discuss what these characters might say to each other about living in ancient Egypt. Perform your interview for the class.

Do It!

Create a Photo-Essay

Find pictures on the Internet of objects that tell about life in ancient Egypt. Use presentation software to create a photo-essay slideshow. Write a few sentences about each object. How does each object help us understand the past?

This artwork depicts a pharaoh's family.

Write It!

Write a List

With a partner, write a list of modern-day objects you would want archaeologists to find years from now. What would these objects teach others about our society? Why is it important for future generations to find these items? Explain your list to the class.

Our Diverse
EARTH

Unit at a Glance
► **Language**: Make an Argument,
Use Appropriate Language,
Science Words
► **Literacy**: Make Connections
► **Content**: Earth

Unit
4

Share What You Know

❶ **Draw** a beautiful place.

❷ **Explain** why it is special to you.

❸ **Share** your drawing with the class.

Build Background: Watch a video about protecting Earth.
Ⓝ NGReach.com

Language Frames

- We should _____ because _____ .
- It is a fact that _____ .
- According to experts, _____ .

Make an Argument

Listen to the argument. Then use **Language Frames** to make your own argument about the best way to protect wildlife.

Save the Gray Wolf (((MP3)))

Some people argue that wolves should be removed from the wild. That would be a tragic mistake. We should allow gray wolves to stay in their natural territory because they are an important part of a balanced ecosystem. Wolves prey on weaker animals like deer. As a result, populations of deer and other animals stay balanced—not too many and not too few. It is a fact that this makes the remaining animals stronger.

Ranchers argue that wolves should be removed because wolves kill their livestock. But that is not the answer. According to experts, a better solution is to teach ranchers how to live with wolves. Then ranchers will lose less livestock, and wolves may get the chance to make a comeback.

Save the Gray Wolf

Science Vocabulary

Key Words

- dependent
- endangered
- extinct
- policy
- recover
- thrive

Key Words

Look at the photographs and read the text. Use **Key Words** and other words to talk about why we should protect animals.

manatee

Problem

The number of manatees in the world is getting smaller, making them an **endangered** species. One cause for this change in numbers is boat traffic, which may injure or kill manatees. If this does not improve, manatees may become **extinct** and no longer exist.

MANATEE ZONE
IDLE SPEED
NO WAKE
· ALL YEAR ·

PERMIT NO. 92-037   62N-22.011 FAC

Action

Manatees are **dependent** on humans because they need our help. We must change the boating **policies**, or laws, to protect manatees.

Solution

When manatees are protected, they will **thrive**, and their numbers will **recover** to the levels they were before.

Talk Together

What should people do to help endangered species thrive? Work with a partner to create an argument that includes a claim, reasons, and evidence. Use **Language Frames** from page 220 and **Key Words** to make your argument.

Author's Viewpoint

Many texts reflect an author's perspective, or **viewpoint**, about a topic. Sometimes, authors directly state their opinions. At other times, you must look for clues, such as the examples the author includes or the words the author chooses. For example, if an author uses the word *impact* to describe the way you affect the world, you can determine that the author believes you have the power to affect the world in an important way.

Look Into the Text

You wash your face, chat with your family, eat your breakfast, and jump on the school bus. Even before you get to school, you have **interacted** with many people and things. Believe it or not, all of the things you do—**your outdoor activities, what you eat and drink, how you travel from place to place**—have an **impact** on the world around you.

"The author includes many **examples** of ways we affect the world."

"Her **word choice** shows that the effect is serious and important."

Map and Talk

A viewpoint chart can help you keep track of words, phrases, and examples that reveal how an author feels about a topic.

Viewpoint Chart

Text Evidence	Author's Viewpoint
"Believe it or not, all of the things you do . . . have an impact on the world around you."	The author *believes* that your actions have strong, important effects on the world.

Talk Together

Do your actions impact the world around you? Discuss your opinions with a partner and record them on a viewpoint chart. List your strongest words and phrases as text evidence and record what they show about your viewpoint. Then use the chart to form an argument about the topic.

More Key Words

Use these words to talk about "A Natural Balance" and "Mireya Mayor."

appeal
(u-**pēl**) *noun*

An **appeal** is a serious request for help. The student made an **appeal** to his teacher for help with a project.

effective
(i-**fek**-tiv) *adjective*

Something that is **effective** has good results. An umbrella is **effective** for keeping dry in the rain.

factor
(**fak**-tor) *noun*

A **factor** is something that can lead to a specific result. Heavy rains were a **factor** in the terrible flooding.

protection
(pru-**tek**-shun) *noun*

Protection keeps people, animals, and things safe. Helmets give **protection** to the bikers' heads.

sustain
(su-**stān**) *verb*

To **sustain** is to continue or keep up an action, event, or thing. The runner drinks lots of water to **sustain** her during the race.

Talk Together

Make a Word Map for each **Key Word**. Then compare your maps with a partner's.

Definition	Characteristics
a thing that keeps someone or something safe	provides safety, security
Word protection	
A roof gives protection from rain.	A lamppost does not give protection from rain.
Examples	**Non-examples**

Add words to My Vocabulary Notebook.
NGReach.com

Learn to Make Connections

Did you ever read something that reminded you of something else? If you did, you made a connection that could help you better understand the text.

How to Make Connections

1. As you read, think about things that relate to the text.
   - **Self to Text (S-T):** Connect something in the text with your experience or knowledge.
   - **Text to Text (T-T):** Explain how the text connects to something else you have read or seen.
   - **Text to World (T-W):** Explain how the text connects to a problem or issue in the world.

2. Decide how each connection helps you better understand the text.

> I read _____.
>
> This reminds me of _____.
>
> This helps me understand _____.

Here's how one student made a connection to a text.

Look Into the Text

> **All across Earth, humans are changing the environment in small and large ways. We cut down trees for lumber to build houses.** We plow fields to grow crops. . . . These activities also affect nonliving things in the environment, such as soil and water.

> I read a magazine article about how trees protect hills from landslides. (T-T)

> "I read **a fact from the text**. This reminds me of **an article I read before**. This helps me understand **why trees are important**."

Making connections as you read can help you make sense of the author's viewpoint. It can also help make the text more understandable and meaningful to you.

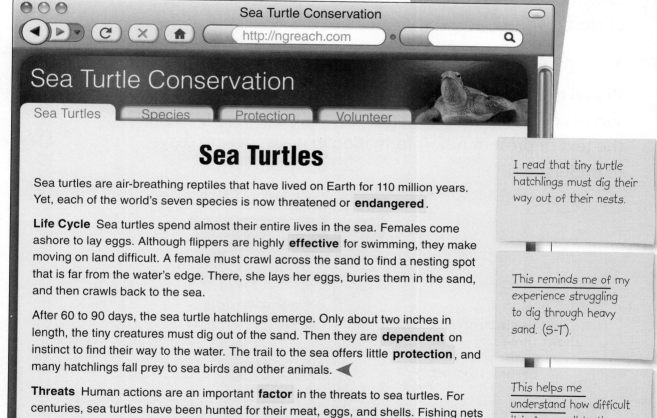

Read the Web article and sample notes. Use **Language Frames** to make connections as you read. Talk with a partner about the connections you made.

Web Article

Sea Turtle Conservation

http://ngreach.com

Sea Turtle Conservation

| Sea Turtles | Species | Protection | Volunteer |

Sea Turtles

Sea turtles are air-breathing reptiles that have lived on Earth for 110 million years. Yet, each of the world's seven species is now threatened or **endangered**.

Life Cycle Sea turtles spend almost their entire lives in the sea. Females come ashore to lay eggs. Although flippers are highly **effective** for swimming, they make moving on land difficult. A female must crawl across the sand to find a nesting spot that is far from the water's edge. There, she lays her eggs, buries them in the sand, and then crawls back to the sea.

After 60 to 90 days, the sea turtle hatchlings emerge. Only about two inches in length, the tiny creatures must dig out of the sand. Then they are **dependent** on instinct to find their way to the water. The trail to the sea offers little **protection**, and many hatchlings fall prey to sea birds and other animals. ◀

Threats Human actions are an important **factor** in the threats to sea turtles. For centuries, sea turtles have been hunted for their meat, eggs, and shells. Fishing nets and lines drown them. Beach activity damages nests and eggs. Furthermore, bright lights can distract hatchlings at night, leading them away from the water.

Solutions Many programs now exist to help **sustain** sea turtle populations. Several countries have banned the harvesting of sea turtles and the sale of turtle-related products. **Appeals** to coastal communities have helped reduce light pollution and raise awareness of nesting grounds. ◀

With careful planning, education, and environmental **policies**, there is hope that the sea turtle population will **recover** and **thrive** once more.

I read that tiny turtle hatchlings must dig their way out of their nests.

This reminds me of my experience struggling to dig through heavy sand. (S-T).

This helps me understand how difficult it is for small turtle hatchlings to emerge from their nests.

◀ = a good place to stop and make a connection

Read an Environmental Report

Genre

Environmental reports are nonfiction. They give facts and information about environmental topics. Authors often inform or alert readers to issues that affect nature.

Text Features

Visual graphics present information in creative formats, such as charts, tables, diagrams, and lists. These may support the text or present new information in ways that are easy to understand.

This visual graphic shows three stages that happen when a species becomes extinct.

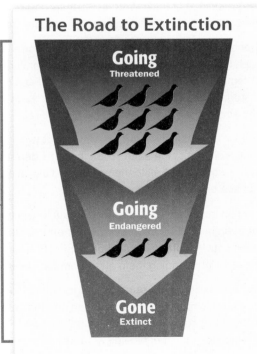

The Road to Extinction

Going Threatened

Going Endangered

Gone Extinct

A Natural Balance

based on a book by Nora L. Deans

NATIONAL GEOGRAPHIC

Green sea turtles swim off the coast of Bora Bora Island. These turtles are endangered in many countries.

Comprehension Coach

Some conservation efforts include relocating sea turtle eggs.

228

Our Effect on the Environment

Beep! Beep! Beep! Your alarm goes off, and you hop out of bed. You wash your face, chat with your family, eat your breakfast, and jump on the school bus. Even before you get to school, you have interacted with many people and things. Believe it or not, all of the things you do—your outdoor activities, what you eat and drink, how you travel from place to place—**have an impact on** the world around you.

The way we live our lives affects the environment. The environment is all of the living and nonliving things around you. All across Earth, humans are changing the environment in small and large ways. We cut down trees for lumber to build houses. We plow fields to grow crops. We pave roads and build parking lots. We pour waste into rivers, lakes, and oceans. We use giant nets and boats to catch huge numbers of fish. Activities like these affect plants and animals. These activities also affect nonliving things in the environment, such as soil and water.

A kayaker passes by trash along the shore of the Anacostia River near Washington, DC.

In Other Words

have an impact on affect or change

▶ **Before You Move On**

1. **Make Connections** According to the text, how do we affect the world around us? What does this remind you of?

2. **Details** What are two specific ways that humans change land and water? How does this impact the environment?

229

Are We Helping or Harming?

Sometimes our actions allow a certain plant or animal population—or the total number of individuals in a group—to get larger. For example, if you planted tulips in your yard, the tulip population in your area would increase. Or if you put seeds out for the birds in your area, the bird population might get larger.

Our activities also can lead to smaller plant and animal populations. What would happen to the plants and animals in a neighborhood park if the park were turned into an apartment building? They would either die or move someplace else. Then the area's plant and animal populations would shrink.

Overhunting, pollution, and other activities sometimes cause the population of a species to become so small that it cannot survive. A species that is in danger of dying out is called an **endangered** species. When a species can no longer survive and dies out completely, it becomes **extinct**. A species that is extinct is gone forever.

▲ Drivers must learn to share the highway with black bears in Nevada.

The Road to Extinction

An easy way to remember the threats facing plants and animals today is HIPPO. It stands for:

- **H**abitat loss–cutting down trees and tearing up the land often leaves plants and animals with no place to live

- **I**ntroduced species–bringing in new life-forms that crowd out or feed on the ones that were there

- **P**ollution–chemicals and wastes that damage or even kill living things

- **P**opulation growth–more and more people who need more food and more land

- **O**ver-consumption–hunting and harvesting more plants or animals than you need

What's Harming the Habitat?

The way we use or pollute natural resources, such as water or land, affects the environment. Several **factors** contribute to the loss of habitats. Habitats are the areas that support plant and animal populations.

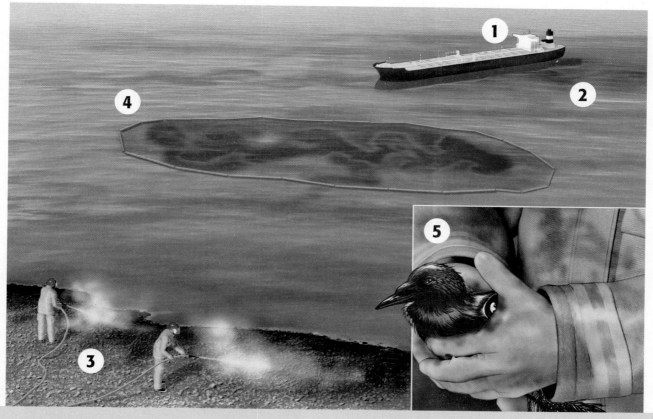

Oil spill emergency

1 Oil spills are major ocean disasters. An oil spill is what happens when a tanker, or large ship, carrying oil gets a hole in it and leaks the oil.

2 A large tanker gets stuck on shallow land. When crew members start to drive the tanker again, they can put a hole in it, leaking the oil.

3 As part of the clean-up effort, oily shore rocks and sand are rinsed with very hot water. Thousands of workers help clean up the spill.

4 **Containment booms** surround large areas of oil.

5 Oil-soaked birds are cleaned with **absorbent pads**. Some survive, but hundreds of thousands die. Sea otters, whales, and schools of fish also die.

In Other Words

Containment booms Floating materials that stop oil from spreading

absorbent pads cloths to soak up the oil

▶ **Before You Move On**

1. **Author's Viewpoint** What does the author think is harming our environment? Use evidence from the text to explain.

2. **Use Text Features** What information does the diagram show about the effects of oil spills on living and nonliving things?

231

Are We Solving the Problem?

As groups of plants and animals began to disappear, people began working on a **policy** to protect these species. In the early 1900s, some laws were passed to protect certain animals. However, the **big breakthrough** came in 1973. This is when the United States government passed the Endangered Species Act. This act lists species that are in danger of becoming extinct. The act also makes it illegal to disturb, harm, pursue, shoot, wound, kill, trap, capture, or collect any of the species on the list. The act protects not only the listed species but also the areas where they live. If a species is **dependent** on a certain habitat, that area needs to be protected, too.

Many species are on the list, but they're not all classified the same way. Species are listed as either "endangered" or "threatened." An endangered species is one in danger of becoming extinct. A threatened species is a species that could become endangered without **protection**.

The U.S. Fish and Wildlife Service (FWS) is the government agency that enforces the Endangered Species Act. Many of the scientists at FWS keep a close watch on endangered and threatened plants and animals. They track the populations of the species on the list. They also collect information about the areas where the species live.

If the collected information from the FWS shows that the population of a threatened species is steadily decreasing, the species could be reclassified as an endangered species. If the population of an endangered species gets larger, it could be downlisted. This means that it is moved one step down to the threatened species list. If the population of a species gets large enough, it could be removed from the list completely.

▼ A threatened species can become **endangered** without **protection**. An endangered species can become **extinct**.

The Road to Extinction

Going
Threatened

Going
Endangered

Gone
Extinct

In Other Words
big breakthrough most important change

Endangered Animals

Habitat loss is the most serious threat facing manatees today.

▲ Black rhinoceros

▲ Mitchell's satyr butterfly

▲ Golden-shouldered parrot

▶ **Before You Move On**

1. **Author's Viewpoint** What evidence from the text shows how the author feels about protecting habitats?

2. **Summarize** Tell in your own words what threats plants and animals face today.

For example, the bald eagle used to be listed as an endangered species. In 1963, there were only 400 pairs of these birds left. By 1995, after many recovery efforts, the bald eagle population had increased enough for the FWS to reclassify the bald eagle from "endangered" to "threatened." Due to government and volunteer efforts, there are about 10,000 pairs today. The bald eagle has now been removed from the endangered and threatened species lists.

Along with the FWS, additional organizations and individuals try to protect endangered species as well. Zoos and aquariums often work together to breed and raise rare and endangered animals. Botanical gardens and other groups raise rare and endangered plants. They also save their seeds.

Not everyone agrees about what is the best way to help an endangered species. Sometimes helping the animals interferes with people's jobs or activities. Like so many cases involving endangered species, survival means balancing the protection of endangered species with people's ways of life.

▲ The aloe's habitat is affected by burning and other kinds of habitat destruction.

▲ Orchid smuggling is leading to the loss of many kinds of wild orchids.

▲ The government began protecting the saguaro cactus when it started to disappear. This has prevented it from becoming endangered.

On June 28, 2007, the bald eagle was taken off the Federal List of **Endangered** and Threatened Wildlife and Plants. The bald eagle will still be protected by the Bald and Golden Eagle **Protection** Act.

How Well Are We Doing?

Good News

- Thanks to the Endangered Species Act, conservation groups and government agencies are working together to protect endangered species.

- Twenty-seven species on the endangered species list, including the gray whale and American alligator, have **recovered** enough to be taken off the list.

- Better **field research techniques** give us faster and better data about endangered species.

- Many groups, including zoos and aquariums that breed rare and endangered species, are trying to help many species survive.

Bad News

- There are many disagreements between organizations and the general public about how best to take care of endangered species.

- More research has to be done before hundreds of plants and animals can be included on the endangered or threatened species lists.

- Since being listed on the endangered species list, 10 species have become extinct. Some scientists think that thousands of unlisted species are becoming extinct each year.

- The presence of an endangered species may **halt a construction project**, cause people to lose their jobs, or even threaten humans' way of life.

In Other Words

field research techniques ways of studying nature

halt a construction project stop work at a building project

▶ **Before You Move On**

1. **Author's Viewpoint** How does the author feel about animals becoming **extinct**? How do you know?

2. **Make Connections** What connection can you make to the facts about the bald eagle populations?

235

A Balancing Act

Wolf Number 9 waits in a pen before her release into Yellowstone.

In 1995, fourteen gray wolves were captured in Canada and moved to Yellowstone National Park in the United States. An important female wolf in this group was called Number 9 by the Yellowstone biologists. She and her mate, Number 10, were **expecting a litter of pups** when Number 10 was killed by hunters.

Just after Number 10 died, Number 9 gave birth to eight pups. They were the first wolf pups born in Yellowstone in more than 60 years. Although her new life in Yellowstone had a hard beginning, Number 9 was able to **thrive** in her new home. During her lifetime, she has given birth to at least six litters of pups.

In Other Words
expecting a litter of pups going to have babies

"If I were going to make a statue to commemorate the wolf reintroduction, it would be a statue of Number 9," says Doug Smith, the biologist in charge of the wolf relocation. "She has **single-handedly** put this population back on its feet."

The Hunters and the Hunted

Gray wolves like Number 9 once roamed throughout North America. Wolves live in packs, or groups, of about six to twenty animals. Each member in a wolf pack helps the group survive. They work together to raise young wolf pups, protect the pack, and find food.

Gray wolves are predators that hunt a variety of prey, such as bison, elk, deer, and moose. At one time, the populations of wolves and their prey were in a natural balance. This means the populations were not too large or too small, and each species was able to survive.

The delicate balance between predator and prey was **disrupted** when European settlers came to North America. Soon, due to human hunters, wolves and many other animals began to disappear. Settlers killed more than 60 million bison. They also killed millions of elk, deer, and other wildlife. The wolves' natural prey became harder to find.

Wolf packs began to hunt livestock, such as cattle and sheep. People depended on that livestock for food, goods, or money. Wolves were then seen as troublesome, and hunters killed the wolves by the thousands. Government agencies even paid hunters bounties, or cash awards, for wolves that were shot.

The government once paid bounties to hunters who shot wolves.

In Other Words
single-handedly by herself
disrupted changed in a negative way

▶ **Before You Move On**

1. **Explain** Why do wolves and their prey need to be in a natural balance?

2. **Author's Viewpoint** What are the author's views on the European settlers? Use evidence from the text to support your answer.

A gray wolf captures its prey.

gray wolf

Making a Return

By the end of the 1930s, most of the gray wolves that once lived in the United States were gone. In the 1960s, the only gray wolves in the U.S. (not including Alaska) were a small number that still lived on either an island in Lake Superior or in Minnesota. By 1965, the government stopped paying wolf bounties. By then, the gray wolf population was in serious trouble.

After the Endangered Species Act was passed in 1973, the gray wolf was classified as an endangered species in 48 states. In 1995, biologists from FWS began the project to reintroduce gray wolves to Yellowstone. The scientists **got permits** to move 31 gray wolves from Canada: 14 were relocated in 1995, and 17 more moved in 1996.

Before releasing the wolves into the park, the biologists attached electronic collars around their necks. The scientists also took careful measurements of each wolf's length, weight, the size of its teeth, and other physical characteristics. These data allowed the scientists to study each wolf and keep track of the entire wolf population.

Today, there are between 400–450 wolves in the **Yellowstone recovery area**. With success, however, also came problems. As the wolves in Yellowstone multiplied, they split into new packs. The packs spread out, and each **claimed its own territory**. Some of the land that the wolves claimed was outside of the park on land owned by ranchers.

▲ the route the wolves traveled to Yellowstone

▶ **Before You Move On**

1. **Use Text Features** What part of the text does the map support? How does the map give information in a different way than the text?

2. **Make Connections** How can you help threatened or **endangered** species?

Trouble on the Ranch

"I never thought the wolf reintroduction was a good idea—they're killers no matter what." These are the words of one rancher **opposed to** the release of the wolves. Many other ranchers felt the same way.

Ranchers are in the business of raising and selling cattle, sheep, and other livestock. On a ranch, losing an animal to a wolf attack is a serious matter. More than 35,000 elk and other prey roam inside Yellowstone, and the wolves are free to hunt these animals. However, wolves sometimes hunt livestock outside the boundaries of the park. Since the gray wolf was an endangered species, ranchers worried about how they would be able to protect their livestock. The ranchers felt the wolves threatened their way of life. They wanted

In Other Words
opposed to who did not agree with

240

Protesters demonstrate against wolves in Ronan, Montana.

Yellowstone, and days after it was released, it was back there killing again—and killed an additional 15."

Each time livestock were killed by wolves, scientists investigated to find out which wolf or wolves had been involved. Researchers tried moving problem wolves to distant wilderness areas. This didn't always work.

Finding New Answers

Over the past several years, many steps have been taken to protect ranchers' livestock. When wolves repeatedly hunt livestock, the problem wolves are killed. Conservation organizations, like the Defenders of Wildlife, pay ranchers for the livestock they lose to wolf attacks. Some ranchers have also chosen to move **their grazing lands** to areas farther away from the wolves. Like so many other cases involving endangered species, survival for all means finding a balance between needs.

The gray wolf is still an endangered species that needs protection. Fortunately, the offspring of Number 9 continue to thrive in Yellowstone today. Through the hard work and compromises of many people, the wolves are again finding a place in the United States. ❖

the wolves removed. An organization called the American Farm Bureau Federation represented the ranchers and worked to stop the wolf reintroduction program.

"We had one Farm Bureau member that had at one point this year 59 **head of ewes** and lambs killed," said Karen Henry, a rancher and president of the Wyoming Farm Bureau in 1997. "They took the wolf back to

In Other Words

head of ewes female sheep

their grazing lands the places where their livestock eat

▶ **Before You Move On**

1. **Explain** What happened during the wolf reintroduction that helped ranchers?
2. **Make Connections** How do the ranchers' problems with the wolves remind you of other world events? Explain.

Think and Respond

Talk About It

Key Words

appeal	policy
dependent	protection
effective	recover
endangered	sustain
extinct	thrive
factor	

1. "A Natural Balance" is an environmental report. Choose one visual graphic from the report and explain how it presents information that helped you better understand what you read.

2. What is author's purpose in writing the report? How **effective** is the author in meeting this purpose? Cite text evidence in your answer.

3. Review the visual graphic of the oil spill on page 231. What words and examples does the author include that explains her viewpoint about oil spills?

4. Animal populations can be classified as "threatened" or "**endangered**." Why is the difference in these terms important?

5. How do humans affect the natural balance of nature in positive and negative ways? Use specific examples from the text to support your response.

6. Do we provide adequate **protection** for animals and their habitats? Make an argument, using text evidence to support your claim.

Learn test-taking strategies and answer more questions.
NGReach.com

Write About It

Write a brochure that could be placed near the habitat of one of the animals from "A Natural Balance." Explain why the animal needs help and what visitors to the area can do to protect the animal. Use at least three **Key Words** and include text evidence to support your ideas.

Manatee Habitat

Manatees are on the Endangered Species List. Help us keep them from going extinct!

It's illegal to:
- **pursue**
- **wound**

Author's Viewpoint

Use a viewpoint chart to record specific text evidence that reveals how the author of "A Natural Balance" feels about the environment.

Viewpoint Chart

Text Evidence	Author's Viewpoint
"Believe it or not, all of the things you do . . . have an impact on the world around you."	*The author believes that your actions have strong, important effects on the world.*

Use your viewpoint chart to help you summarize the author's main argument to a partner. Explain how the author's viewpoint is conveyed in the text and how she uses examples and chooses words that support her claims.

Fluency  Comprehension Coach

Use the Comprehension Coach to practice reading with phrasing. Rate your reading.

Talk Together

How does "A Natural Balance" show the value of diversity in nature? Discuss your ideas with a partner. Use **Key Words** and cite evidence from the text to support your ideas.

Prefixes and Base Words

A **prefix** is a word part that is added to the beginning of a **base word**. To find the meaning of a word with a prefix, think about what each word part means.

EXAMPLES

The prefix *inter-* means "among; between."

| prefix | base word |

inter- + act = interact

The prefix *dis-* means "opposite."

| prefix | base word |

dis- + appear = disappear

Prefix	Meaning	Examples
en-	to put in	enforce, enlist
in-	not	independent, ineffective
over-	too much	over-consumption, overhunting

The chart above shows more prefixes and their meanings. Based on the chart, what do you think the word *overestimate* means?

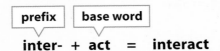

Try It

Read the sentences. Then answer the questions. Use the chart to help you.

> Some <u>endangered</u> species are in trouble of becoming extinct. People need to improve <u>ineffective</u> laws and policies to help these struggling populations.

1. **Look for the prefix *en-*. What is the best meaning for the word <u>endangered</u>?**

   A put in danger

   B causing danger

   C saving from danger

   D classified as dangerous

2. **Look for the prefix *in-*. What is the best meaning for the word <u>ineffective</u>?**

   A not effective

   B very effective

   C used to be effective

   D will become effective

NATIONAL
GEOGRAPHIC

Connect Across Texts You read about the importance of a natural balance. Now read about an explorer who is working to restore a natural balance in rainforests.

Genre An **online article** gives information about a topic. It can include links to other Web pages.

MIREYA MAYOR
EXPLORER/CORRESPONDENT

Mireya Mayor surveys a rainforest in Madagascar.

MIREYA MAYOR
EXPLORER/CORRESPONDENT

| 2013 | 2014 | 2015 |

 » J. MICHAEL FAY
CONSERVATIONIST

 » SALIMA IKRAM
ARCHAEOLOGIST

» JOSEPH LEKUTON
TEACHER

 » MIREYA MAYOR
**EXPLORER/
CORRESPONDENT**

"The rainforest appears to be a gigantic, green **mishmash** of unknowns. We are still discovering new species and who knows what else might be out there. But we do know that every tree and creature in it plays a vital role in our existence. Ensuring their survival helps to ensure ours."

Mireya Mayor has slept in the rainforest among poisonous snakes. She has been chased by gorillas, elephants, and leopards. She even swam with great white sharks! Mayor is a city girl and a former NFL cheerleader. How does she find herself as an explorer in situations like this?

It all began in college. Mayor began studying **primates**. "I was **seized** by the fact that some of these incredible animals are **on the verge of** extinction. And they had never been studied. In some cases not even a mere photograph existed to show their existence. I asked more questions. It became clear to me that much about our natural world still remained a mystery." Mayor decided to dedicate her life to solving that mystery.

Today, Mayor is a Fulbright scholar and a National Science Foundation Fellow. She also appears as a host on the National Geographic *Wild Nights* television series. Each expedition allows

In Other Words

mishmash mixture

primates gorillas and other
    animals like them

seized very interested

on the verge of near

MIREYA MAYOR
EXPLORER/CORRESPONDENT

Click on map for detail

Mayor to teach viewers about a different species of animal that needs our help.

For example, one of Mayor's National Geographic TV expeditions allowed her to go to the Gulf of California. Her goal there was to research the powerful six-foot-long Humboldt Squid. It was a time of personal discovery that gave Mayor the opportunity to climb rocky cliffs and look at untouched tropical ecosystems.

An expedition also led Mayor to Namibia. She went into a veterinarian's haven, or safe place, for leopards. "While caring for the leopards," Mayor explains, "the vet accidentally discovered a cure for fluid in the brain. It is a disease that also occurs in human infants. As a result of our film and the **media attention** it received, new studies are now taking place in children's hospitals. That is why I consider my television work just as important as my **conservation field work**," she notes. "The TV series **sheds light** on the plight of **endangered** species and animals around the world. Television has the power to help people know and connect with these animals and habitats that are disappearing. We may be facing the largest mass extinction of our time. Awareness is crucial. If we don't act now, it will be too late."

In Other Words

media attention positive news stories
conservation field work work to save species in the wild
sheds light focuses attention

▶ **Before You Move On**

1. **Fact/Opinion** What is one fact and one opinion that Mayor expresses?
2. **Explain** Why does Mayor consider her television work just as important as her conservation field work?

MIREYA MAYOR
EXPLORER/CORRESPONDENT

"I had to get that documentation because only then was I able to lobby to have its (the lemur's) habitat fully protected," said Mayor.

Mayor went to Madagascar on another of her National Geographic Explorer expeditions. On that expedition, she discovered a new species of lemur. This discovery brought everyone's attention to Mayor's work. She had to document it. Once it was documented, she could try to obtain **protection** for the animal's habitat. This required grueling fieldwork during the **monsoon** season. "There we were, tromping through remote areas of jungle, rain pouring, tents blowing. We were looking for **a nocturnal animal**. One that happens to be the smallest primate in the world," she says. Her careful research and documentation were important. She was able to convince Madagascar's president to declare the species' habitat a national park. Soon after that, the president also agreed to triple the number of protected areas in the nation. As Mayor reports, one tiny discovery became "a **huge ambassador** for **all things wild** in Madagascar."

Mayor believes that local support for conservation is a key **factor** in bringing about change. "The local people are at the **very core** of **effective** conservation. Without their support, the 'dream' of saving the planet can never become a reality. The rainforest is literally their backyard. Yet many Malagasy kids have

In Other Words

monsoon rainy
a nocturnal animal an animal that is active at night
huge ambassador popular representative
all things wild wildlife
very core most important part

Emerging Explorers

National Geographic's Next Generation

| OUR EXPLORERS | ABOUT THE PROGRAM |

MIREYA MAYOR
EXPLORER/CORRESPONDENT

NEWS

» Emerging Explorers News

» Photo Gallery: Best Mountain Photographs of 2014 Announced

» What Triggers Tornadoes? New Season May Hold Answers

never even seen a lemur. So I organize lots of field trips into the forest. Only by seeing how amazing these creatures are, will kids want to protect them." Mayor stresses the importance of providing education and opportunities for local communities to learn about the threats to animals and how they can help. She believes it will be critical to protecting the planet.

Mayor **circles the globe** on television expeditions, but her heart remains in the rainforests of Madagascar. As she describes it, "This phenomenal natural laboratory could vanish in our lifetime. It could become the stuff of history books, not science books. Until I can walk away . . . and know it's going to be okay, I just can't leave. ❖

Healthy Rainforest

Destroyed Rainforest

▲ Mayor's conservation work makes locals aware that the destruction of the rainforest threatens the lives of plants and animals.

In Other Words

circles the globe travels around the world

▶ **Before You Move On**

1. **Cause/Effect** Name two things Madagascar's president changed as a result of Mayor's work.

2. **Author's Viewpoint** How does the author show how much Mayor cares about her work?

Compare Authors' Viewpoints

Both "A Natural Balance" and "Mireya Mayor" describe the effects that people's activities have on the environment. Work with a partner to complete a Venn diagram that compares the authors' viewpoints. Then put together the details you recorded in the "Both" section to make a generalization, or statement, that is true for both authors.

Venn Diagram

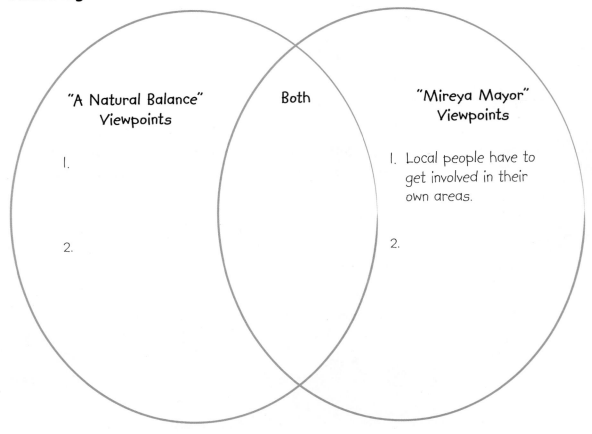

"A Natural Balance" Viewpoints

1.

2.

Both

"Mireya Mayor" Viewpoints

1. Local people have to get involved in their own areas.

2.

Talk Together

How do both texts address the value of diversity and balance in nature? How do they suggest that we should **sustain** a natural balance on Earth? Use **Key Words** and evidence from the text to talk about your ideas with a small group.

Adjectives and Adverbs

You can use **adjectives** and **adverbs** to describe and compare.

Grammar Rules Adjectives and Adverbs

There are similar rules for using **adjectives** and **adverbs** to compare.

	Adjective	Adverb
• To compare two nouns or actions, add **–er**. • For words with three or more syllables, use **more** or **less**.	smaller more incredible less threatening	faster more rapidly less seriously
• To compare three or more nouns or actions, add **–est**. • For words with three or more syllables, use **most** or **least**.	smallest most incredible least threatening	fastest most rapidly least seriously
Some words have special forms for comparing.	good better best bad worse worst many more most	well better best badly worse worst

Read Adjectives and Adverbs

Good writers use adjectives and adverbs to make their writing more precise. Read these sentences from "A Natural Balance." What adjectives and adverbs can you find?

> • Better field research techniques give us faster and better data about endangered species.
>
> • There are many disagreements . . . about how best to take care of endangered species.

Write Adjectives and Adverbs

Write a paragraph that explains why we must help **endangered** species. Include adjectives and adverbs. Then compare your sentences with a partner's.

Use Appropriate Language

Formal Language	Informal Language
• Thank you for _____.	• Thanks!
• May I _____?	• Let's _____.
• Would you mind _____?	• Can you _____?

Listen to the discussions about a proposed hotel development on a beach. Then use **Language Frames** and appropriate language to talk about another environmental issue.

Save Our Beach (((MP3)))

Thank you, City Council members, for allowing me to speak to you this evening. I am here to present objections to the proposed Mega-Hotel on Marsh Beach.

Look on the easel. The left side shows the beach as it is now. The right side shows what the beach would look like with the hotel.

Dude, that hotel would really wreck the beach!

Yeah, we sure couldn't surf there anymore.

Key Words

deforestation

ecological

landscape

management

regulate

Key Words

Look at these photographs and read the captions. Use **Key Words** and other words to talk about forests in the western United States.

▼ For many years, **deforestation** caused **ecological** damage to trees. Entire forests disappeared due to logging and natural fires. Without the trees, many animals and plants suffered.

▲ Today, many of the **landscapes** along the western coast of the U.S. include protected forests that everyone can enjoy.

◀ Since then, many groups have worked with the government to **regulate**, or control, how trees are used and replanted. This kind of careful **management** could help save many forests.

Talk Together

Pretend you are talking to teachers in your school about protecting natural habitats like forests or beaches. Use **Language Frames** from page 252 and **Key Words**. Be sure to use appropriate language for your audience.

Characters' Viewpoints

All people have viewpoints about the world and their own experiences. Characters in stories often have viewpoints, too. As you read, try to determine a character's viewpoint by analyzing the character's dialogue, thoughts, and actions.

Look Into the Text

> Danny watched over his shoulder. **"You really think that's better?" he asked incredulously,** "Oh, well. You know best. **Send away."**
>
> Julian sent the e-mail and then said, "I'd better do my homework." He pulled out his math book. . . .
>
> **Danny sighed heavily and set to work himself, alternately scribbling furiously and singing along with the TV.**

"Danny's **words** show that he is surprised by Julian."

"Danny's **actions** show that he changes his mind and attitude easily."

Map and Talk

A character description chart can help you keep track of characters and their viewpoints based on evidence from the text.

Character Description Chart

Character	Evidence	Character's Viewpoint
Danny	• "You really think that's better?" he asked incredulously.	• Danny is surprised by Julian.

Talk Together

Tell a partner a story about two friends. Include details about what the characters say, think, and do. Have your partner use the information to create a character description chart for one of the characters in your story.

More Key Words

Use these words to talk about *Operation Redwood* and "The Super Trees."

advocate
(**ad**-vu-kāt) *verb*

When you **advocate** something, you support it with words or actions. The dentist **advocates** brushing your teeth twice a day.

intervene
(in-tur-**vēn**) *verb*

When you **intervene**, you do something to change an event or a result. She **intervenes** when her sons argue.

obligation
(o-bli-**gā**-shun) *noun*

An **obligation** is something you must do. It is the boy's **obligation** to take care of the dog.

participate
(par-**ti**-su-pāt) *verb*

When you **participate**, you do something with others. These students **participate** on a sports team.

utilize
(**yū**-ti-līz) *verb*

When you **utilize** something, you use it to do a job. The gardeners **utilize** a shovel to collect leaves.

Talk Together

Make a Vocabulary Example Chart that includes each **Key Word**. Then compare your chart with a partner's.

Word	Definition/Synonym	Example
utilize	use	a pencil to write

Add words to My Vocabulary Notebook.
⊘ NGReach.com

Learn to Make Connections

As you read, make connections between what you already know about a topic and what you read about it. Connecting the text to what you know can help you add to your understanding of the text.

How to Make Connections

1. **Identify the Topic** As you read, figure out the topic—what the selection is mostly about.

2. **Look for Connections** As you read, pay attention to what you already know about the topic.

3. **Build Understanding** Connect what you read with what you know. Then explain how the connection helps you understand the text.

The topic is _____.

I already know _____.

Because I know _____, I understand _____.

Here's how one student made a connection to the text.

Look Into the Text

Dear Mr. Carter,

Maybe I shouldn't call you names, but that's how I feel. I've lived next to Big Tree Grove my whole life, and **you just come in and buy the Greeley land and think you can cut down all the trees**, and you don't even care.

"The topic is cutting down trees. **I read** about the plans for Big Tree Grove. I already know that some people care a lot about trees. Now I understand why the writer is so upset."

Making connections to what you're reading makes the text more interesting and easier to understand.

Talk Together

Read the blog post and sample notes. Use **Language Frames** to make connections as you read. Then talk with a partner about how your connections helped you understand the text.

Blog

Trina's Travels
http://ngreach.com

Trina's Travels

| Blog | About Trina | Past Posts |

Redwood Forest
Tuesday, March 11 | **Author:** <u>Trina</u>

In my latest trip, I traveled up the California coast to visit what remains of the amazing redwoods. As I walked along this beautiful **landscape**, I was humbled. The tallest trees stand over 350 feet high, and many have lived on Earth for more than 2,000 years. ◄

Naturally, I **participated** in some touristy activities as well. I drove my car through the trunk of a living redwood. I even ate lunch inside a redwood tree!

You can imagine how sad I was to learn that only 5 percent of our redwood forests are still standing. After the California Gold Rush, millions of trees were chopped down for farmland and to build homes. This **deforestation** continued until conservationists, such as John Muir, **intervened**. They **advocated** that logging be **regulated** and that land be set aside to conserve wilderness areas. ◄

What happened to the redwood forests is a story that has been repeated throughout human history—and continues today. In fact, without **ecological management**, the world's rainforests could completely disappear in 100 years. To say that no more trees should be cut down is not realistic. We will always need to **utilize** forest products. In addition, our growing population demands more room for farmland, livestock, and people. However, we have an **obligation** to the plant and animal species that depend on forests to do all we can to protect them. ◄

The topic is a trip to a redwood forest.

I already know that redwoods are the tallest trees on Earth.

Because I know how great these trees are, I understand why Trina feels humbled in the forest.

◄ = a good place to stop and make a connection

257

Read Realistic Fiction

Genre

Realistic fiction is a story that seems as if it could be true. The characters, plot, and setting all seem real.

Writing Forms

Authors can use many different writing forms in fiction. Some writers show interaction between characters through a narrator's descriptions or characters' dialogue. Other writers may tell their stories in the forms of letters or journals. In this story, the characters send **e-mails** that include a mixture of formal and informal language.

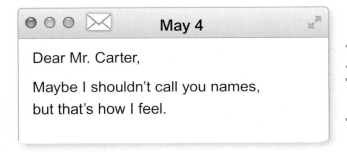

⟩ formal language
greeting

⟩ informal language
in body of e-mail

Dear Mr. Carter,

Maybe I shouldn't call you names, but that's how I feel.

May 4

FROM
OPERATION
REDWOOD

by S. Terrell French

ILLUSTRATED BY ERWIN MADRID

 Comprehension Coach

▶ **Set a Purpose**
Find out how the characters in the
story plan to save the redwoods.

*Julian Carter-Li accidentally reads the following e-mail intended for his uncle. Afraid of getting caught, he deletes the original e-mail to his uncle but forwards a copy of it to his friend, Danny. When Danny responds to the e-mail using Julian's name, the boys find themselves involved in **a quest** to save some of California's oldest redwood trees.*

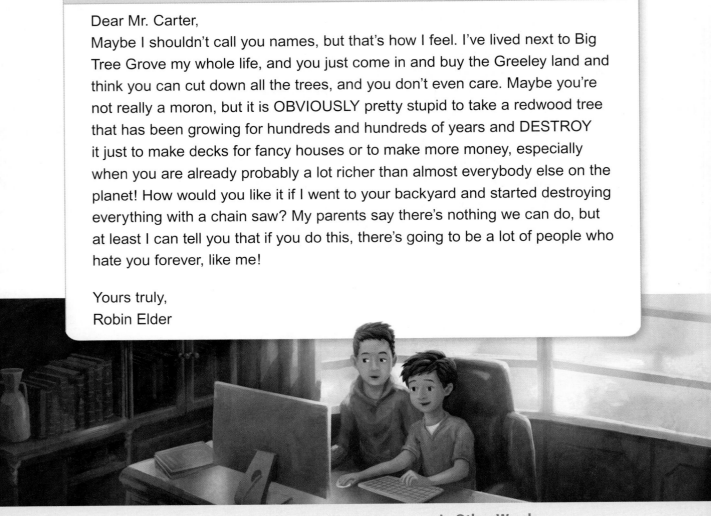

May 4

Dear Mr. Carter,

Maybe I shouldn't call you names, but that's how I feel. I've lived next to Big Tree Grove my whole life, and you just come in and buy the Greeley land and think you can cut down all the trees, and you don't even care. Maybe you're not really a moron, but it is OBVIOUSLY pretty stupid to take a redwood tree that has been growing for hundreds and hundreds of years and DESTROY it just to make decks for fancy houses or to make more money, especially when you are already probably a lot richer than almost everybody else on the planet! How would you like it if I went to your backyard and started destroying everything with a chain saw? My parents say there's nothing we can do, but at least I can tell you that if you do this, there's going to be a lot of people who hate you forever, like me!

Yours truly,
Robin Elder

In Other Words
a quest an exciting adventure

260

Robin,

I am the unfortunate nephew of Mr. Sibley Carter, **aka** the Great and Terrible **Mr. CEO**. I have intercepted your recent message to him. Please reveal your identity and **spell out** in more detail your complaint against Mr. CEO and what sinister deeds he intends to perform. I was forced to destroy your prior message because I feared it might endanger yourself or others. Feel free to speak freely. You can **have utmost confidence** in me. Although we are related by blood, I am no friend of my uncle's. Please have utmost confidence also in my closest friend, Daniel Lopez. I would trust him with my life. You can contact me through him, at this address. Please do not attempt to contact me through my uncle or it could endanger my life and yours.

Your devoted servant,
Julian Carter-Li
P.S. Are you a girl?

"Are you crazy?" Julian said when he'd finished reading the e-mail. "Are you trying to make me look like an idiot?"

"No, trust me," Danny said with enormous sincerity. "It's better this way. She'll take us more seriously."

Julian put his head in his hands. "Danny! You totally **screwed this up**."

In Other Words
aka also known as (abbreviation)
Mr. CEO Boss of the Company
spell out describe
have utmost confidence trust
screwed this up ruined everything

Danny was silent for a moment. "Oh, come on. It's not such a big deal. If you really don't like it, send a **retraction**. You can type it yourself." He stood up and offered Julian the chair.

Very slowly, Julian **pecked out**:

May 5

Dear Robin,
That last e-mail was from my friend Danny. Please ignore it. Sibley Carter is my uncle. I found your e-mail by accident, but I don't understand what you're talking about. Who are you and where's Big Tree Grove and what's the Greeley land and what does my uncle have to do with them? I promise I won't give any information to my uncle. We are not very close.

Sincerely,
Julian Carter-Li

P.S. I really did delete your message to my uncle. I don't think he would have listened to you anyway.

Danny watched over his shoulder. "You really think that's better?" he asked incredulously. "Oh, well. You know best. Send away."

Julian sent the e-mail and then said, "I'd better do my homework." He pulled out his math book. "I have two pages of math for tonight and three still from yesterday."

Danny sighed heavily and set to work himself, alternately **scribbling furiously** and singing along with the TV.

In Other Words

retraction new e-mail to correct what was sent before

pecked out typed

scribbling furiously writing quickly

Dear Julian Carter-Li,

Thank you for your e-mail. Assuming you are who you say you are and you're telling me the truth, I guess I should thank you for deleting that e-mail. I was **having second thoughts** about sending it. I guess I thought Sibley Carter wouldn't pay any attention to my letter, but I was mad and I wanted him to know.

I am 11 years old (12 on July 29th). How old are you? I live on a ranch (more of a farm, really) in Mendocino County. Big Tree Grove is an EXTREMELY rare **stand** of old-growth redwood on the land next to ours. It used to belong to Ed Greeley. He loved Big Tree and was NEVER going to cut it down. Your uncle, obviously, is the CEO of IPX, which is now the owner of the Greeley land. IPX is planning to **CLEAR-CUT the whole stand**! Maybe you can get your uncle to change his mind?

Yours truly,
Robin

P.S. Tell your friend Danny of course I'm a GIRL! And this isn't a JOKE!!!!

May 8

Hey Robin Hood,
I never said it was a joke! Don't you have any sense of humor???

Your everlastingly faithful correspondent,
Señor Daniel Lopez

In Other Words

having second thoughts feeling regret
stand group
CLEAR-CUT the whole stand cut down all of the trees

▶ **Before You Move On**

1. **Character's Viewpoint** What evidence shows how Robin feels about Big Tree Grove?
2. **Make Connections** How does your experience of having been 11 years old help you understand a character's problem?

▶ **Predict**

Will Robin explain why she feels an **obligation** to protect the trees?

○○○ ✉   **May 8**

Dear Robin,

Thanks for writing back. You are probably right that my uncle wouldn't have paid any attention to your letter, but it might have made him mad and gotten you in trouble somehow. I am 12 and in the sixth grade at Filbert Middle School. I'm staying with my uncle because my mom had to go to China (Sibley is my dad's brother). My cousin lives there too. He's only 8, but he's a nice kid. I don't know if I can get my uncle to change his mind about your redwoods. Probably not. Do you like living in the redwoods? I have been to the redwoods at Muir Woods. They are pretty enormous. Have you been there?

Julian

P.S. Danny wants to know if Ed Greeley is dead.

○○○ ✉   **May 11**

Dear Julian,

That is so cool your mom is in China. What's she doing there? And where's your dad?

My family's pretty boring. I have 3 brothers and an annoying little sister. And a father and mother, obviously. Nobody ever goes ANYWHERE. We are home schooled, so I don't go on field trips, and I'm not in any grade, but I'm reading on a 12th grade level. We grow most of our own food, so we hardly ever leave the ranch. But I don't actually mind. I LOVE living in the redwoods. Plus, we have a farm with chickens and goats and stuff. I HATE even going into town (I know you shouldn't say "hate" but it's true). It's so crowded and dirty and ugly. Plus you have to drive FOREVER to get there. May is my favorite month. The flowers are out, and we've got a new baby goat. When I grow up, I'm going to live right here. My dad's going to build me my own house down near the river. I'm already making the blueprints.

I've never been to Muir Woods, but I did a report on John Muir for a contest on California Heroes (unfortunately, I didn't win the Grand Prize). Have you studied him?

Robin

P.S. OBVIOUSLY Ed Greeley has passed away or else Big Tree would not be THREATENED.

May 13

Dear Goat Girl,
OBVIOUSLY we are familiar with John Muir, founder of the Sierra Club and Yosemite National Park. It may interest you to know that I am reading at the level of a certified genius, and my friend, Mr. Carter-Li, has recently been nominated for a Nobel Prize in mathematics.

I don't know if I would actually like to live with chickens. My dad used to have chickens, and he says they are not the brightest creatures on the planet. San Francisco is a very cool city. It has the Golden Gate Bridge. And Alcatraz, the famous prison. Don't forget that millions of people come every year just to see the cool things here.

Signing off from the epicenter of the civilized world,
Danny

P.S. Don't you know it's rude to ask people personal questions?????

Dear JULIAN,

You can tell your FRIEND that a lot of people come to Huckleberry Ranch too. My mom and dad lead seminars on organic gardening and solar power, and we're part of the Farm/Urban Network (FUN). Sometimes in the summer we **host exchange students** through FUN. Of course, we wouldn't want MILLIONS of people here. They'd just trample everything and ruin everything. Then it might look like San Francisco! (Ha-ha!) But we live so far away from town that it's nice to have visitors. My mom loves all our guests (even the BAD ones), and my dad is a natural born teacher. I like the exchange students best because my best friend moved to Phoenix last year so now there's no kids my age nearby.

Has your uncle said anything about Big Tree?
Did I ask something too personal???

Yours truly,
Robin

Dear Robin,

I haven't heard anything from my uncle about Big Tree, but he doesn't really talk much. He's hardly ever home.

My mom is a photographer and she got **a grant** to go to China to do a photographic series on Buddhist temples. My uncle moved to San Francisco from Boston last fall. So my mom asked him if I could stay with them while she's in China. He said yes, but actually I found out he's sending me away to camp for the whole summer. My dad died in a motorcycle crash when I was 7.

I think your house sounds very interesting. Danny and I looked at the website for that exchange program, and there was a picture of your goats! It sounds like FUN (you must get a lot of **puns** about this!).

Julian

In Other Words

host exchange students have students from other countries live with us
a grant money
puns jokes

Dear Julian,

I have to write fast because I have **double chores** today. I got in BIG trouble yesterday because I forgot that I had made this stupid bet with Molly (my SUPER annoying sister), and I lost (which was basically unfair, but that's another story), and I was supposed to milk the goats. They were FINE, of course, but my dad was super angry!

Anyway, I just wanted to say sorry about your dad. That is a real tragedy to lose your father. Maybe in real life your uncle is not such a moron. I may be unfairly judging him and not understanding things from **his shoes**. My mom says I have a tendency to do this. But I don't see how anything could justify cutting down Big Tree Grove. I do apologize if what I said in my e-mail about your uncle hurt your feelings. Obviously, I didn't know YOU were going to read it!

Robin

Dear Robin,

It's OK about my dad. I don't really remember him that much because I was so little when he died. I get in trouble at my uncle's a lot too. My aunt has this point system for everything I do. I'm supposed to get a laptop when I get 25 points, but right now I'm at negative 17. I spend most of my time at Danny's. If you don't go to school, what do you do all day?

Julian

In Other Words
double chores twice as much housework to do
his shoes his viewpoint

Dear Goat Girl,

Since you asked, I'm doing extremely well. Thank you for your concern!

Lose your sympathy for Mr. CEO! I'm sure he doesn't **care 2 cents for** your redwoods. He actually banned me from his mansion because I didn't get my feet off his couch fast enough to satisfy his evil mate. I kid you not, I was wearing socks!!!!

Julian is in DENIAL if he thinks he's ever going to get a laptop because he **gets dinged** a point for the most idiotic things—like saying "yeah" instead of "yes." And let's not forget that Mr. CEO is sending Julian to MATH CAMP!! In FRESNO.

Basically, Sibley's EVIL. You should **bring him down**!!! **On the other hand,** at least he doesn't make Julian milk goats!

Just tellin' it like it is,
Danny

Dear Julian (and Danny),

There's about a million things to do here. Well, obviously, there's a lot of stuff I HAVE to do, like my homework and reports, etc. And planting and weeding and gathering eggs and milking the goats, etc. But there's a lot of fun stuff too, like going to the river or the swimming hole. We bake a lot with my mom, and I'm still working on my blueprints for my house. I bet it's a lot more fun than math camp!

Of course my favorite place to go is Big Tree. Nobody ever goes there except me, and it's the most BEAUTIFUL place on earth. I can bring a book or a snack (I LOVE chocolate chip cookies, do you?). If you saw it, you'd know why I'm so mad at your uncle and IPX!

Speaking of which, even if your uncle is not the nicest man in the world, he can't be entirely heartless. He's taking care of you, right? Couldn't you at least say something to your uncle about Big Tree? If I could speak to him, I'd have plenty to say!

Robin

In Other Words

care 2 cents for care at all about
gets dinged loses
bring him down stop him
On the other hand, However,

▶ **Before You Move On**

1. **Character's Viewpoint** What influen[ce] Robin's views about **deforestation**? G[ive] examples from the text.

2. **Make Connections** How do your ow[n] experiences help you better understa[nd] the characters?

▶ **Predict**
Will the boys figure out a way
to **intervene** and help Robin?

270

Julian sat through the next day of school in a kind of **daze**. As his teachers **droned on and on,** he became fixated on a single depressing thought: If he went to math camp and **Mandarin** camp all summer, he wouldn't have a real summer vacation for more than a year! Two years of school without a break. Meanwhile, there were kids like Robin living in the United States of America who didn't even have to go to school at all! That was injustice!

After school, he just lay on Danny's bed while Danny worked away on the latest e-mail to Robin. When he finished, he read it out loud:

May 25

Dear Robin,
Nothing but bad news here. First, we haven't found out anything about your redwoods. Mr. CEO hasn't said a word. Are you sure you've got the right guy??

Second, even if you DO have the right guy, we're not going to be able to help you much more because it's official: Julian's being shipped off to Math Camp in three weeks. While you're up there having your vacation from not being in school, the Dastardly **Duo**—reaching new heights of evilness—are forcing poor Julian to spend HIS summer vacation doing algebra and learning Chinese!!!

So it looks like you're losing your undercover agent!
Lopez & Carter-Li

In Other Words
daze dream
droned on and on talked and talked
Mandarin Chinese language
Duo Pair

271

Julian watched a hummingbird dip into the feeder by Danny's window. "You know, she doesn't like it when you write like that. She thinks you're making fun of her."

"Aw, she can take it! She's a big girl."

"It would be nice to give her some good news for a change."

"What? Like, 'Julian had a long talk with his uncle and convinced him that cutting down redwood trees is morally wrong'? Be realistic! We're talking about Mr. CEO here!"

"Yeah, I guess."

They turned reluctantly to their homework. With the end of school approaching, their teachers were trying to **cram as much into their heads** as possible. Danny worked conscientiously for half an hour then began to drum a syncopated beat with his pencil against his desk lamp. Finally, he turned to Julian and said, "Heard anything from your mom?"

Julian reached into his back pocket. The postcard was still there, and he unbent it and handed it to Danny.

"Very touching!" Danny said. "'Wish you were here.' Very original."

"Aw, be quiet." Julian studied the golden Buddha. "She's doing good. *She's* not in math camp."

Danny flipped the postcard onto Julian's stomach and turned toward the computer. "New message from Robin Hood! See, if she were offended, she wouldn't write back so quickly."

Julian sat up and looked at the screen:

  May 25

Dear Julian and Danny,
I feel for Julian about math camp. Truly that would be my WORST NIGHTMARE to be **cooped up** in a classroom all day, winter AND summer. I think I would go CRAZY!! I can't even stand to wear shoes for a day!

Hey—I just had the MOST BRILLIANT idea!!! What if you came up here instead?? Then you could see Big Tree Grove for yourself and maybe figure out how to convince your uncle not to cut it down.

On second thought, I guess your uncle isn't going to send you HERE, when WE'RE the ones fighting his logging plan!

OK. **Scratch** that idea. Maybe it wasn't so brilliant after all!

Robin

In Other Words

cram as much into their heads teach them as much

cooped up stuck

Scratch Forget

Julian hadn't even gotten to the end of the e-mail when Danny cried out, "That girl is a genius!"

"Danny!"

"You can go to her house! Instead of math camp! It's perfect!"

"It's not *perfect!* It's crazy!"

"Why?"

"Well, first, I'm all signed up for High Sights Academy. Second, like Robin says, Sibley's not going to send me off to live with his *enemies.*"

"Say it's an exchange program. Through FUN! He won't even know!"

"Come on. It would take Sibley about two seconds to figure out they live next to Big Tree Grove."

"You always **look on the dark side**," Danny said in exasperation. "And you have no sense of adventure! You're the most boring person on Earth. You're going to live the boringest life ever and then bore yourself to death."

"I don't see you running off to Robin's."

"Umm," Danny said in his **airheaded** girl voice, "am I, like, the one being sent to math camp here?"

"Danny, there's no way."

But Julian had **pored over** the pictures of Huckleberry Ranch on the FUN website until he knew them by heart: two goats, an orchard covered in pink blossoms, a mossy waterfall beneath towering redwoods. And, for a moment, he imagined a summer without points, without shoes, without math camp. He could walk down the shady path. Into the forest. Into Robin's redwoods. ❖

In Other Words

look on the dark side think about the negative things

airheaded silly

pored over studied

▶ **Before You Move On**

1. **Character** Why does Robin suggest that Julian visit her at Big Tree Grove?

2. **Make Comparisons** Use text evidence to show how Robin and Danny are similar and different.

274

Meet the Author
S. Terrell French

Like Robin in *Operation Redwood*, S. Terrell French spent her childhood summers swimming, kayaking, and running through forests with bare feet. She says, "The redwood forests along the coast of Northern California are some of the coolest places on earth!" When she grew up, her love for nature grew with her. French became an environmental lawyer. For her first novel, *Operation Redwood*, French chose an ecological topic that was close to her heart—and her home in San Francisco, California. She wanted to show that "the battle over natural resources isn't just something that occurs in faraway places, like the Amazon."

French believes that reading books is an important part of being a writer. Reading many stories inspired her to write her own stories about topics, ideas, and settings that are important in her own life. Perhaps one of her stories will inspire her readers to write about what they love, too.

Writer's Craft

The author sets her story in places that she knows and cares about. In *Operation Redwood*, her characters use e-mails to describe some of these places. Write your own e-mail to a friend. Use informal language and vivid details to describe a special place that you know well.

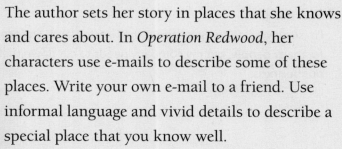

Key Words

advocate	management
deforestation	obligation
ecological	participate
intervene	regulate
landscape	utilize

Talk About It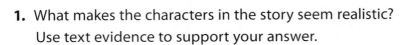

1. What makes the characters in the story seem realistic? Use text evidence to support your answer.

2. The author uses e-mails to tell part of the story. How do the e-mails help you understand each character?

3. Compare Julian's home with Robin's. How do the two environments affect the way they look at the world?

4. Imagine you are Julian. Use appropriate language to speak to your uncle about saving Robin's redwoods.

5. How does Danny feel about living in the city versus living in the country? Use text evidence to determine his viewpoint.

6. Based on what you have read, what can you infer about Robin's parents and their viewpoint about **deforestation** and the **management** of Big Tree Grove? Cite text evidence to support your answer.

Learn test-taking strategies and answer more questions.
NGReach.com

Write About It

Based on what you know about Sibley Carter, how do you think he might have reacted to Robin's original e-mail? Write a response e-mail from Mr. Carter to Robin. Use at least three **Key Words** and appropriate language as you write from Mr. Carter's viewpoint.

May 5

Dear Robin,
I'm sorry you are so upset about the Greeley land. **Deforestation** is difficult for many people, but my company needs to cut down these trees as a part of our business.

Characters' Viewpoints

Use the character description chart to record the dialogue, thoughts, and actions of the characters in *Operation Redwood*. You can add as many details as needed to show the characters' viewpoints.

Character Description Chart

Character	Evidence	Character's Viewpoint
Danny	• "You really think that's better?" he asked incredulously. •	• Danny is surprised by Julian. •
Julian	• •	• •
Robin	• •	• •

Use your character description chart to explain each character's viewpoints to a partner. Use **Key Words**.

Fluency  Comprehension Coach

Use the Comprehension Coach to practice reading with expression. Rate your reading.

Talk Together

Consider the viewpoints of the characters in *Operation Redwood*. Do they feel that diversity in nature is valuable? Discuss your ideas with a partner. Use **Key Words** and evidence from the text in your discussion.

Greek and Latin Roots

Greek and Latin roots can make up English words. A root is a central word part that has meaning, but it is not a complete word. If you know the meanings of word parts like roots, prefixes, and suffixes, you can figure out the meaning of the word.

EXAMPLE

root meaning "together"		root meaning "to protect"		word meaning "to protect together"
con-	+	serv	=	conserve

Root	Orgin	Meaning	Example
eco	Greek	home (environment)	economy
log/logy	Greek	thought, study	dialogue
ven/vent	Latin	come	convene

The chart above shows more Greek and Latin roots and their definitions. The Latin root *ad* means "towards," and the root *voc* means "to call or speak." What do you think *advocate* means?

Try It

Read the sentences. Then answer the questions. Use the chart to help you.

Robin wants to <u>intervene</u> to stop Mr. Carter from clear-cutting the forest. <u>Ecology</u> is important to her because she loves to learn about the forest.

1. The prefix *inter-* means "between." What is the best meaning for <u>intervene</u>?

   A come again

   B come between

   C stop from coming

   D come toward

2. What is the best meaning for the word <u>ecology</u> in the sentence?

   A study of the environment

   B harm to the environment

   C saving the environment

   D in the environment

Connect Across Texts You read about fictional characters fighting **deforestation**. Now learn how real scientists are working to save the forests.

Genre An **essay** is a short nonfiction text that explores a single topic. Photos often provide information about the topic.

The Super Trees

by Joel Bourne

John Muir was one of the first people to **advocate** for protecting California's forests. In 1895, Muir gave a speech to the Sierra Club about the importance of national parks and protections for great trees like the redwoods and sequoias.

"The battle we have fought, and are still fighting, for the forests is a part of the eternal conflict between right and wrong, and we cannot expect to see the end of it. I trust, however, that [we] will not weary in this forest well-doing. The fight for the Yosemite Park and other forest parks and **reserves** is **by no means** over; nor would the fighting cease, however much the boundaries were **contracted**. Every good thing, great and small, needs defense. . . . So we must count on watching and **striving** for these trees, and should always be glad to find anything so surely good and noble to strive for." – John Muir

Scientists investigate a hole in a redwood tree that was caused by a forest fire. This tree has been burned in two fires, but it is still standing.

In Other Words
reserves protected places
by no means not
contracted changed
striving fighting

▶ **Before You Move On**

1. **Paraphrase** In your own words, explain John Muir's viewpoint about protecting forests.

2. **Make Connections** Consider what you know about trees, and read the caption. Why is the tree in this photo unique?

279

Nearly 100 years later, John Muir's work to save the redwoods is carried on by people like Mike Fay. It could be said that the history of modern America is carved in redwood. Mike Fay has spent three decades helping save African forests. He is a Wildlife Conservation Society biologist and National Geographic Society explorer-in-residence.

Mike Fay's love for the **iconic** American trees began a few years ago after he explored the largest intact jungle remaining in Africa. One day while driving along the northern California coast, he found himself gazing at areas of clear-cuts and spindly **second-growth forests**. Another time in a state park, a six-foot-tall slice of an old redwood log on display caught his attention. Near the burgundy center a label read: "1492 Columbus."

"The one that **got me** was about three inches from the edge," Fay says. "Gold Rush, 1849.' And I realized that within the last few inches of that tree's life, we'd very nearly **liquidated** a 2,000-year-old forest."

Mike Fay

◄ By studying the rings formed within trees, scientists are able to estimate the ages of trees.

In Other Words

iconic famous

second-growth forests forests that had been replanted and were growing back

got me made me feel strong emotions

liquidated destroyed

This **landscape** shows clear-cuts in a stand of spruce, fir, and redwood trees.

In the fall of 2007, he **resolved** to see for himself how Earth's tallest forest had been **exploited** in the past and how it is being treated today. He wanted to find out if there was a way to maximize both timber production and the many **ecological** and social benefits that forests provide. Fay started walking at the southern end of the forest. There the trees grow in scattered groves in the Santa Lucia Range and the Santa Cruz Mountains. In small parks like Muir Woods outside San Francisco and Big Basin near Santa Cruz, he encountered a few rare patches of ancient trees. He walked 1,800 miles through forests that had been cut at least once. Many had been cut three times since 1850. This left islands of larger second-growth forest in a sea of mostly small trees.

While Mike was walking, he saw many beautiful sights. Redwoods the size of Saturn rockets sprouted from the ground like giant beanstalks. The trees' trunks were blackened by fire. Some trees had thick, ropy bark that spiraled skyward in candy-cane swirls. Others had huge cavities big enough to hold 20 people. Treetops had plummeted from 30 stories up and were half-buried among the sorrel and sword ferns. They were the **casualties** of powerful wars with the wind, which even now coursed through the tops with creaks and groans.

In Other Words
resolved decided
exploited used
casualties victims

▶ **Before You Move On**

1. **Make Comparisons** How is the information from the photo and caption above different from the text about clear-cut forests?

2. **Explain** How does Mike Fay hope to save the redwoods? Use evidence from the text to support your response.

It was a good year to be walking the redwoods. The Pacific Lumber Company was bankrupt. It had spent more than two decades battling environmentalists and state and federal regulators over its aggressive cutting practices. Most of the remaining **old growth was** protected. However, the **emblematic** species of the great forests continued to lose numbers. Some of them included the northern spotted owls, elusive little seabirds called marbled murrelets, and coho salmon.

Something else was **taking root among** the trees. Environmental groups, consulting foresters, and even a few timber companies and communities agreed that the redwoods were at a historic crossroads. It was a time when society could move beyond the log/don't log debates of decades past. They could embrace a different kind of forestry that could benefit people, wildlife, and perhaps even the planet.

The **mantra** of industrial foresters has long been to grow trees as fast as possible to maximize the return on investment. This method provided a steady flow of wood products to market. Now foresters are changing to a form of single-tree selection. This is more productive in the long run than clear-cutting. Every 10 to 15 years they take about a third of the timber in a stand. They only cut down the least robust trees. This creates more open space and allows the remaining trees to get a greater share of sunlight. This also speeds their growth. Every year, the amount and quality of the standing wood increase. The process can proceed for centuries. The advantages are two-fold: short-term income and a larger payback over the long term.

This change isn't just about wood. Past damage to ecosystems is being repaired. Sediment is being excavated from streams to restore their flow. Trees identified as crucial for wildlife habitat are being preserved.

Mike Fay says, "This isn't about loving big trees. It's about the fact that I spent 333 days walking 1,800 miles through the entire range of the redwoods with a notebook in my hand, documenting details about this ecosystem—and witnessing the aftermath of the cutting of at least 95 percent of the most wood-laden forest on Earth. If you want clean water, salmon, wildlife, and high-quality lumber, you've got to have a forest."

In Other Words
old growth was old forests were
emblematic important
taking root among starting because of
mantra belief

A black bear walks through a redwood forest.

"With increased production for humanity also come healthy ecosystems and global balance. We can—and must—do this not just with our forests and wildlife but also with the fish in our oceans and streams, the soils on our farms, and the grass in our pastures. The redwoods can show us the way." ❖

▶ **Before You Move On**

1. **Author's Purpose** Why does the author end this essay about redwoods with Mike Fay's viewpoint about "global balance"?

2. **Make Connections** What parts of this essay connect to other **ecological** problems you know?

Key Words

advocate	obligation
deforestation	management
ecological	participate
intervene	regulate
landscape	utilize

Compare Genres

Operation Redwood and "The Super Trees" both focus on the importance of redwood forests. Use a comparison chart to show how the selections are similar and different. Then use the comparison to help draw a conclusion that is true for both selections.

Comparison Chart

	Operation Redwood	"The Super Trees"
Genre		
Main Characters or People		biologist and explorer Mike Fay
Text Features and Forms	informal dialogue chatty e-mails illustrations	
Important Events		
Author's or Character's Viewpoint		

Talk Together

Is diversity valuable in a forest? With a partner, discuss how each selection addresses this question. Then use the conclusion you drew above to form a generalization about diversity. Use **Key Words** and evidence from the text to talk about your ideas.

Participial Phrases

A **participle** is a verb form that often ends with **-ed** or **-ing**. It can be used alone or appear at the start of a group of words called a **participial phrase**.

Grammar Rules Participial Phrases

A **participle** or a **participial phrase** acts as an adjective to describe a **noun** or **pronoun**.	The **rustling trees** were huge. Mike had discovered **them growing** gracefully.
Insert a comma (**,**) after a **participle** or a **participial phrase** that begins a sentence.	**Walking** through the forest, Mike saw many trees.
Insert a comma (**,**) both before and after a **participle** or a **participial phrase** that identifies or explains the **noun** or **pronoun** that comes before it.	Now, the **trees, blackened by fire,** were dead.

Read Participial Phrases

Good writers often use participles and participial phrases to make their writing more interesting and descriptive. Read this passage based on *Operation Redwood*. What participles and participial phrases can you find? What extra details do they add?

> Opening my uncle's e-mail, I discovered a note from a girl named Robin. Robin, sounding upset, described my uncle's plans to destroy a stand of redwoods. Armed with a plan, I went to see my uncle.

Write Participial Phrases

Reread page 268 of *Operation Redwood*. Write a summary of the e-mail exchange between Robin and Julian. Include at least one participle and two participial phrases in your sentences. Be sure to use commas correctly. Then compare your sentences with a partner's.

Write as an Advocate

Write an Argument

How can you help endangered animals, plants, or trees? Write an argument that persuades people to find a way to help an endangered species. Post your argument on a blog or bulletin board entitled "Helping Endangered Species."

condor

Study a Model

In an argument, you present your claim, or opinion. You use reasons and evidence to show why readers should agree with your claim and change what they think or do. Read Rafael's argument about helping an endangered species.

Help the California Condor
by Rafael Pincay

Do you want to help endangered animals but don't know how? **You should join Condor Watch to help save the California condor.**

Condor Watch needs volunteers like you. According to the U.S. Fish and Wildlife Service, only about 200 California condors live in the wild. Scientists have installed remote-control cameras to take thousands of photos of condors. Volunteers collect data from the many photos. This data helps scientists understand condor behavior and threats to their survival.

Participating in Condor Watch is easy because all you need is online access. The Web site shows you how to identify condors in a photo and send the information to researchers. You can do real scientific research right from home.

Condor Watch is a great way to help save an animal. **Log on to join Condor Watch today and help save condors!**

Rafael organizes his argument by introducing his **claim**.

In following paragraphs, Rafael clearly organizes the **reasons** for his claim. He develops and supports the reasons with **specific evidence**.

The conclusion tells what **action** Rafael wants people to take.

Prewrite

1. **Choose a Topic** What argument could you make to persuade people to help an endangered plant or animal? Talk with a partner to find an idea.

2. **Gather Information** What reasons will you give to support your claim? What evidence can you give to develop your reasons? Where can you locate credible sources for your reasons and evidence?

3. **Get Organized** Use a chart to help you organize your ideas.

Claim-and-Evidence Chart

Claim	Reasons and Evidence	Action Needed
Joining Condor Watch is a great way to help save California condors.	Condor Watch needs volunteers to collect data from photos of wild condors.	

Draft

Use your claim-and-evidence chart as you write your draft. Begin by stating your claim, or opinion about the topic. Support your claim with reasons and evidence. Then conclude by telling readers what action you want them to take.

Revise

1. **Read, Retell, Respond** Read your draft aloud to a partner. Your partner listens and then retells your main points. Then talk about ways to improve your writing.

Language Frames	
Retell	**Make Suggestions**
• Your claim is _____ . • The reasons and evidence you gave included _____ . • You want people to _____ .	• The relationship between your claim and reasons isn't clear. Could you add a transition, such as _____ ? • Could you add more evidence to support _____ ? • I'm not sure what you want people to do. Maybe you could _____ .

2. **Make Changes** Think about your draft and your partner's suggestions. Use the Revising Marks on page 617 to mark your changes.

   • Make sure your evidence is specific and from a credible source.

   > According to the U.S. Fish and Wildlife Service, only about 200
   > ~~Only a few~~ California condors live in the wild.

   • Did you connect your claims, reasons, and evidence? Would adding transitions make the connections clearer?

   > *because*
   > Participating in Condor Watch is easy. All you need is online access.

   • Make sure that your readers know what action to take.

   > Log on to join Condor Watch today and
   > Help save condors!

Edit and Proofread

Work with a partner to edit and proofread your argument. Pay special attention to adjectives, adverbs, and participial phrases. Use the marks on page 618 to show your changes.

Punctuation Tip

Use punctuation, such as commas, parentheses, or dashes, to set off participial phrases.

Publish

1. **On Your Own** Make a final copy of your argument. Put the key points on note cards and present it to your class as a persuasive speech.

Presentation Tips	
If you are the speaker . . .	**If you are the listener . . .**
Be sure to make eye contact with listeners as you speak. Use appropriate language.	Do you understand all the speaker's reasons? If not, ask questions.
Clarify your ideas and answer listeners' questions or counterarguments with more reasons and evidence.	Evaluate whether the speaker has supported his or her claim with sufficient reasons and evidence.

2. **In a Group** Gather all the arguments from your class. Post them on a class blog or a bulletin board called "Helping Endangered Animals."

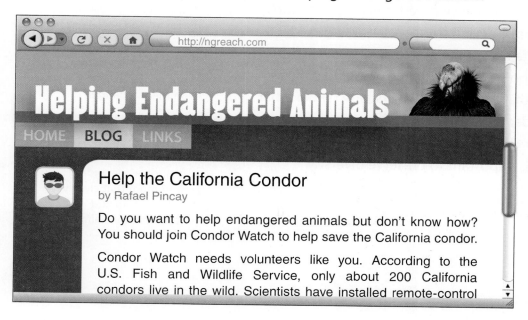

http://ngreach.com

Helping Endangered Animals

HOME   BLOG   LINKS

Help the California Condor
by Rafael Pincay

Do you want to help endangered animals but don't know how? You should join Condor Watch to help save the California condor.

Condor Watch needs volunteers like you. According to the U.S. Fish and Wildlife Service, only about 200 California condors live in the wild. Scientists have installed remote-control

In this unit you found many answers to the **Big Question**. Now use your concept map to discuss it. Think about the different ideas presented in the selections. Why is diversity important, and what we can do to protect our environment?

Concept Map

Is diversity valuable?

Each species of plant and animal teaches us something different.

Performance Task: Argument

Consider what you have learned from the selections and **Small Group Reading** books about diversity on Earth. Write a letter to the editor of your town's newspaper about the importance of saving plants and animals that are in danger. Persuade readers that trees and endangered animals need to be protected. Support your claim with reasons and evidence that show why it is important to preserve diversity.

Checklist

Does your letter to the editor

✓ use text evidence from the selections about saving plants and animals in danger?

✓ include relevant evidence to support your claim?

✓ include a concluding statement that clearly follows from and supports the claim?

Share Your Ideas

Choose one of these ways to share your ideas about the **Big Question**.

Write It!

Write a Speech

Research an animal that is endangered. Write a speech to persuade your classmates to save this animal. Back up your claim with reasons and evidence. Explain what actions students could take. Then present the speech to your class.

Talk About It!

Make a Presentation

Use the Internet to research redwood trees and why they are important to the environment. Use presentation software to include photos and text in your presentation.

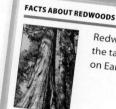

FACTS ABOUT REDWOODS

Redwoods are the tallest trees on Earth.

Do It!

Perform a Skit

Think about the selection *Operation Redwood*. Perform a skit with a group of classmates about what might happen if Julian Carter-Li spends the summer with Robin's family. What could they do to change Uncle Sibley's decision to cut down the redwood trees in Big Tree Grove?

Write It!

Write a Short Story

Imagine that you are exploring Madagascar when you discover a new species. Write a short story about your expedition. What new species did you discover? Why is the discovery of this new species important? In your short story, describe why diversity is important to you and your research.

A Time to
ACT

? BIG Question Why do people take a stand?

Unit at a Glance
▶ **Language**: Ask for and Give Information, Support Opinions, Social Studies Words
▶ **Literacy**: Determine Importance
▶ **Content**: Civil Rights

Unit
5

Share What You Know

❶ **Think** about something unfair that you would like to protest.

❷ **Make** a poster that shows your message of protest.

❸ **Share** with your classmates.

Build Background: Watch a movie about civil rights.
● NGReach.com

Language Frames

- Where did _____ ?
- _____ happened
  _____ .
- Why did _____ ?
- _____ because
  _____ .

Ask for and Give Information

Look at the photograph, and listen to the questions and answers. Then use **Language Frames** to ask for and give more information about the photograph.

Coretta Scott King

Dr. Martin Luther King, Jr.

From Selma to Montgomery ((MP3))

Student: This is a historical photo that shows one of the civil rights marches that took place during the 1960s. Where did this march take place?

Teacher: This march happened on the road to the state capitol of Alabama in the 1960s.

Student: Why did the protesters march that day?

Teacher: They marched because they wanted to protest unfair laws that made it difficult for African Americans in Alabama to vote.

Social Studies Vocabulary

Key Words

boycott

demonstration

discrimination

integrate

prejudice

separate

Key Words

Look at these photographs, and read the captions. Use **Key Words** and other words to talk about how African Americans fought against **prejudice** during the Civil Rights Movement.

▲ Many African Americans faced **discrimination**. They were not allowed to do certain things because of their race, such as drinking out of "white only" water fountains.

▲ In Montgomery, Alabama, African Americans had to ride at the backs of public buses. They started a bus **boycott** by refusing to ride the buses until the law changed.

◀ African American children had to attend **separate** schools that kept them apart from Caucasian children. People held **demonstrations** in protest. They wanted to **integrate** the schools so all children could go to school together.

Talk Together

Based on the information on pages 294–295, talk with a partner about the Civil Rights Movement. Take turns asking for and giving information about how and why African Americans fought against **prejudice**. Use **Language Frames** from page 294 and **Key Words**.

Relate Ideas

The main idea of a text is the most important idea. Most authors introduce a main idea and then elaborate on the main idea by including illustrations and examples. As you read, **relate ideas** like these to better understand what you read.

The 1950s were good years for many Americans. They had jobs that paid well, new homes in the suburbs, and good schools for their children. But African Americans were one group who did not share fully in all this. **In the 1950s, prejudice against African Americans was widespread in the United States. One of the worst results of this prejudice was segregation, the practice of keeping people apart based on race.**

"The **main idea** is about prejudice."

"Segregation is one **example** that relates to prejudice."

Map and Talk

You can use a main idea web to record how details and examples in a text relate to a main idea.

Main Idea Web

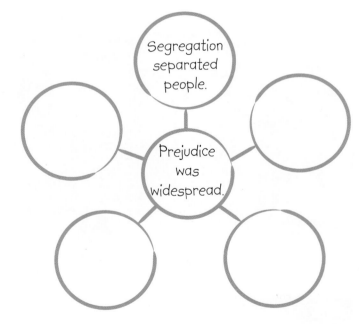

Talk with a partner about an example of prejudice you have experienced or learned about. Work together to record a main idea and at least two related details or examples in a main idea web.

More Key Words

Use these words to talk about "The Civil Rights Movement" and "Rosa Parks: My Story."

endeavor
(in-**de**-vur) *noun*

An **endeavor** is a serious effort. Cleaning the park is a positive **endeavor** for these volunteers.

implement
(**im**-plu-ment) *verb*

When you **implement** a plan, you make it happen. The soccer coach will **implement** new strategies to help his team win more games.

inherent
(in-**her**-unt) *adjective*

If something is **inherent**, it comes naturally. The girl's **inherent** helpfulness shows when she helps her father with yard work.

position
(pu-**zi**-shun) *noun*

A **position** is an official rank or job. The mayor has a high **position** in a town's government.

react
(rē-**akt**) *verb*

When you **react**, you respond to something. This grandmother **reacts** to the flowers by smiling.

Talk Together

Work with a partner. Make a Study Card for each **Key Word**.

> endeavor
> **What It Means:**
> a serious effort
> **Example:**
> climbing a mountain
> **Not an Example:**
> watching television

Add words to My Vocabulary Notebook.
 NGReach.com

Learn to Determine Importance

To determine what's important, you focus on what matters. One way to determine what's important in a text is to look for ideas or concepts that the author repeats. You can also look for section headings that divide a nonfiction selection into its most important ideas. The **details** in each section will support the section's **main idea**.

How to Identify Main Idea and Details

?	**1.** Turn the title, section heading, or subheading into a question. If the section does not have a heading, ask a question about what the section is mostly about.	My question is _____.
👁	**2.** Look for information that answers your question. These are the details.	Detail #1: _____. Detail #2: _____.
💭	**3.** Think about how the details answer your question to determine the main idea.	The main idea is _____.

Here's how one student determined importance.

Look Into the Text

A Divided Society

Jim Crow laws said that blacks and whites must use different schools, restaurants, hotels, theaters, parks, sections of trains and buses, and so on. Even funeral homes and cemeteries were segregated! In the few places where blacks and whites shared public services—such as post offices and banks—**African Americans had to wait for all whites to be served first.**

> My question is: How was society divided?
>
> These details show how society was divided.
>
> The main idea is that society was divided by prejudice and segregation.

Identifying the main idea and important details of a passage helps you determine the most important information in a selection.

Talk Together

Read the history article and sample notes. Use **Language Frames** to determine the main idea and details as you read. Talk with a partner about how you determined importance.

History Article

FREEDOM RIDERS

IN 1960, LAWSUITS, SUCH AS *Boynton v. Virginia*, resulted in a Supreme Court ruling that outlawed segregation at interstate rail and bus stations. The ruling, however, was largely ignored in the South, where **separate** facilities for blacks and whites remained. Rather than holding **demonstrations** or **boycotts** against interstate travel, Freedom Riders hoped to draw attention to the problem. The plan was simple: blacks and whites would travel from Washington, DC, to New Orleans on buses. They would sit together and ignore signs in bus stations that separated blacks and whites. ◄

The first Freedom Riders left Washington, DC, on May 4, 1961, in two buses. The seven black and six white Freedom Riders knew the **inherent** dangers in riding buses together through the South. But they were determined to make a stand against **discrimination**.

While the Freedom Riders faced **prejudice** in South Carolina, the real trouble began when the buses reached Alabama. On May 14, one of the buses was firebombed in Anniston. The Freedom Riders escaped the

burning bus but were beaten when they got out. They did not fight back.

A similar fate awaited the second bus in Birmingham, Alabama. Its passengers were also attacked and beaten. Police were slow to **react**. Many of the Freedom Riders were beaten so badly that they were unable to continue their **endeavor**. ◄

More rides were organized. Again, Freedom Riders were arrested and beaten when they tried to **integrate** bus stations. Again, police failed to protect them. Finally, Attorney General Robert Kennedy used his powerful **position** to provide National Guard support. He also ordered the Interstate Commerce Commission to end segregation in interstate travel. That dictate was **implemented** in September of 1961. ◄

My question is: Who were the Freedom Riders?

Detail #1: They were groups of black and white people.

Detail #2: They rode buses through the South.

The main idea is that black and white people rode buses together to protest segregation in transportation.

◄ = a good place to stop and identify main idea and details

Read a History Article

Genre

A **history article** tells about real events that happened in the past. History articles usually present information in chronological order so that readers can see how events developed through time.

Text Features

Many nonfiction articles use **headings** to divide the text into meaningful sections. Sometimes, a heading will have a **subheading** that gives more specific information about the section's content.

This heading is about the beginning of the Civil Rights Movement.

The Movement Begins

Thurgood Marshall

This subheading shows that Thurgood Marshall was involved with the beginning of the movement.

One group that fought for equality is the National Association for the Advancement of Colored People (NAACP). The NAACP was founded in 1909. Its goal was to obtain equal rights for all people and to eliminate racial hatred and discrimination.

The Civil Rights Movement

by Kevin Supples

On March 7, 1965, 600 people in Alabama began a march to demand civil rights. When they reached the State Capitol building in Birmingham on March 25, there were 25,000 people marching.

America in 1950
A Divided Society

The 1950s were good years for
many Americans. They had jobs that
paid well, new homes **in the suburbs**,
and good schools for their children.
But African Americans were one group
who did not share fully in all this. In
the 1950s, **prejudice** against African
Americans was **widespread** in the United
States. One of the worst results of this
prejudice was segregation, the practice of
keeping people apart based on race.

Segregation was different in different
parts of the United States. The South
was home to more than half of African
Americans. In the South, segregation was
enforced by Jim Crow laws. These laws
had controlled the lives of Southern blacks
since the late 1800s. Jim Crow laws said
that blacks and whites must use different
schools, restaurants, hotels, theaters,
parks, sections of trains and buses, and

▲ A child uses a drinking fountain outside a
North Carolina courthouse.

▲ Signs showed how facilities and areas were
segregated.

In Other Words
in the suburbs outside large cities
widespread very common
enforced supported; made legal

so on. Even funeral homes and cemeteries were segregated! In the few places where blacks and whites shared public services—such as post offices and banks—African Americans had to wait for all whites to be served first.

In the North, segregation happened **by practice and custom**. Many African Americans moved to Northern cities during the 1940s, and whites responded by moving to the suburbs. African Americans found themselves trapped in city slums—poor neighborhoods where housing and schools were bad and where there were few jobs.

Both Northern and Southern segregation were wrong and both forms of segregation denied black people an equality that they had a right to as Americans. In the 1950s, some African Americans were determined to change things. They started the Civil Rights Movement. This **movement** brought together many people and for some, the struggle to win equality became their life's work.

Many Caucasians moved out of Northern cities when African Americans moved in. Neighborhoods like Harlem, New York (pictured), suffered because of a lack of city services. ▶

In Other Words

by practice and custom because of people's beliefs rather than laws

movement organized effort to change society

▶ **Before You Move On**

1. **Make Comparisons** How was segregation different in the North and the South?

2. **Cause/Effect** Why were African Americans determined to change the "divided society"?

The Movement Begins
Thurgood Marshall

One group that fought for equality is the National Association for the Advancement of Colored People (NAACP). The NAACP was founded in 1909. Its goal was to obtain equal rights for all people and to **eliminate** racial hatred and **discrimination**.

The leader of the NAACP's efforts to end segregation was their top lawyer, Thurgood Marshall. He used the law to fight injustice against African Americans. Marshall argued thirty-two cases before the U.S. Supreme Court during his career, and he won twenty-nine of them. Some say that Marshall did more than any other individual to win civil rights for African Americans.

Marshall was born in Maryland in 1908. He was raised in a proud middle-class family. Smart and hard working, he was a fine student. Marshall went to college and later attended law school at Howard University in Washington, DC. Marshall graduated in 1933, first in his class.

Most of Marshall's clients were poor. Some couldn't even pay anything, but Marshall worked hard for them anyway.

He usually won his cases. He became known as **the "little man's lawyer."** Marshall had a good sense of humor. He enjoyed jokes and often used humor to help him get through **hard times**.

◄ **Thurgood Marshall stands in front of the U.S. Supreme Court. Later he was appointed the nation's first African American Supreme Court justice.**

In Other Words
eliminate end
the "little man's lawyer." a lawyer who helped the poor.
hard times bad experiences

"Separate but Equal"

Throughout his career, Thurgood Marshall fought the " **separate** but equal" rule. This rule was created in 1896 by the Supreme Court. It said that states could offer separate services to African Americans and whites as long as the services were close to equal, but actually they often were not.

Many states passed laws saying that **local school districts** could decide whether to have separate schools for blacks and whites. The result was that all schools in the South were segregated. And there was nothing "equal" about the education black children were given in their poor, crowded schools.

After World War II, many Southern states tried to improve their blacks-only schools. They wanted to show that these schools were equal, but their efforts were **too little and too late**. By 1952, there were several court cases about segregated schools. The most famous case involved an eight-year-old girl named Linda Brown.

Linda's family lived close to a public school in Topeka, Kansas, but that school accepted only white students. So Linda had to travel by bus to a blacks-only school. To reach their bus stop, she and her sister had to walk through a dangerous railroad yard. Early in 1951, the Browns and some other African American families decided to take the local school district to court. In July, the local school board promised they would end segregation "as soon as possible." But that wasn't good enough for the Browns.

▼ **Linda Brown (front, center) sits in her segregated classroom.**

In Other Words

local school districts the leaders of schools in each area

too little and too late not enough

▶ Before You Move On

1. **Main Idea/Details** Thurgood Marshall fought hard for civil rights. List two details from the text that support this main idea.

2. **Draw Conclusions** How did the " **separate** but equal" law affect the Browns?

Brown v. Board of Education

The Browns' case became famous and Thurgood Marshall decided to use it to try to end segregated schools everywhere. He brought the case to the Supreme Court. The court decided to group the Browns' case with four others. Their case is known as *Brown v. Board of Education*.

Marshall argued the case before the Supreme Court. He argued that the Fourteenth Amendment of the U.S. Constitution said that states must treat all citizens alike, regardless of race. He said that black children did not receive schooling equal to that given to white children. He also said that black children **thought less of themselves** because they attended poor schools.

Almost three years after Linda Brown's family started the case, a final decision was reached. On May 17, 1954, the Supreme Court ruled that school segregation went against the Constitution.

After the ruling, the government made many school districts **redraw their borders**. Now white and black students would go to school together. This victory was an important step in the fight for civil rights. Many hoped that **integrating** schools would lead to integrating all of society. But there was still a long struggle ahead.

◀ **African American children arrive for class. Segregated schools like this one led to the famous *Brown v. Board of Education* legal case.**

In Other Words
v. (versus) against (in Latin)
thought less of themselves felt unimportant
redraw their borders allow black students to attend

THEN

Linda Brown

A young Linda Brown (left) stands with her younger sister and her parents. Her father, Reverend Oliver Brown, asked, "Why should my child walk four miles when there is a school only four blocks away? Why should I . . . explain to my daughter that she can't attend school with her neighborhood playmates because she is black?"

▲ Linda Brown and her family in the 1950s

NOW

Linda Brown

Today Linda Brown Thompson lives in Topeka, Kansas. She owns an educational consulting firm with her sister. Together, Linda and her sister have spoken about the court case and their experiences across the country. They have also appeared on television and were invited to the White House.

"We lived in the calm of the hurricane's eye, looking out at the storm and wondering how it would end," she recalled on the fiftieth anniversary of the Supreme Court decision to end segregation in public schools.

▲ Linda Brown Thompson, left, signs autographs at the University of Michigan in 2004.

▶ Before You Move On

1. **Relate Ideas** How does the section about Linda Brown on page 307 contribute to the topic of civil rights?

2. **Draw Conclusions** Why was the Browns' case important to the Civil Rights Movement?

The Little Rock Nine

Within a year, some school districts desegregated. Here and there, African American and white students attended school together. But many school districts, especially in the South, found ways to **resist** and delay the Supreme Court ruling.

Little Rock, Arkansas, became a test case for the new ruling because public schools there were ordered to desegregate in September 1957. The local school board agreed, but the governor of Arkansas, Orval Faubus, refused. He was facing a tough re-election fight, and he hoped to win the support of the many white Arkansas voters who still wanted segregated schools.

▼ **National Guard troops stand outside Little Rock's Central High School in 1957.**

In Other Words
resist fight against

When school opened that September, Governor Faubus sent National Guard troops to Central High School. He ordered them to stop nine African American students from entering the newly integrated school. Elizabeth Eckford, one of the **"Little Rock Nine,"** arrived at school alone when a white mob began to scream at her.

For three weeks, the crisis continued. At this point, President Dwight Eisenhower stepped in by placing the Arkansas National Guard under federal control. The nine black students arrived at the school in a U.S. Army car. With soldiers protecting them, the students finally were integrated into the school. Eisenhower had shown that the federal government would protect civil rights.

Later, President Eisenhower wrote a message to parents of the Little Rock Nine. "In the course of our country's progress toward equality of opportunity, you have shown dignity and courage."

◄ **Elizabeth Eckford had to walk past a crowd that shouted insults at her on her first day at Central High School.**

▶ **Before You Move On**

1. **Cause/Effect** How did Governor Faubus **react** to the Supreme Court ruling to desegregate?

2. **Explain** How did President Eisenhower show that the federal government would protect civil rights?

The Struggle Continues

Martin Luther King, Jr.

The legal victory of *Brown v. Board of Education* was just one step in the fight against segregation. It did not change things as quickly as people had hoped.

▼ **Dr. Martin Luther King, Jr.**

African Americans were ready to do more, and they began to organize. At this moment in history, a new leader arrived. He was a young minister named Martin Luther King, Jr.

King was born in 1929 in Atlanta, Georgia, to a middle-class family. He was the son and grandson of Baptist ministers. His mother was a teacher. One of his grandfathers had been a slave. King excelled at school. He began college at the age of fifteen in a program for gifted students. He went to Morehouse College, a well-known all-black school in Atlanta. By the time King was eighteen, he had decided to **follow in his father's footsteps**.

While at Boston University finishing his studies to be a minister, King met Coretta Scott. She was studying voice and piano. The two were married in 1953, and the following year, Reverend King became pastor of a church in Montgomery, Alabama. He quickly became known for his wisdom and powerful preaching. Then in December 1955, an event **took place** that would make Martin Luther King, Jr., a leader of the Civil Rights Movement.

In Other Words
follow in his father's footsteps be a minister like his father
took place happened

Changing the System

Rosa Parks

Montgomery, Alabama, was a segregated city in 1955. African Americans were treated **as second-class citizens** there. The public bus system was a constant reminder of this.

As in many Southern cities, more blacks rode the city buses than whites. Even so, the first ten rows of every bus were reserved for white passengers only. If a bus was crowded and a white passenger needed a seat, blacks had to stand. Black passengers had to pay **their fares** at the front of the bus, but then they had to get off the bus and re-board by the back door. At busy times, the bus sometimes left before everyone who had paid got back on.

On December 1, 1955, an African American woman named Rosa Parks was riding the bus home from work. She was a **seamstress** and also worked at the local NAACP office. Parks had been on her feet all day, and she was tired. She was sitting in the eleventh row—the first row of seats set aside for African American passengers.

The bus was crowded and some black passengers were standing at the back. When a white man boarded and needed a

▲ **Rosa Parks is fingerprinted by the police.**

seat, the bus driver ordered Parks and three other African Americans in her row to stand. She refused to move and the driver called the police.

Parks was arrested for disobeying the law that required African Americans to give up their seats to white people. Two officers took her to the police station where **she was booked**. They then transferred her to the city jail and placed her in a cell.

News of Parks's arrest shocked the African American community. Civil rights supporters saw that this was their chance to change the rules. They asked Martin Luther King, Jr., to be their leader. That evening, Dr. King spoke to a cheering crowd of African Americans, and he called for them to start a bus **boycott**, which meant they would not ride the buses.

In Other Words

as second-class citizens unfairly

their fares for their tickets

seamstress person who sews clothes

she was booked her information was recorded

▶ **Before You Move On**

1. **Sequence** Explain the sequence of events that began with Parks getting on a bus.
2. **Draw Conclusions** Based on evidence from the text, why did civil rights supporters ask King to be their leader?

The Montgomery Bus Boycott

For the next year, very few African Americans rode public buses in Montgomery, Alabama. Most **used car pools** to get to work. The boycott worked. The bus company lost a lot of money. The combination of the city's loss of money and a decision by the Supreme Court forced the Montgomery Bus Company to accept integration.

In June 1956, a federal court ruled that the bus segregation in Alabama was against the Constitution. The city of Montgomery did not **give in** easily. Lawyers for the city took the case to the Supreme Court, but that November, the Supreme Court agreed that segregation on buses was not lawful in the case of *Browder v. Gale*. A little over a year after the day that Rosa Parks refused to move, the Montgomery buses were integrated.

The Montgomery bus boycott was big news. It made Martin Luther King, Jr., famous. *Time* magazine put him on the cover. Requests to speak **poured in** from all over the country, and the publicity also led to boycotts in many other parts of the South.

The Protests

In February 1960, four African American college freshmen in Greensboro, North Carolina, decided to take another step toward equality. They sat down at the whites-only lunch counter in a

In Other Words
used car pools rode together in cars
give in quit fighting
poured in came in

312

▲ Thousands of African Americans walked to work during the Montgomery bus **boycott**.

Woolworth's store and politely ordered coffee and donuts. The students were refused service. At that time, many department stores across the country had lunch counters, but most Southern lunch counters did not serve food to African Americans. Blacks were free to shop at the stores but could not eat there.

To protest, the four students sat at the counter for the rest of the afternoon. They returned the next day. This time, twenty more students came with them and each day, more people—both black and white—joined the "sit-in." By Saturday, hundreds **jammed** the lunch counters.

The events in Greensboro became news. At first, white business leaders refused to **bend to** the protest. But then black citizens set up a boycott of local stores. Stores began losing money and finally, on July 25, 1960, the first black person was served lunch at Woolworth's.

During the next eighteen months, thousands of people **staged** sit-ins all over the South. Most of those taking part were black students. Both Martin Luther King, Jr., and Thurgood Marshall supported these nonviolent protests. African Americans had found a new and powerful way to be heard.

▲ Dr. Martin Luther King, Jr., speaks at a rally during the bus boycott.

▶ **Before You Move On**

1. **Summarize** In your own words, explain why the bus **boycott** was so effective.
2. **Make Inferences** Why did white people join the black protesters at the lunch counter sit-ins?

313

Achieving the Dream

The Civil Rights Act

In the fall of 1960, John F. Kennedy was elected president of the United States. Kennedy won 70 percent of the black vote. He had shown that he would support ending segregation. Kennedy did not make changes quickly, but he did appoint more African Americans to high federal **positions** than any president before him. Kennedy appointed Thurgood Marshall to be a federal judge.

In June 1963, President Kennedy demanded that Congress pass a strong civil rights bill. In a speech to the nation he asked, "Are we to say to the world—and much more importantly to each other—that this is the land of the free, except for the Negroes?"

To persuade Congress to pass the bill, civil rights leaders A. Philip Randolph and Bayard Rustin organized a huge march on Washington, DC. On August 28, more than 250,000 people—both African Americans and whites—came together in the nation's capital. **Labor unions** and religious leaders joined the protest.

It was the largest show of support for the Civil Rights Movement so far. The march ended at the Lincoln Memorial. For three hours, the crowd listened to a lot of speeches. People were getting sleepy and restless when the last speaker, Martin Luther King, Jr., came to the microphone. His famous "I Have a Dream" speech **electrified** the crowd.

A few months after the March on Washington, President Kennedy was assassinated. His vice-president, Lyndon Johnson, **succeeded him**. President Johnson passed the Civil Rights Act of 1964. The new law banned segregation in public places, and it also banned unfair treatment of workers based on their color, sex, religion, or national origin. ❖

◀ **Dr. Martin Luther King, Jr., smiles and waves at the huge crowd gathered at the March on Washington.**

In Other Words

Labor unions Groups who wanted civil rights for workers
electrified excited
succeeded him became the next president

▶ **Before You Move On**

1. **Relate Ideas** How did President Kennedy affect the Civil Rights Movement?
2. **Details** In what ways did the Civil Rights Movement succeed? Use evidence from the text to explain your answer.

Talk About It

1. History articles give information about real events from the past. How have the real events described in "The Civil Rights Movement" affected your school and community today?

2. Review the photographs and captions about Linda Brown and Elizabeth Eckford. Ask for and give information about their school experiences.

3. Analyze how the section on Thurgood Marshall relates to the topic of civil rights. How does this section help you understand a main idea in the text?

4. Compare Rosa Parks and the students at the Woolworth's lunch counter. Cite specific evidence from the text to support your comparisons.

5. How were nonviolent protests, such as **boycotts** and sit-ins, effective **endeavors** during the Civil Rights Movement? Use text evidence to support your answer.

6. Was it more effective for civil rights activists to challenge segregation in court or to challenge it with boycotts or sit-ins? Use text evidence to support your judgment.

Learn test-taking strategies and answer more questions.
NGReach.com

Write About It

Write a paragraph to give information about the accomplishments of the Civil Rights Movement. Cite examples from the text. Use at least three **Key Words**.

> During the Civil Rights Movement, African Americans fought **prejudice** and **discrimination**.

Relate Ideas

Use the main idea web to relate details and examples to a main idea in "The Civil Rights Movement."

Main Idea Web

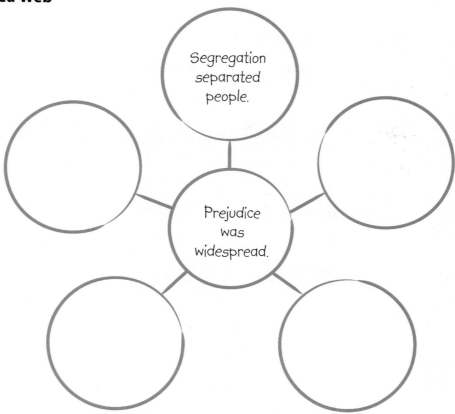

Use your main idea web to summarize the article with a partner. Use **Key Words**.

Fluency  Comprehension Coach

Use the Comprehension Coach to practice reading with intonation. Rate your reading.

Talk Together

Why did civil rights activists decide to take a stand in "The Civil Rights Movement"? Discuss your ideas, using **Key Words** and text evidence.

Word Origins

Many words have roots that come from other languages. **Roots** are word parts that have meanings but cannot be used without other word parts. Use a root word and another word part to figure out the meaning of the example below.

EXAMPLE

| prefix meaning "before" | root meaning "to tell" |

pre-   +   dict   =   **predict**

Root	Origin	Meaning	Example
civ-	Latin	citizen	civilian
jud-, judic-	Latin	judge	judicial
part-, par-	Latin	portion or part	partition
pos-	Latin	put or place	pose

The chart above shows some other common roots. Based on the Latin root *pos-*, what do you think *position* means?

Try It

Read the sentences. Then answer the questions. Use the chart to help you.

Thurgood Marshall fought <u>prejudice</u> against African Americans. In one Supreme Court case, he argued that <u>separate</u> schools were illegal.

1. **Look at the root *judic-*. What is the best meaning for the word <u>prejudice</u>?**

   A judge unfairly

   B judge before a court

   C judge before knowing

   D judge favorably

2. **Look at the root *par-*. What is the best meaning for the word <u>separate</u>?**

   A apart

   B alone

   C joined

   D unfair

Connect Across Texts You read about Rosa Parks's arrest. Now read about the same events from her viewpoint.

Genre A **memoir** is the story of a person's life, written by that person.

From
ROSA PARKS: MY STORY
BY Rosa Parks

When I got off from work that evening of December 1, I went to Court Square as usual to catch the Cleveland Avenue bus home. I didn't look to see who was driving when I got on, and by the time I recognized him, I had already paid my fare. It was the same driver who had **put me off** the bus back in 1943, twelve years earlier. He was still tall and heavy, with red, rough-looking skin. And he was still mean-looking. I didn't know if he had **been on that route** before—they switched the drivers around sometimes. I do know that most of the time if I saw him on a bus, I wouldn't get on it.

In Other Words
put me off made me leave
been on that route driven those roads

▶ **Before You Move On**

1. **Details** When did the events of this memoir take place? Use evidence from the text to support your answer.
2. **Make Inferences** What would Parks have done if she had noticed the bus driver immediately? How do you know?

319

I saw **a vacant** seat in the middle section of the bus and took it. I didn't even question why there was a vacant seat even though there were quite a few people standing in the back. If I had thought about it at all, I would probably have **figured** maybe someone saw me get on and did not take the seat but left it vacant for me. There was a man sitting next to the window and two women across the aisle.

The next stop was the Empire Theater, and some whites got on. They filled up the white seats, and one man was left standing. The driver looked back and noticed the man standing. Then he looked back at us. He said, "Let me have those front seats" because they were the front seats of the black section. Didn't anybody move. We just sat right where we were, the four of us. Then he spoke a second time: "Y'all better **make it light** on yourselves and let me have those seats."

The man in the window seat next to me stood up, and I moved to let him pass by me, and then I looked across the aisle and saw that the two women were also standing. I moved over to the window seat. I could not see how standing up was going to "make it light" for me. The more we **gave in and complied**, the worse they treated us.

2013

USA | FOREVER

Rosa Parks

a stamp to commemorate Rosa Parks's 100th birthday in 2013 ▶

In Other Words
a vacant an empty
figured guessed that
make it light make it easy
gave in and complied did what they wanted

I thought back to the time when I used to sit up all night and didn't sleep, and my grandfather would have his gun right by the fireplace, or if he had his one-horse wagon going anywhere, he always had his gun in the back of the wagon. People always say that I didn't give up my seat because I was tired, but that isn't true. I was not tired physically, or no more tired than I usually was at the end of a working day. I was not old, although some people have an image of me as being old then. I was forty-two. No, the only tired I was, was tired of giving in.

The driver of the bus saw me still sitting there, and he asked was I going to stand up. I said, "No." He said, "Well, I'm going to have you arrested." Then I said, "You may do that." These were the only words we said to each other. I didn't even know his name, which was James Blake, until we were in court together. He got out of the bus and stayed outside for a few minutes, waiting for the police.

As I sat there, I tried not to think about what might happen. I knew that anything was possible. I could be **manhandled** or beaten. I could be arrested. People have asked me if it occurred to me then that I could be the test case the NAACP had been looking for. I did not think about that at all. In fact if I had let myself think **too deeply** about what might happen to me, I might have gotten off the bus. But I chose to remain.

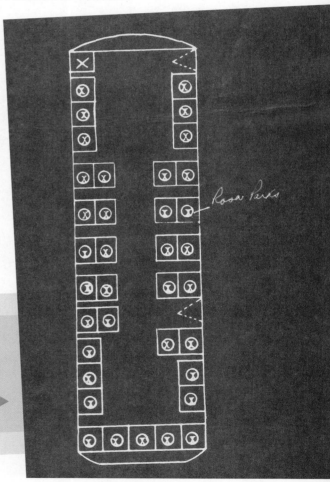

▶ a diagram of the bus and the location of Rosa Parks's seat ▶

▶ Before You Move On

1. **Summarize** How was Parks's decision different from the decisions of others around her?
2. **Analyze Argument** What reason does Parks give for refusing to give up her seat?

321

▲ black and white passengers on a public bus in 1956

◀ the bus that Rosa Parks rode

Meanwhile there were people getting off the bus and asking for **transfers**, so that began to loosen up the crowd, especially in the back of the bus. Not everyone got off, but everybody was very quiet. What conversation there was, was in low tones; no one was talking out loud. It would have been quite interesting to have seen the whole bus empty out. Or if the other three had stayed where they were, because if they'd had to arrest four of us instead of one, then that would have given me a little support. But it didn't matter. I never thought **hard** of them at all and never even bothered to criticize them.

Eventually two policemen came. They got on the bus, and one of them asked me why I didn't stand up. I asked him, "Why do you all push us around?" He said to me, and I quote him exactly, "I don't know, but the law is the law and you're under arrest." One policeman picked up my purse, and the second one picked up my shopping bag and **escorted** me to the squad car. In the squad car they returned my personal belongings to me. They did not put their hands on me or force me into the car. After I was seated in the car, they went back to the driver and asked him if he wanted to **swear out a warrant**. He answered that he would finish his route and then come straight back to swear out the warrant. I was only **in custody**, not legally arrested, until the warrant was signed.

As they were driving me to the city desk, at City Hall, near Court Street, one of them asked me again, "Why didn't you stand up when the driver spoke to you?" I did not answer. I remained silent all the way to City Hall.

the police report that details the events of Rosa Parks's arrest ▶

POLICE DEPARTMENT
CITY OF MONTGOMERY

Complainant _____ J.F.Blake _____ (wm) _____ Da

Address _____ 27 No. Lewis St.

Offense _____ Misc.

Address _____ Reported By _ S

Date and Time Offense Committed _____ 12-1-55 _____ 6:06 pm

Place of Occurrence _____ In Front of Empire Theatre _____ (On Mont,

Person or Property Attacked

How Attacked

Person Wanted

Value of Property Stolen

_____ Value Recovered

Details of Complaint (list, describe and give value of property sto

We received a call upon arrival the bus operator said he

sitting in the white section of the bus, and would not mo

We (Day & Mixon) also saw her.

The bus operator signed

In Other Words
transfers tickets to change to different buses
hard badly
escorted led
swear out a warrant officially complain about me
in custody being held at the police station

▶ **Before You Move On**

1. **Cause/Effect** How did Parks's refusal to give up her seat affect her and those around her?

2. **Make Inferences** Based on what you have read, why did Parks remain quiet on the way to City Hall?

As we entered the building, I asked if I could have a drink of water, because my throat was real dry. There was a fountain, and I was standing right next to it. One of the policemen said yes, but by the time I bent down to drink, another policeman said, "No, you can't drink no water. You have to wait until you get to the jail." So I was denied the chance to drink a sip of water. I was not going to do anything but wet my throat. I wasn't going to drink a whole lot of water, even though I was quite thirsty. That made me angry, but I did not respond.

At the city desk they filled out the necessary forms as I answered questions such as what my name was and where I lived. I asked if I could make a telephone call and they said, "No." Since that was my first arrest, I didn't know if that was more **discrimination** because I was black or if it was **standard practice**. But it seemed to me to be more discrimination. Then they escorted me back to the squad car, and we went to the city jail on North Ripley Street.

I wasn't frightened at the jail. I was more **resigned** than anything else. I don't recall being real angry, not enough to have an argument. I was just prepared to accept whatever I had to face. I asked again if I could make a telephone call. I was ignored.

They told me to put my purse on the counter and to empty my pockets of personal items. The only thing I had in my pocket was a tissue. I took that out. They didn't search me or handcuff me.

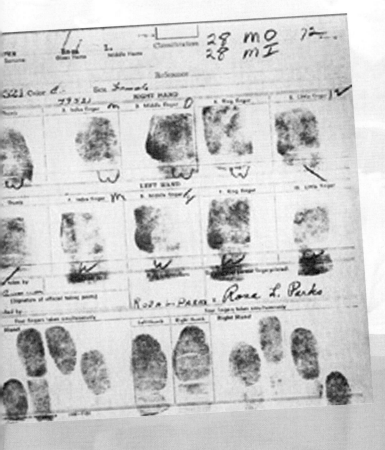

◄ **Rosa Parks's fingerprint sheet from her arrest**

In Other Words

standard practice how they treated all people

resigned accepting

I was then taken to an area where I was fingerprinted and where **mug shots** were taken. A white **matron** came to escort me to my jail cell, and I asked again if I might use the telephone. She told me that she would find out.

She took me up a flight of stairs (the cells were on the second level), through a door covered with iron mesh, and along a **dimly lighted corridor**. She placed me in an empty dark cell and slammed the door closed. She walked a few steps away, but then she turned around and came back. She said, "There are two girls around the other side, and if you want to go over there with them instead of being in a cell by yourself, I will take you over there." I told her that it didn't matter, but she said, "Let's go around there, and then you won't have to be in a cell alone." It was her way of being nice. It didn't make me feel any better.

As we walked to the other cell, I asked her again, "May I use the telephone?" She answered that she would check.

There were two black women in the cell that the matron took me to, as she had said. One of them spoke to me and the other didn't. One just acted as if I wasn't there. The one who spoke to me asked me what had happened to me. I told her that I was arrested on the bus. ❖

Rosa Parks's official mug shot ▶

In Other Words
mug shots photographs for police records
matron female guard
dimly lighted corridor dark hallway

▶ **Before You Move On**

1. **Explain** How did Parks **react** to the police officers and jail experience? Use text evidence to support your answer.

2. **Main Idea/Details** Rosa Parks faced **discrimination**. List two details to support this main idea.

Key Words

boycott	integrate
demonstration	position
discrimination	prejudice
endeavor	react
implement	separate
inherent	

Compare Accounts

The history article, "The Civil Rights Movement," by Kevin Supples, and Rosa Parks's memoir, "Rosa Parks: My Story," both describe social injustices and **discrimination** . Use a Venn diagram to compare and contrast how the authors of each selection describe Rosa Parks's experience. Then evaluate the two accounts, and discuss which viewpoint is more effective.

Venn Diagram

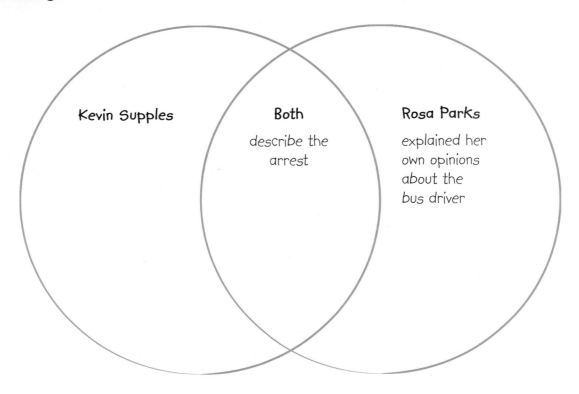

Kevin Supples

Both
describe the arrest

Rosa Parks
explained her own opinions about the bus driver

Talk Together

Think about the history article and the memoir. Why do people like Rosa Parks take a stand in difficult situations? Use **Key Words** and specific examples and evidence from the text to talk about your ideas with a partner.

Verb Tenses

The **tense** of a verb tells when an action happens.

Grammar Rules Verb Tenses

• For most verbs, add **–ed** to show past tense.	People **called** Thurgood Marshall the "little man's lawyer."
• For some verbs, change the base word before you add **–ed**.	Marshall **worried** about the effects of segregation on African American students.
• Irregular verbs have **special forms** to show past tense.	Marshall **brought** the Browns' case to the Supreme Court. They **won**.
• Use the helping verb **will** before the **main verb** to show future tense.	Rosa Parks's quiet act of protest **will inspire** people for a long time.
• You can also use **am going to**, **are going to**, or **is going to** before a **main verb**.	We **are going to study** the Montgomery bus boycott next February.

Read Verb Tenses

Good writers use correct verb tenses to tell about events. Read this passage from the memoir. What verbs tenses can you find? How can you tell the difference?

> She walked a few steps away, but then she turned around and came back. She said, "There are two girls around the other side, and if you want to go over there with them instead of being in a cell by yourself, I will take you over there."

Write Verb Tenses

Write about an event that occurred during the Civil Rights Movement and how it relates to current events. Include at least two past, present, or future tense verbs. Compare your sentences with a partner's.

Language Frames

- In my opinion, _____ .
- Based on _____ , I conclude that _____ .
- I am convinced that _____ .

Express and Support Opinions

Look at the photo, and listen to the student's opinions. Then use **Language Frames** to express your own opinions about the topic and support them with facts and evidence.

Children Shouldn't Have to Work (((MP3)))

In my opinion, one of the most serious issues in the world is child labor because children must work at jobs that are dangerous, keep them out of school, and stop them from having normal childhoods.

You may think this only happens in faraway countries, but based on historical articles I have read, I conclude that child labor was a huge problem in U.S. history, too. In the early 1900s, many children worked long hours for little pay.

Fortunately, laws now protect children's rights in the U.S., but I believe our work is not done because there are still millions of children in the world who need the same protection. Now that we know about their problems, I am convinced that it's our duty to help them.

Social Studies Vocabulary

Key Words

declaration

defensively

humanity

indignation

innocence

Key Words

Look at these pictures, and read the captions. Use **Key Words** and other words to talk about child labor.

▲ In 1989, many countries signed United Nations agreements and made strong verbal and written **declarations** that officially stated the need to stop child labor around the world.

▲ Unfortunately, millions of children were still forced to work. Factory owners weren't giving children the basic rights of **humanity**. They treated children horribly, making them work long hours in unsafe conditions.

▲ Over time, many people learned about child labor in various countries. They were horrified and felt intense **indignation** and anger.

▲ Factory owners maintained their **innocence** by claiming child labor wasn't their fault. They **defensively** stated that very poor parents made their children work. Many children around the world still work today.

Talk Together

Should people take a stand to end child labor in the world? With a partner, use **Language Frames** from page 328 and **Key Words** to express and support your opinion.

329

Theme

In a story, a **theme** is a general truth or important idea about life or the world. Some stories can include multiple themes. Authors usually don't state a theme directly. Instead, readers must look for details from the title, setting, characters, and plot to determine the theme.

Look Into the Text

That same evening, after dinner, **Iqbal made a solemn declaration** to the men and women who were meeting in the big downstairs room: **"I want to stay and help you free all the children who are slaves in Pakistan."**

"Iqbal's **actions** and **dialogue** give clues about the theme."

Map and Talk

A theme chart can help you collect details that hint at a story's theme. As you read, think about how the details work together to convey a message.

Theme Chart

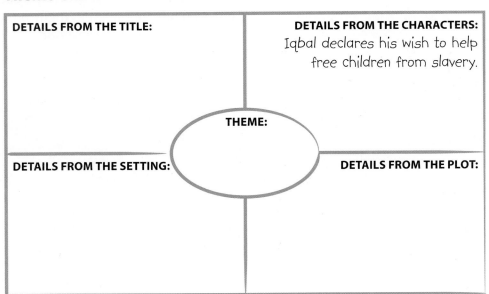

DETAILS FROM THE TITLE:	DETAILS FROM THE CHARACTERS: Iqbal declares his wish to help free children from slavery.
THEME:	
DETAILS FROM THE SETTING:	DETAILS FROM THE PLOT:

Talk Together

Talk with a partner about a familiar story that features a courageous person. Create a theme chart with details that help you understand the theme.

More Key Words

Use these words to talk about *Iqbal: A Novel* and *Roll of Thunder, Hear My Cry.*

authority
(u-**thor**-u-tē) *noun*

When you have **authority**, you have the power to make decisions and direct other people's actions. The teacher has the **authority** to make rules in the classroom.

commitment
(ku-**mit**-munt) *noun*

A **commitment** is a promise to do something. This woman made a **commitment** to volunteer to feed the homeless on weekends.

intention
(in-**ten**-shun) *noun*

An **intention** is an aim or purpose. The runner practices hard because his **intention** is to compete in the Olympics in the future.

presume
(pri-**züm**) *verb*

When you **presume**, you think something is true without being certain. The judge will **presume** that this prisoner is innocent until he is proven guilty.

reinforce
(rē-un-**fors**) *verb*

When you **reinforce** something, you make it stronger. The builders can **reinforce** the floor by adding extra supports.

Talk Together

Work with a partner. Role-play a scene in which two people discuss ways to help others. Use at least two **Key Words** in the scene.

> I made a commitment to help others.

> It is my intention to volunteer, too.

Add words to My Vocabulary Notebook.
NGReach.com

331

Learn to Determine Importance

One way to determine what matters in a text is to pay attention to the most important events and details. Then you can **summarize** this information in your own words.

How to Summarize

1. Identify the topic. Ask, "What is the text mostly about?"

> The topic is _____ .

2. Look for important events and other details.

> Detail #1 is _____ .
> Detail #2 is _____ .

3. Tell about the most important events and details in your own words.

> The _____ is about _____ .

Here's how one student summarized the text.

Look Into the Text

> **Iqbal** **stood up and drew himself to his tallest**, which actually wasn't very tall. **He looked immensely tall to us**, though, as if he could touch the ceiling.
>
> **"I'm not afraid," he said. "I'm not afraid of anybody."** **They believed him.**

> The topic is a boy named Iqbal.

> These details show what Iqbal does and how people react.

> The text is about how Iqbal is determined and respected.

Summarizing the text helps you identify the most important events and details in a text. It can also help you remember what you have read.

Talk Together

Read the editorial and sample notes. Use **Language Frames** to determine importance and summarize the text with a partner.

Editorial

WORLD TIMES NEWSPAPER

Iqbal Masih: A Bonded Child Laborer

In 1994, 12-year-old Iqbal Masih stood on a Boston stage and made a powerful **declaration** against child labor. His journey had been a long, painful one, **reinforced** by his stunted growth and the scars on his hands. Masih was born in Pakistan in 1982, but his childhood **innocence** did not last for long. At age four, Masih became a bonded laborer. He was given to a carpet factory owner to work off a family debt.

Masih and other children were forced to work 12 hours a day in a dirty, airless room. The children quickly learned not to question **authority**. If they made mistakes, they were beaten, burned, or locked in dark closets. They acted **defensively** to protect themselves from attacks. Still, Masih found it hard to control his **indignation** at his treatment. ◄

At age 10, Masih gained his freedom with the help of the Bonded Labor Liberation Front (BLLF). The BLLF had made a **commitment** to fight child labor in Pakistan. Its members worked to free child laborers and to give them food, shelter, and schooling.

You might **presume** that Masih would be ready to lead an easier life, but he had firm **intentions** to end child slavery. He wanted to save other children from the harm he had suffered. He uncovered illegal factories for the BLLF and made speeches against child slavery. In 1994, Masih received the Reebok Human Rights Youth in Action Award for his work. He flew to Boston to accept the award. There he spoke about his life and what he had learned about **humanity** during his fight for children's rights. ◄

The topic is Iqbal Masih and child labor.

Detail #1 is that Iqbal suffered from working.

Detail #2 is that child laborers were treated horribly.

The first section is about how Masih lived in slavery.

◄ = a good place to stop and summarize important events and details

333

Read Biographical Fiction

Genre

Biographical fiction is a story that is based on a real person's life. The main people and events are real, but the story is fiction because the author creates some of the details, such as specific dialogue that people say or a fictional narrator who tells the story.

Setting

The setting of a story is *where* and *when* it takes place. This story takes place in Pakistan during the 1990s. Because this was a real time and place, the setting influenced the characters and plot events.

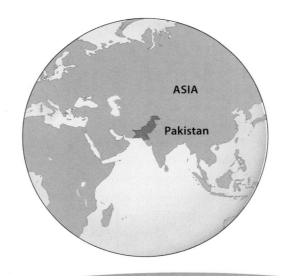

From

Iqbal
A Novel

by Francesco D'Adamo
TRANSLATED BY ANN LEONORI

Comprehension Coach

▸ **Set a Purpose**
Find out about an important **commitment** that a boy named Iqbal makes.

Young Iqbal Masih is a bonded slave in Pakistan, forced to weave carpets for the evil factory owner Hussain Khan until the boy can pay off his family's debts. Iqbal escapes and returns with the police and the leader of the Liberation Front to free the other child laborers. His friend, Fatima, tells the story of their new lives at the Liberation Front headquarters, where the children must decide how to use their newfound freedom.

That same evening, after dinner, Iqbal made a **solemn declaration** to the men and women who were meeting in the big downstairs room: "I want to stay and help you free all the children who are slaves in Pakistan."

Eshan Khan looked at him and smiled.

"That's not possible, Iqbal. You were very courageous when you rebelled and helped us rescue your companions, but you can't stay here with us. You belong to your family. What would your father and mother say if we didn't take you home to them?"

"What good will it do me to go home, if after a year or even sooner I'm a slave again? Or Maria, or Fatima? Or the others? How many children are out there working the way we were?"

"We don't know for sure. There are hundreds of **clandestine** carpet factories just in Lahore, and in the countryside there are the **brick-making kilns**. Up toward the mountains there are the mines. And then there are the farm slaves . . . tens of thousands of children, hundreds of thousands, maybe . . . ."

In Other Words
solemn serious, important
clandestine secret
brick-making kilns ovens in which clay is
   baked to form bricks ▶

336

"You want to free them," said Iqbal. "And, so do I."

Maria and I watched, our mouths wide open, we were so impressed. Iqbal was talking like an adult.

"Think it over, Eshan," one of the men said. "The boy is clever and could be useful. You know how hard it is to get the **magistrates** to **intervene**. Iqbal could sneak in and talk to the children, who would trust him. He can find the proof we need. If it hadn't been for him, we would never have been able to stop Hussain Khan."

Eshan Khan continued to shake his head.

"No. He'd have to learn so many things . . ."

"I'll learn," Iqbal promised. "I've already learned to read and write. Well . . . a little, anyway."

"It's too dangerous. The carpet merchants and the kiln owners are very powerful. The moneylenders are influential. The police tend to protect them—you've already seen that. And the magistrates just **look the other way**. All of us here have been threatened and **persecuted**. No, we can't allow it."

Iqbal stood up and drew himself to his tallest, which actually wasn't very tall. He looked immensely tall to us, though, as if he could touch the ceiling.

"I'm not afraid," he said. "I'm not afraid of anybody."

They believed him.

▼ carpet-weaving loom

In Other Words

magistrates local officers

intervene act

look the other way ignore the problem

persecuted treated unfairly or harshly

Iqbal went home to visit his family. Ten days later Eshan Khan brought him back, and he spent the rest of the day closed up in his room. Toward evening he came out and said, "My mother cried and my father was frightened for me, but now they understand my choice, and they approve. I've promised that I'll go back as often as I can, especially for our holidays, but I want to stay here, Fatima. I want to study. I want to learn everything I can. I want to be a famous lawyer and free all the children in Pakistan."

"Good for you, Iqbal!" exclaimed Maria.

I said the same, but my voice **trembled**.

Iqbal did study. We all did. He also took part in the meetings of the Liberation Front, listening so carefully that his forehead would become wrinkled with the effort to understand.

Less than a month after we had been rescued, Iqbal managed to sneak into a carpet factory that was hidden in a damp cellar in the northern outskirts of Lahore. He found thirty-two children covered with **scabies** and wounds, so thin their ribs almost cut through their skin. He spoke to them. He showed them the scars on his hands to win their trust, and he took photos of the chains, the looms, the water seeping in. The place was raided three days later by some men from the Liberation Front, accompanied by a magistrate and policemen, who arrested the **proprietor** and freed the children.

In Other Words
trembled sounded afraid
scabies itchy skin rashes
proprietor owner

All that night and throughout the next day Maria and I worked alongside Eshan Khan's wife and the other women, carrying pots of hot water back and forth for baths and making beds for the new arrivals.

Were they ever dirty! It was hard to believe that *we* were like that when we arrived.

Iqbal continued to take his declaration seriously. Over the next few months, he helped close eleven more factories. Almost two hundred children were **liberated**. They all passed through Headquarters, which at times looked like an orphanage! They were cared for and then sent back to their families. All the children told the same story, "our" story. They came from isolated villages in the middle of the countryside; there was a bad harvest or an illness, and the families had to ask **for loans** from the moneylenders. Then the families had to **bond their children** to pay back the debt.

Iqbal wanted to do more.

"We have to **hit** the moneylenders," Iqbal said. "They're to blame for everything."

By now he had taken his place in the meetings of the adults, speaking up with **authority**. He was tireless. The minute he finished one mission, he began another.

"We have to send them all to prison, every single one!" he would say.

Maria and I were uncomfortable when he was out **scoping** illegal factories. We worried and waited anxiously for his return.

In Other Words
liberated freed
for loans to borrow money
bond their children force their children to work
hit stop, punish
scoping looking for

▶ **Before You Move On**

1. **Character** Why does Iqbal decide to stay and work on freeing more children?
2. **Theme** What actions does Iqbal take that may provide clues to the theme of the story?

▶ **Predict**

Find out about the dangers Iqbal
faces because of his **commitment**.

One night he didn't come home and we were afraid something had happened to him. He returned the next morning with a black eye and a cut on his cheek.

"I found another workshop," he said, "but they caught me. They smashed the camera, too. Let's just wait a few days, then I'll go back."

Eshan Khan was proud of him and treated him like a son. And Maria and I were treated like daughters. We had everything we needed, but still I fretted sometimes. Iqbal's and my paths were going in different directions, and I felt that soon we would have to separate. I was also occupied by thoughts of my family. Sooner or later my relatives would be found. What would I do then?

But there were problems much more important than mine. Eshan Khan was worried. "We have to be careful," he said, "Because *they*, the moneylenders and the people who get rich by **exploiting** children, won't give in so easily. The more children we liberate, the more exploiters we accuse, the more they will try to silence us. That's what they're afraid of . . . **our voice**. They get rich and fatten where there's silence and ignorance."

One evening I overheard Eshan Khan talking softly to his wife.

"It's Iqbal who worries me. By now they know him. They know that it's thanks to him that we can find them. He's so enthusiastic, but **he's rash**. We'll have to be more cautious."

Soon there were two men on guard in the big downstairs room.

One night something woke us. We heard strange noises, then gunshots. Then there were shouts and the sound of running feet.

"What's happening?" we asked.

No one answered.

Out in the street some people shook their fists at us, and there were

---

In Other Words

exploiting using and hurting
our voice us telling the truth about them
he's rash he acts before he thinks

340

tough-looking men on the sidewalk in front of Headquarters. They would stand there for hours, watching us go in and out.

When I thought about Eshan Khan's *they*, I thought of Hussain Khan, but I also realized *they* had to be something even bigger and much worse.

Then came the **episode** in the market to **reinforce** my fears.

Even in a city as big and modern as Lahore, the outdoor market is the true center of life and activity. Sooner or later during the day everybody passes through, perhaps to shop and meet friends, perhaps simply to look at people. **Periodically** the activists of the Liberation Front would go to the market, where they would build a little platform to speak from. Over the platform they hung a banner that said NO MORE CHILD LABOR, and there were signs with **slogans** against bonded labor and slavery.

In Other Words
episode event
Periodically Sometimes
slogans messages

The volunteers distributed handouts exactly like the one Iqbal had brought back to us at Hussain Khan's. The men gave short speeches, using a big trumpet-thing they called a megaphone.

A little crowd always gathered. The merchants, especially the richest ones, ridiculed and insulted the speakers. They even threw things at them. The majority of the audience listened **passively**. Only a few had enough **nerve** to show timid approval. These were usually farmers or laborers, usually people who understood what it meant to lose a child in that way. At least, that's what Iqbal *told* us, for Maria and I weren't allowed to go. They said it was too dangerous.

That day Iqbal spoke, too. He stood balanced precariously on a fruit crate, holding the heavy megaphone. Despite his shyness and embarrassment, despite the shouting, the whistling, and the racket of the onlookers,

▲ megaphone

he managed to talk about his experience. He spoke about Hussain Khan and the carpet factory, about children chained to their looms. Then he **named names**. He shouted all the names he had heard during the meetings at Headquarters, the names of the great moneylenders, the names of rich, important, mysterious men who lived in luxury in the center of town, who traveled, who had business all over the world: Eshan Khan's *they*.

He called them **flesh merchants**, exploiters, **vultures**.

A riot broke out in the square. A small group tried to attack the platform, pushing, slapping. The police had to intervene, not very willingly.

In Other Words
passively without commenting
nerve courage
named names said the names of the guilty men
flesh merchants people who sell other people
vultures birds that feed on dead animals

They weren't in the square, of course. They don't go to the open-air market, but evidently they have lots of supporters.

The next morning, Eshan Khan came in with a pile of newspapers under his arm. There were articles in all of Lahore's papers, and also in a Karachi paper. Two of them even had printed photos of Iqbal, standing on the platform with that funny trumpet-thing in front of his mouth.

One of the papers called him "the courageous child who had **denounced his oppressors**," and another talked about the "shameful exploitation of a child's **innocence**."

"This is a good thing, isn't it, Father?" he asked Eshan Khan. "You said that *they* keep getting stronger thanks to ignorance and silence. Well, this isn't silence."

"Yes, Iqbal," Eshan Khan said, "this is good for **our cause**."

But he didn't seem convinced. He looked worried.

In Other Words

denounced his oppressors publicly blamed the people who had hurt him

our cause the work we are doing to end child slavery

▶ **Before You Move On**

1. **Explain** According to Eshan Khan, what keeps the factory owners and moneylenders strong?

2. **Theme** What does Iqbal do and say at the market? What clues do they give about the theme of the story?

I remember that period so well. Iqbal was happy, enthusiastic about everything, hungry and thirsty for anything new.

We were beginning to get used to our new life, to freedom. We could go out whenever we wanted . . . well, almost. Eshan Khan's wife **kept a close eye on** us. Once she gave us some money and we went to the movies. It was just like Karim said. We saw an Indian film that lasted four hours and I cried the whole time. Iqbal was nasty and wouldn't go see it a second time. We discovered television. We listened to strange music that came from far away—from America, they said.

Iqbal was full of plans for the future. He talked about them to Maria and me. He wasn't afraid of all the new things. I was, at least a little. Everything was happening so fast, or maybe I was afraid the happy dream would end, too fast.

One day a foreign person in strange clothes came to Headquarters. He said he was an American reporter. He interviewed Iqbal and Eshan Khan for two hours. A few days later an international **correspondent** came.

"When people **abroad** know about our cause, they'll help us and we'll be safer," said Eshan Khan.

One night we were awakened by loud explosions. We could hear screams and see flames rising up to the windows on the second floor. We tried to go downstairs but Eshan Khan stopped us.

"You stay here!" he roared.

Someone had thrown two **incendiary** bombs against Headquarters. A man was injured and had to go to the hospital. *They* had sent a warning.

In Other Words
kept a close eye on carefully watched
correspondent reporter
abroad from other countries
incendiary explosive fire

One dull, rainy day at the beginning of November, Eshan Khan called Iqbal and me into his personal office. We entered the small, whitewashed room, which was almost empty and very neat. It stood in complete contrast to the rest of the house, which was full of papers, signs, color, and confusion. Here was a desk under neat piles of papers, a telephone, a chair that didn't look very comfortable, makings for tea, and a strong smell of tobacco. Eshan Khan was walking impatiently back and forth, his eyes shining. He was holding a big brightly colored ball. We had already seen it a few times and we thought, *Oh, no! Another geography lesson.*

Eshan Khan spun the ball and showed us a big area colored yellow. "This is the United States," he said. "It's a big and important country."

"I know," said Iqbal, hoping to avoid a lesson. "It's the place where they make the songs."

"Where there's Hollywood and the movie stars," I said to help him.

Ignoring our show of knowledge of American culture, Eshan Khan pointed to a small black spot on the edge of an enormous sea.

"This city is Boston," he continued. "Every year a company called Reebok awards a prize that's called 'Youth in Action.' It's given to a young person who has done something **of merit** in any country in the world."

"I know Reebok," insisted Iqbal. "They make shoes. I've wanted a pair for months, but they're too expensive."

"The prize is fifteen thousand dollars."

"How many rupees is that?" I asked.

"More than we can imagine. This year the prize has been awarded to Iqbal."

Silence.

"To me?" Iqbal asked, confused.

"Yes, and do you know what it means? It means that now you're known all over the world and so is our fight against child labor. It means that from now on, *they* will have to be careful before they try to **touch us** in any way. It's a victory, Iqbal, and it's all thanks to you. You and I will go to Boston to receive the prize. But first"—Eshan Khan turned the globe—"we'll stop here."

He pointed to another country.

"This is Sweden," he said.

▲ Visby, Sweden

In Other Words
of merit valuable, important
touch us hurt or bother us

"And what's that?"

"A country where it's very cold. It's in Europe. There's going to be an international conference on labor problems. People will be coming from all over the world. They want to hear you speak."

"Me?"

We were **astonished**. It was like a dream. It was difficult for us to believe that others, in that faraway and unknown place called the world, knew about us and our suffering. We were **nobodies, wretches** who just a year before had been working at our looms, some of us chained to them. And all those people wanted to listen to Iqbal!

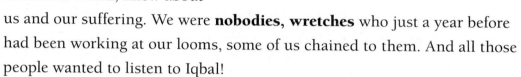

"There's more," said Eshan Khan. "A university near Boston has given you a scholarship. It means you'll be able to **get a degree**. Didn't you say you want to become a lawyer?"

Iqbal nodded without speaking.

"But . . . that means . . . we'll have to go . . . "

"We'll be away almost a month," said Eshan Khan. "Just wait. You'll like traveling. You'll see so many new things. When we get back you'll begin your studies, and later on you can go visit your family. You must be happy."

"I am happy," answered Iqbal, "but I want to stay here, with you and Fatima and Maria. I want to free more children."

In Other Words
astonished surprised
nobodies, wretches people no one cared about
get a degree graduate from college

347

"You'll still be helping us. You're important. But later on, if you become a good lawyer, you'll be even more useful.

"Today there's good news for Fatima, too. We've found your village, and your family. You'll be going home."

My heart jumped. Home! I could hardly remember it. And my mother? And my brothers and sisters?

Suddenly I wanted to cry, but I felt silly. Why should I want to cry at good news? I was about to return home—free! Iqbal was going to receive a rightful reward for what he had done. Everything was going well. Whoever could have **foreseen all this** when we were working like slaves for Hussain?

I did cry, and it was because I was so happy.

The next two weeks just flew by. The big pink house boiled over with activity, everyone running from one end to the other, getting things ready for the journey. Reporters from Pakistan and abroad wanted to know about the prize. The garden was always full of people. For me, every sunset held sadness and hope.

How much longer before Iqbal left? Nine days.

I have memories of Eshan Khan talking into three microphones. Of a stranger wandering around, taking photos of all of us. I should have made him give me one—at least I'd have that now. I remember the women kneeling with pins in their mouths, fitting the Western-style suit that Iqbal would wear at the ceremony. It had

In Other Words
foreseen all this known this would happen

a jacket, trousers, and a vest, all in a heavy dark blue material. It would be cold where he was going.

One day I came upon Iqbal, all alone in the middle of an empty room, while he was practicing the speech he would give in Sweden and in Boston. He **tripped over** every sixth word, and then said, "Come on, Fatima, help me!" so I took the written speech and, reading a little slowly, gave him the right cues.

" . . . *Every day in Pakistan seven million children get up in the dark before dawn. They work all day, through evening. They make rugs, they make bricks, they work the fields, they go down into the mines. They don't play or run or shout. They never laugh. They're slaves and they wear chains on their feet. . . .*

" . . . *So long as there's a child in this world who is* **deprived of** *his childhood, a child who is beaten, violated, or exploited, nobody can say:* It's not my business. *That's not true. It's your business, too. And it's not true that there's no hope. Look at me. I had hope. You, ladies and gentlemen, you must have courage. . . . "*

Iqbal Masih accepts his Reebok Human Rights Award in Boston on December 7, 1994. ▶

▶ **Before You Move On**

1. **Make Inferences** Why does Eshan Khan encourage Iqbal to become a lawyer instead of staying in Pakistan?

2. **Summarize** In your own words, tell the most important details in Iqbal's speech.

Epilogue

Iqbal Masih was murdered on Easter Sunday in 1995, in Muritke, a village some thirty kilometers from Lahore, Pakistan. He was about thirteen.

His murderers have never been discovered.

"He was killed by the **Carpet Mafia**," Eshan Khan declared.

Iqbal's name has become the symbol of the battle to liberate millions of children throughout the world from violence and slavery. ❖

▲ **Iqbal Masih**

In Other Words

Carpet Mafia carpet factory owners and moneylenders that Iqbal was trying to stop

Meet the Author

Francesco D'Adamo

Francesco D'Adamo has published several popular fiction books for young adults. He enjoys telling stories from an outsider's perspective, as he did in *Iqbal: A Novel*. D'Adamo believes that stories about people like Iqbal Masih can challenge readers to make the world a better place and encourage them "to be curious and restless, trying to understand what kind of a world we're living in and what they can do."

D'Adamo has a passion for storytelling that keeps him writing. He believes that if you have a story to tell, you must write it before doing anything else. He calls writing "the sacred flame." What story do you have burning in you?

Writer's Craft

The author uses strong, direct words to start the story. For example, Iqbal declares: "I want to stay and help you free all the children who are slaves in Pakistan." How does this strong opening grab your attention? Write a brief speech about your beliefs on an issue, including a strong opening.

Key Words

authority	indignation
commitment	innocence
declaration	intention
defensively	presume
humanity	reinforce

Talk About It

1. *Iqbal: A Novel* is biographical fiction. It adds fictional details to facts about the life of the real Iqbal Masih. Which parts of the story are factual and which are most likely fictional? Give examples from the text.

2. Is Iqbal's **commitment** to freeing child laborers in Pakistan brave or foolish? Express and support your opinion using examples from the story.

3. Compare Iqbal and the factory owners. Use text evidence to identify their motivations and **intentions** for child laborers.

4. A girl named Fatima narrates the story. How does her character change as the story's plot unfolds? Use text evidence to support your answer.

5. Based on what you have read and what you know, what can you infer about families like the Masihs who have to bond their children to factory owners?

6. What conclusions can you draw about how the government of Pakistan views child labor? Base your conclusion on evidence from the text.

Learn test-taking strategies and answer more questions.
 NGReach.com

Write About It

Imagine you are a journalist visiting the open-air market in Lahore when Iqbal bravely addresses the crowd. How would you report the story? Write a news report to share your observations. Use at least three **Key Words**.

> **"Declarations Against Child Labor"**
>
> LAHORE, PAKISTAN. A small riot broke out yesterday when a young boy named Iqbal Masih accused factory owners of robbing children of their **innocence** by forcing them to work in factories.

Theme

Use the theme chart to record clues from the story that help convey an important theme, or message, in *Iqbal: A Novel*.

Theme Chart

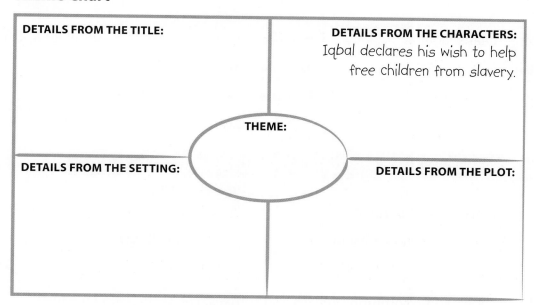

DETAILS FROM THE TITLE:

DETAILS FROM THE CHARACTERS:
Iqbal declares his wish to help free children from slavery.

THEME:

DETAILS FROM THE SETTING:

DETAILS FROM THE PLOT:

Use your theme chart to explain one of the story's themes to a partner. Describe how you used clues from the story to determine the theme.

Fluency  Comprehension Coach

Use the Comprehension Coach to practice reading with expression. Rate your reading.

Talk Together

How do the characters in *Iqbal: A Novel* take a stand against injustice even when faced with serious obstacles? Discuss your ideas with a partner. Use **Key Words** and evidence from the text.

Word Parts

Adding a **word part** to a base word changes the meaning of the base word. Knowing common **prefixes** and **suffixes** can help you understand new words. Use word parts to figure out the meanings of the examples below.

EXAMPLES

The prefix *re-* means "again."

prefix	base word

re- + use = reuse

The suffix *-ate* means "having or containing."

base word	suffix

fortune + ate = fortunate

Prefix/ Suffix	Origin	Meaning	Example
re-	Latin	again	rewind, rearrange
in-	Latin	not, lack of	injustice, inaccurate
-ate	Latin	to have or to contain	fortunate, affectionate
-ity	Latin	state or quality	captivity, opportunity

The chart above shows some common prefixes and suffixes. The suffix *-ation* means "the act or result of." What do you think the word *declaration* means?

Try It

Read the sentences. Then answer the questions. Use the chart to help you.

Iqbal fought against the <u>inhumanity</u> of the factory owners towards the child laborers. He was <u>passionate</u> about setting the slaves free.

1. **Look for the prefix *in-*. What is the best meaning for the word <u>inhumanity</u>?**

   A   lack of cruelty

   B   lack of people

   C   lack of creativity

   D   lack of respect

2. **Look for the suffix *-ate*. What is the best meaning for <u>passionate</u>?**

   A   lacking passion

   B   understanding passion

   C   ignoring passion

   D   feeling passion

Connect Across Texts You read about how Iqbal fought for children's rights. Now read how a family challenges **discrimination** against schoolchildren in the 1930s.

Genre A **historical fiction** story takes place during a real time in the past. The characters, plot, and setting all seem real.

From Roll of Thunder, Hear My Cry

by Mildred D. Taylor
ILLUSTRATED BY ROBERT BARRETT

"Cassie Logan?"

I looked up, startled.

"Cassie Logan!"

"Yes, ma'am?" I jumped up quickly to face Miss Crocker.

"Aren't you willing to work and share?"

"Yes'm."

"Then say so!"

"Yes'm," I murmured, sliding back into my seat as Mary Lou, Gracey, and Alma giggled. Here it was only five minutes into the new school year and already I was in trouble.

▶ **Before You Move On**

1. **Preview** Based on the illustration, what can you learn about the setting of the story?
2. **Make Inferences** What is Cassie's attitude toward school? Cite evidence from the text to support your answer.

355

By ten o'clock, Miss Crocker had rearranged our seating and written our names on her seating chart. I was still sitting beside Gracey and Alma but we had been moved from the third to the first row in front of a small potbellied stove. Although being **eyeball to eyeball with** Miss Crocker was nothing to look forward to, the prospect of being warm once the cold weather set in was nothing to be **sneezed at** either, so I resolved to make the best of my rather **dubious** position.

Now Miss Crocker made a startling announcement: This year we would all have books.

Everyone gasped, for most of the students had never handled a book at all besides the family Bible. I admit that even I was somewhat excited. Although Mama had several books, I had never had one of my very own.

"Now we're very fortunate to get these readers," Miss Crocker explained while we eagerly **awaited the unveiling**. "The county superintendent of schools himself brought these books down here for our use and we must take extra-good care of them." She moved toward her desk. "So let's all promise that we'll take the best care possible of these new books." She stared down, expecting our response. "All right, all together, let's repeat, 'We promise to take good care of our new books.'" She looked sharply at me as she spoke.

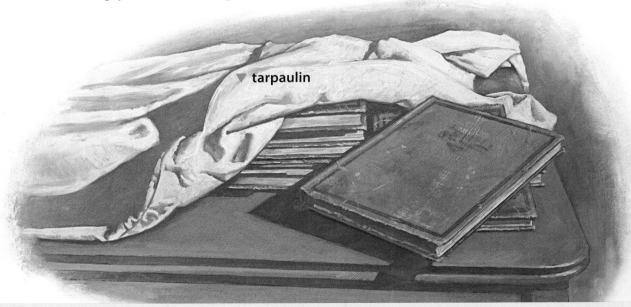

tarpaulin

In Other Words
eyeball to eyeball with so close to
sneezed at given up
dubious awkward, uncomfortable
awaited the unveiling waited to see the books

"WE PROMISE TO TAKE GOOD CARE OF OUR NEW BOOKS!"

"Fine," Miss Crocker beamed, then proudly threw back the tarpaulin.

Sitting so close to the desk, I could see that the covers of the books, a motley red, were badly worn and that the gray edges of the pages had been **marred** by pencils, crayons, and ink. My anticipation at having my own book **ebbed to a sinking** disappointment. But Miss Crocker continued to beam as she called each fourth grader to her desk and, recording a number in her roll book, handed him or her a book.

As I returned from my trip to her desk, I noticed the first graders anxiously watching the disappearing pile. Miss Crocker must have noticed them too, for as I sat down she said, "Don't worry, little ones, there are plenty of readers for you too. See there on Miss Davis's desk." Wide eyes turned to the covered teacher's platform directly in front of them and an audible sigh of relief swelled in the room.

I glanced across at Little Man, his face lit in eager excitement. I knew that he could not see the soiled covers or the marred pages from where he sat, and even though his **penchant** for cleanliness was often annoying, I did not like to think of his disappointment when he saw the books as they really were. But there was nothing that I could do about it, so I opened my book to its center and began browsing through the spotted pages. Girls with blond braids and boys with blue eyes stared up at me. I found a story about a boy and his dog lost in a cave and began reading while Miss Crocker's voice **droned on monotonously**.

Suddenly I grew conscious of a break in that monotonous tone and I looked up. Miss Crocker was sitting at Miss Davis's desk with the first-grade books stacked before her, staring fiercely down at Little Man, who was pushing a book back upon the desk.

"What's that you said, Clayton Chester Logan?" she asked.

The room became gravely silent. Everyone knew that Little Man was in big trouble for no one, but no one, ever called Little Man "Clayton Chester" unless she or he meant serious business.

In Other Words

marred ruined

ebbed to a sinking changed to a feeling of

penchant need, desire

droned on monotonously was boring to listen to

▶ **Before You Move On**

1. **Make Inferences** Why is Miss Crocker so excited about the books?

2. **Summarize** Why is Cassie disappointed by the books? Use text evidence as you retell the important details.

Little Man knew this too. His lips parted slightly as he took his hands from the book. He quivered, but he did not take his eyes from Miss Crocker. "I—I said may I have another book please, ma'am," he squeaked. "That one's dirty."

"Dirty!" Miss Crocker echoed, **appalled** by such **temerity**. She stood up, gazing down upon Little Man like a bony giant, but Little Man raised his head and continued to look into her eyes. "Dirty! And just who do you think you are, Clayton Chester? Here the county is giving us these wonderful books during these hard times and you're going to stand there and tell me that the book's too dirty? Now you take that book or get nothing at all!"

Little Man lowered his eyes and said nothing as he stared at the book. For several moments he stood there, his face barely visible above the desk, then he turned and looked at the few remaining books and, seeming to realize that they were as badly soiled as the one Miss Crocker had given him, he looked across the room at me. I nodded and Little Man, glancing up again at Miss Crocker, slid the book from the edge of the desk, and with his back straight and his head up returned to his seat.

Miss Crocker sat down again. "Some people around here seem to be **giving themselves airs**. I'll tolerate no more of that," she scowled. "Sharon Lake, come get your book."

I watched Little Man as he scooted into his seat beside two other little boys. He sat for a while with **a stony** face looking out the window; then, evidently accepting the fact that the book in front of him was the best that he could expect, he turned and opened it. But as he stared at the book's inside cover, his face clouded, changing from sulky acceptance to puzzlement. His brows furrowed. Then his eyes grew wide, and suddenly he sucked in his breath and sprang from his chair like a wounded animal, flinging the book onto the floor and stomping madly upon it.

In Other Words
appalled disgusted
temerity boldness
giving themselves airs thinking they are better than others
a stony an angry

Miss Crocker rushed to Little Man and grabbed him up in powerful hands. She shook him vigorously, then set him on the floor again. "Now, just **what's gotten into you**, Clayton Chester?"

But Little Man said nothing. He just stood staring down at the open book, shivering with **indignant** anger.

"Pick it up," she ordered.

"No!" defied Little Man.

"No? I'll give you ten seconds to pick up that book, boy, or I'm going to get my **switch**."

In Other Words

what's gotten into you why are you acting like this

indignant intense

switch weapon to punish you

▶ **Before You Move On**

1. **Author's Style** How does the author show the feeling, or mood, in the classroom?

2. **Character** How would you describe Miss Crocker? Use text evidence to support your answer.

Little Man bit his lower lip, and I knew that he was not going to pick up the book. Rapidly, I turned to the inside cover of my own book and saw immediately what had made Little Man so furious. Stamped on the inside cover was a chart which read:

PROPERTY OF THE BOARD OF EDUCATION
Spokane County, Mississippi
September, *1922*

CHRONOLOGICAL ISSUANCE	DATE OF ISSUANCE	CONDITION OF BOOK	RACE OF STUDENT
1	*September 1922*	*New*	*White*
2	*September 1923*	*Excellent*	*White*
3	*September 1924*	*Excellent*	*White*
4	*September 1925*	*Very Good*	*White*
5	*September 1926*	*Good*	*White*
6	*September 1927*	*Good*	*White*
7	*September 1928*	*Average*	*White*
8	*September 1929*	*Average*	*White*
9	*September 1930*	*Average*	*White*
10	*September 1931*	*Poor*	*White*
11	*September 1932*	*Poor*	*White*
12	*September 1933*	*Very Poor*	*nigra*

The blank lines continued down to line 20 and I knew that they had all been reserved for black students. A knot of anger swelled in my throat and held there. But as Miss Crocker directed Little Man to bend over the "whipping" chair, I put aside my anger and jumped up.

"Miz Crocker, don't, please!" I cried. Miss Crocker's dark eyes warned me not to say another word. "I know why he done it!"

"You want **part of this switch**, Cassie?"

"No'm," I said hastily. "I just wanna tell you how come Little Man **done what he done**."

"Sit down!" she ordered as I hurried toward her with the open book in my hand.

Holding the book up to her, I said, "See, Miz Crocker, see what it says. They give us these ole books when they didn't want 'em no more.

She regarded me impatiently, but did not look at the book. "Now how could he know what it says? He can't read."

"Yes'm, he can. He been reading since he was four. He can't read all them big words, but he can read them columns. See what's in the last row. Please look, Miz Crocker."

This time Miss Crocker did look, but her face did not change. Then, holding up her head, she gazed unblinkingly down at me.

"S-see what they called us," I said, afraid she had not seen.

"That's what you are," she said coldly. "Now go sit down."

I shook my head, realizing now that Miss Crocker did not even know what I was talking about. She had looked at the page and had understood nothing.

"I said sit down, Cassie!"

I started slowly toward my desk, but as the hickory stick **sliced the tense air**, I turned back around. "Miz Crocker," I said, "I don't want my book neither."

The switch landed hard upon Little Man's upturned bottom. Miss Crocker looked questioningly at me as I reached up to her desk and placed the book upon it. Then she swung the switch five more times and, discovering that Little Man had no **intention** of crying, ordered him up.

"All right, Cassie," she sighed, turning to me, "come on and get yours."

In Other Words

part of this switch to be punished also

done what he done did something you thought was wrong

sliced the tense air came down to hit Little Man

▶ **Before You Move On**

1. **Theme** How is the theme of prejudice conveyed through the school books?

2. **Interpret** What does Miss Crocker mean when she says to Cassie, "come on and get yours"?

By the end of the school day I had decided that I would tell Mama everything before Miss Crocker had a chance to do so. From nine years of **trial and error**, I had learned that punishment was always less severe when I poured out the whole truth to Mama on my own before she had heard anything from anyone else. I knew that Miss Crocker had not spoken to Mama during the lunch period, for she had spent the whole hour in the classroom preparing for the afternoon session.

As soon as class was dismissed I sped from the room, weaving a path through throngs of students happy to be free. But before I could reach the seventh-grade-class building, I had the **misfortune to collide with** Mary Lou's father.

Mr. Wellever looked down on me with surprise that I would actually bump into him, then proceeded to lecture me on the virtues of watching where one was going. Meanwhile Miss Crocker briskly crossed the lawn to Mama's class building. By the time I escaped Mr. Wellever, she had already disappeared into the darkness of the hallway.

Mama's classroom was in the back. I crept silently along the quiet hall and peeped cautiously into the open doorway. Mama, pushing a strand of her long, crinkly hair back into the chignon at the base of her slender neck, was seated at her desk watching Miss Crocker thrust a book before her. "Just look at that, Mary," Miss Crocker said, thumping the book twice with her forefinger. "A perfectly good book ruined. Look at that broken binding and those foot marks all over it."

Mama did not speak as she studied the book.

"And here's the one Cassie wouldn't take," she said, placing a second book on Mama's desk with an outraged slam. "At least she didn't have a tantrum and stomp all over hers. I tell you, Mary, I just don't know what got into those children today. I always knew Cassie **was rather high-strung**, but Little Man! He's always such a perfect little gentleman."

Mama glanced at the book I had rejected and opened the front cover so that the offensive pages of both books faced her. "You say Cassie said

In Other Words
trial and error making mistakes
misfortune to collide with bad luck to meet
was rather high-strung could get angry easily

it was because of this front page that she and Little Man didn't want the books?" Mama asked quietly.

"Yes, **ain't that something**?" Miss Crocker said, forgetting her teacher-training-school diction in her **indignation**. "The very idea! That's on all the books, and why they got so upset about it I'll never know."

"You punish them?" asked Mama, glancing up at Miss Crocker.

"Well, I certainly did! Whipped both of them good with my hickory stick. Wouldn't you have?" When Mama did not reply, she added **defensively**, "I had a perfect right to."

"Of course you did, Daisy," Mama said, turning back to the books again. "They disobeyed you." But her tone was so quiet and **noncommittal** that I knew Miss Crocker was not satisfied with her reaction.

"Well, I thought you would've wanted to know, Mary, in case you wanted to **give them a piece of your mind** also."

Mama smiled up at Miss Crocker and said rather absently, "Yes, of course, Daisy. Thank you." Then she opened her desk drawer and pulled out some paper, a pair of scissors, and a small brown bottle.

In Other Words
ain't that something can you believe that
noncommittal unconcerned, calm
give them a piece of your mind yell at them

▶ **Before You Move On**

1. **Make Inferences** How does Miss Crocker expect Mama to respond to Cassie and Little Man's behavior?

2. **Draw Conclusions** Why is Mama quiet and calm as Miss Crocker tells her what has happened?

Miss Crocker, **dismayed** by Mama's seeming unconcern for the seriousness of the matter, thrust her shoulders back and began moving away from the desk. "You understand that if they don't have those books to study from, I'll have to fail them in both reading and composition, since I plan to base all my lessons around—" She stopped abruptly and stared in amazement at Mama. "Mary, what in the world are you doing?"

Mama did not answer. She had trimmed the paper to the size of the books and was now dipping a gray-looking glue from the brown bottle onto the inside cover of one of the books. Then she took the paper and placed it over the glue.

"Mary Logan, do you know what you're doing? That book belongs to the county. If somebody from the superintendent's office ever comes down here and sees that book, you'll be in real trouble."

Mama laughed and picked up the other book. "In the first place no one cares enough to come down here, and in the second place if anyone should come, maybe he could see all the things we need—current books for all of our subjects, not just somebody's old throwaways, desks, paper, blackboards, erasers, maps, chalk . . . " **Her voice trailed off** as she glued the second book.

In Other Words
dismayed upset
Her voice trailed off She stopped speaking

364

"Biting the hand that feeds you. That's what you're doing, Mary Logan, biting the hand that feeds you."

Again, Mama laughed. "If that's the case, Daisy, I don't think I need that little bit of food." With the second book finished, she stared at a small pile of seventh-grade books on her desk.

"Well, I just think you're spoiling those children, Mary. They've got to learn how things are sometime."

"Maybe so," said Mama, "but that doesn't mean they have to accept them . . . and maybe we don't either."

Miss Crocker **gazed suspiciously at** Mama. Although Mama had been a teacher at Great Faith for fourteen years, ever since she had graduated from the Crandon Teacher Training School at nineteen, she was still considered by many of the other teachers as a **disrupting maverick**. Her ideas were always a bit too radical and her statements a bit too **pointed**. The fact that she had not grown up in Spokane County but in the Delta made her even **more suspect**, and the more traditional thinkers like Miss Crocker were wary of her. "Well, if anyone ever does come from the county and sees Cassie's and Little Man's books messed up like that," she said, "I certainly won't accept the responsibility for them."

"It will be easy enough for anyone to see whose responsibility it is, Daisy, by opening any seventh-grade book. Because tomorrow I'm going to 'mess them up' too."

Miss Crocker, finding nothing else to say, turned imperiously and headed for the door. I dashed across the hall and awaited her exit, then crept back.

Mama remained at her desk, sitting very still. For a long time she did not move. When she did, she picked up one of the seventh-grade books and began to glue again. I wanted to go and help her, but something warned me that now was not the time to make my presence known, and I left.

I would wait until the evening to talk to her; there was no rush now. She understood. ◆

In Other Words
gazed suspiciously at did not seem to believe
disrupting maverick rulebreaker
pointed direct, strong
more suspect harder to trust

▶ **Before You Move On**

1. **Use Text Evidence** How does Mama feel about "the way things are"? Give examples from the text to support your answer.

2. **Character's Motive** Why does Mama "mess up" the books? Is that what she is really doing? Explain.

Key Words

authority	indignation
commitment	innocence
declaration	intention
defensively	presume
humanity	reinforce

Compare Themes

Both *Iqbal: A Novel* and *Roll of Thunder, Hear My Cry* are stories about young characters who take a stand. Read the themes listed in the comparison chart and add two of your own. Determine if each theme applies to the story, and then explain how it is developed using specific evidence from the text. Work with a partner to complete the chart. Then discuss the themes and whether they are still true in your community.

Comparison Chart

Themes	Iqbal: A Novel	Roll of Thunder, Hear My Cry
People should stand up to injustices.	Yes. Iqbal bravely "names names" at the open-air market.	
Taking a stand can cause problems.		

Talk Together

Think about both stories and the chart above. How do the themes help you understand why each character takes a stand? What issues do they have in common? Discuss your ideas with a partner. Use **Key Words** and evidence from the text.

Perfect Tense Verbs

Perfect tense verbs show how actions are related to one another in time.

Grammar Rules Perfect Tense Verbs

Tense	When Do You Use It?	Examples
Present Perfect	• Use for actions that began in the past and are still going on	Little Man **has disliked** dirty things since he was a boy.
	• Use for actions that happened at an unknown past time	The books **have been used** by many other students in the past.
Past Perfect	• Use for actions completed before another past action	The other students **had accepted** their books before Cassie opened hers.
Future Perfect	• Use for actions that will happen before a future time	By the next day, Mama **will have changed** all the books.

Read Perfect Tense Verbs

Good writers choose verb tenses carefully to show when story events happen. Read this passage from *Roll of Thunder, Hear My Cry*. How does the author's use of verb tenses help you understand the timing of events?

> Rapidly, I turned to the inside cover of my own book and saw immediately what had made Little Man so furious. . . . The blank lines continued down to line 20 and I knew that they had all been reserved for black students.

Write Perfect Tense Verbs

Discuss Miss Crocker's conversation with Mama. Then write sentences that describe why the children were upset about the books and what Mama intends to do. Use perfect tense verbs in each sentence. Compare your sentences with your partner's.

Write as a Citizen

Write an Argument

What can you do to take a stand and help your fellow citizens? Write a speech that persuades people to take action.

Study a Model

In an argument, you present your claim, or viewpoint. You use reasons and evidence to show why others should agree with your claim and change what they think or do. Read Michael's argument about one way he wants others to take action.

Do the Right Thing!
by Michael Napp

Have you ever seen an accident or spotted a stranger who was hurt or sick? What did you do? Some people just look the other way. **I believe that bystanders have a responsibility to help in these situations in any way they can.**

Bystanders should help those in need **because it is the right thing to do.** They should treat others the way they would want to be treated.

Another reason to help is that **bystanders can save lives**. In many cases, someone may die without immediate medical help. For example, if a bystander gives CPR to a heart attack victim right away, the victim's chance of survival is doubled or tripled, according to the American Heart Association. Even bystanders who don't know much about CPR or first aid can help by calling 911.

So the next time you see an accident or a sick or injured stranger, don't look the other way. Stop and help!

The introduction captures readers' attention with thought-provoking questions. Then Michael clearly states his **claim**.

Signal words connect the claim and the **reasons** for the claim.

Michael develops and supports the reasons with relevant evidence.

The conclusion follows from the argument and tells what action Michael wants people to take.

Prewrite

1. **Choose a Topic** What persuasive argument could you make to convince others to take action? Talk with a partner to find an idea.

Language Frames	
Tell Your Ideas	**Respond to Ideas**
• One thing I feel strongly about is _____ . • One way to take action is _____ . • I'd like to persuade people to _____ .	• I'm not clear about your viewpoint about _____ . Can you clarify? • I'm not sure exactly what you want people to do about _____ . Can you tell me more?

2. **Gather Information** What reasons and evidence will you use to support your claim? Where can you locate credible sources for your evidence?

3. **Get Organized** Use a chart to organize your ideas.

Claim, Reasons, and Evidence Chart

Claim	Reasons and Evidence	Action Needed
Bystanders have a responsibility to help when they see a person in need.	It is the right thing to do.	

Draft

Use your chart and the reasons and evidence you collected to write your draft.

- Begin by stating your claim, or viewpoint.

- Support your claim with reasons and evidence.

- Conclude by telling readers what you want them to think or do.

Revise

1. **Read, Retell, Respond** Read your draft aloud to a partner. Your partner listens and then summarizes your main points in his or her own words. Then talk about ways to improve your writing.

Language Frames	
Summarize	**Make Suggestions**
• The _____ is about _____ .	• The beginning of your argument would be more engaging if you _____ .
• Your claim is _____ .	• The relationship between your claim and reasons isn't clear. Could you add a signal word, such as _____ ?
• The reasons you gave to support your claim are _____ .	
• You want people to _____ .	• Could you add more evidence to develop your idea about _____ ?

2. **Make Changes** Think about your draft and your partner's suggestions. Use the Revising Marks on page 617 to mark your changes.

   • Does your argument begin in an engaging way? Start with a thought-provoking question or statement to catch your readers' attention.

   > Have you ever seen an accident or spotted a stranger who was hurt or sick? What did you do?
   > ~~People may see accidents or strangers who are hurt or sick.~~

   • Did you connect your claim and reasons? Would adding signal words make the connections clearer?

   > Bystanders should help others who are injured or sick. *because* It is the right thing to do.

370

Edit and Proofread

Work with a partner to edit and proofread your argument. Pay special attention to verb tenses and agreement. Use the marks on page 618 to show your changes.

Use the marks on page 618 to show your changes.

Publish

1. **On Your Own** Make a final copy of your argument. Put the key points on note cards and present the argument to your class as a persuasive speech.

Presentation Tips	
If you are the speaker . . .	**If you are the listener . . .**
Speak clearly at a good pace to keep the speech lively.	Listen for the speaker's main argument and support. Take notes to record the most important ideas.
Use visuals to present and elaborate on your ideas in a clear and understandable way.	Do you understand the speaker's reasons and evidence? Ask questions for clarification.

2. **With a Group** Gather all the arguments from your class to create a special-edition newspaper. Add pictures and other articles related to your topics. Print copies of your newspaper to share around school.

DO THE RIGHT THING!
by Michael Napp

Have you ever seen an accident or spotted a stranger who was hurt or sick? What did you do? Some people just look the other way. I believe that bystanders have a responsibility to help in these situations in any way they can.

Bystanders should help those in need because it is the right thing to do. They should treat others the way they would want to be treated.

Another reason to help is that bystanders can save lives. In many cases, someone may die without immediate medical help. For example, if a bystander gives CPR to a heart attack victim right away, the victim's chance of survival is doubled or tripled, according to the American Heart Association. Even bystanders who don't know much about CPR or first aid can help by calling 911.

So the next time you see an accident or a sick or injured stranger, don't look the other way. Stop and help! ■

BIG Question

Why do people take a stand?

Talk Together

In this unit, you found many answers to the **Big Question**. Now use your concept map to discuss it. Think about the different reasons for taking a stand that were presented in the selections. What did the people or characters take a stand for, and why?

Idea Web

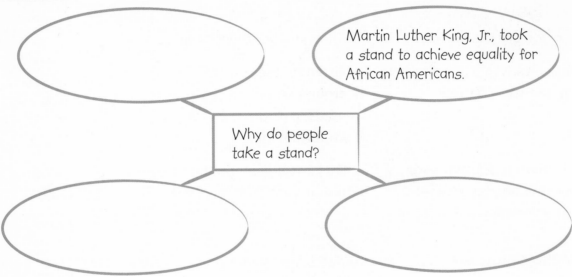

Martin Luther King, Jr., took a stand to achieve equality for African Americans.

Why do people take a stand?

Performance Task: Argument

Consider the people you learned about who took a stand, including people and characters in the **Small Group Reading** books. Imagine your class is going to honor one of these people. Whom would you choose to honor? Why? Write a blog entry for your class Web site that makes an argument for honoring your person.

Checklist

Does your argument

- ✓ use text evidence from the selection about this person?
- ✓ include relevant evidence to support your claim?
- ✓ include a concluding statement that clearly follows from and supports the claim?

372

Share Your Ideas

Choose one of these ways to share your ideas about the **Big Question**.

Write It!

Write a Biography

Research one of the leaders from the Civil Rights Movement. Write a brief biography of this person's life. Include photos, documents, or illustrations that give more information about how this person took a stand.

Talk About It!

Conduct a Debate

Choose an important problem or issue in your school or town. Divide into two teams. One team will take a stand in support of the issue, and one team will take a stand against it. Help your team research your side of the issue. Use what you have learned throughout this unit to help your team try to win the debate.

Do It!

Create a Photo Slideshow

Find pictures on the Internet that show important events in the Civil Rights Movement or the global fight against child labor. Use presentation software to create a photo slideshow. Write information about each photo. Then conduct your presentation.

FAMILIES MARCHED FOR CIVIL RIGHTS

People marched for:
• The right to vote
• The right to a good education.
• The right to be treated with respect.

Write It!

Write a Letter

Write a letter to Cassie from *Roll of Thunder, Hear My Cry* to tell her how you feel about her situation. Respond to how Cassie, Little Man, and Mama took a stand. Share details with Cassie about a time that you've taken a stand. Compare and contrast how your experiences were alike or different.

Food for Thought

? BIG Question

How can we feed a growing planet?

Unit 6

Share What You Know

❶ **Think** about five foods you love.

❷ **Make** a card for each food. Draw, label, and describe it. Imagine these are the only five foods you get for the rest of your life.

❸ **Trade** two cards with classmates. Explain why you traded.

Build Background: Watch a video about food.
NGReach.com

Language Frames

- Everyone thinks _____.
- While some people think _____, others believe _____.
- _____ says _____, but _____ and _____ say _____.

Paraphrase

Listen to several different viewpoints on school lunch and then hear how Sia paraphrases her friends' viewpoints. Use **Language Frames** to paraphrase information in a discussion about food.

School Lunch ((MP3))

Ryan: I want a slice of pizza. I know it's real food because I can see the cheese, peppers, onions, and tomato sauce.

Kayla: I'm not sure if the pizza is made of all good food. Maybe they added other ingredients to the tomato sauce, like sugar. I just get foods I know don't have added ingredients—like apples and salad.

Noah: I bring my own lunch. Then I know for sure what's in it.

Sia: All of my friends are concerned about what is in their lunches. Everyone thinks it is important to choose foods with good ingredients. While some of my friends trust what they see, others believe it is better to know for sure what they are eating.

Social Studies Vocabulary

Key Words

donate

equip

inspiration

nutritious

practical

welfare

Key Words

Read the blog post about a school garden. Use **Key Words** to talk about ways the school helps its community.

Victory Middle School News

Blog | About Victory Middle School | Archives

Join Our Garden Club

Wednesday, March 9

You are invited to join our school's Garden Club! Two local businesses have been kind enough to **donate** extra gardening tools to our club. The businesses will supply and **equip** us with all of the tools and seeds we need to grow **nutritious**, healthy foods.

The Garden Club takes the food we grow to people in need all around our city. You can learn **practical**, helpful skills and contribute to the health and **welfare** of others by simply spending a few hours a week with us! We welcome your new ideas and creative **inspiration**, too. Together, we can make this garden even more amazing!

Talk Together

How do organizations like the Garden Club help feed a growing planet? Share your thoughts in a group. Then work with a partner to paraphrase several of your classmates' perspectives. Use **Language Frames** from page 376 and **Key Words**.

Plot and Character

The **plot** is the series of events that happen in a story. The **characters** think, say, or do things in response to the events. As you read, look for how characters respond to important story events.

In the excerpt below, the narrator is a girl named Kim who doesn't have a way to remember her father who died years ago.

Look Into the Text

> I thought about how my mother and sisters remembered my father . . . I'd been born eight months after **he'd died**. . . . I dug six holes. All his life in Vietnam my father had been a farmer. Here our apartment house had no yard. But in that vacant lot **he would see me. He would watch my beans break ground and spread, and would notice with pleasure their pods growing plump** .

"The **event** is that Kim's father has died."

"Kim's **response** is to remember her father by growing bean plants."

Map and Talk

A double sequence chain can help you keep track of important events from the story and how a character responds to each event.

Double Sequence Chain

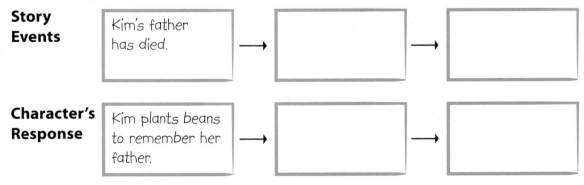

Story Events			
Kim's father has died.	→		→

Character's Response			
Kim plants beans to remember her father.	→		→

Talk Together

Tell a partner a story from your own life. Have your partner use a double sequence chain to record the events of your story and your responses.

378

More Key Words

Use these words to talk about *Seedfolks* and "Soup for the Soul."

---

devote
(di-**vōt**) *verb*

To **devote** means to give your time or attention to something. The girl **devotes** her free time to helping at the animal shelter.

envision
(in-**vi**-zhun) *verb*

To **envision** means to picture something in your mind. He can **envision** winning first place.

eventually
(i-**ven**-shu-wu-lē) *adverb*

When something happens **eventually**, it happens at a later time. The seedling will **eventually** grow into a flower.

---

incentive
(in-**sen**-tiv) *noun*

An **incentive** is something that makes you want to take action. The sale at the store gave customers an **incentive** to buy more shirts.

supplement
(**su**-plu-munt) *noun*

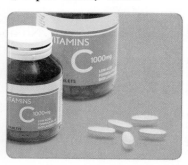

A **supplement** is something that is added to meet a need. A person who needs more vitamins in his or her diet may take a vitamin **supplement**.

Talk Together

Write a question using one or two **Key Words**. Have your partner answer. Take turns until you have used all of the words twice.

Questions	Answers
What is an incentive to devote more time to practicing a sport?	With practice, I would eventually become a better player.

Add words to My Vocabulary Notebook.
 NGReach.com

Learn to Make Inferences

Writers don't always tell you everything you need to know. Sometimes you need to fill in the missing information, or **make inferences**, when you read.

How to Make Inferences

👁	**1.** Look for ideas and information that the author emphasizes.	I read _____.
☁	**2.** Think about your own experiences with the topic or detail.	I know _____.
🧩	**3.** Combine what you know with what you read. Make a guess about what the author means but isn't stating directly.	I can infer that _____.

Here's how one student made an inference.

Look Into the Text

> I stood before our **family altar**. It was dawn. No one else in the apartment was awake. **I stared at my father's photograph**—his thin face stern, lips latched tight, his eyes peering permanently to the right. I was nine years old and still hoped that perhaps his eyes might move. Might notice me.

"I read **details** about an altar and photo.

"**I know that some families have altars for people who have died.**"

"**I can infer that the narrator's father has died.**"

Authors don't always state everything directly. Look for the information the author does provide, and make an inference by combining your experience with the text evidence.

Talk Together

Read the realistic fiction story and sample notes. Use **Language Frames** to make inferences as you read. Then talk with a partner about the inferences you made and how you made them.

Realistic Fiction

A Garden of Understanding

by Willa Jean Matthews

I crumpled up the letter I'd been writing to my grandmother and tossed it into the trash. We'd moved to the city this past winter when Mom was offered a new job, and I missed Grams terribly. Still, I couldn't send her another letter telling her how unhappy I was when I knew she was waiting to hear that I had **eventually** settled in. ◀

"Willa Jean," Mom called, interrupting my thoughts. "I'm not letting you **devote** another Saturday to staring out that window. Put on your oldest clothes and a jacket. You're coming with me." The suggestion jolted me out of my gloom. Mom had been so busy with her new job that I wasn't sure she had even noticed my misery. ◀

Three blocks later, we arrived at a corner lot where several of our neighbors were already gathered. It was hard to **envision** why everyone was standing in a dirty, trash-filled lot, but it soon became clear. Our neighbor, Mr. Himura, explained that the city had given us shovels, rakes, and trash bags as an **incentive** to clean up the lot and start a community garden. The city's only request was that we **donate** part of the food from our garden to **supplement** the city's food bank for the poor.

"Sounds like a lot of hard work," Mom said doubtfully, but I was excited. Working in the garden with Grams had always been our special time together, and I missed kneeling next to her and digging in the sun-warmed soil. ◀

"What should we plant?" Mom asked.

"Tomatoes," I answered. Grams had always made the most delicious sandwiches from the tomatoes in her garden.

"I miss those sandwiches," Mom said softly, "and I miss Grams, too." I hugged her. Maybe this garden would grow a new understanding between us.

I read that Willa Jean doesn't want to write another sad letter to Grams.

I know that my parents worry about me when they know I am unhappy.

I can infer that Willa Jean doesn't want Grams to worry that she still feels unhappy in the new city.

◀ = a good place to stop and make an inference

381

Read Realistic Fiction

Genre

Realistic fiction tells about events that could really happen. The characters, plot, and setting all seem real.

Characters' Viewpoints

A character's viewpoint is how the character thinks and feels about someone or something in the story. An author can reveal a character's viewpoint through the character's actions, dialogue, thoughts, and responses to plot events. As you read, look for clues that help you identify a character's viewpoint.

It seemed like hours and hours before we had the ground finished. We rested a while. Then my father asked if I was ready. I thought he meant ready to plant our seeds. **But instead, we turned another square of ground. Then another after that. Then three more after that**. . . .

from
Seedfolks

by Paul Fleischman

ILLUSTRATED BY KATHLEEN KINKOPF

▶ **Set a Purpose**
Find out why a group of neighbors
starts a community garden.

Kim

I stood before our family altar. It was dawn. No one else in the apartment was awake. I stared at my father's photograph—his thin face stern, lips latched tight, his eyes peering permanently to the right. I was nine years old and still hoped that perhaps his eyes might move. Might notice me.

The candles and the incense sticks, lit the day before to mark his death anniversary, had burned out. The rice and meat offered him were gone. After the evening feast, past midnight, I'd been awakened by my mother's crying. My oldest sister had joined in. My own tears had then come as well, but for a different reason.

I turned from the altar, tiptoed to the kitchen, and quietly **drew** a spoon from a drawer. I filled my lunch thermos with water and reached into our jar of dried lima beans. Then I walked outside to the street.

The sidewalk was completely empty. It was Sunday, early in April. An icy wind teetered trash cans and turned my cheeks to marble. In Vietnam we had no weather like that. Here in Cleveland people call it spring. I walked half a block, then crossed the street and reached the **vacant lot**.

I stood tall and **scouted**. No one was sleeping on the old couch in the middle. I'd never entered the lot before, or wanted to. I did so now, picking my way between tires and trash bags. I nearly stepped on two rats gnawing and froze. Then I told myself that I must show my bravery. I continued farther and chose a spot far from the sidewalk and hidden from view by a rusty refrigerator. I had to keep my project safe.

In Other Words
drew took
vacant lot empty area of land
scouted looked around

I took out my spoon and began to dig. The snow had melted, but the ground was hard. After much work, I finished one hole, then a second, then a third. I thought about how my mother and sisters remembered my father, how they knew his face from every angle and **held in their fingers** the feel of his hands. I had no such memories to cry over. I'd been born eight months after he'd died. Worse, he had no memories of me. When his spirit hovered over our altar, did it even know who I was?

I dug six holes. All his life in Vietnam my father had been a farmer. Here our apartment house had no yard. But in that vacant lot he would see me. He would watch my beans break ground and spread, and would notice with pleasure their pods growing plump. He would see my patience and my hard work. I would show him that I could raise plants, as he had. I would show him that I was his daughter.

My class had sprouted lima beans in paper cups the year before. I now placed a bean in each of the holes. I covered them up, pressing the soil down firmly with my fingertips. I opened my thermos and watered them all. And I **vowed to** myself that those beans would thrive.

Virgil

My father, he always has a smile on his face and a plan moving in his head. We were standing together on the sidewalk while the men were clearing the lot. I was watching the rats running for their lives. They were shooting off every which way. A couple of dealers came over, the ones always bragging about how bad they are. A rat ran right up one of their legs. The dude screamed, just like women do with a mouse in cartoons, only louder. Shook his leg like his toe was being electrocuted. That rat flew off and dove down a storm drain. I looked at my father. That's when I saw that he hadn't **paid the rat any mind**. Hadn't even turned his head. His eyes were stuck completely on the garden land being uncovered. He had a two-foot-wide smile on his face.

My father drove a bus back in Haiti. Here he drives a taxi. That night he drove himself way across town to borrow two shovels from a friend of his. The next morning was the first day without school. I was done with fifth grade forever. I'd planned on sleeping till noon to celebrate. But when it was still half dark my father shook my shoulder. School was over, but that garden was just starting.

We walked down and picked out a place to dig up. The ground was packed so hard, the tip of my shovel bounced off it like a **pogo stick**. We tried three spots **till** we found one we liked. Then we walked back and forth, picking out broken glass, like chickens pecking seeds. After that we **turned the soil**. We were always digging up more trash—bolts and screws and pieces of brick. That's how I found the **locket**. It was shaped like a heart and covered with rust, with a broken chain. I got it open. Inside was this tiny photo of a

In Other Words
paid the rat any mind even noticed the rat
pogo stick jumping toy
till until
turned the soil made the soil ready for planting
locket small jewelry case

girl. She was white, with a sad-looking face. She had on this hat with flowers on it. I don't know why I kept it instead of tossing it on our trash pile.

It seemed like hours and hours before we had the ground finished. We rested a while. Then my father asked if I was ready. I thought he meant ready to plant our seeds. But instead, we turned another square of ground. Then another after that. Then three more after that. My father hadn't been smiling to himself about some little garden. He was thinking of a farm, to make money. I'd seen a package of seeds for pole beans and hoped that's what we'd grow. They get so tall that the man in the picture was picking **'em** way at the top of a ladder. But my father said no. He was always asking people in his cab about how to get rich. One of 'em told him that fancy restaurants paid lots of money for this baby lettuce, smaller than the regular kind, to use in rich folks' salads. The fresher it was, the higher the price. My father planned to pick it and then race it right over in his cab. Running red lights if he had to.

In Other Words
'em them

Lettuce seeds are smaller than sand. I felt embarrassed, planting so much ground. No one else's garden was a quarter the size of ours. Suddenly I saw Miss Fleck. I hardly recognized her in jeans. She was the strictest teacher in Ohio. I'd had her for third grade. She pronounced every letter in every word, and expected you to talk the same way. She was tall and even blacker than my father. No slouching in your seat in her class or any kind of rudeness. The other teachers seemed afraid of her, too. She walked over just when we finished planting.

"Well, Virgil," she said. "You seem to have **claimed** quite a large *plantation* here."

That's just what I was afraid of hearing. I looked away from her, down at our sticks. We'd put 'em in the ground and run string around 'em, cutting our land up into six pieces. I didn't know why, till my father stepped forward.

In Other Words
claimed taken
plantation *piece of land*

"Actually, madam, only this very first area here is ours," he said. He had on his biggest smile. He must have remembered her. "The others we have planted at the request of relatives who have no tools or who live too far."

"Really, now," said Miss Fleck.

"Yes, madam," said my father. He pointed at the closest squares of land. "My brother Antoine. My auntie, Anne-Marie."

My eyes opened wide. They both lived in Haiti. I stared at my father, but he just kept smiling. His finger pointed farther to the left. "My Uncle Philippe." He lived in New York. "My wife's father." He died last year. "And her sister." My mother didn't have any sisters. I looked at my father's smiling face. I'd never watched an adult lie before.

"And what did your *extended* family of gardeners ask you to plant?" said Miss Fleck.

"Lettuce," said my father. "All lettuce."

"What a coincidence," she said back. She just stood, then walked over to her own garden. I'm pretty sure she didn't believe him. But what principal could she send him to?

That lettuce was like having a new baby in the family. And I was like its mother. I watered it in the morning if my father was still out driving. It was supposed to **come up** in seven days, but it didn't. My father couldn't figure out why. Neither of us knew anything about plants. This wrinkled old man in a straw hat tried to show me something when I poured out the water. He spoke some language, but it sure wasn't English. I didn't get what he was babbling about, till the lettuce finally came up in wavy lines and bunches instead of straight rows. I'd washed the seeds out of their places.

The minute it came up, it started to **wilt**. It was like a baby always crying for its milk. I got sick of hauling bottles of water in our shopping cart, like I was some old lady. Then the heat came. The leaves shriveled up. Some turned yellow. That lettuce was dying.

In Other Words
come up start growing above the ground
wilt droop; look unhealthy

My father practically cried, looking at it. He'd stop by in his cab when he could, with two five-gallon water containers riding in the back instead of passengers. Then bugs started eating big holes in the plants. I couldn't **see** anyone buying them from us. My father had promised we'd make enough money to buy me an eighteen-speed bike. **I was counting on it.** I'd already told my friends. My father asked all his passengers what to do. His cab was like a library for him. Finally, one of 'em told him that spring or fall was the time to grow lettuce, that the summer was too hot for it. My father wasn't smiling when he told us.

I couldn't believe it. I stomped outside. I could feel that eighteen-speed slipping away. I was used to seeing kids lying and making mistakes, but not grown-ups. I was mad at my father. Then I sort of felt sorry for him.

That night I pulled out the locket. I opened it up and looked at the picture. We'd studied Greek myths in school that year. In our book, the goddess of crops and the earth had a sad mouth and flowers around her, just like the girl in the locket. I scraped off the rust with our dish scrubber and shined up that locket as bright as I could get it. Then I opened it up, just a crack. Then I whispered, "Save our lettuce," to the girl.

In Other Words

see envision; imagine

I was counting on it. I was sure I would get it.

▶ **Before You Move On**

1. **Make Inferences** Why is Kim **devoted** to making sure the lima beans grow? Base your inference on evidence from the text.

2. **Plot/Character** How does Virgil respond to his father's actions? Use evidence from the text to support your answer.

▶ **Predict**
Will Amir have more success with
the garden than Virgil?

In India we have many vast cities, just as in
America. There, too, you are one among millions. But
there at least you know your neighbors. Here, one
cannot say that. Here you have a million crabs living in
a million **crevices**.

When I saw the garden for the first time, so
green among the dark brick buildings, I thought
back to my parents' Persian rug. It showed climbing
vines, rivers and waterfalls, grapes, flower beds, singing
birds, everything **a desert dweller** might want. The garden's green was
as soothing to the eye as the deep blue of that rug. I'm aware of color—I
manage a fabric store. But the garden's greatest benefit, I feel, was not relief
to the eyes, but to make the eyes see our neighbors.

I grew eggplants, onions, carrots, and cauliflower. When the
eggplants appeared in August they were pale purple, a strange and eerie
shade. Very many people came over to ask about them and talk to me.
I recognized a few from the neighborhood. Not one had spoken to me
before—and now how friendly they turned out to be. The eggplants
gave them an excuse for breaking the rules and starting a conversation.
How happy they seemed to have found this excuse, to let their natural
friendliness out.

In Other Words
crevices small places
a desert dweller someone who lives in the desert

Those conversations tied us together. In the middle of summer someone dumped a load of tires on the garden at night, as if it were still filled with trash. A man's four rows of young corn were crushed. In an hour, we had all the tires by the curb. We were used to helping each other by then. A few weeks later, early in the evening a woman screamed, down the block from the garden. A man with a knife had taken her purse. Three men from the garden ran after him. I was surprised that I was one of them. Even more surprising, we caught him. A teenager named Royce held the man to a wall with his pitchfork until the police arrived. I asked the others. Not one of us had ever chased a criminal before. And most likely we wouldn't have except near the garden. There, you felt part of a community.

I came to the United States in 1980. Cleveland is a city of immigrants. The **Poles** are especially well known here. I'd always heard that the Polish men were tough steelworkers and that the women cooked lots of cabbage. But I'd never known one—until the garden. She was an old woman whose space bordered mine. She had a seven-block walk to the garden, the same route I took. We spoke quite often. We both planted carrots. When her hundreds of seedlings came up in a row, I was very surprised that she did not thin them—pulling out all but one healthy-looking plant each few inches, to give them room to grow. I asked her. She looked down at them and said she knew she ought to do it, but that this task reminded her too closely of her concentration camp, where the prisoners were inspected each morning and divided into two lines—the healthy to live and the others to die.

Her father, an orchestra violinist, had spoken out against the Germans, which had caused her family's arrest. When I heard her words, I realized how useless was all that I'd heard about Poles, how much **richness** it hid, like the worthless shell around an almond. I still do not know, or care, whether she cooks cabbage.

In Other Words
Poles people from Poland
richness truth; important information

392

In September, Royce and a Mexican man collected many bricks from up the street and built a big barbecue. A bit later their friends began arriving. One brought a guitar, another played violin. They filled a folding table with food.

It was a **harvest festival**, like those in India, though no one had planned it to be. People brought food and drinks and drums. I went home to get my wife and son. Watermelons from the garden were sliced open. The gardeners proudly showed off what they'd grown. We traded harvests, as we often did. And we gave food away, as we often did also—even I, a businessman, trained to give away nothing, to always make a profit. The garden provided many excuses for breaking that particular rule.

In Other Words

harvest festival celebration of the food we had grown

Many people spoke to me that day. Several asked where I was from. I wondered if they knew as little about Indians as I had known about Poles. One old woman, Italian I believe, said she'd admired my eggplants for weeks and told me how happy she was to meet me. But something bothered me. Then I remembered. A year before she'd claimed she'd received the wrong change in my store. She'd gotten quite angry and called me—despite her own accent—a dirty foreigner. Now that we were so friendly with each other, I dared to remind her of this. Her eyes became huge. She apologized to me over and over again. She kept saying, "Back then, I didn't know it was you. . . ." ❖

▶ **Before You Move On**

1. **Make Inferences** Why doesn't Amir care whether or not the Polish woman cooks cabbage?

2. **Theme** How does the community garden bring people together? Cite text evidence.

Meet the Author

Paul Fleischman

"Ideas are everywhere," says Paul Fleischman. "As my father says, the trick is turning them into something." Fleischman grew up in Monterey, California. He helped his dad with the family's printing press. His father read to him often, and because of this, Fleischman "grew up knowing that words felt good in the ears and on the tongue, that they were as much fun to play with as toys."

Today, Fleischman is an author and award-winning poet. He feels that being a writer is exciting and fun, but he also admits that it takes a lot of work. He says, "I typically write 10 hours a day, five or six days a week. I'm a slow writer. That's what it takes for me to get books written." Perhaps some of his readers can discover the excitement, fun, and hard work of writing, too.

Writer's Craft

Fleischman thinks words are "as much fun to play with as toys." In *Seedfolks*, when Virgil says the lettuce is "crying for milk," the author plays with personification. Writers sometimes use personification to give human qualities to animals, objects, or ideas. Write a description that uses personification to tell about an everyday object in a unique way.

Key Words

devote	inspiration
donate	nutritious
envision	practical
equip	supplement
eventually	welfare
incentive	

Talk About It 💬

1. *Seedfolks* is realistic fiction. In what ways are the characters from the story similar to people you know in real life?

2. Paraphrase the different perspectives the characters have about the garden lot. How are the characters' feelings and opinions alike or different?

3. How do the characters react to gardening failures and successes? Cite at least two examples from the story.

4. What do Kim, Virgil, and Amir have in common? Cite evidence from the text to support your conclusion.

5. Using evidence from the text, compare Kim and Amir's **inspirations** for gardening.

6. Amir and the Polish woman come from different cultural backgrounds. How do their different experiences affect their viewpoints?

Learn test-taking strategies and answer more questions.
🌐 NGReach.com

Write About It 🖊

Write an email from Virgil to one of his relatives to share information about the community garden. Use at least three **Key Words** and information from the text.

● ● ● ✉   Garden   ↗

Dear Uncle Philippe,
Father and I **devote** every spare moment to our garden now. We planted a whole bunch of lettuce seeds. Father hopes that, **eventually**, we'll make a ton of money by selling the lettuce to restaurants.

Plot and Character

Use a double sequence chain to record important events in *Seedfolks* and the characters' responses to those events. Use one set of boxes for each character.

Double Sequence Chain

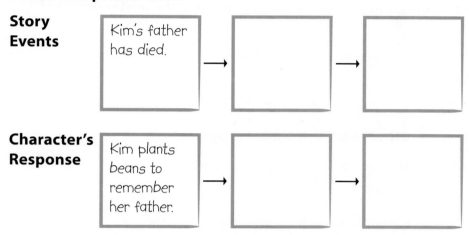

Story Events

| Kim's father has died. | → | | → | |

Character's Response

| Kim plants beans to remember her father. | → | | → | |

Use your double sequence chain to summarize the events and the characters' reactions. Explain how all of these events lead to the resolution, or ending, with Amir's story. Work with a partner, and use **Key Words**.

Fluency  Comprehension Coach

Use the Comprehension Coach to practice reading with intonation. Rate your reading.

Talk Together

How does *Seedfolks* provide ideas for how we can feed a community? Discuss your ideas with a partner. Use **Key Words** and evidence from the text to support your ideas.

Multiple-Meaning Words

Some words are spelled the same way but have different meanings. When you read a **multiple-meaning word**, you can use a dictionary and context clues to help you figure out which meaning best fits in the sentence.

Use the dictionary entries and context clues below to determine the best meaning of *mark* in this sentence:

> The shovel barely left a <u>mark</u> in the hard soil.

[1]**mark \mark ** *noun* **1:** a scratch or dent **2:** a grade or score

[2]**mark \mark ** *verb* **1:** to remember or honor **2:** to write on something

[1]**turn \turn** *verb* **1:** to move around something **2:** to dig up or plow

[2]**turn \turn** *noun* **1:** a rotation or spin **2:** a chance to do something

Try It

Read the sentences. Then answer the questions. Use the dictionary entries to help you.

> Kim lit candles to <u>mark</u> her father's death anniversary. Later, she took lima beans and water out to the empty lot. She used a spoon to <u>turn</u> the soil and plant the beans. Then she watered them.

1. **What is the best meaning of the word** <u>mark</u> **as it is used in the sentence?**

   A to remember or honor

   B to write on something

   C a scratch or dent

   D a grade or score

2. **What is the best meaning of the word** <u>turn</u> **as it is used in the sentence?**

   A to move around something

   B to dig up or plow

   C a rotation or spin

   D a chance to do something

Soup for the Soul

by Kristin Donnelly
from the pages of *Food and Wine Magazine*

Mary Ellen Diaz's food is good enough for Chicago's best restaurants. Instead, she gives meals away to people in need.

▶ **Before You Move On**

1. **Predict** Preview the photos and captions. What do you predict this interview will be about? Explain your prediction.

2. **Paraphrase** In your own words, restate the introduction on this page. Explain what Diaz is doing to help others.

"Pie is a symbol of community, and giving the first slice is like giving the best," says Mary Ellen Diaz.

Diaz is the founder of an innovative Chicago soup kitchen called First Slice. "This organization gives **the first slice** to people who rarely get anything special," says Diaz A former chef at Chicago's acclaimed North Pond restaurant, Diaz feeds 400 homeless people each week, preparing delicious meals with fresh, locally grown, mostly **organic** ingredients—dishes like butternut squash soup or spicy multigrain-vegetable soup.

First Slice soup kitchen is successful partly because of generous people who work as volunteers, **donate** money, or become customers. Diaz opened a restaurant called First Slice Pie Café. It serves a seasonal menu including **made-from-scratch** pies. Diaz also started a program that allows busy families to help the hungry. At the same time, they are making their own schedule a little bit easier. Families may sign up to receive three gourmet meals a week. Every meal is nourishing, balanced, and from local organic ingredients. **Profits go** toward both the private chef service and the soup kitchen.

▲ Mary Ellen Diaz uses her skills as a chef to help people.

In Other Words

the first slice the best or most important part

organic chemical-free

made-from-scratch homemade and not store-bought

Profits go The money earned from the program goes

Q. *What inspired you to leave your job as a chef and **launch** First Slice?*

A: I had a great restaurant career, but I felt like I had to make a choice about whether or not to stay. I wanted to be home at night reading books to my little girl instead of **slaving away** in the kitchen. I was also reading a lot about Jane Addams. She ran her own community kitchen that served food to people living on the street. She also helped women who were trying to **enter the workforce**. Jane Addams is still very much the **inspiration** for First Slice. I also started volunteering in soup kitchens, and I realized feeding forty to fifty people takes talent. I never thought of using my skills that way until then.

Q: *What kind of food do you cook at First Slice?*

A: We made a lot of Cajun food to feed **displaced victims of** Hurricane Katrina. We also get a lot of requests for food with Latin flavors, dishes that might use tortillas. Smothered pork chops are really popular. A pot of greens is definitely a big thing, because most people on the street don't have access to farm-fresh produce. It's interesting: A lot of our clientele grew up in rural communities, and they know more about growing fruit and vegetables than I do. They ask really specific questions about the soil and the farming methods. It's wonderful that we can make that fresh-from-the-farm connection.

▲ **A student volunteer helps prepare a meal at First Slice.**

In Other Words

launch start

slaving away always working hard

enter the workforce get jobs

displaced victims of people who had no homes because of

▶ **Before You Move On**

1. **Confirm Prediction** What is the author's purpose for this interview? How can you tell?

2. **Cause/Effect** What motivated Diaz to start First Slice? Name at least two reasons based on evidence from the text.

Q: *Where do most of your ingredients come from?*

A: I use a lot of the same local suppliers that I did when I was a restaurant chef. The farmers I work with are community-based and **a bit quirky and anti-establishment**, like me.

Q: *Is soup a big part of your program?*

A: Definitely. In the fall and winter we serve soup on a street corner every Tuesday night to homeless youth. We probably have thirty different recipes. We hide a lot of vegetables in our soups—I **play the same game** with the kids on the streets that I do with my own two kids. They might think they're eating just cheddar cheese soup, but it's been thickened with vegetables like butternut squash.

Q: *What's the biggest lesson you've learned since starting First Slice?*

A: The smallest things can help change somebody's life. Saying hello to a homeless person instead of looking away. Or cooking something really simple and giving it to a homeless person so she feels good.

Q: *How do you work with volunteers?*

A: There's a food writer who comes in four hours a week and all she does is roll pie dough for us. She just loves pie dough. We serve a lot of pie, and making pie dough is really **therapeutic**. There's a man who comes in and just wants to chop onions. He recently applied for a job at a new gourmet store. He didn't get it, but I was thrilled that chopping onions gave him the confidence to start looking for a job; he's been out of work for so many years.

In Other Words

a bit quirky and anti-establishment do things differently

play the same game do the same thing

therapeutic relaxing

Q: What's the best way for people to help feed the homeless?

A: Make a connection with a **food pantry** and find a way to donate **nutritious** food. Fresh fruit and vegetables are always appreciated. Canned beans are always great to have around. Rice, dried grains, canned tomatoes, and jarred salsa are also good to have. I have issues with the fact that the first thing I see in most food pantries are **overstarched, oversugared things**. Homeless people need nutritious food as much as anyone, even more.

Q: What do you eat to stay healthy?

A: A lot of salads, like one with carrots from the farm, radishes, organic greens, blue cheese, spiced pecans and pepitas [pumpkin seeds]—with bacon on the side.

Q: How do you find balance in your life between work and family?

▲ **Mary Ellen Diaz encourages students of all ages to get involved with feeding the world.**

A: What's neat is that I can bring my kids to anything we do at First Slice; they love what I do and they love to come with me. The people **get a kick out of** them, and **vice versa**. My daughter mentioned to me this morning that when it's her birthday, she is going to have a party and ask people to bring her a toy that she can donate to kids in need. How great is that? ❖

▶ **Before You Move On**

1. **Problem/Solution** How does Diaz make sure that the kids she serves get enough vegetables?

2. **Viewpoint** Which words let you know that Diaz is proud of the way her work influences her children?

Respond and Extend

Key Words

devote	inspiration
donate	nutritious
envision	practical
equip	supplement
eventually	welfare
incentive	

Compare Viewpoints

Both *Seedfolks* and "Soup for the Soul" include viewpoints about the benefits of gardens and **nutritious** meals.

With a partner, look for details in the text that help show the viewpoints. Use a comparison chart to compare viewpoints and the details from both texts. Then synthesize, or combine, the ideas in the chart to form a generalization that is true about food or communities.

Comparison Chart

Seedfolks Kim	*Seedfolks* Virgil	*Seedfolks* Amir	"Soup for the Soul" Mary Ellen Diaz
Viewpoint: feels the garden will bring her closer to her dead father and help her father get to know her	**Viewpoint:**	**Viewpoint:**	**Viewpoint:**
Details: • •	**Details:** • •	**Details:** • •	**Details:** • •

Talk Together

Based on what you have read in the two selections, what are the most effective ways for everyday people to help feed their communities? Use **Key Words** and evidence from both selections to talk about your ideas.

Pronouns

When nouns and pronouns agree, they both refer to the same person, place, or thing. The noun is the **antecedent**, and the **pronoun** refers to it.

Grammar Rules **Pronouns**

A **pronoun** and its **antecedent** must agree in number and person.

• Use a **singular pronoun** for one person or thing.	**Diaz** is a chef. **She** started First Slice.
• Use a **plural pronoun** for more than one person or thing.	**Volunteers** are helpful. **They** do a lot.
• Use **I** and **me** to refer to yourself. Use **we** and **us** to refer to yourself and one or more people.	**Diaz** said, "**I** had a great career."
• Use **you** to address one or more persons.	**Sofia**, are **you** inspired by Ms. Diaz?
• Use **he**, **she**, **him**, and **her** to refer to another person. Use **they** and **them** to refer to more than one person.	The **boys** said **they** would volunteer.
• Use **it** and **them** to refer to a thing or things.	Diaz makes **soup**. The kids like **it**.

Read Sentences with Pronouns

Good writers switch between pronouns and antecedents to make their writing sound more natural. Read this passage from Virgil's story in *Seedfolks*. Identify the pronouns and antecedents.

> My father had promised we'd make enough money to buy me an eighteen-speed bike. I was counting on it. I'd already told my friends. My father asked all his passengers what to do.

Write Sentences with Pronouns

Reread page 389 of *Seedfolks*. Write four sentences to describe what Virgil does. Use at least three pronouns and antecedents. Then compare your sentences with a partner's.

Language Frames

- I think you should
  _____ .

- One reason that you
  should _____ is
  because _____ .

- In fact, there is evidence
  that _____ .

- It's very important that
  _____ .

Persuade

Listen to how one friend persuades another to volunteer. Then use **Language Frames** to convince someone to volunteer in your community.

Help End Hunger (((MP3)))

Emilio: I can't help out today because I planned to see a movie.

Sarah: I think you should volunteer today instead. One reason that you should volunteer is because many people in our community do not have enough food to feed their families. We can help.

Emilio: That is a good reason.

Sarah: In fact, there is evidence that about 842 million people don't get enough to eat each day! It's very important that we try to help feed them.

Emilio: Well, you convinced me! I can see a movie anytime. I want to volunteer today, too. How can I help?

Sarah: We are collecting canned food for a food drive at school. You can help collect canned food from home, friends, and neighbors.

Social Studies Vocabulary

Key Words

gene

global

organic

poverty

production

virus

Key Words

Hunger is a **global** issue that affects millions of people in the world. Look at the cause-and-effect diagram. Then read about some solutions.

GLOBAL ISSUE: HUNGER

Cause	Effect	Effect
Millions of people live in **poverty**, without enough money for basic needs, such as food.	Without money or food, people experience hunger.	Without proper food or nutrition, people cannot fight **viruses** and may become very sick.

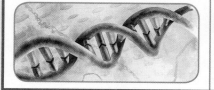  

GLOBAL SOLUTIONS

Solution	Pro	Con
Use science to modify **genes**—the codes in plant and animal cells—and control how food grows. 	Food genes can be modified, or changed, to help plants grow faster and bigger. 	No one knows for sure if genetically modified food causes health problems. 
Increase **organic**, non-chemical farming methods. 	Food grown without chemicals can be more nutritious and healthful. 	Organic food may take longer to grow. This slower **production** often increases cost.

Talk Together

Which solution is the most effective way to end global hunger? Try to persuade a partner to agree with your viewpoint. Use **Language Frames** from page 406 and **Key Words** to explain your ideas.

Argument

When writers make an **argument**, they state a claim about a topic. Then they support the claim using reasons and evidence. Some writers use facts to support their claims; others use opinions. As you read, evaluate each of the author's claims. Study the text to determine which arguments are supported by reasons and evidence and which arguments are not.

Look Into the Text

Science and technology help modern farmers raise more food.

One important way is by inventing **new machines and equipment that are better and faster** than old ones. For example, a **machine called a combine can harvest ears of corn from cornstalks, cut the corn kernels off the ears, and store the kernels in the machine in a matter of seconds.**

"The **claim** that science and technology help raise more food is supported by **facts** about a combine."

Map and Talk

An argument chart can help you evaluate a writer's claims, or arguments. Use the chart to record a writer's claim, the support he or she provides, and whether the support is fact or opinion.

Argument Chart

Argument/Claim	Support	Type of Evidence
Science and technology help farmers raise more food.	• A combine can harvest corn and store it in seconds.	• Fact

Talk Together

What can students do to help reduce global hunger? Make a claim based on your answer. Give support for your claim while your partner records it in an argument chart. Is your support based more on facts or opinions?

More Key Words

Use these words to talk about "Feeding the World" and "How Altered?"

controversy
(**kon**-tru-vur-sē) *noun*

A **controversy** is a disagreement between groups of people. Cutting down the trees caused a **controversy**.

crucial
(**kroo**-shul) *adjective*

Something that is **crucial** is necessary or very important. It is **crucial** to drink water when you are hiking.

eliminate
(i-**li**-mu-nāt) *verb*

To **eliminate** means to take out or leave out. He was **eliminated** from the spelling contest after he missed a word.

innovative
(**i**-nu-vā-tiv) *adjective*

Something **innovative** uses new ideas. The new glass building has an **innovative** design.

modified
(**mo**-du-fīd) *adjective*

If something is **modified**, a part of it has been changed. The **modified** bus has a lift to raise and lower wheelchairs.

Talk Together

Make a Vocabulary Example Chart that includes a row for each **Key Word**. Then compare your chart with a partner's.

Word	Definition	Example from My Life
crucial	important	bring lunch money to school

Add words to My Vocabulary Notebook.

NGReach.com

Learn to Make Inferences

Writers don't always tell you everything you need to know. Sometimes you need to fill in the missing information, or **make inferences**, when you read.

How to Make Inferences

👁	**1.** Look for important ideas and details.	I read _____ .
☁	**2.** Think about what the author suggests but does not state directly. Make an inference based on the text and what you already know.	I can infer that _____ .
☁	**3.** Think again. Is your inference supported by text evidence?	My inference is supported by _____ .
🧩	**4.** Keep reading to put new ideas together and build on your earlier inference.	I read on and can add _____ .

Here's how one student made an inference.

Look Into the Text

· **Humans produce more food than ever before—17 percent more calories are available per person today than 30 years ago.** If this food were divided equally, everyone would have enough.

· There are only about **half as many underfed people today as there were in 1970**.

> I read details that tell how much food people are growing.

> I can infer that people now have more access to more food.

> My inference is supported by this evidence about underfed people.

Making inferences can help you better understand what an author is trying to say. As you read, look for details that you can use to add to or change your inferences.

Talk Together

Read the editorial and sample notes. Use **Language Frames** to make inferences as you read. Talk with a partner about the inferences you made and how you made them.

Editorial

WORLD TIMES NEWSPAPER

End World Hunger

Hunger is more than the feeling you get when you miss an after-school snack. It's a **global** problem that affects one in eight people around the world. Every year, more than half a million people die from hunger. That's more than the amount of people who die from the measles **virus**, or diseases such as meningitis or hepatitis. It's **crucial** that we **eliminate** this deadly problem. ◀

One of the biggest problems with hunger is that it creates a cycle of **poverty** and more hunger. People who can't afford to buy nutritious food often become weak and ill. They are unable to work and can't support their families. Often, children must work in fields or factories to earn money for food. For boys and girls who do attend school, hunger can make it difficult for them to focus and learn. Poor health and lack of education makes it harder for these children to get jobs in the future, which makes the cycle of hunger continue. ◀

Innovative scientific advances have helped scientists fight the hunger problem. By changing the **genes** of plants, such as cotton, corn, and soybeans, scientists have helped farmers grow stronger, better crops. These crops have helped provide more food and higher profits for farmers around the world. However, genetically **modified** (GM) crops are not without **controversy**. Some people don't trust these altered crops. They worry the foods are unsafe. Still, GM crops are becoming more popular and accepted each year because they are helping to feed so many people. ◀

Hunger isn't an easy problem to overcome, but change is possible. There is more food available than ever before, and the number of people living with hunger has gone down. If we can join together and continue to find better ways to get food to the people who need it, we can end world hunger in the future.

I read that hunger affects one in eight people.

I can infer that hunger is a problem we need to solve quickly.

My inference is supported by evidence: that hunger is killing more people today than three of the world's deadliest viruses and diseases.

I read on and can add that we can't solve hunger without getting rid of poverty, too.

◀ = a good place to stop and make an inference

411

WORLD HUNGER

Read a Persuasive Article

Genre

In a **persuasive article**, the author tries to convince readers that certain topics, opinions, or actions are important.

Persuasive Language

Authors use persuasive language to convince readers to agree with their viewpoint. Persuasive language can include facts or opinions. **Facts** are persuasive because they use solid reasons, statistics, and backup from experts. **Opinions** appeal to a reader's emotions, use strong words, and usually give a personal viewpoint.

solid reasons

expert backup

statistic

> **Poverty, war, and poor farming practices** are among the reasons that people go hungry. In some parts of the world, there are millions of hungry people. **According to the United Nations**, Asia has the largest number of underfed people—**about half a billion**.

strong words and a personal viewpoint

> **We would be wise** to explore all of the **good ideas**, whether from organic and local farms or high-tech and conventional farms, **and blend the best of both**.

NATIONAL
GEOGRAPHIC

Feeding the
WORLD

Article adapted from National Geographic materials by
Peter Winkler, **Kathleen Simpson**, and **Jonathan Foley**

Comprehension Coach

▶ **Set a Purpose**
Find out why food issues are
a **global** problem.

TABLE FOR NINE BILLION

Four new babies—hungry and thirsty—
are born every second. Earth has over seven
billion people today and may have nine billion
by 2050. Can we feed them all?

The average adult needs between
2,200 and 2,900 calories each day, and
also requires a variety of vitamins, minerals,
and other nutrients to stay healthy. For many
people, having enough food to meet those
requirements isn't a problem; for others, it is.

Poverty, war, and **poor farming practices**
are among the reasons that people go hungry.
In some parts of the world, there are millions
of hungry people. According to the United
Nations, Asia has the largest number of
underfed people—about half a billion. Africa
comes next with about 200 million hungry
people. The debate over how to address the
global food challenge has become polarized,
pitting conventional agriculture and global
commerce against local food systems and
organic farms. We would be wise to explore
all of the good ideas, whether from organic
and local farms or high-tech and conventional
farms, and blend the best of both.

▲ **free soup line in Manila, Philippines**

In Other Words

poor farming practices people
    farming incorrectly

pitting forcing the competition of

HOW WELL ARE WE DOING?

Good News

- Humans produce more food than ever before—17 percent more calories are available per person today than 30 years ago. If this food were divided equally, everyone would have enough.

- There are only about half as many underfed people today as there were in 1970.

- Better seeds, machines, fertilizers, and **pesticides** have hugely increased the amount of food farmers can grow.

Bad News

- Every day, roughly 870 million people don't get enough to eat. About 200 million are hungry children. Poverty is the principal cause of hunger.

- Some farmers can't afford the new seeds, machines, and chemicals that create larger crops.

- The increased use of pesticides and fertilizers used in modern farming may **pose** risks to human health and the environment.

- Farmers and other food producers must consider the benefits and costs of new technologies.

In Other Words
pesticides chemicals used to protect plants
pose create

▶ **Before You Move On**

1. **Draw Conclusions** Based on what you have read, why do you think it is difficult to divide all the food equally to stop **global** hunger?

2. **Use Text Features** How do the two lists help you better understand important food issues?

HUNGER IN OUR WORLD

Hunger is a problem in many countries. This map shows how hunger affects our world.

NORTH AMERICA

SOUTH AMERICA

UNITED STATES   An estimated 13.5 million Americans—most of whom have low incomes—live in food deserts, where sources of nutritious food are distant or difficult to reach.

HAITI   Haiti is one of the world's poorest countries, and about one-third of Haiti's people suffer from food insecurity—**lack of access to** sufficient nutritious food.

BOLIVIA   In Bolivia, one of the poorest countries in Latin America, two-thirds of the people **live below the poverty line**. Many cannot afford to purchase adequate food.

WEST AFRICA   Millions of farmers in West Africa struggle to feed their families. Côte d'Ivoire, the world's leading producer of cocoa, has one of the world's highest poverty rates.

In Other Words

lack of access to they are unable to get

live below the poverty line do not make enough money for basic daily living

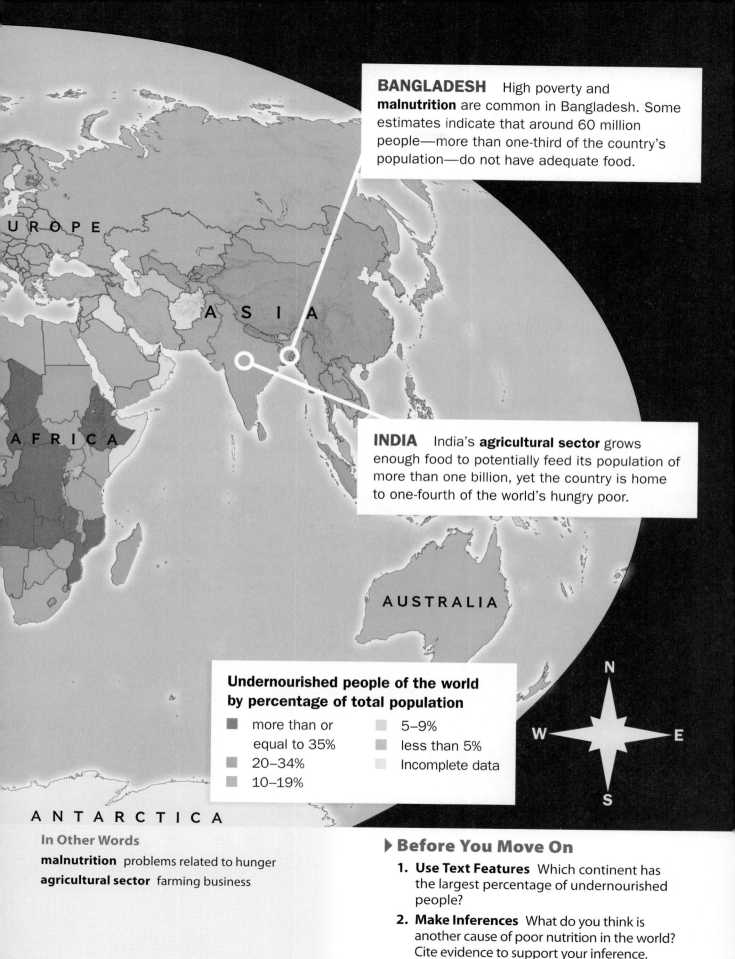

BANGLADESH High poverty and **malnutrition** are common in Bangladesh. Some estimates indicate that around 60 million people—more than one-third of the country's population—do not have adequate food.

EUROPE

ASIA

AFRICA

INDIA India's **agricultural sector** grows enough food to potentially feed its population of more than one billion, yet the country is home to one-fourth of the world's hungry poor.

AUSTRALIA

Undernourished people of the world by percentage of total population

- more than or equal to 35%
- 20–34%
- 10–19%
- 5–9%
- less than 5%
- Incomplete data

N
W E
S

ANTARCTICA

In Other Words

malnutrition problems related to hunger
agricultural sector farming business

▶ **Before You Move On**

1. **Use Text Features** Which continent has the largest percentage of undernourished people?

2. **Make Inferences** What do you think is another cause of poor nutrition in the world? Cite evidence to support your inference.

INDUSTRIAL FARMING: HIGH TECH AND HIGH COST

Science and technology help modern farmers raise more food. One important way is by inventing new machines and equipment that are better and faster than old ones. For example, a machine called a combine can harvest ears of corn from cornstalks, cut the corn kernels off the ears, and store the kernels in the machine in a matter of seconds. All of this happens while the farmer drives through the field. Combines can harvest multiple crops, such as corn, soybeans, and wheat.

But modern farm equipment comes at a high price. Combines cost between $320,000 and $500,000 today. Add to this amount the costs of fuel to run the machines and repairs when needed. While high-tech machines **increase efficiency**, many small farmers cannot afford the high cost.

Modern farmers also get help from biologists and chemists. Scientists have developed powerful fertilizers that encourage plant growth. At the same time, pesticides protect crops from insects and diseases. These innovations have helped modern farmers to increase their **production**, but they have also raised questions about modern farming practices.

The "green revolution" that started in the 1960s increased **yields** in Asia

A helicopter sprays pesticides on apple trees to protect them from disease.

In Other Words
increase efficiency help farmers produce more
yields the amount of healthy crops

combines harvesting wheat

field erosion

and Latin America by using better crop varieties and more fertilizer, irrigation, and machines. However, it had major environmental costs. Environmentalists warn that today's Americans use too many chemicals. Farmers, lawn-care companies, and backyard gardeners rely heavily on pesticides to protect their plants.

Problems occur when chemicals meant to kill pests also harm or kill other animals. One pesticide used to fight gypsy moth **infestations** also destroyed harmless butterflies. There is also the potential risk of pesticides seeping into our food or water. While not all of these chemicals may be harmful, some are. **Opponents of industrial farms** argue that the increased use of chemicals is too risky.

Farmers also face the challenge of keeping their land healthy. Earlier generations of farmers plowed vast areas of land. This practice sometimes led to erosion, or the wearing away of the soil. Farmers today use a variety of techniques to protect the soil, including leaving plant roots in the ground to help hold the soil in place. But many industrial farms now focus on growing a single crop to increase their production. Over time, this practice can begin to rob the soil of needed nutrients.

In Other Words

infestations invasions

Opponents of industrial farms People who do not support large companies that farm

▶ **Before You Move On**

1. **Analyze Claims** What are the advantages of high-tech farming? Use evidence from the text to support your answer.

2. **Explain** What are some environmental issues caused by industrial farming?

Insects can ruin a crop of corn. They **burrow** into the ears and stalks until the corn is ruined, the leaves drop to the ground, and the stalks fall over in the wind. A whole season's worth of the farmer's work, time, and money is wasted. Genetic scientists wrestled with this problem and came up with an answer. They transferred **genes** from bacteria with natural insect-fighting abilities into the **DNA** of corn plants. The result was a corn plant that kills insects that feed on it, yet does not harm people who later eat the corn.

Since the 1990s, scientists have been modifying genes in plants. Farmers have planted corn with built-in bug-killers, papayas that resist plant diseases, and soybeans that are not harmed when fields are sprayed with weed-killers. In the United States, genetically **modified** (GM) crops are so common that most people eat them every day. Most consumers do not even know when they are eating GM foods because they are not labeled.

Around the globe, many experts worry about how GM crops will affect the

genetically modified plants in test tubes

In Other Words
burrow dig
DNA genetic code

environment. They fear that **pollen** from insect-killing crops could blow onto nearby weeds. Butterflies and other creatures might eat this pollen and die. They worry that nearby weeds could absorb the pollen from GM crops and grow into **"superweeds"** that might take over an ecosystem. Some people also fear that these new foods may contain allergens, or substances that cause allergic reactions. Other people look forward to the day when genetically modified crops might solve many of the world's problems.

Scientists **sharply** disagree about the safety of genetically modified food. Supporters point out that any new plant variety has to be rigorously tested before it can be approved for **human consumption**. They argue that high-tech foods are a safe way to improve agriculture. Some experts point out that genetically modified corn and soybeans have been widely used in the United States since 1996. They say no one has suffered as a result.

Critics warn that it's dangerous to put genes into species where they don't belong. Genes tell the cells in plants or animals how to grow. Some scientists argue that we cannot know for sure how the mixing of genes will affect plants or animals **in the long term.** With that in mind, many people worry about the safety of genetically modified foods.

How does eating genetically modified food affect people? The U.S. Department of Agriculture says that GM foods are just as safe as non-GM foods, but no one knows for sure. Only time will tell. Whether GM plants are a problem or a solution, they are already part of our lives.

In Other Words

pollen powder

"superweeds" weeds that are hard to kill

sharply strongly

human consumption people to eat

in the long term over a long period of time

▶ **Before You Move On**

1. **Analyze Claims** Some experts argue that genetically engineered foods are safe. List evidence that supports this argument.

2. **Author's Viewpoint** How does the author feel about genetically modified foods? Cite evidence that supports your answer.

SUSTAINABLE FARMING: A RETURN TO THE PAST?

Sustainable farming focuses on the wise use of natural resources to prolong the life of the environment. Sustainable agriculture includes organic farming. Organic farmers emphasize the use of renewable resources and the

conservation of soil and water. Organic foods are grown without the use of human-made chemicals, such as fertilizers or pesticides. Sustainable farming methods support natural processes. Farmers minimize plowing and water use. They help keep soil healthy by planting fields with different crops year after year. They avoid using pesticides by working with insects and plants that naturally **repel** the crop-destroying pests.

Since the 1900s, a staggering 75 percent of the world's total crop diversity has disappeared from farmers' fields. In developing countries, small farms provide up to 80 percent of the total food supply. These rural, poor farms are also the ones most affected by weather and climate. Growing a greater variety of plants can help small farmers achieve a more varied and nutritious diet. It also increases the productivity of their land with smaller amounts of water, fertilizer, and energy. Growing a variety of crops also makes a farmer better able to handle changes in rainfall or temperature.

Critics of sustainable agriculture claim that its methods result in lower crop production and higher land use. They believe that using only these methods will lead to food shortages for the world's population. Supporters claim that recent evidence suggests that, over time, sustainable farms can be as productive as the industrial farms and with less impact on the environment. Also, though small farms **lag** behind industrial farms in the amount they produce, they often deliver more food that ends up feeding people.

rooftop organic farm in New York City

In Other Words

repel resist or fight against

lag are farther

▶ **Before You Move On**

1. **Explain** How does **organic** farming use natural resources? Use evidence from the text to support your answer.
2. **Make Inferences** Why are small farms so important to **global** food **production**?

A FIVE-STEP PLAN TO FEED THE WORLD

You've just read about three methods of farming being used globally today: industrial farming, genetically modified foods, and sustainable farming. Scientists differ about which method will provide enough food to feed the world's increasing population.

Jonathan Foley is the director of the Institute on the Environment at the University of Minnesota. He led a team of scientists to research an answer to this question: How can the world double the amount of food available while also reducing the harm to the environment that agriculture causes?

The team came up with five steps:

1. **Stop cutting down forests to increase farmland.**
2. **Instead, grow more on existing farmland.**
3. **Combine the best of current farming methods to use resources more efficiently.**
4. **Begin to change our diets.**
5. **Reduce our food waste.**

The first two steps focus on producing more crops on existing farmland rather than clearing more land for farming. Farming of both livestock and crops already uses more than 38 percent of ice-free land on the planet. Most of the land cleared has not been used to grow food but rather

A World Demanding More

By 2050 the world's population will likely increase by about 35 percent.

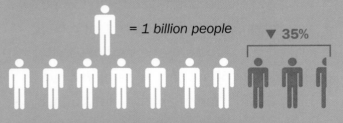

= 1 billion people   ▼ 35%

To feed that population, crop production will need to double.

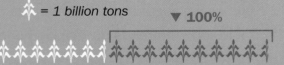

= 1 billion tons   ▼ 100%

Why? Production will have to **far outpace** population growth as the developing world grows **prosperous** enough to eat more meat.

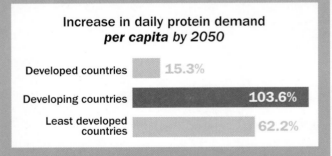

Increase in daily protein demand *per capita* by 2050

Developed countries	15.3%
Developing countries	103.6%
Least developed countries	62.2%

In Other Words
far outpace grow more quickly than
prosperous wealthy
per capita for each person

to produce timber or food for livestock. Increasing production on less productive farms in developing countries, such as Africa and Latin America, is especially important. Step three suggests increasing food production by combining high-tech farming systems with methods borrowed from organic farming. Industrial farming is finding new ways to reduce its use of chemicals and **minimize its impact on** the environment. Using these improved methods with organic farming methods can greatly reduce the use of water and chemicals.

Steps four and five ask us to look at what we eat and how much we eat. Today, only 55 percent of the world's crop calories feed people directly. The rest are fed to livestock or turned into biofuels and industrial products. Finding more efficient ways to grow meat and reducing the amount of meat in our diets could increase the available amount of food across the planet. Food waste is also an issue. In rich countries, a lot of food goes to waste in homes, restaurants, and supermarkets. In poorer countries, food is often lost due to **unreliable storage** and slow transportation. Decreasing the amount of food we waste could be one of the most effective tools we have.

According to Foley and his team, these five steps could more than double the world's food supplies and reduce the environmental impact of agriculture. We need to think about finding a balance between producing more food and sustaining the planet for future generations. And we need to do it now. ❖

More than 1,000 women and children line up for food in Yama, which is a village in the country of Niger.

In Other Words

minimize its impact on lessen any harm to

unreliable storage storerooms that are unprotected

▶ **Before You Move On**

1. **Make Inferences** Why would decreasing food waste help to increase food supplies?

2. **Viewpoint** Why is Dr. Foley concerned about the impact of agriculture on the environment?

425

Talk About It

1. How do the authors use persuasive language to develop the arguments in the article? Cite text evidence to support your answer.

2. Which features of the persuasive article do you think will have the greatest impact on readers? Use text evidence to support your answer.

3. Pretend you are trying to convince a farmer to stop the **production** of genetically **modified** crops on his farm. Which facts from the text would you use to persuade the farmer?

4. Some people claim that **organic** farming is a possible solution to the **global** problem of hunger. Is this claim supported by facts in the article? Explain your answer.

5. Choose one claim from the "Good News" and "Bad News" list on page 415. How do the authors support this claim later in the article?

6. What conclusion can you draw about the authors' viewpoints about food issues? What text evidence confirms this conclusion?

Learn test-taking strategies and answer more questions.
NGReach.com

Write About It

Write a letter for your school newspaper to help raise awareness about the issues mentioned in the article. Use at least three **Key Words** and text evidence.

Dear Victory Middle School students,

It is so important that our countries produce enough crops to **eliminate** world hunger. However, there is a lot of **controversy** about farming right now. I'm writing this letter to tell you what the problems are and how we might be able to solve them.

Argument

Use an argument chart to keep track of the claims and supporting evidence in "Feeding the World."

Argument Chart

Argument/Claim	Support	Types of Evidence
Science and technology help farmers raise more food.	• A combine can harvest corn and store it in seconds. •	• Fact •
	• •	• •
	• •	• •

Map and Talk

Talk with a partner. Use your argument chart to summarize the article's claims and the evidence that supports them. Use **Key Words**.

Fluency  Comprehension Coach

Use the Comprehension Coach to practice reading with phrasing. Rate your reading.

Talk Together

Which details from "Feeding the World" help explain ways that we can feed a growing planet? Discuss your ideas with a partner. Use **Key Words**.

Multiple-Meaning Words

You can use context clues to try to figure out the meaning of a **multiple-meaning word**. Then check the meaning in a dictionary.

Read the following sentence:

> The <u>practice</u> of using genetically modified crops is so common in the U.S. that most people buy and eat GM foods every day.

The words *common* and *every day* are context clues that help you figure out that *practice* means "a repeated action." Use the dictionary entries to confirm your guess.

> ¹**practice** \ **prak**-tus \ *verb* **1:** to do over and over to become skilled
> **2:** to work at as a profession
>
> ²**practice** \ **prak**-tus \ *noun* **1:** the usual way of doing something
> **2:** a repeated action

Try It

Read the sentences. Then answer the questions.

> Scientists carefully analyze the process of food <u>production</u>, including how crops are grown and sent to different places. They investigate farming <u>practices</u> in order to find the best way for farmers to grow the most crops for the most people.

1. **Which is the meaning of the word <u>production</u> as it is used in the sentence?**

   A a performance

   B a written or artistic work

   C a natural process for making something

   D a process of making or growing something

2. **Which is the meaning of the word <u>practices</u> as it is used in the sentence?**

   A to do over and over to become skilled

   B to work at as a profession

   C the usual way of doing something

   D a repeated action

NATIONAL GEOGRAPHIC

HOW ALTERED?

ADAPTED FROM NATIONAL GEOGRAPHIC MATERIALS
by Jim Richardson and Jennifer Ackerman

Can **biotech** foods help feed the world? "Eight hundred million people on this planet are **malnourished**, and the number continues to grow," says Channapatna Prakash. Prakash is an agricultural scientist at the Center for Plant Biotechnology Research at Tuskegee University.

In Other Words

biotech genetically modified

malnourished unhealthy from not eating enough food

▶ **Before You Move On**

1. **Make Inferences** Can you likely trust Prakash's claims? Why or why not?
2. **Make Connections** What kinds of emotions might you feel if you were constantly hungry? Explain.

Prakash and many other scientists believe that **genetic engineering** of foods can help meet the problems of food shortage and hunger. It can increase crop yields and offer crop varieties that resist pests and disease. It can also provide ways to grow crops on land that would otherwise not support farming because of drought or poor soil conditions. Prakash says, "This technology is easy for farmers to use. The farmers just plant the seeds, and the seeds bring new features in the plants."

However, Prakash also states that biotechnology isn't a cure for world hunger, but it is an important tool. In order to end world hunger, we must include soil and water conservation, pest management, and other methods of sustainable agriculture.

Critics fear that genetically engineered products are being rushed to **market** before their effects are fully understood. There is intense debate in North America and Europe about the value and impact of genetically engineered food crops. Just what are genetically **modified** foods? Who is eating them? What do we know about their benefits and their risks? What effect might these plants have on the environment? Can they help feed and preserve the health of Earth's growing population?

More than 60 percent of all **processed** foods on U.S. supermarket shelves contain ingredients from engineered soybeans, corn, or **canola**. Some of these foods include pizza, chips, cookies, ice cream, and salad dressing. Are biotech foods safe for humans? Yes, as far as we know.

"Risks exist everywhere in our food supply," points out Dean DellaPenna, plant biochemist. "With genetically engineered foods we minimize risks by doing rigorous

In Other Words
genetic engineering altering the genes
market stores
processed altered or changed
canola oil made from plant seeds

430

testing." DellaPenna believes that genetically engineered foods are the key to **the next wave of advances** in agriculture and health.

Scientists, such as Prakash and DellaPenna, believe the benefits of using technology to help our food supply **far outweigh** any possible risks. Using science to strengthen the growth of plants is one way genetic engineering can help feed our growing planet. However, some critics of genetic engineering argue that there is

enough food in the world. They believe that redistributing existing food supplies is the solution to hunger and malnutrition.

Can biotech foods harm the environment? It depends on whom you ask. Most scientists agree that the main safety issues of genetically engineered crops involve the environment. Many ecologists believe that the most damaging environmental impact of biotech crops may be **gene flow**. Could the genes that give engineered plants resistance to insects, disease, or harsh growing conditions also give weeds the same features? In developing countries, **staple crops** are more frequently planted near wild relatives. The risk of gene transfer is higher. No known superweeds from biotech crops have emerged, yet, but it may just be a matter of time.

Can biotech foods end world hunger and improve the lives of people? This remains to be seen. Their potential is enormous, yet they carry risks. We may **pay for** accidents or errors in judgment in ways we cannot yet imagine. But the biggest mistake of all would be to blindly reject or accept this new technology. We must analyze carefully how, where, and why we introduce genetically altered products. We must test them thoroughly and judge them wisely. Then we can weigh their risks against their benefits to those who need them most.

In Other Words

the next wave of advances new improvements
far outweigh are greater than
gene flow the transfer of features from plant to plant
staple crops crops that are eaten the most
pay for suffer because of

▶ **Before You Move On**

1. **Explain** What does Prakash mean when he says that biotech is a tool and not a cure?
2. **Details** What do ecologists feel is the worst problem that biotech crops could cause? Cite text evidence in your response.

IN FAVOR OF GENETICALLY MODIFIED FOODS
New technology can help protect against hunger.

Florence Wambugu, *The Washington Post*

I was one in a family of nine children growing up on a small farm in Kenya's highlands. I learned firsthand about the enormous challenge of **breaking the cycle of poverty** and hunger in rural Africa. In fact, the reason I became a plant scientist was to help farmers like my mother. My mother sold the only cow our family owned to pay for my secondary education. This was a sacrifice because I, like most children in Kenya, was needed on the farm.

I have since made it my mission to alert others to the urgent need for new technology in Africa. New technology can help protect against hunger, environmental damage, and poverty. African growers desperately need access to the best management practices and fertilizer. They need better seeds and biotechnology to help improve crop **production**. Crop production is currently the lowest in the world **per** unit area of land. Traditional agricultural practices continue to produce only low yields and poor people. These practices will not be sufficient to feed the additional millions of people who will live on the continent fifty years from now. So the question becomes, why aren't these types of biotechnology applications more readily available to African farmers? The priority of Africa must be to feed its people and to sustain agricultural production and the environment.

The people of Africa cannot wait for others to debate the **merits of** biotechnology. America and other developed nations must act now to **allocate** technologies that can prevent suffering and starvation.

In Other Words
breaking the cycle of ending
per for each
merits of good things about
allocate give other countries

AGAINST GENETICALLY MODIFIED FOODS

Genetically modified food is a risky form of technology.

Michael Bloch, *Oak High School Gazette*

Genetically modified (GM) food is not the best way to feed the world. In my opinion, GM food is a harmful and risky form of technology.

I do not think we should genetically modify our food because it harms plant and animal life. GM plants can accidentally mix with wild plants. When this happens, superweeds, or giant weeds, may grow. Farmers need to use stronger forms of pesticide to kill superweeds. Stronger pesticides are bad for other plants and for the air we breathe.

Animals are also affected by GM foods. Some GM corn crops are a major health risk to animals that eat them. A study done in the U.S. showed that 44 percent of caterpillars of the monarch butterfly died when fed large amounts of pollen, or powder, from GM corn.

We know that GM foods negatively affect plant and animal life. It is important to think about the risks GM foods pose to humans as well. Many experts caution against GM foods. Ronnie Cummins of the Organic Consumers Association warns, "We are rushing **headlong** into a new technology. We are courting disaster if we don't **look before we leap**." Furthermore, Dr. Mae-Wan Ho, a geneticist and physicist, cautions that, "Genetic engineering is inherently dangerous."

Since nearly half the U.S. corn and soybean crops are now genetically modified, we must act now. We do not know the health effects of these foods. Until we do, it is in everyone's interest to find better ways of feeding the world. ❖

a researcher studies genetically modified rice plants at Cornell University

In Other Words
headlong too fast
look before we leap study GM foods first

▶ **Before You Move On**

1. **Make Judgments** Who has the more convincing argument? Support your judgment with evidence from the text.

2. **Make Comparisons** How are the two viewpoints similar? Identify examples from the texts.

433

Respond and Extend

Key Words

controversy	modified
crucial	organic
eliminate	poverty
gene	production
global	virus
innovative	

Compare Arguments

Both "Feeding the World" and "How Altered?" discuss the benefits and risks of using various farming methods to fight **global** hunger and **poverty** . Compare two arguments presented in each text and the evidence that supports each argument. Then synthesize, or combine, the information to form a generalization that is true about the arguments in both selections.

Comparison Chart

	Argument	Evidence, Reasons, or Facts
"Feeding the World"	1.	• •
	2.	• •
"How Altered?"	1. GM foods can help with problems of food shortage and hunger.	• Genetic modifications increase crop yields. •
	2.	• •

Talk Together

What suggestions does each persuasive article give for feeding a growing planet? Use **Key Words** and evidence from the text to talk about your ideas.

Different Kinds of Pronouns

Different kinds of **pronouns** are used in different situations.

Grammar Rules Different Pronouns

• Use an **indefinite pronoun** when you're not naming a specific person or thing. Examples: **all, both, nothing, anything, everyone, someone, somebody, something**.	**Something** must be done about world hunger. **Everyone** deserves healthy food.
• Use a **demonstrative pronoun** to connect to an antecedent without naming it.	**This** is a huge global problem. **That** might be one solution.
• **Reflexive pronouns** and **intensive pronouns** refer back to nouns or other pronouns in a sentence. These pronouns end with **–self** or **–selves**.	
• Use a **reflexive pronoun** when the object refers back to the **subject**.	**I** ask **myself** how I can help solve the problem.
• Use an **intensive pronoun** to emphasize a **noun** or a **pronoun** in a sentence.	**Scientists themselves** disagree about the safety of GMOs.

Read Different Kinds of Pronouns

Good writers use a variety of pronouns to avoid repetition and make the writing more interesting. Read this passage based on "Feeding the World." Identify the different pronouns. How does the writer avoid repetition?

> Can anything be done to make sure everyone has enough food?
> Researchers constantly ask this. Dr. Jonathan Foley himself
> proposed an interesting plan.

Write Different Kinds of Pronouns

Reread pages 424–425 of "Feeding the World." Write a paragraph that explains how you can participate in the Five-Step Plan. Use different kinds of pronouns. Then compare your paragraph with a partner's.

435

Write as a Citizen

Write an Editorial

Write an editorial about genetically modified foods (GMs) to persuade people to think the way you do.

A lab worker checks GM plants for diseases.

Study a Model

An editorial is a kind of persuasive essay. In an editorial, you use a formal tone to express your viewpoint, or claim. Then you support your claim with reasons and evidence. Read Tom's editorial about labeling GMs.

What's in That Tomato?

If you are a health-conscious shopper, you probably read the nutrition label before buying a food product. But what about the information that food companies omit from the labels? Many foods are genetically modified, but shoppers have no idea what they are putting into their carts. I believe that all genetically modified foods should be clearly labeled.

Food labels inform people about what is going into their food. Genetically modified foods (GMs) are developed by placing a gene from one plant into another plant. **More than 60 percent of all processed foods in the U.S. contain genetically engineered ingredients.** But there are no long-term studies on how these new plants affect humans. Until these studies are conducted, labeling GMs can help people decide for themselves whether they want to risk eating GMs.

If you also believe that GMs should be clearly labeled, please join me in writing to government agencies and food companies. Together, we can let them know how we feel about this issue.

Tom clearly introduces his **claim.**

Tom gives **reasons** for his claim. He develops and supports the reasons with relevant evidence, including examples, facts, and statistics.

The **conclusion** restates Tom's claim and tells what action he wants people to take.

Prewrite

1. **Choose a Topic** Think about food-related issues you have learned about. What ideas do you have about them? Talk with a partner to find a viewpoint, or claim.

<table>
<tr><td colspan="2" align="center">**Language Frames**</td></tr>
<tr><td>**Tell Your Ideas**

• One thing I've learned about _____ is _____ .

• One thing I feel strongly about is _____ .

• I'd like to persuade people to _____ .</td><td>**Respond to Ideas**

• I don't understand your opinion. Can you explain _____ ?

• I don't think I agree with your reason because _____ .

• What facts will you use to persuade readers?</td></tr>
</table>

Use sentences like these to choose your topic.

2. **Gather Information** What reasons will you give to support your claim? What convincing evidence will you use to persuade the readers to accept your viewpoint?

3. **Get Organized** Use an author's viewpoint chart to help organize and develop your claim, support, and conclusion.

Author's Viewpoint Chart

Claim	Facts or Other Support	Action Needed
Genetically modified foods should be labeled.	• There have been no long-term studies about the effects of GM crops. •	

Draft

Use your chart to write your draft.

- Begin by stating your claim, or viewpoint.

- Support your claim with persuasive language that includes facts and evidence.

- Conclude by telling readers what you want them to do.

Revise

1. **Read, Retell, Respond** Read your draft aloud to a partner. Your partner listens and then retells your main points. Then talk about ways to improve your writing.

Language Frames	
Retell	**Make Suggestions**
• Your claim is _____ .	• Could you add examples, facts, or statistics to support _____ ?
• The reasons you gave included _____ .	• Sometimes your style is a little informal. Maybe you could say _____ instead?
• Your conclusion asks people to _____ .	• I'm not exactly sure what you want people to do. Could you make the conclusion stronger by _____ ?

2. **Make Changes** Think about your draft and your partner's suggestions. Use the Revising Marks on page 617 to mark your changes.

    • Make sure you have used appropriate language for a formal style. Look for places to change contractions and other informal language.

    > But what about the information that food companies don't put _{omit from} on the labels?

    • Did you include relevant examples, facts, or statistics? Would adding them help support your reasons and evidence?

    > Genetically modified foods (GMs) are developed by placing a gene from one plant into another plant. In fact, more than 60 percent of all processed foods in the U.S. contain ingredients that have been genetically engineered.

Edit and Proofread

Work with a partner to edit and proofread your essay. Pay special attention to the correct use of indefinite, demonstrative, reflexive, and intensive pronouns. Use the marks on page 618 to show your changes.

Grammar Tip

Avoid pronoun confusion. Use subject and object pronouns correctly. Make sure that each pronoun's antecedent is clear.

Publish

1. **On Your Own** Make a final copy of your editorial. Put the key points on note cards and present it to your class as a persuasive speech.

Presentation Tips	
If you are the speaker . . .	**If you are the listener . . .**
Use formal language to fit the context of your speech.	Think about what you do not understand. Pose questions related to the topic.
Answer listeners' questions or counterarguments with specific examples, facts, and statistics.	Decide which parts of the speaker's argument are supported by reasons and evidence and which are not.

2. **In a Group** Gather all the editorials from your class. Send them to the editor of a local newspaper or post them on a class blog.

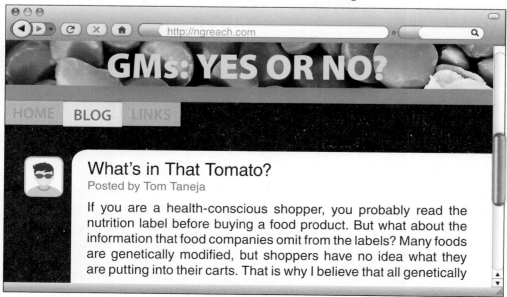

http://ngreach.com

GMs: YES OR NO?

HOME   BLOG   LINKS

What's in That Tomato?
Posted by Tom Taneja

If you are a health-conscious shopper, you probably read the nutrition label before buying a food product. But what about the information that food companies omit from the labels? Many foods are genetically modified, but shoppers have no idea what they are putting into their carts. That is why I believe that all genetically

BIG Question

How can we feed a growing planet?

Talk Together

In this unit you found many answers to the **Big Question**. Now use your concept map to discuss it with the class. Think about how the selections presented different ways of addressing the global food shortage problem.

Problem-and-Solution Chart

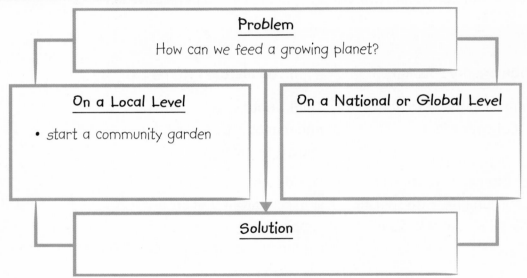

Problem

How can we feed a growing planet?

On a Local Level

• start a community garden

On a National or Global Level

Solution

Performance Task: Argument

Think about the different solutions to solving the problem of world hunger that you read about, including those in the **Small Group Reading** books. What do you think your community could do to help feed a growing planet? Write a letter to your mayor that makes an argument for your idea.

Checklist

Does your argument

- ✔ use evidence from the selections about feeding a growing planet?

- ✔ clearly introduce your claim?

- ✔ include relevant evidence to support your claim?

- ✔ include a concluding statement that clearly follows from and supports the claim?

Share Your Ideas

Choose one of these ways to share your ideas about the **Big Question**.

Write It!

Write a Blog Entry

Write a blog entry that features projects and organizations that help to end world hunger. Are there some projects in your area that help to end hunger? Find pictures to include in your blog entry. If possible, post your work on your classroom's Web site.

Talk About It!

Give a Speech

Develop a speech about inventions that have improved farming practices, like the treadle pump. Use presentation software to create a slideshow to accompany your speech. Present it to the class.

FARMING INVENTIONS
- treadle pump
- cotton gin
- thresher

Do It!

Make a Map

Draw a map of your town that includes a new community garden. Plot out what you would grow in each section. What can you plant that could be served in school lunches? Include a compass rose, map symbols, and a key to explain what each symbol stands for.

Write It!

Write a Song

Work with a partner to write a song, rap, or chant about why it is important to end hunger. Include details about the problem of hunger and what can be done to end it. Perform your song or chant with your partner.

Ancient China

BIG Question

Why should we study ancient cultures?

Unit at a Glance
▶ **Language:** Interpret Images, Summarize, Social Studies Words
▶ **Literacy:** Synthesize
▶ **Content:** Ancient China

Unit
7

Share What You Know

❶ **Think** about why people study ancient cultures.

❷ **List** some things that people can learn from studying ancient cultures.

❸ **Share** your list with the class.

Build Background: Watch a video about ancient China
🌐 **NGReach.com**

Language Frames

- This image shows
  _____ .

- The _____ in the
  image mean(s)/show(s)
  that _____ .

- The image is important
  because _____ .

- The image helps me
  understand _____ .

Interpret Images

Listen to how one student interprets this historical Chinese painting. Then use **Language Frames** to interpret an image in your own way.

food stand

furniture store

sedan chair to carry passengers

A Glimpse into the Past ((MP3))

This image shows a street scene in the city of Suzhou, China, hundreds of years ago. The food stand, the furniture store, and the people's activities in the image show that some things in Suzhou were similar to modern life. You can still find examples of those things in China today. However, the people's clothing, the style of the buildings, and the sedan chair in the image show ways in which life in Suzhou was different.

The image is important because it gives many details about the past. I can compare life in China long ago with modern life today. The image helps me understand what everyday life might have been like for people who lived in China hundreds of years ago.

Social Studies Vocabulary

Key Words

ancestor

conquest

empire

infrastructure

revolt

Key Words

Look at the painting and read the description of dynasties in ancient China.
Use **Key Words** and other words to talk about ancient China.

Ancient China

This painting is from the Sung dynasty, which lasted from 960 C.E. to 1279 C.E.
Ancient China had many different dynasties. A dynasty is a line of rulers from the
same family. A powerful dynasty could last hundreds of years as newer family
members built upon the successes of the **ancestors** who had come before them.
A Chinese **empire** was a large area controlled by the ruling family. The empire
could grow with each successful **conquest** in battles to take over other lands.
Different kinds of **infrastructure**, such as bridges and roads, were signs of a
strong empire. But a dynasty might end if others tried to take control by starting
a **revolt** to fight against the ruling family.

Talk Together

How does this painting help you understand more about life in ancient China?
Use **Language Frames** from page 444 and **Key Words** to interpret the image
and discuss this question with a group.

Relate Ideas

Many writers of nonfiction give information about key individuals who greatly affected the time in which they lived. The author introduces the person and then elaborates on the information by giving examples and anecdotes, or stories, that illustrate the person's characteristics. As you read, **relate ideas** in the text that show the person's strengths, weaknesses, and contributions to society.

Look Into the Text

Before the time of Qin Shihuang . . . there was no China. Instead, there were seven separate kingdoms. . . . **The kingdom of Qin was the fiercest; soldiers received their pay only after they had presented their generals with the cut-off heads of enemy warriors**. By 221 B.C., **the ruler of the Qin kingdom had "eaten up his neighbors** like a silkworm devouring a leaf," according to an ancient historian. **The name China comes from Qin.**

"This **evidence** tells about Emperor Qin's soldiers, victories, and impact on China."

Map and Talk

A text evidence chart can help you organize information about an individual, idea, or event. After completing the chart, analyze the evidence to understand more about the subject.

Text Evidence Chart

Person's Qualities	Text Evidence
brutal, mean	Qin's soldiers had to cut off their enemies' heads.

Talk Together

Talk with a partner about another historical figure you have studied. Use a text evidence chart to list the person's qualities in the first column. Then list evidence that demonstrates those qualities in the second column.

More Key Words

Use these words to talk about *The Emperor's Silent Army* and "A Silent Army."

aspect
(**a**-spekt) *noun*

An **aspect** is a part, or feature, of something. One **aspect** of friendship is comforting your friends if they are sad.

assemble
(u-**sem**-bul) *verb*

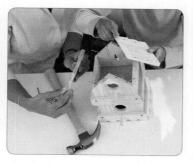

To **assemble** means to put together. They use a hammer and nails to **assemble** the birdhouse.

domain
(dō-**mān**) *noun*

A **domain** is the area that is controlled by a person or a group of people. The stage is the singer's **domain**.

foundation
(fown-**dā**-shun) *noun*

A **foundation** is the base on which something rests. Many homes are built on concrete **foundations**.

unify
(**yū**-nu-fī) *verb*

To **unify** means to bring together as one. The two railway lines **unify** onto a single track.

Talk Together

Work with a partner. Make an Expanded Meaning Map for each **Key Word**.

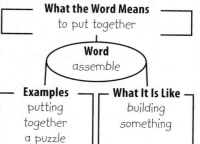

What the Word Means
to put together

Word
assemble

Examples
putting together a puzzle

What It Is Like
building something

Add words to My Vocabulary Notebook.

NGReach.com

Learn to Synthesize

Good readers synthesize, or put together, information as they read. You can **draw conclusions** by combining details from different parts of the text to come up with new ideas that the author does not state directly.

How to Draw Conclusions

	1. As you read, notice a detail that seems important in the text.	I read _____.
	2. Look for another detail about the same topic that seems important.	I also read _____.
	3. Put the details together, and decide what the details mean.	My conclusion is that _____.

Here's how one student drew a conclusion.

Look Into the Text

The king of Qin now ruled over an immense empire—around one million square miles . . . To the ruler of Qin, **being called king was no longer grand enough. He wanted a title that no one else had ever had before.** What he chose was Qin Shihuang. This means **"first emperor, God in Heaven, and Almighty of the Universe"** all rolled into one.

"I read **details** about how Qin wanted a special name."

"I also read **examples** of powerful names he chose. "

"My conclusion is that Qin thought he was more powerful than anyone in the universe."

Drawing conclusions as you read can help you figure out information that the author does not state directly.

Talk Together

Read the biography and sample notes. Use **Language Frames**
to help you draw conclusions as you read. Talk with a partner
about the conclusions you made and how you made them.

Biography

Emperor Qin

Emperor Qin Shihuang was born with the name Ying Zheng in 259 B.C. His father was the king of the Qin state. Ying Zheng grew up during a time when China was divided into seven separate states that had been at war for centuries. From a young age, Ying Zheng studied the history of the Qin state and the lives of his **ancestors**. He also learned about the art, or process, of war.

In 246 B.C., Ying Zheng became king when his father died. When Ying Zheng was 22, he gained full power of the Qin state and set out to conquer the other six states. His first **conquest** was the Han state. Then, one at a time, he defeated the remaining five states. By 221 B.C., Yin Zheng was able to **assemble** all the states into one. He named the new **empire** Qin after his original state. Then he changed his name to Qin Shihuang, which means "The First Emperor of Qin." ◀

Once he was the emperor, Qin Shihuang made many changes to **unify** his empire. He standardized coins, weights, measures, and written Chinese characters. He also strengthened the **infrastructure** of his empire by building canals and roads to connect the states in his **domain**.

One well-known **aspect** of Qin's leadership was that he was a harsh ruler. He ordered that a great wall be built to keep invaders out of his land. Some historians believe that over 300,000 workers died while working on this huge, dangerous project. Today, the Great Wall of China is built on the **foundation** of Qin Shihuang's original wall. ◀

Qin Shihuang died in 210 B.C. at the age of 49. Just three short years after his death, a **revolt** brought an end to the dynasty that Qin Shihuang believed would last for thousands of years. ◀

I read that Qin's father was the King of their state.

I also read that Qin changed his name to say he was the first emperor.

My conclusion is that Qin thought he was a better, more powerful ruler than his father.

◀ = a good place to stop and draw a conclusion

Read a History Article

Genre

A **history article** is nonfiction. It tells about people, places, and events in the past. History articles often include images from a time period to give more detailed information about historical events or figures.

Text Features

In *The Emperor's Silent Army*, there are many **images** of the leader, Qin Shihuang, in stone engravings, paintings, fabric weaves, and bronze models. These pictorial representations can help you better understand the culture and time in which Qin Shihuang lived. This art also shows how people perceived Qin Shihuang and how artists were instructed to represent him.

This stone engraving is a modern interpretation of how Qin Shihuang looked.

This ancient bronze model shows how emperors traveled at that time.

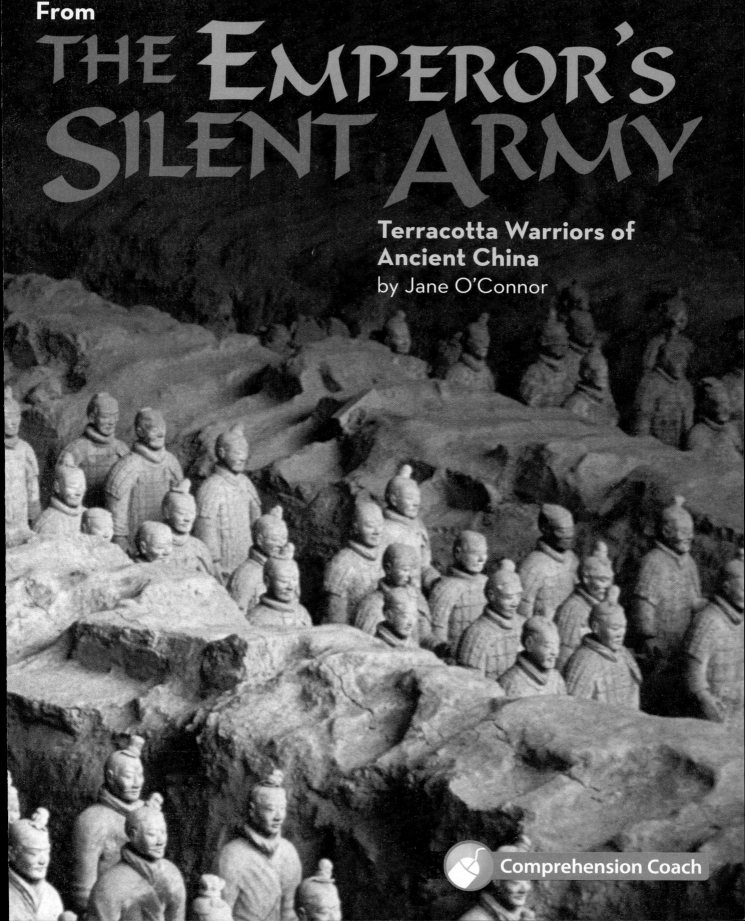

From

THE EMPEROR'S SILENT ARMY

Terracotta Warriors of Ancient China

by Jane O'Connor

Comprehension Coach

▶ **Set a Purpose**

Learn how Qin Shihuang planned to continue his **conquest** from the grave.

Before the time of Qin Shihuang (pronounced *chin shir-hwong*), who lived from 259 to 210 B.C., there was no China. Instead, there were seven separate kingdoms—each with its own language, currency, and ruler. For hundreds of years they had been fighting one another. The kingdom of Qin was the fiercest; soldiers received their pay only after they had presented their generals with the cut-off heads of enemy warriors. By 221 B.C., the ruler of the Qin kingdom had "eaten up his neighbors like a silkworm devouring a leaf," according to an ancient historian. The name China comes from Qin.

The king of Qin now ruled over an immense **empire**—around one million square miles that stretched north and west to the Gobi desert, south to present-day Vietnam, and east to the Yellow Sea. To the people of the time, this was the **entire civilized world**. Not for another hundred years would the Chinese know that empires existed beyond their boundaries. To the ruler of Qin, being called king was no longer grand enough. He wanted a title that no one else had ever had before. What he chose was Qin Shihuang. This means "first emperor, God in Heaven, and Almighty of the Universe" all **rolled into one**.

But no title, however superhuman it sounded, could protect him from what he feared most—dying. More than anything, the emperor wanted to live forever. According to legend, a magic elixir had granted eternal life to the people of the mythical Eastern Islands. Over the years, the emperor sent expeditions out to sea in search of the islands and the magic potion. But each time they came back empty-handed.

In Other Words

entire civilized world only place where people were known to live

rolled into one together

statue of Qin Shihuang

452

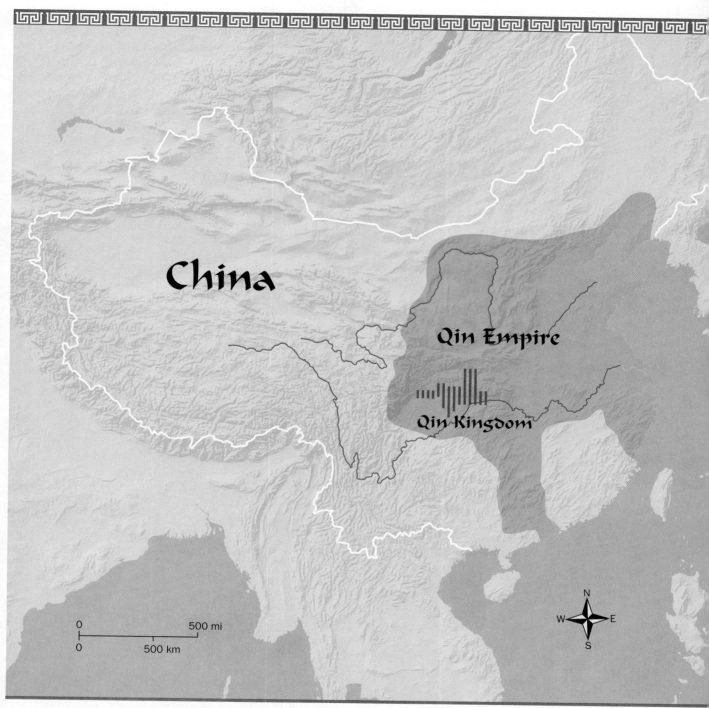

▲ This map shows the Qin **empire** in brown and the Qin kingdom in stripes.

▶ **Before You Move On**

1. **Figurative Language** Explain what it means that Qin had "eaten up his neighbors like a silkworm devouring a leaf."

2. **Use Text Features** What information does the map show that is not included in the text?

453

This painting from the seventeenth century shows the first emperor carried in a covered litter called a palanquin.

If he couldn't live forever, then Qin Shihuang was determined to live as long as possible. He ate powdered jade and drank mercury in the belief that they would prolong his life. In fact, these "medicines" were poison and may have caused the emperor to fall sick and die while on a tour of the easternmost outposts of his empire. He was forty-nine years old.

If **word of** Qin Shihuang's death got out while he was away from the capital there might be a revolt . So his ministers kept the news a secret. With the emperor's body inside his chariot, the entire party traveled back to the capital city. Meals were brought into the emperor's chariot; daily reports **on affairs of state** were delivered as usual—all to keep up the appearance that the emperor was alive and well. However, it was summer, and a terrible smell began to come from the chariot. But the clever ministers found a way to **account for** the stench. A cart was loaded with smelly, salted fish and **made to precede** the chariot, overpowering and masking any foul odors coming from the dead emperor. And so Qin Shihuang returned to the capital for burial.

▲ This is a modern stone engraving that depicts the first emperor of China.

In Other Words
word of the news about
on affairs of state about the government
account for explain
made to precede traveled in front of

▶ **Before You Move On**

1. **Use Text Features** Study the painting on page 454. What does the painting help you understand about the life of an emperor?

2. **Explain** How did Qin Shihuang's fear of death affect his life? Cite text evidence.

▲ For thousands of years, the Chinese have made silk fabric. This detail of a silk robe shows an embroidered dragon, the symbol of Chinese emperors.

▲ On long journeys, the emperor would have slept in a covered carriage like this half-scale model made from bronze in the third century B.C.

The tomb of Qin Shihuang had been under construction for more than thirty years. It was begun when he was a young boy of thirteen and was still not finished when he died. Even incomplete, the emperor's tomb was enormous, larger than his largest palace. According to legend, it had a domed ceiling **inlaid** with clusters of pearls to represent the sun, moon, and stars. Below was a gigantic relief map of the world, made from bronze. Bronze hills and mountains rose up from the floor, with rivers of mercury flowing into a mercury sea. Along the banks of the rivers were models of the emperor's palaces and cities, all exact **replicas** of the real ones.

In ancient times, the Chinese believed that life after death was not so very different from life on earth. The soul of a dead person could continue to enjoy all the pleasures of everyday life. So people who were rich enough constructed elaborate, underground tombs filled with silk robes, jewelry with precious stones, furniture, games, boats, chariots—everything the dead person could possibly need or want.

In Other Words
inlaid decorated
replicas copies

▶ **Before You Move On**

1. **Make Inferences** Study the photograph and caption on page 456. Why do you think dragons were the symbol for emperors?

2. **Relate Ideas** How does Qin Shihuang's tomb reflect his personality in life? Cite specific evidence from the text.

457

Qin Shihuang knew that **grave** robbers would try their best to loot the treasures in his tomb. So he had machines put inside the tomb that produced the rumble of thunder to scare off intruders, and mechanical crossbows at the entrance were set to fire arrows automatically should anyone dare trespass. The emperor also made certain that the workers who carried his coffin in to its final resting place never revealed its exact **whereabouts**. As the men worked their way back through the tunnels to the tomb's entrance, a stone door came crashing down, and they were left to die, sealed inside the tomb along with the body of the emperor.

Even all these **measures**, however, were not enough to satisfy the emperor. And so, less than a mile from the tomb, in underground trenches, the **terracotta** warriors were stationed. Just as flesh-and-blood troops had protected him during his lifetime, the terracotta troops were there to protect their ruler against any enemy for all eternity.

Qin Shihuang became emperor because of his stunning victories on the battlefield. His army was said to be **a million strong**. In every respect except for number, the terracotta army is a faithful replica of the real one.

So far, terracotta troops have been found in three separate pits, all close to one another. A fourth pit was discovered, but it was empty. The entire army faces east. The Qin kingdom, the emperor's homeland, was in the northwest. The other kingdoms that had been conquered and had become part of his empire lay to the east. So Qin Shihuang feared that any enemy **uprising** would come from that direction.

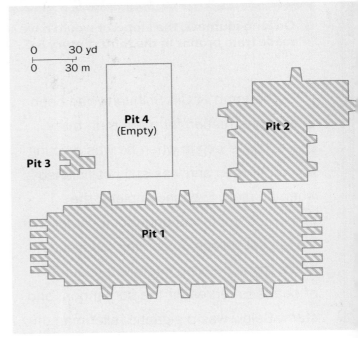

▲ **This diagram shows the four pits that have been discovered. Only Pits 1, 2, and 3 contain terracotta figures.**

The first pit is by far the biggest, more than two football fields long, with approximately 6,000 soldiers and horses. About 1,000 have already been excavated and restored. None of the soldiers in the army wears a helmet or carries a shield—proof of the Qin soldiers' fearlessness. But the archers stationed in the front lines don't wear any armor either. They needed to be able to move freely in order to fire their arrows with accuracy. And so these frontline sharpshooters, who were the first targets of an approaching enemy, also had the least protection.

Following the **vanguard** are eleven long columns of foot soldiers and lower-ranking officers, the main body of the army, who once carried spears, battle-axes, and **halberds**. The soldiers are prepared for an attack from any direction.

Those in the extreme right and extreme left columns face out, not forward, so that they can block enemy **charges** from either side. Last of all comes the rear guard, three rows of soldiers with their backs to the rest of the army, ready to stop an attack from behind.

▲ In Pit 1, three rows of unarmored soldiers are followed by the main body of the army.

In Other Words
vanguard first group of warriors
halberds sharp, spiked weapons
charges attacks

▶ **Before You Move On**

1. **Draw Conclusions** Did Qin Shihuang trust his tomb's internal safety measures? Cite evidence from the text.

2. **Analyze** How did Qin Shihuang's actions reflect his concerns that people might **revolt** against him?

▲ The chariots that originally followed the horses rotted away long before the discovery of the terracotta army.

Stationed at various points among the foot soldiers are about fifty charioteers who drove wooden chariots. Each charioteer has a team of four horses and is dressed in full-length armor. In some carts, a general rides beside the charioteer, ready to beat a drum to signal a charge or ring a bell to call for **a retreat**.

The long, rectangular arrangement of soldiers in Pit 1 follows a real battle formation used to defeat real enemies in ancient times. It is called a sword formation, with the frontline archers representing the tip of the sword, the chariots and columns of foot soldiers forming the blade, and the rear guard the handle.

In Other Words
a retreat the army to get back

▲ Low-ranking infantrymen wore no armor.

Pit 2 is far smaller than Pit 1. With an estimated 900 warriors of all different ranks, Pit 2 serves as a powerful back-up force to help the larger army in Pit 1. There are also almost 500 horses—about 350 chariot horses and more than 100 cavalry horses.

◀ This drawing shows what a wooden chariot would have looked like.

▶ **Before You Move On**

1. **Relate Ideas** How does information about the terracotta soldiers show Qin Shihuang's attention to detail?

2. **Explain** What is the purpose of Pit 2? Use evidence from the text in your answer.

The terracotta horses are Mongolian ponies, not very big, but muscular and full of power. With their flaring nostrils, bared teeth, and bulging eyes, the chariot horses all look as if they are straining to gallop across a battlefield. The mane of each chariot horse is trimmed short and its tail is braided. That is so it won't get caught in the **harness**.

By the time of the first emperor, soldiers on horseback were replacing war chariots. It was hard for even the most experienced drivers to manage a chariot over bumpy, rock-strewn ground. **Cavalrymen** could move much more swiftly and easily. Their horses had fancy saddles decorated with rows of nail heads and tassels, but no **stirrups**—they hadn't **come into use** yet.

▲ **The terracotta horses are life-size.**

In Other Words
harness straps used to control the horse
Cavalrymen Soldiers riding horses
stirrups straps to hold the riders' feet
come into use been created

Pit 3, by far the smallest, contains fewer than seventy warriors and only one team of horses. Archeologists think that Pit 3 represents army headquarters. That's because the soldiers are not arranged in an attack formation.

Instead, they face one another in a U shape, as if they are busy consulting among themselves. Although the officers at command central would not **engage in hand-to-hand combat**, the fate of the thousands of troops in Pit 1 and Pit 2 **rests in their hands**.

Altogether, the three pits of warriors and horses make up an unstoppable army. All the warriors are stationed strategically, exactly as they would have been on a real battlefield. For example, rows of kneeling soldiers with crossbows alternate with rows of standing archers. This way, while one row is firing, the other row has time to reload their bows. The crossbow was by far the most powerful weapon of the time. The Chinese were using crossbows as early as 400 B.C. In Europe, however, crossbows didn't come into use for at least another 1,300 years.

In earlier times in ancient China, real soldiers and horses were killed and buried alongside their dead ruler. But by the time of Qin Shihuang, this horrible custom was no longer so common. Instead, clay or wooden figurines were substituted for human sacrifices. Once the figures were buried underground, it was believed that they would come to life magically and protect the dead emperor both from real attackers hoping to **ransack** his tomb and from any evil spirits wanting to harm his **immortal soul**.

Interestingly, there is not a single word about the buried army in any records from ancient times. Why was this? Was the creation of the clay soldiers simply not worthy of mention? Or was the emperor making sure that nobody knew about his ultimate secret weapon? ❖

▲ Unlike most of the figures, who stand stiffly, face forward, this archer is in a much more natural pose.

In Other Words

engage in hand-to-hand combat fight people directly

rests in their hands is their responsibility

ransack steal or break items in

immortal soul soul that would live forever

▸ **Before You Move On**

1. **Use Text Evidence** What does the information about Pit 3 illustrate about Qin Shihuang's actions and motives?
2. **Visualize** How do the descriptions of the soldiers help you picture their placement and duties in the emperor's army?

Talk About It

1. History articles can help readers learn new information about places or people from the past. What new information did you learn about ancient China in *The Emperor's Silent Army*?

2. Why might there have been a **revolt** if people had discovered Qin Shihuang's death while he was away from the capital?

3. Review the description of Pit 1 on pages 459–460. Imagine you are in Pit 1, looking at the soldiers. Describe how your visualization makes you feel and how this helps you understand the text.

4. Interpret the drawing on page 461. What does it help you understand about chariots?

5. Which **aspect** of Qin Shihuang's life best explains why he is a key individual in China's history? Explain your answer, using evidence from the text.

6. Qin Shihuang was a very clever man. How do the plans for his tomb support this claim? Cite text evidence in your answer.

Learn test-taking strategies and answer more questions.
⊘ NGReach.com

Write About It ✐

What else would you like to learn about Qin Shihuang? Write a letter to the author of *The Emperor's Silent Army* to ask for information. Use at least three **Key Words** and details from the article in your letter.

Dear Ms. O'Connor,

I would like to learn more about Qin Shihuang's **empire**.

I would especially like to know more details about how

Qin Shihuang was able to **unify** all of those kingdoms into one.

Relate Ideas

Use a text evidence chart to relate ideas about Qin Shihuang from *The Emperor's Silent Army*. Record examples and anecdotes that the author includes to illustrate the emperor's strengths, weaknesses, and contributions to society.

Text Evidence Chart

Person's Qualities	Text Evidence
brutal, mean	Qin's soldiers had to cut off their enemies' heads.

Use your text evidence chart to analyze Qin Shihuang with a partner. Explain why he was a key individual in Chinese history and how the author's examples and anecdotes elaborate on these ideas. Use **Key Words**.

Fluency  Comprehension Coach

Use the Comprehension Coach to practice reading with phrasing. Rate your reading.

 **Talk Together**

Does *The Emperor's Silent Army* help you understand why we should study ancient cultures? Why or why not? Discuss your ideas with a partner. Use **Key Words** and support your ideas with details from the selection.

Context Clues

When you read an unfamiliar word, look for clues in the nearby text. **Context clues** are words and phrases that may help you figure out the meaning of the new word.

Type of Context Clue	Signal Words	Example
Definition Clue: explains the word directly in the text	*is, are, was, called, means, refers to, or*	An **ancestor** *is* a member of the family who has lived and died in the past.
Synonym Clue: gives a word or a phrase that means almost the same thing	*also, like*	*Like* many other kingdoms, the **empire** was made up of several small states.
Antonym Clue: gives a word or phrase that means almost the opposite	*but, unlike*	The king tried to **unify** his people, *but* they remained divided.

EXAMPLE

> Legends told of an elixir, or magic potion, that gave eternal life to anyone who drank it.

In the sentence above, the phrase *or magic potion* is a definition clue that can help you figure out that *elixir* means "a magical drink."

Try It

Read the sentences. Then answer the questions.

> Like all the other gatherings, the people assembled to hear the emperor speak. He honored their ancestors, who had come before them.

1. **Use context clues. What is the best meaning for the word assembled?**

   A expected
   B listened
   C came together
   D scattered

2. **Use context clues. What is the best meaning for the word ancestors?**

   A great rulers of other kingdoms
   B family members born earlier
   C people who gather together
   D emperors who win wars

NATIONAL GEOGRAPHIC

Connect Across Texts You learned why Qin Shihuang built his terracotta army in the past. Now read how workers are preserving the Emperor's army today.

Genre A **history article** gives detailed information about a specific historical place, event, or person.

A SILENT ARMY
by Jacqueline Ball and Richard Levey

It was 1974. In Xi'an (pronounced *shee-an*), 930 km (580 miles) southwest of Beijing, some farmers were digging a well. Reaching a level 4.6 meters (15 feet) below ground, they uncovered a fragment of pottery that looked like the head of a very large sculpture of a man. The farmers could tell right away that this pottery was more important than finishing the well. They told a local official, who instantly called in archaeologists.

▶ **Before You Move On**
1. **Make Inferences** Why did the farmers know that the statue was important?
2. **Use Text Features** Study the image. How does it support the information about the sculpture?

▲ The sculpture of an archer lies in a partially excavated section of Pit 2. Other figures guarding Qin Shihuang's tomb included cavalry troops, charioteers, and infantrymen.

Working like crime scene investigators, the archaeologists carefully excavated the area around the farmers' well. They found many statues of soldiers made of a red clay called terracotta. They also found clay horses and chariots. It was as if a whole army lay beneath the earth. The site is only a mile from the main tomb of the First Emperor of China, Qin Shihuang, who lived from 259 B.C. to 201 B.C. They knew this massive group of sculptures must be part of his tomb **complex**.

Over the next six years, the investigators detected three underground pits covering more than 22,000 square meters (200,000 square feet). Ranged over this huge space were about 8,000 terracotta warriors and horses buried in tunnels or rooms that were separated by walls made of **rammed** earth. Some figures stood tall, and others kneeled. Horses galloped or waited in harnesses.

In Other Words
complex area
rammed tightly packed

HOW THEY WERE MADE

Each sculpture was life-size. Actually, the soldiers were even bigger than life. They stood about 1.8 meters (six feet) tall, which was taller than most Chinese people were at the time they were made. This would have made them seem especially strong and powerful. Each figure's face had a different expression, hairstyle, and clothing. Each one was marked with his army rank.

From studying the way the warriors were made, archaeologists concluded that Qin's **craftsmen** had an extremely high level of technical skills. The various parts of the sculptures—legs, arms, bodies, fronts of heads, and backs of heads—were made in separate molds. Then each warrior was glued together.

Over the molded parts, craftsmen attached individually sculpted ears, noses, hair, and facial expressions. They also attached military armor, belts, and other precise costume details. They then **fired** the completed sculptures in a pottery **kiln** and painted the finished products. As a result of such careful attention to detail, no two warriors or horses are exactly the same.

It appears that the craftsmen who made the sculptures were proud of their work. The name of the person who built each figure was found inscribed on the warrior's robe, leg, or armor.

In Other Words
craftsmen sculptors; artists
fired baked
kiln oven

▲ This life-size archer once held a real crossbow in his hands. Some experts consider him to be the best crafted of all the terracotta soldiers.

▶ **Before You Move On**

1. **Explain** How did archaeologists make a connection between the terracotta army and the tomb of Qin Shihuang?

2. **Use Text Features** How does the archer statue shown above demonstrate the "attention to detail" described in the text?

469

THE FIRST EMPEROR

The Qin dynasty ruled about 2,200 years ago. It was around this time that historians began to put together a written record of China's history. So we have more than **turtle shells** to help us interpret the terracotta warriors and understand the Emperor's life.

From the time he was a child, Ying Zheng planned ahead. When he inherited the throne of the Qin (pronounced *chin*) kingdom at age 13, he ordered workers to begin building his tomb. Then he got busy conquering the many neighboring kingdoms in the enormous plains around the Yellow River. Eventually, Ying united the kingdoms into an **empire**. He took the name Qin Shihuang, "First Emperor of Qin." Historians believed that the name Qin is the source of the word "China."

THE GREAT WALL

Qin Shihuang's reign lasted 37 years. During much of that time, the dynasty was either at war or defending its borders from invaders. Under his rule, several sections of the defensive wall built over the previous centuries were rebuilt, strengthened, connected, and extended into what we know today as the Great Wall of China.

In Other Words

turtle shells the writing that ancient Chinese historians recorded on turtle shells and bones

470

▲ Although Qin Shihuang's tomb has never been excavated, an artist has illustrated how the tomb might look, based on historical descriptions of the interior.

▶ **Before You Move On**

1. **Draw Conclusions** Review the information about Qin Shihuang on page 470. What kind of ruler was he?

2. **Interpret** Study the painting. What does it help you understand about the first emperor?

PREPARING THE TOMB

While the Great Wall was visible for many miles and remains an important symbol of China, Qin Shihuang's tomb was even more amazing. Over the course of his reign, some 700,000 workers were involved in its construction. A historian of the time recorded that pearls were placed in the ceiling of his burial chamber to represent the stars. A map of the Qin Empire, with its rivers and lakes filled with liquid mercury, was said to have been carved into the floor of the tomb. It is believed that the Emperor felt so strongly about keeping the details of the tomb's construction a secret that he had thousands of workers buried alive when the tomb was sealed.

Though archaeologists know the location of this tomb, they haven't yet found the entrance. They must be very careful when they do find it. If it really contains rivers of mercury, it will be poisonous to anyone who enters.

It may come as no surprise that Qin Shihuang was a feared and hated ruler. Perhaps he realized this and also planned on bringing protection with him to the afterlife. The Emperor always thought big. He brought not just some soldiers but an entire army.

▲ Workers try to piece together one of the terracotta warriors found in Pit 1. Thousands of figures **await eventual reconstruction.**

In Other Words
await eventual reconstruction are waiting to be put back together

472

THE TERRACOTTA ARMY TODAY

Archaeologists are still digging up terracotta soldiers. In fact, in the 30 years since the army was discovered, only 1,000 of the estimated 8,000 soldiers have been uncovered. But the terracotta army is also one of the most popular tourist destinations in China. It is facing a dangerous, modern enemy. In the 1990s, the Chinese government erected enormous buildings over the dig site to protect the warriors from the weather. They also allowed 1.5 million visitors each year to come and watch the ongoing excavation.

But the site is in Xi'an, which is one of the most polluted cities in the world. In addition, all those visitors breathing in a closed building have added a lot of moisture to the air. The moisture got so bad that **mold** has grown on many of the statues.

Qin Shihuang clearly thought that 8,000 terracotta soldiers were enough to defend him in the afterlife. However, it doesn't look as if he considered who would defend those soldiers. Conservationists, or professionals who

▲ A few of the soldiers still show their original paint. Technicians use the latest techniques to determine how the soldiers were painted.

work to preserve important historical artifacts, are working now to figure out how to reduce the amount of damage that pollution and visitors do to this ancient army. Only then can the soldiers continue to stand guard well into the future. ❖

In Other Words
mold a plant-like organism

▶ **Before You Move On**

1. **Relate Ideas** What examples does the author include to show how the Emperor's army contributed to modern China?

2. **Draw Conclusions** How might the complex be saved? Cite text evidence to support your conclusion.

Respond and Extend

Key Words

ancestor	empire
aspect	foundation
assemble	infrastructure
conquest	revolt
domain	unify

Compare Details

Both *The Emperor's Silent Army* and "A Silent Army" provide information about Qin Shihuang and his terracotta army. Use a comparison chart to compare how the two authors presented the information in similar or different ways. Then analyze the information in the chart to draw conclusions about Emperor Qin's rule.

Comparison Chart

	The Emperor's Silent Army	"A Silent Army"
History of Qin Shihuang's Life	Details: • • •	Details: • ruled about 2,200 years ago • •
Qin Shihuang's Tomb	Details: • • •	Details: • • •
Qin's Terracotta Army	Details: • • •	Details: • • •

Talk Together

Analyze the information from both texts. How do they show ways that historians and archaeologists work together to help us learn about ancient China? Use **Key Words** and cite evidence from the text as you discuss and compare your ideas with a partner's.

Pronoun Agreement

A **pronoun** usually refers back to a noun. This noun is called the antecedent. The type of pronoun you use depends on how it is used in a sentence.

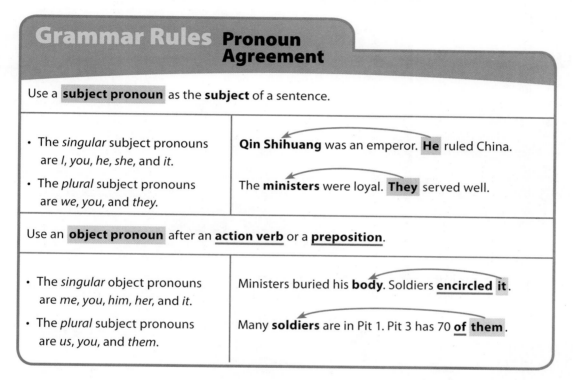

Grammar Rules **Pronoun Agreement**

Use a **subject pronoun** as the **subject** of a sentence.

• The *singular* subject pronouns are *I, you, he, she,* and *it.*	**Qin Shihuang** was an emperor. **He** ruled China.
• The *plural* subject pronouns are *we, you,* and *they.*	The **ministers** were loyal. **They** served well.

Use an **object pronoun** after an **action verb** or a **preposition**.

• The *singular* object pronouns are *me, you, him, her,* and *it.*	Ministers buried his **body**. Soldiers **encircled it**.
• The *plural* subject pronouns are *us, you,* and *them.*	Many **soldiers** are in Pit 1. Pit 3 has 70 **of them**.

Read Sentences with Pronouns

Writers use pronouns to keep from repeating words too often. Read this passage from "A Silent Army." Which words are used to avoid repetition?

> Though archaeologists know the location of this tomb, they haven't yet found the entrance. They must be very careful when they do find it. If it really contains rivers of mercury, it will be poisonous to anyone who enters.

Write Sentences with Pronouns

Reread pages 472–473 of "A Silent Army." Write a paragraph explaining the challenges that archaeologists face as they excavate the terracotta army. Include at least two subject pronouns and two object pronouns. Trade paragraphs with a partner. Underline each pronoun and circle its antecedent. Make sure that the pronouns and antecedents match.

Language Frames

- The main idea/event is
  _____.
- The person/character
  _____.
- To summarize, _____.

Summarize

Listen to the folk tale "The Ungrateful Tiger." Then listen to how one student summarizes the story. Use **Language Frames** to summarize another folk tale you know.

The Ungrateful Tiger ((MP3))

One night, a tiger falls into a hole. He tries to get out but can't.

In the morning, a man passes by. The tiger promises to be grateful if the man helps him get out. So the man helps the tiger climb out.

Once the tiger is out, he roars that he will eat the man.

Just then, a clever rabbit comes along and tricks the tiger.

The tiger falls back into the hole. The rabbit and the man leave the tiger to his fate.

ℭ

To summarize, when an ungrateful tiger threatens to eat the man who helped him, a clever rabbit tricks the tiger and saves the man's life.

476

Social Studies Vocabulary

Key Words

despair

invasion

legendary

precious

subordinate

Key Words

Read the story and study the illustrations. Use **Key Words** and other words to talk about how traditional stories can add to our understanding of history.

A Legendary Emperor

Emperor Yao was well loved and **precious** to his people. He chose to live in a small hut instead of a huge palace. If anything bad happened in his empire, he blamed himself.

Emperor Yao had a son named Danzhu who was not kind. Danzhu only cared about money. He gave orders to his father's loyal **subordinates**, or servants, for his own selfish reasons.

Emperor Yao knew that his son's greedy attitude would be as hurtful as a forceful **invasion** into his peaceful country by an evil, new ruler.

Emperor Yao **despaired** at the upsetting thought of leaving his empire to Danzhu. He bravely broke tradition and gave his empire to a kind and humble young man named Shun. This **legendary** action is remembered to this day.

Talk Together

Summarize the text about Emperor Yao with a partner. Use **Language Frames** from page 476 and **Key Words** as you retell the most important events in your own words.

Elements of Fiction

Some fiction writers use a literary device called an **embedded story**. This is a story that is included within the main story. Embedded stories can help build background for the main story, provide an example or illustration of something in the main story, or help the main story's plot move forward toward a resolution of the characters' problems.

"Ba, you said you would tell me the Old Man of the Moon story again today."

"More stories!" Ma said, and her chopsticks struck the inside of her empty rice bowl resentfully . . .

Ma shook her head and sighed, but said nothing, so Ba began.

The Story of the Old Man of the Moon

Once there was a magistrate who was quite powerful and proud. . . .

"The text of the main story includes a story title to show where the embedded story begins."

Map and Talk

A double plot diagram can help you keep track of an embedded story. As you read the main story, think about how the embedded story influences the main story's characters and plot.

Double Plot Diagram

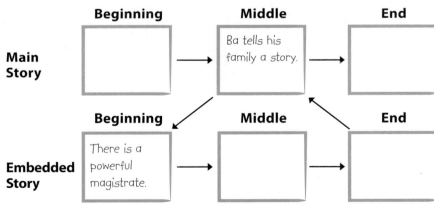

Talk Together

Tell a partner about an important day in your life. Explain the entire day's events as the main story. Tell an embedded story about something in the past that will give your listener more background about you or the event. Share enough details so that your partner can fill in a double plot diagram.

More Key Words

Use these words to talk about *Where the Mountain Meets the Moon* and "Mu Lan."

expertise
(**ek**-spur-tēz) *noun*

Expertise is special knowledge or skill. A black belt shows a high level of **expertise** in karate.

inquiry
(**in**-kwu-rē) *noun*

An **inquiry** is a question or investigation. The police will hold an **inquiry** to ask people how the accident happened.

integrity
(in-**te**-gru-tē) *noun*

Integrity is behaving in a way that is honest, fair, or right. The girl showed **integrity** by returning the wallet she found.

pose
(pōz) *verb*

To **pose** means to stand still in a certain position. The boy **poses** like a superhero.

promote
(pru-**mōt**) *verb*

To **promote** means to give someone a higher rank or position. The colonel will **promote** the general to a higher rank.

Talk Together

Work with a partner. Write a question using at least one **Key Word**. Your partner answers your question using a different **Key Word**, if possible. Use each word twice.

Question: Why might someone be <u>promoted</u>?

Answer: A worker may show a special <u>expertise</u> at his or her job.

Add words to My Vocabulary Notebook.
NGReach.com

Learn to Synthesize

As you read, you can **form generalizations**, or general statements, about people, things, or situations. Valid, or true, generalizations should be based on what you read as well as your own observations.

How to Form Generalizations

📖	**1.** As you read, look for details that are about the same idea.	I read _____.
💭	**2.** Add related examples from your own experience or knowledge.	I know _____.
🧩	**3.** Make a general statement that seems true based on evidence from the text and your knowledge.	I can generalize that _____.

Here's how one student formed a generalization.

Look Into the Text

Every morning, before the sun rose, Minli, her mother, and her father began work in the fields. It was planting season, which was especially grueling. The mud stuck to their feet like glue and each seedling had to be painstakingly planted by hand. When the hot sun burned overhead, Minli's knees shook from weariness.

"I read **details** about the family's hard work."

"I know that ancient Chinese farmers did not have many advanced tools."

"I can generalize that farming was extremely difficult work in ancient China."

Forming generalizations can help you better understand the ideas and concepts presented in a text. Remember that valid generalizations should always be supported by evidence in the text.

Talk Together

Read the folk tale and sample notes. Use **Language Frames** to
form generalizations as you read. Talk with a partner about the
generalizations you formed and how you made them.

Folk Tale

Good Luck
or
Bad Luck?

Long ago, a wise, old man lived in the open plains beyond the Great Wall of
China. The things that were most **precious** to him were his son and his horses. People
appreciated the old man's **expertise** and **integrity** and traveled from far and wide to
buy horses from him. ◀

One day, one of the man's **subordinates** accidentally left the stable door open.
The man's favorite stallion, a horse **legendary** for its beauty and speed, escaped. While
others would have **despaired**, the old man remained calm. He said to his neighbors,
"Why be upset? No one knew the horse would escape. What's done is done."

A few days later, the stallion returned with a dazzling, white mare. After an **inquiry**
to make sure that no one had lost a horse, the man added the rare white horse to his
stable. The man's neighbors were delighted at his good luck, but the wise man remained
calm. "Who knows why this horse has come to me," he said. "What will be will be." ◀

Two weeks later, the man's son fell while riding the beautiful, white horse. The son
broke his leg and walked with a limp from that time forward. The old man did not get
angry at the white horse, nor did he feel sorrow for his son. The neighbors said, "It would
have been better if this horse had never come to you."

But the man merely shrugged and said "Accidents will happen." When the family
posed for a portrait, the wise man stood with one hand resting on his favorite horse and
the other on his son's shoulder.

Two years later, an enemy invaded the man's country. All of the man's neighbors
were **promoted** into military positions and had to go to fight against the **invasion**, but
his son was not included because of his limp. While many lost their lives, the son's life
was saved. Sometimes it's hard to tell the difference between good luck and bad luck! ◀

I **read** that people
traveled from far away to
buy horses from the man.

I **know** that my parents
like working with honest
people, too.

I can **generalize** that
most people prefer to
do business with people
they trust.

◀ = good place to stop and form a generalization

481

Read a Fantasy

Genre

A **fantasy** story is fiction. It includes made-up events that could not happen in real life. Fantasy stories often include talking animals, magical settings, or characters with special powers.

Dialogue

Authors can show their characters' thoughts, feelings, and traits through their dialogue. Pay attention to what characters say and how they say it.

> **"How could you spend your money on that?!"** Ma said, **slapping the rice bowls on the table**. "On something so useless? And we will have to feed it! There is barely enough rice for us as it is."
>
> **"I will share my rice with it,"** Minli **said quickly**. "The goldfish man said that it will bring fortune to our house."

Ma's dialogue and actions convey anger.

Minli's dialogue and actions show she is trying to please Ma.

FROM
Where the
Mountain
Meets the
Moon

by Grace Lin
illustrated by Marina Seoane

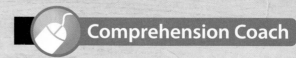
Comprehension Coach

Every morning, before the sun rose, Minli, her mother, and her father began work in the fields. It was planting season, which was especially grueling. The mud stuck to their feet like glue and each seedling had to be painstakingly planted by hand. When the hot sun burned overhead, Minli's knees shook from weariness. She hated the feeling of thick, soggy mud on her hands and face; and many times she wanted to stop in irritation and exhaustion. But seeing her parents' bent backs, patiently working, made her **swallow her complaints** and continue.

As soon as the sun began to set, Minli's parents sent her home to make dinner and to rest while they continued to work in the thick mud. They would not come home until the sun had completely disappeared from the sky.

At home, Minli washed her face and hands and feet; and even though all the water in the basin turned brown, she still felt like she was covered in mud. Her arms and legs were so tired that she felt like an old crab crawling on rocks. As she looked at herself reflected in the dark water, she saw Ma's frown on her face.

Ma is right, Minli thought. *What a poor* **fortune** *we have. Every day, Ba and Ma work and work and we still have nothing. I wish I could change our fortune.*

At that very moment, Minli heard a faint murmuring sound that she had never heard before, like a song chanted from the clouds. Curious, she opened the door to see what the noise was.

And there, on the road in front of her house, she saw a small stranger calling out quietly. "Goldfish," he was saying softly, as if he were **coaxing** his fish to swim. "Bring fortune into your home."

In Other Words
swallow her complaints not
    complain aloud
fortune luck
coaxing encouraging

484

Minli and the villagers stared as he wheeled his cart. Even though the village was by a river, it had been many years since anyone had seen a glimpse of a goldfish. The fish in the Jade River were brown and gray, like the village. The goldfish man's cart was full of bowls of flashing fish that glittered like jewels.

His gentle calling drew Minli to him like a moth to a lit lantern. "How does a goldfish bring fortune into your home?" Minli asked.

The goldfish man looked at her; the sun setting behind him made him glow bright red and yellow. "Don't you know?" he asked her. "Goldfish means plenty of gold. Having a bowl of goldfish means your house will be full of gold and **jade**."

As Minli stared into his bowls with her shining black eyes, a brilliant orange fish stared back at her with its shining black eyes. And then quickly, so quickly that Minli barely thought about it, she turned into the house and grabbed the two copper coins from the white rabbit rice bowl.

In Other Words
◀ **jade** **precious** stones that are used for jewelry and carvings

"I'll buy that one," Minli said, and she pointed at the fiery orange fish with the black eyes and fin that had **caught her eye**.

The other village children looked at her enviously while the watching adults shook their heads. "Minli," one neighbor said, "don't believe his impossible talk. A goldfish won't bring fortune. Save your money."

But Minli was not discouraged and she held out her copper coins to the goldfish man. He looked at her and smiled. Then he took one coin, picked up the fishbowl, and gave it to her.

"May it bring you great fortune," he said. And with a small bow to the villagers, he wheeled out of the village. In moments, he disappeared from view into the shadow of Fruitless Mountain, and if it wasn't for the goldfish Minli had in her hands, all would have thought he was a dream.

But the goldfish was real, and when her parents returned from the fields for dinner they were not happy to learn that Minli had spent her money on it.

"How could you spend your money on that?!" Ma said, slapping the rice bowls on the table. "On something so useless? And we will have to feed it! There is barely enough rice for us as it is."

"I will share my rice with it," Minli said quickly. "The goldfish man said that it will bring fortune to our house."

"Fortune!" Ma said. "You spent half the money in our house!"

"Now, Wife," Ba said, sitting quietly, "it was Minli's money. It was hers to do with as she wished. Money must be used sometime. What use is money in a bowl?"

"It is more useful than a goldfish in a bowl," her mother said **shortly**.

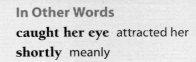

In Other Words
caught her eye attracted her
shortly meanly

"Who knows," Ba said. "Maybe it will bring fortune to our house."

"Another impossible dream," Ma said, looking at the plain rice in her bowl with bitterness. "It will take more than a goldfish to bring fortune to our house."

"Like what?" Minli asked. "What do we need to bring fortune here?"

"Ah," Ba said, "that is a question you will have to ask the Old Man of the Moon."

"The Old Man of the Moon again," Minli said, and she looked at her father. "Ba, you said you would tell me the Old Man of the Moon story again today."

"More stories!" Ma said, and her chopsticks struck the inside of her empty rice bowl resentfully. "Haven't we had enough of those?"

"Now, Wife," Ba said again, "stories cost us nothing."

"And gain us nothing as well," Ma said.

There was **a stony** silence as Ba looked sadly into his rice bowl. Minli tugged at his sleeve. "Please, Ba?" she said.

Ma shook her head and sighed, but said nothing, so Ba began.

The Story of the Old Man of the Moon

Once there was a **magistrate** who was quite powerful and proud. He was so proud that he demanded constant respect from his people. Whenever he made a trip out of the city, no matter what time of day or night, people were to leave their homes, get on their knees, and make deep bows as he passed, or else face the brutal punishment of his soldiers. The magistrate was fierce in his anger as well as his pride. It is said he even expected the monkeys to come down from the trees to bow to him.

In Other Words
a stony an uncomfortable
magistrate city leader

489

The magistrate was harsh with his **subordinates**, ruthless to his enemies, and pitiless to his people. All feared his wrath, and when he roared his orders the people trembled. Behind his back, they called him Magistrate Tiger.

Magistrate Tiger's most coveted wish was to be of royal blood. His every decision was crafted for that purpose; every manipulation was part of a strategy to achieve acceptance into the **imperial** family. As soon as his son was born, he began to make trips and **inquiries** to gain influence, in hopes that he could marry his son to a member of the imperial family.

One night, as the magistrate traveled through the mountains (again on a trip to gain favor for his son's future marriage), he saw an old man sitting alone in the moonlight. The old man ignored the passing horses and carriages, the silk brocade and the government seal, and simply continued reading a large book in his lap, **placidly fingering** a bag of red string beside him. The old man's **indifference** infuriated Magistrate Tiger and he ordered the carriage to stop. However, even the halting noises did not make the old man look up.

Finally, Magistrate Tiger exited his carriage and went to the old man, still engrossed in his book.

"Do you not bow to your magistrate?!" he roared.

The old man continued to read.

"What are you reading that is so important?" the magistrate demanded, and looked at the pages of the book. It was full of scribbles and scrawls that were not of any language the magistrate knew of. "Why, it's just nonsense written in there!"

"Nonsense!" the old man said, finally looking up. "You fool. This is the Book of Fortune. It holds all the knowledge of the world—the past, present, and future."

In Other Words
imperial ruling
placidly fingering gently touching
indifference lack of interest

The magistrate looked again at the marks on the page. "I cannot read it," he said.

"Of course not," the man said. "But I, the Old Man of the Moon, Guardian of the Book of Fortune, can read it. And with it, I can answer any question in the world."

"You can answer any question in the world?" the magistrate **scoffed**. "Very well. Who will my son marry when he is **of age**?"

The Old Man of the Moon flipped the pages of the book. "Hmm," he said to himself. "Yes, here it is . . . your son's future wife is now the two-year-old daughter of a grocer in the next village."

In Other Words
scoffed said rudely
of age old enough; a man

▶ **Before You Move On**

1. **Generalize** What statement can you make about people who have an attitude like Ma's?

2. **Genre** How is the writing style of the embedded story different than the main story? Cite specific examples.

▶ **Predict**
Will the Old Man of the Moon's
prediction come true?

"The daughter of a grocer!" the magistrate spat.

"Yes," the Old Man of the Moon continued. "Right now she is wrapped in a blue blanket embroidered with white rabbits, sitting on the lap of her blind grandmother in front of her house."

"No!" the magistrate said. "I won't allow it!"

"It's true . . ." the Old Man said. "They are destined to be husband and wife. I, myself, tied the red cord that binds them."

"What red cord?" Magistrate Tiger demanded.

"Do you know nothing? I tie together everyone who meets with these red threads." The Old Man sighed, holding up his bag full of red string. "When you were born, I tied your ankle to your wife's ankle with a red thread, and as you both grew older the line became shorter until you eventually met. All the people you've met in your life have been brought to you by the red cords I tied. I must have forgotten to tie the end of one of the lines, which is why you are meeting me now. I won't do that again."

"I don't believe you," the magistrate said.

"Believe or don't believe," the Old Man said, standing up and putting the big book on his back, "we have reached the end of our thread and I will now leave."

The magistrate stared in **dumbfounded** silence as the Old Man of the Moon walked away up the mountain.

"Crazy old man," the magistrate said finally. "What a waste of my time!"

The magistrate returned to his carriage and continued on. But as they drove through the next village, he saw an old blind woman holding a baby girl in front of a house. The girl was wrapped in a blue blanket embroidered with white rabbits, just as the Old Man of the Moon had said.

Magistrate Tiger burned with anger. "I will not let my son marry a grocer's daughter!" he vowed. So, after he arrived at his guesthouse, the magistrate secretly ordered one of his servants to return to the grocer's home and stab the girl with a knife. *That will take care of her*, he thought to himself.

In Other Words
dumbfounded amazed

Many years later, Magistrate Tiger had his dream fulfilled. He was finally able to **obtain a match** for his son with one of the emperor's many granddaughters, and his son would inherit the rule of a remote city. On the wedding day, Magistrate Tiger bragged to his son about how he had arranged the marriage and **outwitted** the Man of the Moon. The son (who was not like his father) said nothing, but after the wedding ceremony, sent a trusted servant to find the grocer's family to **make amends**. In the meantime, he became acquainted with his bride and was happy to find that both were pleased with each other. He found his new wife beautiful, the only oddity about her being that she always wore a delicate flower on her forehead.

"Dear Wife," he said, "Why do you always wear that flower? Even to sleep, you never remove it."

"It is to hide my scar," she said, touching her forehead in embarrassment. "When I was a child no older than two, a strange man stabbed me with a knife. I survived, but I still have this scar."

And at that moment, the trusted servant came rushing in. "Master," he said, "I made the inquiries you asked for. In a flood many years ago, the grocer's family perished—except for the daughter. The king of the city (the emperor's ninth son) then adopted the daughter and raised her as his own . . . and that daughter is your wife!"

"So the Old Man of the Moon was right!" Minli said.

"Of course he was," Ba replied. "The Old Man of the Moon knows everything and can answer any question you ask."

"I should ask him how to bring fortune to our house!" Minli said. "He would know, I'll ask him. Where do I find him?"

In Other Words
obtain a match get a wife
outwitted been smarter than
make amends apologize

"They say he lives on top of Never-Ending Mountain," Ba said. "But no one I have ever spoken to knows where that is."

"Maybe we can find out," Minli said.

"Oh, Minli!" Ma said impatiently. "Bringing fortune to our house! Making Fruitless Mountain bloom! You're always wishing to do impossible things! Stop believing stories and stop wasting your time."

"Stories are not a waste of time," Ba said.

"Stories," Ma said, slapping her hands against the table, making the water in the fishbowl sway as she stood up and left the table, "are what wasted money on this goldfish."

Minli stared down at her rice bowl; the few white grains left sat like **precious** pearls at the bottom of her bowl. Ba patted her arm. "Eat all your rice, Daughter," he said, and with his shaking hands, he scooped the last of his own rice to feed the fish.

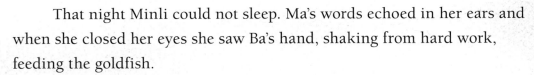

That night Minli could not sleep. Ma's words echoed in her ears and when she closed her eyes she saw Ba's hand, shaking from hard work, feeding the goldfish.

"Ma is right," Minli thought to herself, "the goldfish is just another mouth to feed. I can't let Ba feed the goldfish. Ma and Ba work so hard for every grain of rice, Ba shouldn't have to feed the goldfish, too."

Minli slipped quietly out of her bed and crept to the table where the goldfish was. They stared at each other and Minli knew what she had to do. Quickly, slipping on her shoes and jacket, she took the goldfish and left the house.

It was late. The village was quietly asleep and the stars above filled the sky like spilled salt on dried seaweed. Minli's footsteps seemed to hush the night as she made her way toward the Jade River.

At the edge of the river, Minli looked at her goldfish one last time. The moon shone above so even in the darkness of the night, the fish seemed to burn a bright orange. Its black eyes sparkled at her.

"I'm sorry I can't keep you," Minli whispered. "I hope you will be all right in the river." And with those words, she emptied the bowl into the water. For a moment the fish seemed shocked and was still, like a flickering flame on a match. Then it wiggled in the water and swam in circles, a joyful fire twirling in the water.

Minli watched it and sighed. As the sound faded into the night, Minli realized it was an echo of her mother's impatient, frustrated noise. "Ma will never stop sighing unless our fortune changes. But how will it ever change?" Minli asked ruefully. "I guess that is just another question for the Old Man of the Moon. Too bad no one knows how to get to Never-Ending Mountain to ask him anything."

The fish stopped swimming and looked up at Minli. "I know where it is," it said. The female voice was high and soft, like the wind whistling through the reeds of the water.

Minli stared. "Did you say something?" she asked.

"Yes," the fish said. "I know how you can get to Never-Ending Mountain and ask the Old Man of the Moon a question."

"You're a talking fish?" Minli asked, **her words tumbling into each other** with excitement. "How can you talk?"

"Most fish talk," the fish said, "if you are willing to listen. One, of course, must want to hear."

"I do," Minli said, enthralled and eager. This was just like one of Ba's stories! She **bubbled with** excitement. "How do you know the way to Never-Ending Mountain?"

In Other Words

her words tumbling into each other
speaking quickly

bubbled with felt so much

"I've swum all the oceans and rivers, except for one," the fish said, "and on my way to the last, the goldfish man caught me. I **despaired** in his cart, for I have seen and learned much of the world, including the way to Never-Ending Mountain. Since you have set me free, I will tell you."

"You've swum all the oceans and rivers?" Minli asked. The questions spilled like overflowing water. "Which river haven't you seen? Why have you traveled so much? Where is Never-Ending Mountain? When did . . . "

"This river is the one river I have not swum," the fish interrupted, "and I have waited a long time to see it. So I would like to start as soon as possible. You can ask the Old Man of the Moon all your other questions. Let me tell you the way to him so I can be off."

Minli nodded and asked no more. She realized she was having a conversation with a goldfish, which was very unusual, so she decided to listen. ❖

▶ **Before You Move On**

1. **Confirm Prediction** Was the Old Man of the Moon's prediction correct? What affected the couple's fate?

2. **Character** Minli is willing to set the goldfish free for her family. What does this evidence tell you about Minli?

Meet the Author

Grace Lin

AWARD WINNER

When Grace Lin was young, her mother used to hide collections of Chinese folk tales in their bookshelves for her daughter to discover and read for herself. As a result, Lin grew up with a love of cultural folk tales and storytelling. Her Newberry Honor novel *Where the Mountain Meets the Moon* combines both of these interests in a way that one reviewer has called "a tribute to storytelling."

Lin believes that storytelling is more important than ever in our modern society. "I am hoping that with all of today's technology, the tradition of sharing stories has become even more important. As wonderful as virtual connections are, nothing compares to real-life sharing." Like Lin, look for stories that you treasure. You may find new ways to tell the old stories you love the most.

Writer's Craft

Authors sometimes use characters' dialogue and actions to show what the characters are like. For example, Ma's dialogue and actions show that she is an angry, resentful person. Find examples from the story that show what Ba is like.

Then write a conversation between two people who are discussing a magical event. Use dialogue and actions to show what each character is like.

Key Words

despair	legendary
expertise	pose
inquiry	precious
integrity	promote
invasion	subordinate

Talk About It 💬

1. What elements of Minli's story help you determine that it is fantasy? Cite at least three examples from the text.

2. What ideas does the story present about storytelling and magic? Use evidence from the text to form a generalization about fantasy stories.

3. Think about the most important events in "The Story of the Old Man of the Moon." Summarize the embedded story in your own words.

4. How does Minli change from the beginning to the end of the story? Cite text evidence to show how the story events cause her to react and change.

5. Analyze the purpose of the embedded story. How does it contribute to the development of the main story?

6. Why do you think parents tell their children stories? Form a generalization that is supported by evidence from the text.

Learn test-taking strategies and answer more questions.
🌐 **NGReach.com**

Write About It ✏️

Think about what Ma and Ba might say if they learned Minli had spoken with the goldfish. Write a short dialogue between them. Use at least three **Key Words**.

> "I just heard Minli was talking to the goldfish!" Ma yelled.
>
> "I didn't know our **precious** daughter could speak to fish," Ba replied calmly.

Elements of Fiction

Use a double plot diagram to record the events from the main story and the embedded story in *Where the Mountain Meets the Moon*. Think about how the embedded story affects Minli and leads to the main story's resolution.

Double Plot Diagram

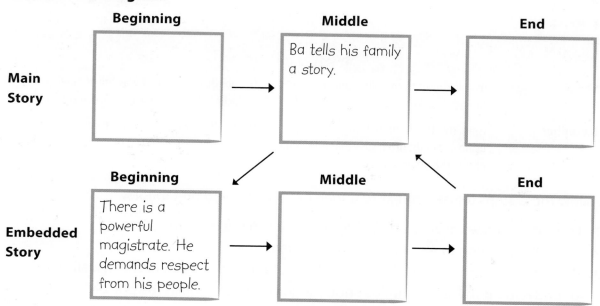

Main Story

Beginning

Middle
Ba tells his family a story.

End

Embedded Story

Beginning
There is a powerful magistrate. He demands respect from his people.

Middle

End

Work with a partner. Use your double plot diagram to summarize the two stories and discuss how they relate to each other. Tell how the embedded story helps the plot of the main story unfold. Use **Key Words**.

Fluency  Comprehension Coach

Use the Comprehension Coach to practice reading with expression. Rate your reading.

Talk Together

Think about the themes, or lessons, within *Where the Mountain Meets the Moon*. Why do cultures create folk tales that teach lessons? What modern-day stories teach similar lessons? Discuss your ideas with your partner. Use **Key Words** and evidence from the text.

Figurative Language

As you read, you may find many phrases with meanings that are different from the literal, or actual, meanings of the words by themselves. This is called **figurative language**. Figurative language can help readers visualize, or create a picture of, what is happening in the story. Similes and metaphors are two kinds of figurative language.

EXAMPLES

Type of Figurative Language	Explanation	Example
Simile	uses *like* or *as* to compare two or more things	The goldfish man's cart was full of bowls of flashing fish that glittered *like* jewels.
Metaphor	compares two or more things without using *like* or *as*; often says that one thing *is* or *was* the other thing	The goldfish *was* a joyful fire twirling in the water.

Follow these steps to use context to understand similes and metaphors.

1. Look at sentences nearby. See if they give clues to the meaning.
2. Predict a meaning that might fit in the context.
3. Reread the sentence to see if the simile or metaphor helps you better visualize or understand the story. If it does not, ask someone to explain the phrase.

Try It

Read the sentences. Then answer the questions. Use the chart and steps to help you.

When Ma saw the fish, she was as angry as a roaring lion. Minli was a statue—frozen in place—while Ma yelled at her.

1. **What is the best meaning for the simile she was as angry as a roaring lion?**

   A Ma was angry about a roaring lion.

   B Ma turned into an angry lion.

   C Ma acted very angrily.

   D Ma roared to sound like a lion.

2. **What is the best meaning for the metaphor Minli was a statue?**

   A Minli stood very still.

   B Minli ran away from Ma.

   C Minli hid behind a statue.

   D Minli turned into a statue.

Connect Across Texts You read about a girl trying to change her fortune. Now read about how one brave woman changed the course of history.

Genre A **drama** is a story that is intended to be performed for an audience. A script is the written form of the play and includes dialogue and stage directions.

Mu Lan
The Girl Who Knew No Fear

A Chinese folk tale retold by Joyce McGreevy   ILLUSTRATED BY LAURA PEREZ

CHARACTERS

NARRATOR 1
NARRATOR 2
FATHER
MOTHER
MU LAN
MESSENGER
GENERAL HUA
SOLDIER 1
SOLDIER 2

SCENE 1

[**SETTING** *The play begins in a peaceful farming village in China in the 1100s, during the Song dynasty. MU LAN, a young woman, is at home. She has long hair and wraps a beautiful robe or shawl around her shoulders. She is seated on a cushion, studying a scroll. NARRATOR 1 and NARRATOR 2 stand off to one side and speak directly to the audience.*]

▶ **Before You Move On**

1. **Drama** How does the Characters list prepare you to read the play?
2. **Setting** What do you know about the setting so far? Cite text evidence that helps you picture the time and place.

503

NARRATOR 1: Long ago, when many an ancient story was as new as the first grass in spring, there lived a girl named Mu Lan.

NARRATOR 2: She lived in a quiet village in China, where farmers' fields spread out in all directions like embroidered cloths of green and gold. No star in the heavens was ever as brilliant as Mu Lan.

NARRATOR 1: From the time that she was a child, Mu Lan demonstrated a tremendous capacity for learning. With her quick **wit** and her restless wonder, Mu Lan could follow a line of thought, no matter how complex, as easily as a bird in flight distinguishes its invisible path. She admired new ideas the way some people admire a beautiful sunrise.

NARRATOR 2: Picture her now as she was then.

[FATHER *and* MOTHER *enter. They are proud of* MU LAN.]

FATHER: Mu Lan, your mother and I are pleased with your devotion to your studies. You behave with respect to your teachers, and you work tirelessly at your lessons. So we were wondering—

MOTHER: Now that you have learned to read and write, to recite our history, and to map many lands—

FATHER: What would you like to study next?

MU LAN: [*begins pacing the room as she thinks over the question*] Well, I do love the arts.

MOTHER: Good, very good.

FATHER: Which arts would you like to learn?

MOTHER: Painting and sculpting?

FATHER: Singing and dancing?

MU LAN: [**posing** *like a kung fu master*] I would like to learn the martial arts!

[MOTHER *and* FATHER *exchange looks of utter surprise, appear to consider the matter, and then smile in agreement.*]

NARRATOR 1: And so she did.

[*As* NARRATOR 1 *and* NARRATOR 2 *speak,* MU LAN ***mimes appropriate actions***.]

NARRATOR 2: Thereafter, her mother and father **took it upon themselves** to teach her everything she wanted to know.

In Other Words
wit intelligence
mimes appropriate actions *acts out what they are saying*
took it upon themselves did everything they could

NARRATOR 1: They taught her to run with speed and stamina . . . to swim with graceful and powerful strokes . . . and to ride on horseback with **unwavering poise**.

FATHER: You can do it, Mu Lan!

NARRATOR 2: They taught her how to **wield a sword of great heft** . . . how to use a bow and arrow.

MOTHER: Keep your aim steady, Mu Lan!

NARRATOR 1: They taught her to stand tall.

[MU LAN *puts hands on hips, stands straight.*]

FATHER: Look everyone in the eye, Mu Lan!

MOTHER: You are strong, Mu Lan!

[MOTHER, FATHER, *and* MU LAN *exit.*]

NARRATOR 1: As the seasons passed, Mu Lan learned more and more.

NARRATOR 2: She was as skillful as the silent tiger that moves undetected through the deep forest, hunting, hunting.

NARRATOR 1: She was as patient as the noble crane that vigilantly watches the still water, waiting, waiting.

NARRATOR 2: She wanted to know many things, but there was one thing, and one thing only, that she absolutely refused to know.

NARRATOR 1: [*proudly*] She refused to know fear.

▶ **Before You Move On**

1. **Character** Describe Mu Lan based on evidence from the text. Include details about how she has developed these traits.

2. **Generalize** Why are narrators an important part of dramas? Use evidence from this play to support your answer.

SCENE 2

[**SETTING** *Same place, one year later.*]

[MU LAN *and* MOTHER *enter.* MOTHER *wears a plain shawl and her hair is pulled into a simple bun.* MOTHER *carries a basket with a small blanket over it.*]

NARRATOR 1: One day, a messenger arrived in the quiet village.

[MESSENGER *enters.*]

NARRATOR 2: He brought terrible news.

MESSENGER: Greetings to all, but alas, I bring terrible news.

NARRATOR 2: See, I told you!

NARRATOR 1: Shh! You're interrupting the scene!

MESSENGER: [*glances at* NARRATOR 2, *annoyed*] As I was saying, I bring terrible news. Hordes of invaders—coldhearted and arrogant men who have not the least respect for our laws—are streaming down from the mountains like a rushing river in full flood.

MOTHER: Oh no! Where are the invaders now?

MESSENGER: They are close and getting closer. Their horses are galloping as loudly as thunder and moving across the land as quickly as wildfire.

MU LAN: We must defend ourselves.

MESSENGER: Yes, for I fear their **ferocity** will be **unyielding**. I therefore require every man and boy in this house to join General Hua's army.

MOTHER: Alas, my husband is ill. So he must fight a different kind of battle to get well again. Until then, he does not have the strength you need.

MU LAN: But I do.

MESSENGER: *You?* Don't make me laugh. You're a girl.

MU LAN: Yes, I know. I also know how to defend my people.

MESSENGER: Miss, I am sure you know many things, but the law says that only men are permitted to join the army.

In Other Words
ferocity power; strength
unyielding unstoppable

MU LAN: Messenger, please tell me, who is obligated to follow the laws of our land, men or women?

MESSENGER: Foolish question! All men and all women must follow the laws of our land.

MU LAN: I see. And who makes the laws of our land, the laws that govern all men and all women?

MESSENGER: All men and all . . . men.

[MU LAN *and* MOTHER *exchange looks of obvious amusement.*]

MESSENGER: [*embarrassed and frustrated*] I'm just the messenger! I must hurry to the next village. Do you have a brother?

MU LAN: Yes, but—

MESSENGER: Good. Tomorrow I will return. Tell your brother to be attired in his soldier's clothing and **standing to attention** with his sword and his shield. Until then!

[MESSENGER *exits.*]

NARRATOR 1: Now, it is true that Mu Lan had a brother, and his name was Mu Li.

NARRATOR 2: However, Mu Li was still . . . a baby!

[MOTHER *removes the blanket and* **coos lovingly** *to indicate that a baby is nestled inside the basket.*]

NARRATOR 1: Why, there were flowers in the field that were older than Mu Li!

NARRATOR 2: But the messenger did not know this. So Mu Lan came up with a plan.

MOTHER: No, Mu Lan, I know what you are thinking, and you cannot do this. You cannot lie.

MU LAN: Mother, I will not lie. I will simply show what is true—that I can defend my people as well as any man.

[MU LAN *and* MOTHER *exit.*]

In Other Words
standing to attention ready to fight
coos lovingly makes loving sounds

▶ **Before You Move On**

1. **Author's Purpose** Why does the author include the interaction between the narrators and the messenger on page 506?

2. **Explain** What argument does Mu Lan make to explain why she should be able to join the army?

NARRATOR 1: But how would Mu Lan do this?

NARRATOR 2: The messenger did not understand that Mu Lan possessed a warrior's skills. He could see only a pretty, young woman who had beautiful hair and who wore fine clothing.

NARRATOR 1: [*in an aside to* NARRATOR 2] Ugh, don't you just hate when that happens?

NARRATOR 2: [*with a sigh*] Oh, I know. Anyway, when the messenger returned—

NARRATOR 1: He expected to see a warrior, and thus a warrior is just what he saw.

[MU LAN *enters dressed as a soldier. Her long hair is hidden under a soldier's hat.*]

MESSENGER: Greetings! You must be Mu Li, the brother.

MU LAN: Actually, I—

MESSENGER: Let's go!

MU LAN: Messenger, before we go, please let me be so bold as to ask you. Am I truly a soldier?

MESSENGER: You certainly look like a soldier, and you clearly stand like a soldier. Now tell me truthfully—are you brave enough to defend your people?

MU LAN: Yes, I am.

MESSENGER: Are you skilled enough to defend your people?

MU LAN: Yes, I am.

MESSENGER: Then I officially declare you a soldier. Now hurry!

[*As* MU LAN *and* MESSENGER *march,* SOLDIER 1 *and* SOLDIER 2 *enter.* SOLDIERS *and* NARRATORS *join in the march.*]

SCENE 3

[**SETTING** *The northern wilderness, far from the village.* **Rugged terrain**.]

NARRATOR 1: For many days and nights, Mu Lan and the other soldiers traveled toward the border, **steadfast in all weathers.**

SOLDIER 1: We traveled up into mountains.

SOLDIER 2: We traveled down into valleys.

NARRATOR 2: At long last, they came to the north, where danger was waiting for them.

NARRATOR 1: The enemy soldiers were relentless, and the fighting was fierce.

MU LAN: [*directly to audience*] But I was not afraid.

MESSENGER: We had never seen such a magnificent warrior.

[GENERAL HUA *enters.* ALL *immediately stand at attention.*]

GENERAL HUA: What news, Messenger?

MESSENGER: General Hua, we have a powerful warrior **in our midst**.

[ALL *look at* MU LAN.]

SOLDIER 1: All soldiers are called upon to be brave, but Mu Li has more bravery than the ocean has water.

SOLDIER 2: All soldiers are required to be skilled, but Mu Li has more skills than the sky above our head has stars.

[SOLDIER 1 *looks up at the sky and mimes counting stars, as if to verify this information.*]

GENERAL HUA: So you are Mu Li. Well, well—

MU LAN: Actually, I—

MESSENGER: [*sternly*] Shh! Never interrupt the General—not ever!

GENERAL HUA: [*to* MU LAN] Soldier, help figure out the next strategy.

NARRATOR 1: And so Mu Lan did just that.

In Other Words

Rugged terrain. Rocky roads.

steadfast in all weathers marching through any kind of weather

in our midst with us

sternly strongly, forcefully

▶ **Before You Move On**

1. **Describe** How does the tone of Mu Lan's responses to the messenger change as the play moves forward?

2. **Character** What is one of Mu Lan's strengths? Give an example from the text.

NARRATOR 2: As a result, General Hua's army won battle after battle. So it happened that one day—well, see for yourself.

MESSENGER: Men! General Hua has reached an important decision.

GENERAL HUA: [*to* MU LAN] Soldier, by your diligent efforts, meticulous planning, and exemplary bravery, it is evident that you are a leader. I **promote** you to Commanding Officer.

MU LAN: Thank you, General. I accept this honor **on behalf** of my family and our people.

[NARRATORS ***resume*** *a position outside of the action.*]

NARRATOR 1: It was a proud moment for Mu Lan.

NARRATOR 2: But the war was not over yet.

NARRATOR 1: It went on, for many years, separating all of the soldiers from their loved ones.

NARRATOR 2: Then it went on—and on—for many more years, separating many a soldier from his life.

[MESSENGER *and* SOLDIERS *march with grim determination.* GENERAL HUA *takes out a map, which he and* MU LAN *appear to study together.*]

SCENE 4

[**SETTING** *Same place, years later.*]

NARRATOR 1: One day, Commanding Officer Mu Li made an extraordinary discovery.

MU LAN: Do you see that mountaintop?

SOLDIER 1: I see many mountains, Commanding Officer.

MU LAN: [*points*] Look up.

NARRATOR 2: The men **raised their gazes** higher . . . and higher.

MU LAN: Do you see the mountaintop jutting high above the clouds? Look up . . . up . . . up. THERE!

SOLDIERS, MESSENGER, GENERAL HUA: [*startled, reacting all at once*] Oh! Ah! Er? What! What? Is it—?

MU LAN: [*calmly*] Yes, it is the camp of our enemy.

SOLDIER 1: **No wonder** we are unable to reach them!

SOLDIER 2: There is no way for us to get up that cliff to their camp.

In Other Words
on behalf in the name
resume *go back to*
raised their gazes looked up
No wonder So that is why

SOLDIER 1: Well, how did the enemy's army get up there?

GENERAL HUA: On their side of the border, there is a gentle slope that leads gradually up to the top.

SOLDIERS: [*sheepishly*] Oh.

MESSENGER: But on our side, there is only a steep and rocky precipice that no man can walk. There is nothing that we can do.

MU LAN: It's true that no man can walk up a cliff. But I know who can. Listen.

[*Offstage: goats* **bleating** *loudly.*]

SOLDIER 1: [*in disbelief*] Goats? Goats! How can goats possibly be of help to us?

MU LAN: Go gather some lanterns from the villagers, and I will show you. Hurry!

[ALL *but the* NARRATORS *exit.*]

SCENE 5

[**SETTING** *Near the base of the cliff, that night.*]

NARRATOR 1: When the soldiers returned, **night had fallen**. Mu Lan told the soldiers to hang a lantern on the horns of each of the goats.

NARRATOR 2: Then she sent the goats up the side of the mountain, to climb steadily higher and higher.

[SOLDIERS, MESSENGER, GENERAL HUA, *and* MU LAN *enter and look up toward the cliff.*]

GENERAL HUA: Commanding Officer, I'm afraid I don't see how your strategy can help us.

MESSENGER: No one is afraid of goats!

[MESSENGER *and* SOLDIERS *start to laugh.*]

SOLDIER 1: In this dark, I cannot even see the goats, only the glow of the lanterns.

SOLDIER 2: [*more and more amused*] Why, for all that the enemy knows, those goats could just be soldiers . . .

In Other Words
sheepishly embarrassed
bleating making sounds
night had fallen it was night

▶ **Before You Move On**

1. **Setting** How do the setting updates help you to better understand the play?
2. **Paraphrase** In your own words, explain why it's so difficult for Mu Lan's army to defeat the enemy.

SOLDIER 1: Yes, from here they resemble nothing so much as soldiers, each one holding up a lantern.

MESSENGER: [*giggling*] Just like hundreds and hundreds of soldiers moving up the mountain.

GENERAL HUA: Now I understand your strategy!

[ALL *stop laughing.*]

NARRATOR 1: Sure enough, when the enemy saw the lanterns move up the cliff, they came to the conclusion—a false conclusion—that General Hua's army was attacking.

SOLDIER 1: Oh, no! The enemy army is rolling boulders down the cliff.

SOLDIER 2: Look out!

NARRATOR 2: But the goats were unstoppable and simply jumped over the boulders and kept on going!

SOLDIER 1: Now our enemies are shooting their arrows.

SOLDIER 2: How rude!

NARRATOR 2: But the sure-footed goats dodged **nimbly** between the arrows and simply kept on climbing!

In Other Words
nimbly quickly and easily

SOLDIER 1: Listen to our enemies.

[ALL *listen and stare.*]

SOLDIER 1: They sound . . . terrified!

SOLDIER 2: I can hear them calling, but I don't understand their language.

MU LAN: Good Messenger, please translate. What are the enemy soldiers saying?

MESSENGER: [*pauses to listen and then translates*] "How can human beings jump over rolling boulders? Mere humans cannot, therefore these must not be ordinary **mortals**! They must in fact be **immortal gods** sent down from heaven!"

SOLDIER 1: What else are they saying?

MESSENGER: "Run for your lives!"

[SOLDIERS *start to run away.*]

MU LAN: Not you, silly.

[MU LAN *points up the cliff.*]

MU LAN: Them.

SOLDIERS: Oh, sorry.

GENERAL HUA: Look! Listen! The enemy soldiers are in retreat!

NARRATOR 1: After that, the enemy army was too afraid to resume the battle.

[*A scroll is tossed onto the stage.* MESSENGER *picks it up and reads it.*]

MESSENGER: General and Commanding Officer, the enemy has sent us a message. They're asking if our two countries could live in peace.

SOLDIER 1: Sounds good to me. Fighting is **such a pain**.

SOLDIER 2: Oh, I agree. I'd like to **take up** fishing or maybe learn to paint.

[SOLDIERS *freeze as they realize that* MU LAN *and* GENERAL HUA *are staring at them with stern looks on their faces.*]

GENERAL HUA: Commanding Officer, what do you think?

MU LAN: General, I think that the bravest thing of all is learn to live in peace—even with people who we do not always understand.

GENERAL HUA: I agree. Messenger, go and tell the enemy—I mean, kindly reassure our neighbors—that the war is finally over.

[ALL *cheer.*]

In Other Words

mortals humans

immortal gods gods who can never be killed

such a pain so hard

take up learn; try

▶ **Before You Move On**

1. **Summarize** How is the enemy fooled by the goats? Cite text evidence.
2. **Make Inferences** Explain the hidden meaning in Mu Lan's response when General Hua asks her what she thinks.

NARRATOR 1: But the General still had more he wished to say.

GENERAL HUA: Commanding Officer, I invite you to accompany me to the palace and meet the Emperor. When I inform him of your **bravery** and praise your honor and skill, he will give you a great reward. You will become rich.

MU LAN: General, I thank you, and I thank the Emperor, but I do not wish for riches. I wish only for one thing.

GENERAL HUA: Name it.

MU LAN: I want the law to allow women to defend their people— our people.

SOLDIER 1: [*amused*] A woman soldier? Preposterous!

SOLDIER 2: [*scornful*] That could never be!

MESSENGER: [*puzzled*] Who could even imagine such a thing?

GENERAL HUA: Commanding Officer, show me a woman who has endured as much

hardship as you have, or a woman who is as brave as you, or a woman who has your skills and your strategies. Show me such a woman, and I will personally ask the Emperor to change the law.

[MU LAN *sets aside her disguise and removes her soldier's hat to reveal her long hair.* ALL *gasp in surprise.*]

MESSENGER: Mu Lan! I remember you! Why, I met you all those many years ago!

MU LAN: [*smiling*] I am glad that you have not forgotten me, good Messenger, for I have been right here by your side ever since!

514

MESSENGER: Oh, right.

GENERAL HUA: [*stunned*] Well! This is a surprise! I . . . I must go inform the Emperor of this development at once! There will be consequences!

MESSENGER: What consequences?

SOLDIERS: Yes, what consequences?

GENERAL HUA: [*pauses for a very long time as* ALL *wait in growing suspense for his answer*] Why, the law will have to change, of course. Fair is fair. Well done, Commanding Officer Mu Lan!

[GENERAL HUA *salutes* MU LAN, *and* ALL *cheer*.]

NARRATOR 1: From that day on, the story of Mu Lan spread throughout the land and around the world. Each version of the story inspired another version of the story, for just as no two musicians ever play the same song in quite the same way, each new teller embellished the tale with characters, plot changes, dialogue, and other details of his or her own. Yet the heroism of Mu Lan always shone through.

NARRATOR 2: Today, wherever young people are not afraid to learn new things . . .

NARRATOR 1: To do what is right . . .

[MOTHER *and* FATHER *enter*.]

MOTHER: To stand tall for what they believe . . .

FATHER: To look everyone in the eye . . .

NARRATOR 1: We say that they are . . .

NARRATOR 2: As brave as Mu Lan.

MU LAN: [*directly to audience*] What brave thing do *you* want to do? ❖

▶**Before You Move On**

1. **Generalize** What does General Hua's decision suggest about the role of women at that time?

2. **Theme** What evidence from the play supports a theme about the equality of men and women?

Compare Experiences

Where the Mountain Meets the Moon is a fantasy story, and "Mu Lan" is a play. After listening to *Where the Mountain Meets the Moon* on the **Selection MP3** and observing your class performance of the play, create a comparison chart. Compare your reading experience with your viewing and listening experience for each of these texts. Then form a generalization about the two genres.

Comparison Chart

Title	Reading Experience	Viewing and Listening Experience
Where the Mountain Meets the Moon	• • •	• • •
"Mu Lan"	• Sometimes, it was hard to read because of the character names and play directions. • •	• • •

Talk Together

What did *Where Mountain Meets the Moon* and "Mu Lan" teach you about ancient China? What new information did you learn from the listening and viewing experience for each genre? Use **Key Words**, text evidence, and your chart to talk about your ideas.

Prepositional Phrases

A **prepositional phrase** starts with a **preposition** and ends with a noun or pronoun. If the prepositional phrase ends with a pronoun, use an object pronoun.

Grammar Rules Prepositional Phrases

Use a **prepositional phrase** to	
• show location.	Mu Lan gazed at the mountaintop **above the clouds**.
• show direction.	The enemy could attack **from it**.
• show time.	**After a long night,** Mu Lan shared her plan.
• give details.	Some soldiers laughed **at Mu Lan's suggestion**.

Read Prepositional Phrases

Writers use prepositional phrases to add details that make sentences clearer and more interesting. Read this passage from "Mu Lan." Identify the prepositional phrases you find. What kind of details does each prepositional phrase add?

> **NARRATOR 1:** For many days and nights, Mu Lan and the other soldiers traveled toward the border, steadfast in all weathers.
>
> **SOLDIER 1:** We traveled up into mountains.
>
> **SOLDIER 2:** We traveled down into valleys.
>
> **NARRATOR 2:** At long last, they came to the north, where danger was waiting for them.

Write Prepositional Phrases

Think about Mu Lan's belief that women should be allowed to serve in the army. Write a paragraph that explains her reasons for feeling as she does. Make your sentences interesting by using different kinds of prepositional phrases to add details. Then compare your paragraph with a partner's.

Write as a Storyteller

Write a Narrative

Write a retelling of a folk tale you know well. You will share your retelling with a group of younger students.

Study a Model

When you retell a story, you create a narrative using your own words. Read how Amanda retells the story of "Mu Lan," a Chinese folk tale.

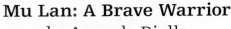

Mu Lan: A Brave Warrior
by Amanda Diallo

Long ago, in ancient China, there lived a brave and clever girl named Mu Lan. One day, a messenger warned that enemies were invading their land. General Hua needed every man to join his troops. Mu Lan wanted to defeat the invaders, too, but the law stated that women could not fight. So she disguised herself as a male warrior and fought alongside the General's men.

One day, Mu Lan discovered the camp of their enemy! The way to the mountain camp was **steep and littered with rocks**. She **attached glowing lanterns to the horns of some goats** and sent them up the mountain. Thinking that General Hua's men carried these lanterns, the **enemy soldiers sent boulders and arrows flying** at the goats. But the goats kept advancing. Terrified, the enemy army fled and asked for peace.

The General wanted to reward Mu Lan with riches, but she asked that the law be changed so that women could become soldiers. Then Mu Lan revealed her true identity as a woman. General Hua was convinced. He changed the law, allowing women to fight as warriors.

Amanda begins the story by introducing the **setting** and the **characters**.

Amanda focuses on just one central problem, or **conflict**.

Amanda includes **descriptive details** about the setting and story events.

Prewrite

1. **Choose a Topic** What folk tale would you like to retell? Choose one that you know well so that you can use specific details from the original story.

<table>
<tr><td colspan="2" align="center">**Language Frames**</td></tr>
<tr><td>**Tell Your Ideas**</td><td>**Respond to Ideas**</td></tr>
<tr><td>

• One folk tale I like is _____ .

• A summary of this story is

  _____ .

• The part of the story that interests me most is _____ .

• I'd also like to include _____ .

</td><td>

• I've never read _____ .
  Why do you want to retell it?

• The part about _____ sounds exciting. Can you tell me more?

• What details will you use?

</td></tr>
</table>

2. **Gather Information** What will you include from the original story? Write specific details you will use to develop the setting, characters, and events.

3. **Get Organized** Use a chart to help you organize details about the main characters in your folk tale.

Character Chart

Character	Motivation	Actions	Traits
Mu Lan	wants to join the army, but only men are allowed to fight	disguises herself as a male warrior	

Draft

Use your character chart as you write your draft. In the first paragraph, introduce your narrator, setting, and characters. Introduce the conflict early in your story. Then add details to make your story exciting, fun, or interesting. Remember to organize events logically to show how the conflict is resolved.

Writing Project, continued

Revise

1. **Read, Retell, Respond** Read your draft aloud to a partner. Your partner listens and then retells your story. Then talk about ways to improve your writing.

Language Frames	
Retell	**Make Suggestions**
• In summary, your story is about _____ . • Your setting is _____ , and your characters are _____ . • First, _____ . Next, _____ . Then, _____ . Finally, _____ .	• I'm interested in your setting. Can you add details about _____ ? • Could you be more specific about _____ ? • I'm not sure how the conflict was resolved. Maybe you could _____ .

2. **Make Changes** Think about your draft and your partner's suggestions. Use the Revising Marks on page 617 to mark your changes.

   • Can you add details that tell more about your characters?

   > brave and clever
   > Long ago, in ancient China, there lived a girl named Mu Lan.

   • Can you add descriptive details to help your reader picture the setting and the story's events?

   > steep and littered with rocks.
   > The way up to the mountain camp was difficult.

   • Make sure that you describe the conflict clearly.

   > , but the law stated that women could not fight.
   > Mu Lan wanted to defeat the invaders, too.

Edit and Proofread

Work with a partner to edit and proofread your story. Pay special attention to how you use pronouns and prepositional phrases. Use the marks on page 618 to show your changes.

Use the marks on page 618 to show your changes.

Publish

1. **On Your Own** Make a final copy of your story. Choose a way to share your work with your classmates. You can read it aloud or act it out.

Presentation Tips	
If you are the speaker . . .	**If you are the listener . . .**
Be sure to change your tone to emphasize questions and exclamations.	A folk tale often teaches a lesson. Listen for details that explain or teach through characters' actions.
Make eye contact with your listeners to help them stay connected.	Smile or nod to show the speaker that you are following and enjoying the story.

2. **In a Group** Folk tales are usually passed on by storytellers. Arrange to visit a class of younger children and share your stories with them. Afterwards, ask them to draw pictures to go with your stories. Then post both the stories and the pictures on your school's Web site.

The Story of Mu Lan

BIG Question

Why should we study ancient cultures?

Talk Together

In this unit you found many answers to the **Big Question**. Now use your concept map to discuss it. Think about the different people and ways of life that were presented in the selections. What did you learn about the culture of ancient China?

KWL Chart

Why should we study ancient cultures?		
What I <u>Know</u>	What I <u>Want</u> to Know	What I <u>Learned</u>
I know China is in Asia. I have seen pictures of the Great Wall of China.	I want to learn why the Great Wall was built.	

Performance Task: Narrative

Consider what you learned about ancient China and the Chinese culture through the selections and the **Small Group Reading** books. Choose one of the people or characters you read about. Imagine that this person meets the Old Man of the Moon from *Where the Mountain Meets the Moon*. Write a short story to describe how the Old Man of the Moon helps this person.

Checklist

Does your narrative

- ✓ clearly describe character and setting?
- ✓ clearly develop the sequence of events?
- ✓ include transition words, descriptive details, and sensory language?

522

Share Your Ideas

Choose one of these ways to share your ideas about the **Big Question**.

Write It!

Write a New Scene

After reading "Mu Lan," think about what happens when Mu Lan returns home from her adventures. Write a new scene for the play about her return home. Think about the new characters Mu Lan might meet along the way. How does her courage in battle inspire her family and friends?

Talk About It!

Give a Presentation

Work with a small group to find photos on the Internet that show artifacts from ancient China. Use presentation software to create a virtual museum. When you present your slideshow to the class, explain what each piece tells you about ancient China.

A *ban liang* from the Qin dynasty

Do It!

Create a Time Line

Work with a partner to find information and photos about important events in China during Qin's lifetime. Use presentation software to create and present a time line that shows your findings.

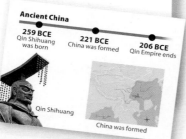

Ancient China

259 BCE Qin Shihuang was born

221 BCE China was formed

206 BCE Qin Empire ends

Qin Shihuang

China was formed

Write It!

Write a Journal Entry

Imagine you are one of the archaeologists working to uncover the terracotta army. Write a journal entry that describes your work and your impressions of the soldiers, horses, and chariots you are uncovering. What can the army teach you about ancient China?

Earth

AND BEYOND

? BIG Question How does studying Earth tell us about other planets?

Unit

8

Share What You Know

❶ **List** landforms you know on Earth.

❷ **Draw** an imaginary planet. Include some of the landforms.

❸ **Describe** the planet to the class.

Build Background: Watch a video about Earth and planets.

⊘ NGReach.com

Clarify and Verify

Listen to a discussion about Mars and Earth. Then use **Language Frames** with a partner to clarify and verify information you know about space.

Earth and Mars ((MP3))

Teacher: Earth and Mars have similar landform features.

Mark: What are "landform features"? Do you mean mountains? I read somewhere that Mars has huge mountains.

Teacher: That is true, but it's not just mountains. Mars also has gullies, deep canyons, and volcanoes that resemble those found on Earth.

Esther: How do we know about features on Mars when no one has ever been there?

Teacher: Some things can be observed from powerful telescopes on Earth. We also depend on information sent from the Mars rovers that are on the surface of the planet now. In fact, I checked for the latest information by looking on the NASA Web site last night. It's filled with up-to-date information about Mars.

Mark: I never knew that Earth and Mars were so similar.

Teacher: We all have a lot to learn about Mars.

Key Words

composition

crater

erode

geologic

survey

terrain

Key Words

Look at this illustration and read the captions. Use **Key Words** and other words to talk about how studying Earth helps us learn about other planets.

▼ Scientists study the **geologic**, or physical, features of Mars.

This bowl-shaped area is a **crater** that was probably made when something from space hit the surface of Mars.

Did wind or water **erode** away parts of Mars's surface, like this channel? Scientists are working to find the answer.

The **terrain**, or land, is rocky.

The **composition** of this rock includes minerals and metals.

The rovers on Mars **survey**, or examine, the surface of the planet.

Talk Together

How does studying Earth's features help us learn about other planets like Mars? Discuss this question with a group using **Language Frames** from page 526 to clarify and verify the information.

Compare and Contrast

Authors organize text to show how ideas are connected. They **compare** to connect ideas that are similar and **contrast** to connect ideas that are different. Authors may use a comparison-and-contrast structure across sections, paragraphs, and sentences. You can study the similarities and differences of two or more things and then use the information to make an inference, connection, conclusion, or generalization about the topic.

In the passage below, look for signal words that compare and contrast two volcanoes.

Look Into the Text

After studying thousands of photos of Olympus Mons and **comparing them to** volcanoes on Earth, scientists have concluded that, **like** Mauna Loa, Olympus Mons is a shield volcano. **Based on this comparison**, they infer that Mars may have a volcanic "hotspot" **like** the kind found beneath Mauna Loa. **Unlike** Hawaii, **however**, you probably wouldn't want to go to Olympus Mons for a tropical vacation. For one thing, it is far too cold!

" **Comparison signal words** show how the two volcanoes are similar."

" **Contrast signal words** show how they are different."

Map and Talk

A comparison-contrast chart can help you compare and contrast information about two or more things. After you complete the chart, use the information to make a statement that synthesizes an idea about the topic.

Comparison-Contrast Chart

	Mauna Loa Volcano	Olympus Mons Volcano	Comparison or Contrast
Location	Hawaii, Earth	Mars	Both planets have volcanoes.
Type	shield volcano		

Talk Together

Describe two places. Your partner completes a comparison-contrast chart with information from your descriptions. Then use the information to make a statement that is true about both places.

Academic Vocabulary

More Key Words

Use these words to talk about "Finding Mars on Earth" and "Here, There, and Beyond."

analogy
(u-**na**-lu-jē) *noun*

An **analogy** is a type of comparison. This **analogy** shows how food is fuel to the body like gas is fuel for a car.

distinct
(di-**stinkt**) *adjective*

When something is **distinct**, it is easy to notice. The leaf is **distinct** because it has colors that are very different from the red leaves around it.

simulate
(**sim**-yū-lāt) *verb*

To **simulate** something is to create an imitation of it. The girl's model **simulates** what happens during a volcanic eruption.

structural
(**struk**-chu-rul) *adjective*

Structural relates to the way something is built or put together. The wooden frame is the **structural** support of the house.

transform
(trans-**form**) *verb*

To **transform** something is to change it. A gardener **transformed** this old car into a flower planter.

Talk Together

Use a **Key Word** to write a question for your partner to answer. Use each **Key Word** twice.

Questions	Answers
How can weather cause <u>structural</u> damage to a home?	A tornado can <u>transform</u> a house into a pile of rubble.

Add words to My Vocabulary Notebook.
 NGReach.com

529

Reading Strategies

- Plan and Monitor
- Visualize
- Ask Questions
- Make Connections
- Determine Importance
- Make Inferences
- Synthesize

Choose Reading Strategies

Good readers use many strategies to understand the meanings of different texts. As you read, choose which strategies to use and when to use them.

How to Choose Reading Strategies

1. As you read, think about what you are trying to understand in the text.

I want to know _____.

2. Decide which strategies you can use to help you understand that part of the text. You may decide to change or combine strategies as you read.

I can _____.

3. Think about how each strategy helps you better understand the text.

This strategy helps me _____.

Here's how one student chose a reading strategy to use.

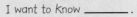
Look Into the Text

A long time ago, science fiction writer H.G. Wells imagined that there were **intelligent beings living on Mars**. They were **scientifically advanced**, but they **lived on a desolate, dying planet**. "[They] regarded this earth with **envious eyes**," he wrote.

"I read **details** about 'intelligent beings.' I want to know what they might do."

"I can connect this idea to a book I read about Martians that visited Earth."

"This strategy helps me understand what the intelligent beings might do."

When you read, choose the best reading strategy to help you understand the text. Sometimes you may need to switch or add a strategy as you read on.

Talk Together

Read the science article and sample notes. Use **Language Frames** as you choose a variety of reading strategies to use as you read. Then talk to a partner about the strategies you used.

Science Article

CURIOSITY
Lands on **MARS**

On August 6, 2012, NASA began its latest and most advanced study of Mars with the landing of the rover Curiosity. The successful landing in Gale **Crater** marked the end of a 99-million mile journey through space and the beginning of a new one over the uncharted **terrain** of the Red Planet. ◄

Mars has long fascinated scientists. Although it is very different from Earth in terms of size, temperature, and atmosphere, Mars shares many of the same **geologic** features that we see on Earth. Volcanoes, canyons, and other landforms can be found on Mars, with many **structural** similarities to those on Earth. Scientists use the information to make **analogies** that compare the landforms on each planet and ask many questions about our neighbor in space. For example: Could ancient rivers have **eroded** Mars's great canyons, too? ◄

Since we can't yet send people to Mars, rovers like Curiosity help us gather critical information because they can **simulate** an actual visit. Curiosity

is equipped with 17 cameras that can **survey** the vast terrain. It also has tools that analyze the **composition** of soil and rock samples. Scientists can then review the results and determine whether they are the same or **distinct** from the elements on Earth. These discoveries could **transform** the way scientists think about Mars. ◄

Scientists don't know exactly what information Curiosity will uncover. Someday we may even find evidence of the "intelligent beings" once described by science fiction writers, such as H.G. Wells. Steve Squyres, the lead scientist on the Mars Exploration Rover Mission, isn't afraid of the unexpected. "You take what Mars gives you," he said. "If we knew what we were going to find, it wouldn't be this much fun."

I want to know more about rovers.

I can ask a question: *What does a rover do?* Then I can read on to find the answer.

This strategy helps me know what kind of information to look for as I read on.

◄ = a good place to choose a reading strategy to check for understanding

Read a Science Article

Genre

A **science article** is expository nonfiction that gives facts and information about the natural world. Science writers often include technical terms to explain natural processes or research procedures.

Text Feature

An **infographic** is a visual image, such as a chart or diagram, that can be used to represent information, knowledge, or data. It conveys complex information quickly and easily.

This **chart** compares information about Mars and Earth.

	Mars	**Earth**
Atmosphere	Carbon dioxide (95.32%) Nitrogen (2.7%) Argon (1.6%) Oxygen (0.13%) Nitric oxide (0.01%)	Nitrogen (77%) Oxygen (21%) Argon (1%) Carbon dioxide (0.038%)

Finding
Mars
on
Earth

by G. K. Gilbert

A long time ago, science fiction writer H.G. Wells imagined that there were intelligent beings living on Mars. They were scientifically advanced, but they lived on a desolate, dying planet. "[They] **regarded** this earth with **envious** eyes," he wrote.

At the time, Wells didn't know what the surface of Mars looked like up close or its **composition** . Nobody did. Instead, astronomers gazed through telescopes at **stark, one-dimensional images**, trying to picture Mars's **terrain** . Were there mountains on Mars? Canyons, perhaps? Or was it just a flat, dusty ball, hurtling through space?

To help answer their questions, people compared the things they saw through their telescopes with more familiar features on Earth. They saw vaguely white masses, for example, and thought of Earth's familiar polar ice caps. They noticed mysterious, curving lines and envisioned the canals people had built on Earth. All the while, they yearned to explore Mars more closely.

Many years later, in 1971, **a space probe** called Mariner 9 got close—to within 13 football fields of Mars's surface. Its images amazed scientists. The photos revealed volcanoes, canyons, and even ice caps—a fantastic new world, both **alien** and strangely familiar. Mariner 9 was followed by a parade of **orbiters and landers** that, over time, created a detailed picture of Mars—one beyond the wildest dreams of early astronomers.

There is one thing that hasn't changed since those early days, though. Researchers continue to make comparisons. They **puzzle over** photographs, matching the **geologic** features they see on Mars to those of Earth. What they are finding is that Mars is not the strange, mystifying world we once imagined it to be. In fact, in some cases, it's as familiar as the ground beneath our feet.

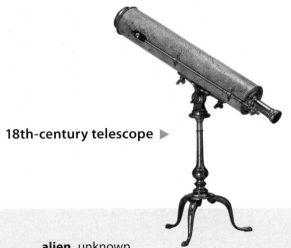

18th-century telescope ▶

In Other Words
regarded looked at
envious greedy
stark, one-dimensional images flat images
  that did not show much information
a space probe an unmanned spacecraft

alien unknown
orbiters and landers space vehicles
puzzle over closely study

McMath-Pierce Solar Telescope,
Kitt Peak National Observatory, Arizona

VOLCANOES:
FIERY FOUNTAINS

Step out onto the gentle, rocky slope of Hawaii's Mauna Loa Volcano. A warm wind whips through your hair as you stare out at the vast Pacific Ocean. The day is clear and calm, and it may be difficult to believe that you are also standing on the largest active volcano on Earth.

You should definitely **keep your eye out**, though. The last time Mauna Loa erupted was in 1984, and it is overdue for another blow. When it erupts again, magma, or melted rock from Earth's upper mantle, will spew out of Mauna Loa as lava.

Why does Mauna Loa keep growing? Well, it is a special kind of volcano called a shield volcano. Shield volcanoes form from a very liquid-like lava that, once it emerges from the volcano, can travel a long way over Earth's surface. As the lava cools and hardens into rock, it will make the volcano even bigger.

In Other Words
keep your eye out watch closely

▶ **Before You Move On**

1. **Make Inferences** Describe what it would be like to be an early astronomer who could only study Mars through a telescope.

2. **Summarize** After comparing features of Mars and Earth, what have modern researchers learned?

This process makes most shield volcanoes very wide but with a **low profile** and a dome shape, just like a knight's shield. Shield volcanoes generally erupt a lot, so many, like Mauna Loa, continue to grow.

Mauna Loa is special in another way, too. Most of Earth's volcanoes form at the boundaries between Earth's tectonic plates, which are the places where huge chunks of Earth's crust meet and slide past each other. Mauna Loa, however, did not form at one of these active tectonic boundary areas. Instead, it formed on one of Earth's hotspots. Hotspots occur above an area called a mantle plume, which is an extremely hot region inside Earth that pushes close to the surface. Magma generated by the hotspot pushes to Earth's surface and forms volcanoes.

Mauna Loa Volcano is certainly large, but it is practically a baby in comparison to Olympus Mons Volcano on Mars. While Mauna Loa stands at 9 km (5.6 miles) above sea level and reaches 120 km (75 miles) across, Olympus Mons is **a whopping** 22 km (14 miles) high and 700 km (435 miles) across. Not only is Olympus Mons the largest volcano on Mars, it is the largest volcano in the entire solar system. Even though it is no longer erupting, Olympus Mons was once a massive, active volcano. How did this giant form, and what can it teach us about Martian geology?

To answer this question, we must return to Mauna Loa. Although it is millions of miles from Olympus Mons, the two volcanoes share many similarities. They both have broad, gently sloping sides, long flows of lava, and many lava channels.

Airliners' average cruising height, about 35,000 ft.

Sea level (on Earth)

Sea floor (on Earth)

In Other Words
low profile short height
a whopping an impressive

One major difference between Mauna Loa and Olympus Mons is size, of course, but that can be explained by gravity. Gravity is the universal attraction between all things, and on Mars it is weaker than on Earth. This allowed Olympus Mons, and all volcanoes on Mars, to build up without collapsing under the weight of accumulating lava.

After studying thousands of photos of Olympus Mons and comparing them to volcanoes on Earth, scientists have concluded that, like Mauna Loa, Olympus Mons is a shield volcano. Based on this comparison, they infer that Mars may have a volcanic "hotspot" like the kind found beneath Mauna Loa. Unlike Hawaii, however, you probably wouldn't want to go to Olympus Mons for a tropical vacation. For one thing, it is far too cold!

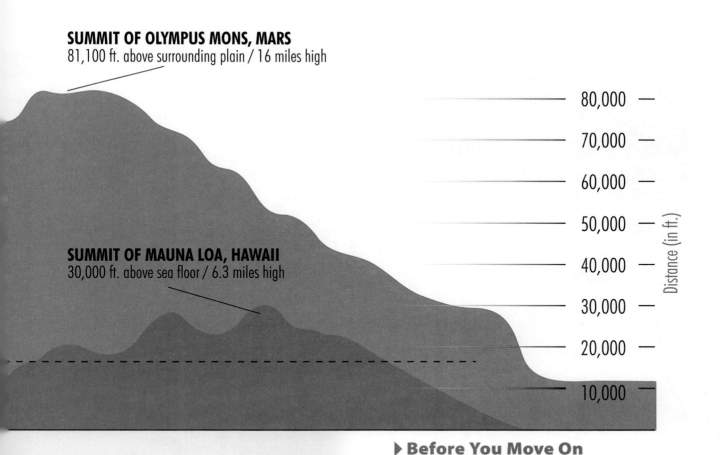

SUMMIT OF OLYMPUS MONS, MARS
81,100 ft. above surrounding plain / 16 miles high

SUMMIT OF MAUNA LOA, HAWAII
30,000 ft. above sea floor / 6.3 miles high

Distance (in ft.)

80,000

70,000

60,000

50,000

40,000

30,000

20,000

10,000

▶ **Before You Move On**

1. **Make Inferences** How can studying Mauna Loa help us learn more about Olympus Mons? Cite examples from the text.

2. **Compare/Generalize** Compare Mauna Loa and Olympus Mons. Make a statement that is true for both volcanoes.

▶ CANYONS: LAYERS OF HISTORY

We have visited Earth's largest volcano. Now, let's take a trip to one of its largest canyons. Stand at the rim of the Grand Canyon and **feast your eyes on** a geologist's dream—layer after colorful layer of limestone, sandstone, granite, shale, and other rocks. The Grand Canyon, which winds its way for 446 km (277 miles) through the desert of the American southwest, is like looking at a cross-section of Earth's history—the lower you go, the further into the past you travel.

Look over the rim and see if you can find the Colorado River. It twists and curls along the bottom of the canyon like a bright blue ribbon. Now imagine its cool, inviting waters. Maybe you'd like to **take a dip**? Well, you'll have to prepare yourself for a long dive. The mighty Colorado River carved this canyon through erosion, which is the action of a river cutting through rock. Over the past six million years, the river has weathered and **eroded** a **chasm** some 1,800 meters (1.1 miles) deep. Studying the Grand Canyon is one of the best ways to learn about our planet—and Mars.

Marble Canyon,
Grand Canyon National Park, Arizona

In Other Words
feast your eyes on look at
take a dip go swimming
chasm canyon

538

Hebes Chasma, an enclosed trough in Valles Marineris

Mars has a "Grand Canyon," too. It's called Valles Marineris, named for the Mariner 9 probe that first spotted it. If you wanted to dive down into the deepest part of Valles Marineris, however, you would have to go a lot deeper than the Grand Canyon— 7 km (4.5 miles) deeper, to be exact.

Composed of several giant, interconnected canyons, Valles Marineris stretches across an area the size of the United States. Near the supersized canyon there is an enormous volcanic rise, called the Tharsis Bulge, which scientists believe hints at Valles Marineris' origins. That's because, unlike the Grand Canyon, which formed through erosion, Valles Marineris formed through faulting, which is movements of the planet's crust.

But let's **survey** Nanedi Vallis near the east end of Vallis Marineris. Nanedi Vallis is about the same size as the Grand Canyon, and it has the Grand Canyon's same steep walls and small channel. Its familiar shape suggests to some scientists that, like the Grand Canyon, it formed through weathering and erosion. In fact, some have even called it the Grand Canyon's cosmic twin.

Imagine for a moment that you are peering down into Nanedi Vallis canyon instead of the Grand Canyon. Behind you, the pale sun glows pink, shining light on the layers of colorful rock. Now stare down into the bottom of the canyon. Maybe you can picture an ancient Martian river?

▶ **Before You Move On**

1. **Contrast/Infer** How were the Grand Canyon and Vallis Marineris formed in different ways? How did this affect the two canyons?

2. **Visualize** Which details help you picture Nanedi Vallis on Mars?

CRATERS: CRADLES OF LIFE?

Where there is water, there is life. We know that is true on Earth. So if there were rivers on ancient Mars, does that mean there was life there, as well? (And could that life still be there now?) Those are questions scientists are trying to answer, and one of their most important sources of information is **craters**.

If you have ever punched your fist into the sand, then you already understand a lot about one kind of crater—the impact crater. Impact craters are simply low areas created by the impact of objects from space.

Impact craters are like ponds or lakes—they are natural, low places for water to settle and be contained. And just like in ponds and lakes, naturally occurring materials from the environment, called sediments, sink to the bottoms of crater lakes.

On Canada's Devon Island, for example, Haughton Crater contains sediments—the **footprint of** an ancient lake that dried up long ago. Scientists are especially interested in these sediments because Devon Island has several similarities to Mars, including craters and a cold climate.

Haughton Crater, Devon Island, Canada

In Other Words
footprint of leftover materials from

Run down into Haughton Crater to discover the crater lake sediments for yourself. You'll want to run fast so you can increase your body temperature. Devon Island, like Mars, is bitterly cold.

Now take off your glove and dig your hand into the thick, fine-grained dirt at the bottom of Haughton Crater. You are holding rock sediments that drifted down through water, probably as an ice cap melted long ago.

Recently, the Curiosity rover did exactly what you are doing now, except it was inside a crater on Mars. It dug its mechanical arm into the bottom of Gale Crater, a crater in Mars's southern hemisphere, and discovered similar rock sediments. Tests proved that they were composed of mudstone, which is a kind of rock formed from mud.

Scientists are **tantalized** by the mudstone samples. The mudstone suggests that there was once mud inside Gale Crater—which means there was probably water. If Gale Crater was the bowl, they wonder, what did it contain? Could it have held a kind of **Martian primordial soup of life**?

NASA's Curiosity rover on Mars

In Other Words

tantalized excited

Martian primordial soup of life ancient Martian life-form

▶ **Before You Move On**

1. **Explain** How does the **analogy** of punching a fist into the sand help to explain an impact crater?

2. **Use Text Features** How does the photo of the Curiosity rover show and extend the information in the text?

WATER FEATURES: A FLOOD OF SIMILARITIES

The canyons and craters on Mars seem to **whisper of** a time when water flowed on its surface, like it does on Earth today. There are some features on Mars, however, that don't just whisper about the presence of water, they shout it out.

Take a look at a photo of Mars's Eberswalde Crater, for example. Do you see the dozens of curved pathways, spreading outward like a fan? What Earthly water feature do they remind you of? If you answered **a river delta**, then you are thinking like a scientist.

Now check out Mars's Newton Crater. Do you see the long, fingerlike pathways descending into it? Compare those to the melt water gullies found on Devon Island.

They look similar, don't they? The gullies on Devon Island were formed when snow on cold, north-facing slopes slowly melted, creating pathways for melt water to flow down into the crater. Scientists wonder if the same process might have once taken place on Mars.

Let's survey photos of salty minerals in the Terra Sirenum region of Mars. On Earth, salts can form when underground water associated with volcanic activity bubbles to the surface and then **evaporates**, leaving the salt behind. Salts can also collect when the water in a surface pond or lake slowly evaporates, such as the lake that once existed in Badwater Basin, in Death Valley, California.

Eberswalde Delta, Mars

Lena River Delta, Russia

Newton Crater, Sirenum Terra, Mars

Northwest Passage Devon Island, Cana

In Other Words

whisper of tell a bit about

a river delta an area where a river spreads out over the edge of land

evaporates dries away

542

They are not shown here, but there seem to be prominent **outflow channels** in the Chryse Planitia region on Mars. They are too large to have been formed by the slow work of a river. They remind many scientists of an area in eastern Washington State called the Channeled Scablands, which formed at the end of the last **glaciation**, about 15,000 years ago.

Back then, a glacial ice dam **plugged** an ancient lake. Whenever the ice dam collapsed, torrents of water came roaring across the landscape, shaping huge valleys, house-sized potholes, and building-sized ripple marks. Many scientists think the many regions of Mars with possible outflow channels were shaped by the same thing that shaped the Scablands—megafloods.

Finally, consider one of Mars's most famous features—the "blueberries." Unlike the soft, sweet fruit found on Earth, Martian blueberries are hard and probably taste like minerals. That's because they contain hematite, which is a mineral often found in hot springs and other **waterlogged** areas on Earth.

At Utah's Grand Staircase-Escalante National Monument, for example, thousands of marble-sized hematite balls were exposed when water eroded the softer surrounding sandstone in which they formed. Some scientists think that the Martian hematite "blueberries" could have been formed in the same way.

Terra Sirenum region, Mars **Badwater Basin, Death Valley, California**

"Blueberries" on "Chocolate Hills," Mars **Grand Staircase-Escalante National Monument, Utah**

In Other Words

outflow channels areas where water flowed
glaciation ice age on Earth
plugged blocked
waterlogged soaked or watery

▶ **Before You Move On**

1. **Summarize** What evidence have scientists discovered to suggest that Mars may have once held water?

2. **Use Text Features** How do the photos and captions provide information in a way that is different from the text?

OBSERVER BEWARE: IS SEEING BELIEVING?

The possible water features on Mars are truly amazing. Scientists marvel at them. **They ooh, and they ahh**. Some scientists are even moved to tears. The canyons, deltas, gullies, and channels all seem to suggest that Mars may have once been warm enough, and its atmosphere dense enough, to have supported flowing water. In other words, Mars may have once been much more like Earth.

Still, scientists understand that these observations and comparisons are just the first steps in the scientific process. The scientific method **dictates** that scientists must prove their **hypotheses** with investigations and evidence before reaching a conclusion.

Take the Martian blueberries, for example. They may look like Earth's hematite balls, but some scientists say they are too small to make a definite comparison. They point out that some Martian blueberries are too shiny. This suggests that they were not formed from

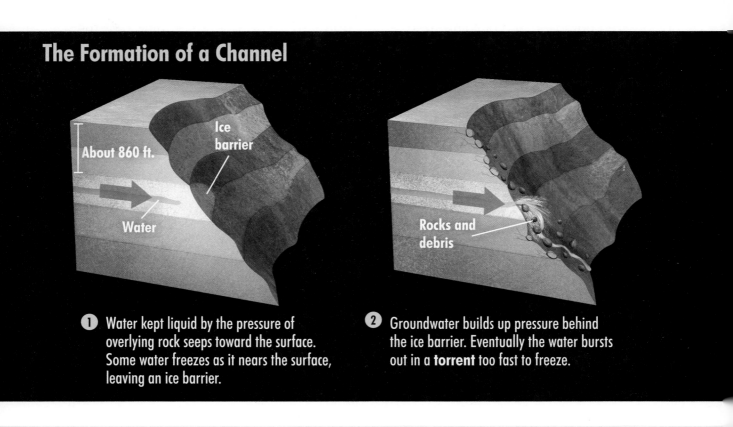

The Formation of a Channel

About 860 ft.

Ice barrier

Water

Rocks and debris

1 Water kept liquid by the pressure of overlying rock seeps toward the surface. Some water freezes as it nears the surface, leaving an ice barrier.

2 Groundwater builds up pressure behind the ice barrier. Eventually the water bursts out in a **torrent** too fast to freeze.

In Other Words

They ooh, and they ahh. They are very impressed.

dictates insists

hypotheses ideas and theories

torrent rush of water

erosive processes at all, like the hematite balls on Earth, but are actually the remains of small meteorites, or objects from space.

And the gullies on Mars? Scientists have questions about those, too. They appear to have been formed by water erosion, but that water may not have come from flowing water on Mars's surface. Scientists have **detected** evidence of possible water below the surface of Mars. That water may, on occasion, be exposed temporarily at the surface.

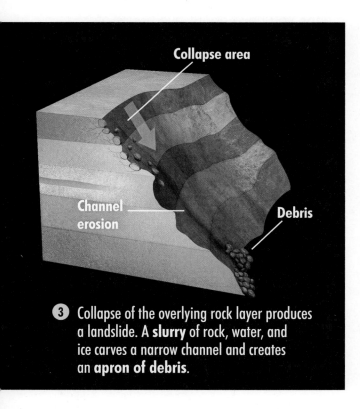

Collapse area

Channel erosion

Debris

3 Collapse of the overlying rock layer produces a landslide. A **slurry** of rock, water, and ice carves a narrow channel and creates an **apron of debris**.

In fact, scientists are starting to question the idea that early Mars had as much surface water as its photos seem to suggest. They have analyzed mineral data gathered by orbiters and have discovered that Mars's most ancient clay minerals could only have formed under extremely high temperatures and from water pressures underground. In other words, they probably did not form on the surface of Mars.

What about the streambeds and river channels? Surely those prove the existence of long-term, flowing water on the surface. Some scientists say no. They argue that those features may have formed during brief, violent events, such as volcanic eruptions or asteroid impacts. They point back at Canada's Devon Island, where strange, vein-like valleys were probably created by a massive ice melt caused by the heat of the impact that created Haughton Crater.

In Other Words
detected found
slurry wet mixture
apron of debris area where the rock and sediments collect

▶ **Before You Move On**

1. **Evaluate** Which argument provides the best evidence against the presence of water on the surface of Mars? Explain.

2. **Use Text Features** Which **geologic** features and processes does the diagram explain?

545

DIFFERENT, YET SIMILAR

So Mars is different from Earth—we know that. Scientists need to be careful not to draw false **analogies**. Still, as our information about Mars increases, scientists and **laypeople** alike cannot help but to **speculate** and to dream. Could it be that our planetary cousin in the sky is more closely related to our home planet than we thought? A brother, perhaps?

In the spirit of speculation, let's take one last field trip. Let's go somewhere on Earth that's so extreme, so remote, and so strange that it is like going to Mars without leaving our planet. Let's go to the Dry Valleys of Antarctica.

To get there, we'll have to take an airplane and then a helicopter. The Dry Valleys lie in a coastal corner of the continent, near the East Antarctic Ice Sheet. Cut off from the ice sheet by large mountains and powerful, **katabatic winds**, the Dry Valleys are one of the few places in Antarctica with permanently exposed ground.

Mars may have many places like the Dry Valleys. It certainly has winds, which can become powerful enough to cover the entire planet in dust. It also has polar ice caps, similar to the giant ice cap that covers Antarctica. And, of course, it's cold on Mars, too—very, very cold.

Let's have our helicopter set us down on in Taylor Valley, the largest of the three dry valleys. Look up at the **mouth of the valley**. Do you see the icy terminus, or end, of the Taylor Glacier? When ice breaks off the glacier, it sublimates. This means it turns from a solid to a vapor, bypassing the liquid stage—just the way ice does on Mars.

Now step out of the helicopter and start walking. It is early spring, which means you have about five hours of sunlight. Like the polar regions of Mars, much of Antarctica is dark during the winter months. And **watch that** 150-mile-per-hour wind gust! Here, like on Mars, powerful winds surge down from the ice sheet, scouring the landscape and drying everything in their path.

The cold, dry environment of this area acts as a **natural preservative**. Unlike most places on Earth, where the stories of the past have been lost to decomposition and erosion, the Dry Valleys are frozen in time, just like Mars seems to be. This doesn't mean there isn't life here, however.

In Other Words

laypeople nonscientists
speculate make guesses
In the spirit of speculation, To test the idea,
katabatic winds winds that move downward
mouth of the valley area where the valley begins

watch that be careful about the
natural preservative way to keep things from changing over time

	Mars	**Earth**
Atmosphere	Carbon dioxide (95.32%) Nitrogen (2.7%) Argon (1.6%) Oxygen (0.13%) Nitric oxide (0.01%)	Nitrogen (77%) Oxygen (21%) Argon (1%) Carbon dioxide (0.038%)
Distance from Sun (average)	227,936,637 km (142,633,260 miles)	149,597,891 km (92,955,820 miles)
Gravity	0.375 that of Earth	2.66 times that of Mars
Surface Temperature	-81 degrees F (-63 degrees C)	57 degrees F (14 degrees C)
Length of Day	24 hours and 37 minutes	Slightly less than 24 hours

Canada Glacier

In Other Words
microorganisms tiny living things
at the top of the food chain a top predator
inhospitable difficult

If you look at the rock with a microscope, you will see **microorganisms** between the grains. Some of the microorganisms are thousands of years old. And do you see that glacier near the top of the valley? There are microbes living there, too, some in near darkness. Scientists have even discovered a microscopic worm here that can survive years of being freeze-dried, or in a frozen state. This worm is **at the top of the food chain** in this dry, frigid place.

Take a look around you one last time. Congratulations, you have finally found the closest place to Mars on Earth. If there are microorganisms surviving in this **inhospitable** place, then why not on Mars? After years of comparing geologic features on the two planets, scientists now believe that life on Mars is possible. But is it there? Only the observations and investigations of future scientists will tell us for sure. Perhaps one of those scientists will be you. ❖

◀ **Taylor Valley, Dry Valleys, Antarctica**

▶ **Before You Move On**

1. **Explain** Why should scientists avoid drawing false **analogies** between Mars and Earth?

2. **Use Text Features** According to the chart and the text, what would make it difficult for humans to survive on Mars?

Think and Respond

Talk About It 💬

1. "Finding Mars on Earth" uses infographics to give information. Compare the diagram on pages 536–537 with the chart on page 547. How do they present similar information in different ways?

2. Review pages 542–545. What questions could you ask a scientist in order to clarify the arguments about the existence of water on Mars?

3. The author uses a compare-and-contrast text structure to write about **geologic** and **structural** features on Mars and Earth. Explain how making a comparison helped you synthesize information about the planets.

4. What is the author's viewpoint about whether life ever existed on Mars? Support your answer by citing specific evidence from the text.

5. Which **analogy** in the science article best helped you understand an unfamiliar scientific concept or term?

6. Is studying Earth an effective way to learn about a planet like Mars? Make an argument to present your opinion. Use text evidence to illustrate and elaborate on your claim.

Learn test-taking strategies and answer more questions.
🌐 NGReach.com

Write About It ✏️

Write a comparison-contrast paragraph to explain how one **geologic** feature (volcano, canyon, **crater**) on Mars is similar to and different from a similar feature on Earth. Use **Key Words** in your paragraph and cite evidence from the text to support your comparison.

> The **terrains** of Mars and Earth share many similarities, but they also have **distinct** differences.

Compare and Contrast

Review one section in "Finding Mars on Earth." Then create a chart that compares the **geologic** landforms or **terrain** on Earth and Mars.

Comparison-Contrast Chart

Section 1: Fiery Fountains

	Mauna Loa Volcano	Olympus Mons Volcano	Comparison or Contrast
Location	Hawaii, Earth	Mars	Both planets have volcanoes.
Type	shield volcano		
Temperature			
Height			

Use your comparison-contrast chart to discuss a **geologic** feature found on both planets. Then synthesize the information you recorded in the chart to form an overall generalization about the feature. Use **Key Words** in your discussion.

Fluency  Comprehension Coach

Use the Comprehension Coach to practice reading with intonation. Rate your reading.

Talk Together

How does comparing something unknown to something we know help us understand both things better? Include **Key Words** and evidence from the text as you discuss your ideas with a partner.

Context Clues

Some nonfiction texts include technical terms and unfamiliar vocabulary. To figure out what new words mean, look for **context clues**. These are nearby words and phrases that give clues to the meaning of a word. The chart below shows two kinds of context clues.

Type of Clue	Signal Words	Example
Restatement Clue: gives the meaning of a **challenging word** in a different way, usually after a comma	*or*	Scientists study ways that natural forces **transform**, *or* change, the terrain of a planet.
Example Clue: gives an example of what the **challenging word** means	*for example, such as, including*	The **composition** of the rocks, *including* the contents of metal and minerals, shows how the rocks were formed.

How the Strategy Works

Follow these steps to use context clues.

1. Read the words nearby or in the next sentence and look for signal words.

2. Predict what the word means.

3. Try out your predicted meaning to see if it makes sense.

4. Check a dictionary to confirm or revise your definition.

Try It

Read the sentences. Then answer the questions. Use the chart and strategy steps.

Scientists believe that Mars and Earth share similar **geologic** features, including volcanoes and craters. Scientists **survey**, or carefully study, these features.

1. Based on the examples, which of these is most likely a geologic feature?

   A air   **C** Earth

   B a star   **D** a mountain

2. What is the meaning of the word survey as it is used in the sentence?

   A take apart   **C** examine

   B think about   **D** test

Connect Across Texts You read about similarities and differences between Earth and Mars. Now read about the rest of the planets and other objects in our solar system.

Genre A **science article** is nonfiction. It tells facts about topics in the natural world.

Here, There, and Beyond

by Glen Phelan

The Sun

Mercury

Venus

Earth

Mars

Jupiter

Saturn

Uranus

Neptune

Earth's neighbors are all the objects in our solar system, and these objects include planets. There are eight planets in our solar system, and they all **revolve** around the sun. Scientists put these planets into two groups: the four planets closest to the sun make up one group, and the four planets farthest from the sun make up the second group.

▲ Earth

Planets Closest to Our Sun

The four planets closest to the sun—Mercury, Venus, Earth, and Mars—have a lot in common. They are mostly made of rock and metal, so they all have hard, uneven **terrains** . Because of their **compositions** , the planets closest to the sun have high densities. This means that these planets are made of condensed, or tightly packed, materials.

In addition to sharing common **structural** features, the rocky planets closest to the sun are alike in other ways. They are small in comparison to most other planets in our solar system, and they have fewer moons. They also share the quality of having short "years" with relatively quick revolutions around the sun.

▲ **The rocky surface of Mars**

In Other Words
revolve travel in a curved path

Even though they have many similarities, each of these four planets differ individually from the others in its group. For example, each planet has a different kind of atmosphere. An atmosphere is a blanket of gas that covers a planet. Mercury has almost no atmosphere, and both Venus and Mars have atmospheres that are mainly carbon dioxide. Earth's atmosphere is primarily nitrogen and oxygen.

Different gases trap different amounts of heat from the sun, which means that each planet also has a different temperature. Venus is the hottest planet because it has a thick and heavy atmosphere covered with clouds. This dense atmosphere traps energy from the sun, creating a **greenhouse effect**. This makes Venus's surface temperature hotter than most ovens!

There are other differences among these rocky planets. Each is a different size, and each one has different surface features. In addition, Earth and Mars spin at about the same rate—one rotation every 24 hours—but Mercury and Venus both take months to rotate just once.

▲ A detailed view of Venus's taken in ultraviolet light to show its cloudy upper atmosphere

THE PLANETS **CLOSEST** TO THE SUN

Mercury Venus

Earth Mars

How Are They Similar?

- **Surface** They are rocky and solid.
- **Rings** They do not have planetary rings.
- **Moons** They have few or no moons.
- **Size** They are small compared to other planets—less than 8,000 miles **in diameter**. Even so, Earth is more than 2.5 times larger than Mercury!

How Are They Different?

- **Planet Life** Earth is the only planet known to have living things.
- **Temperatures** In this group, Venus is the hottest planet (average temperature: 867° F) while Mars is the coldest planet (average temperature: -85° F).
- **Locations** Mercury is closest to the sun, while Mars is farthest from the sun.

In Other Words
greenhouse effect warmer surface temperature
in diameter across from one side to the other

▶ **Before You Move On**

1. **Text Structure** How does the introduction at the top of page 552 contribute to your understanding of the overall science article?

2. **Make Inferences** Why would it be impossible for humans to live on Mercury, Venus, and Mars today?

Planets Farthest from Our Sun

The next group of four planets is Jupiter, Saturn, Uranus, and Neptune. These planets are huge in comparison to the first group. Unlike the planets closer to the sun, these planets do not have compositions of rock or other solid matter. They lack solid, well-defined surfaces. Their atmospheres are mostly made of gases, so many scientists call these planets "gas giants."

Gas giants have many moons and rings that are made of dust and rocks. The rings of some gas giants are difficult to see, while those of other planets, such as Saturn, are visible from Earth.

Although the gas giants share many similarities, each planet is unique. Some of the gas giants have storms on their surfaces. For example, the orange-red oval shown on Jupiter is a storm that has lasted more than 300 years.

Gas giants can also move through space in different ways. Uranus spins on its side, like a rolling ball instead of a spinning top. It is the only planet in our solar system that spins this way.

THE PLANETS **FARTHEST** FROM THE SUN

Jupiter

Saturn

Uranus

Neptune

How Are They Similar?

- **Rings** They are surrounded by rings.
- **Atmosphere** They have thick atmospheres made mostly of gases.
- **Movement** They travel around the sun in almost circular paths.
- **Moons** They have many moons.
- **Size** They are large compared to other planets—up to 88,900 miles in diameter.

How Are They Different?

- **Rings** Saturn's rings are the easiest to see from Earth.
- **Storms** Jupiter and Saturn have more storms than Uranus and Neptune.
- **Colors** Jupiter has shades of white, orange, brown, and red while Neptune is blue in color.
- **Temperatures** In this group, Neptune is the coldest planet (average temperature: -328° F) while Jupiter is the warmest planet (average temperature: -166° F).
- **Size** Jupiter is so large that all of the other planets could fit inside of it.

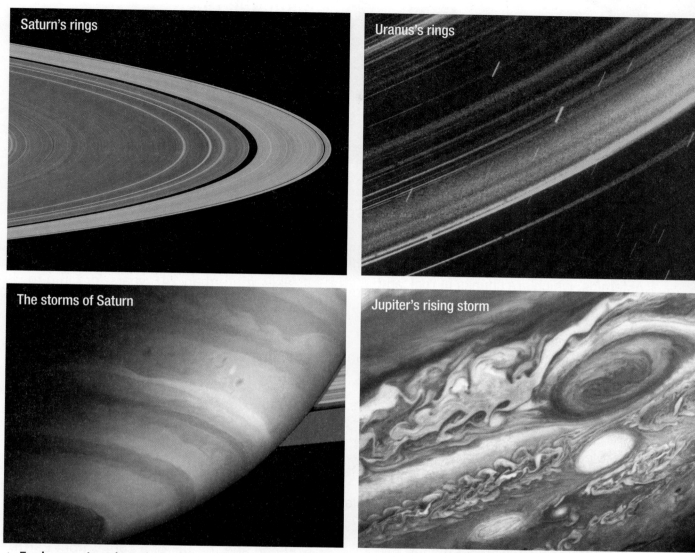

▲ Each gas giant has rings, but only some gas giants have storms on their surfaces.

▶ **Before You Move On**

1. **Use Text Features** What are some of the unique features of Jupiter? Use evidence from the chart to support your answer.

2. **Draw Conclusions** Would space travelers be able to land on these four planets to study them? Use text evidence to explain.

▲ This large asteroid travels around the sun.

Asteroids and Meteoroids

Asteroids, which are chunks of rock and metal, are other neighbors in our solar system. Like planets, asteroids orbit our sun, and most are found between Mars and Jupiter. Some asteroids are as small as houses, while others are much larger. One asteroid is the size of Texas!

Meteoroids are chunks of **debris** in space that are smaller than asteroids. Some meteoroids are tinier than ants, while others are as big as buses. Sometimes a meteoroid falls towards a planet. A meteoroid that strikes a planet is called a meteorite. Sometimes you can see these objects **streaking** across the sky before they hit Earth. People call them "shooting stars."

Icy Objects—Dwarf Planets and Comets

Pluto was once considered the ninth planet in our solar system, but scientists have determined that Pluto is too small to be classified as a planet. Pluto is now called a dwarf planet.

Pluto is not rocky like Earth, nor is it made of gas like Saturn. Pluto has a small, rocky center that is covered with ice, so it resembles a giant snowball in space. Pluto is farther from the sun than Neptune, and it takes more than 248 years for Pluto to travel once around the sun.

Comets, which are large chunks of ice, gas, dust, and rock, also exist in our solar system. Comets are usually found far from the sun. However, when a comet gets close to the sun, the ice on its surface becomes gas. The gas forms an atmosphere, called a coma, around the comet. Some of this gas is pushed from the comet into space, forming the tail of the comet. Occasionally, you can see the tail of a comet from Earth.

In Other Words
debris leftover or extra materials
streaking flying quickly

Pluto and three of its moons: Charon, Nix, and Hydra

Pluto

Nix

Hydra

Charon

Human and Nonhuman Observers

Scientists study objects in our solar system using special tools, such as telescopes. When viewed through a telescope, faraway objects look closer, and details of planets and other space objects are easier to spot. While most telescopes are on Earth, we also have some telescopes in space. Space telescopes are often much larger and can reveal important discoveries, such as the collapse of a comet.

Spacecraft also help us learn more about our neighbors in space. Manned spacecraft carry scientists and astronauts who study our solar system from high above Earth. Spacecraft that do not have people on board are called probes. Probes take pictures, make measurements, and then send the information back to Earth. ❖

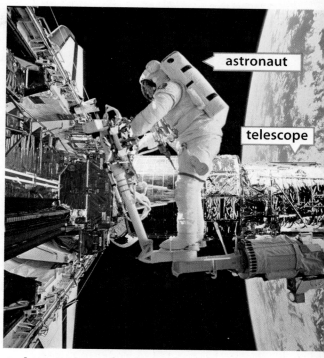

▲ **An astronaut checks a telescope in space.**

▲ **Spacecraft, like this probe, help scientists learn more about the solar system.**

▶ Before You Move On

1. **Make Inferences** How might Pluto's distance from the sun affect its temperature?

2. **Form Generalizations** What advantages do probes have over manned spacecraft? Use evidence from the text.

Respond and Extend

Key Words

analogy	simulate
composition	structural
crater	survey
distinct	terrain
erode	transform
geologic	

Compare Information

The authors of "Finding Mars on Earth" and "Here, There, and Beyond" both use text and infographics to compare objects in our solar system. Work with a partner to complete a comparison chart that shows how information is presented in each selection. Then use the information to form a generalization about how authors use different types of text features and formats to help you understand a topic.

Comparison Chart

	Examples in "Finding Mars on Earth"	Examples in "Here, There, and Beyond"	How Features Give Information
Text	descriptions of geologic features		
Photos and Captions		photos of planets and space objects	
Charts			
Diagrams			

Talk Together

Talk with a partner about a planet in our solar system that you would like to explore. How do the two selections and your knowledge of Earth help you better understand this planet? Use **Key Words** and examples from the text to talk about your ideas.

Compound and Complex Sentences

A **compound sentence** combines two independent clauses, or sentences. A **complex sentence** combines an independent clause and one or more dependent clauses.

Grammar Rules Compound and Complex Sentences

For Compound Sentences: • Use a <u>comma</u> plus a **conjunction** like *and, or, but,* or *so* to join two **independent clauses**.	Earth has water, **but** Mercury does not.
For Complex Sentences: • Join an **independent clause** to a **dependent clause** that cannot stand alone.	Mercury is very hot because it is very close to the sun.
• If the <u>dependent clause</u> comes first, put a <u>comma</u> after it.	As the moon circles Earth, gravity keeps it in orbit.

Read Compound and Complex Sentences

Writers mix simple sentences with compound and complex sentences to change the pacing of their writing and add variety. Read this passage from "Here, There, and Beyond." Identify any compound sentences and complex sentences.

> Unlike the planets closer to the sun, these planets do not have compositions of rock or other solid matter. They lack solid, well-defined surfaces. Their atmospheres are mostly made of gases, so many scientists call these planets "gas giants."

Write Compound and Complex Sentences

Write a short paragraph that describes one or more of the planets. Include at least one compound sentence and one complex sentence. Compare with a partner.

Comparison Words	Contrast Words
similar	although
common	by contrast
as well as	however
likewise	despite

Make Comparisons

Listen to a comparison of two kinds of rock formations. Then use **Language Frames** to make your own comparisons. (((MP3)))

STONE TOWERS

Hoodoos and stalagmites are two types of rock formations. The two are similar because they are both towers of minerals that form naturally. Another thing they have in common is that both are formed by the movement of water over time.

Hoodoos and stalagmites have significant differences, too. Although hoodoos are found above ground, stalagmites are found only in caves.

Most hoodoos are formed when rainwater washes away softer rock, leaving behind harder rock columns. By contrast, limestone stalagmites are formed when water picks up minerals and then drips down onto a cave floor. When the water dries, hard minerals are left behind. Over time, the layers of minerals grow into stalagmites which rise up from the cave floor.

stalagmite

Cat Ba National Park, Quang Ninh

hoodoo

Bryce Canyon National Park, Utah

Science Vocabulary

Key Words

cavern

formation

navigation

passage

subterranean

Key Words

Look at the caving brochure and read the text. Use **Key Words** and other words to talk about what you might see on an amazing adventure.

CAVES

LET'S TAKE A JOURNEY

beneath the surface of the Earth into a **subterranean** cave. The sights underground will amaze you.

For **navigation**, we have headlamps, a compass, and a detailed map. These tools should help us find our way.

BE CAREFUL!

The **passage** you take through the rocks is slippery and narrow, but it leads to a huge, open **cavern**.

Dripping water formed the unusual rock **formations** in this cavern.

Talk Together

What details do you notice about the locations in the **subterranean** journey? Use the **Comparison and Contrast Words** from page 560 and **Key Words** to compare two different **formations**.

Word Choice

Authors choose their words and language carefully to help readers understand the events, setting, and characters in their stories. Their **word choice** can also affect the mood, which is the feelings that readers experience as they read the story.

Look Into the Text

> . . . A vast, limitless expanse of water, the end of a lake if not of an ocean, was spread before us. The indented shore consisted of a beautiful, soft golden sand mixed with small shells from creatures of a past age. The waves broke constantly and echoed in the cavern.

"The **description** includes words that make the water seem huge and endless compared to the characters."

Map and Talk

A word choice chart can help you analyze the language in a story. Identify powerful words and specific descriptions from the text. Then determine how the word choice affects the mood of the scene and your response.

Word Choice Chart

Story Language	What the Words Describe	Mood	Impact on Reader
"vast, limitless expanse of water"	a large body of water	worried, nervous	The description makes me feel nervous about what will happen in the large, unfamiliar place.

Talk Together

Tell a partner about an event in your school or community. Use specific, vivid details to describe the event in a way that will make your partner feel happy. Your partner completes a word choice chart based on your descriptions. Then your partner describes the same event to make you feel a different mood.

More Key Words

Use these words to talk about *Journey to the Center of the Earth* and "Deep Into Darkness."

circumstance
(**sur**-kum-stants) *noun*

A **circumstance** is a fact or event that affects something. Extreme weather **circumstances** prevented us from traveling.

constant
(**kon**-stunt) *adjective*

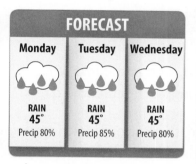

FORECAST

Monday	Tuesday	Wednesday
RAIN 45°	RAIN 45°	RAIN 45°
Precip 80%	Precip 85%	Precip 80%

Something **constant** is continuous or happens all the time. The **constant** rain this week may cause flooding.

estimate
(**es**-tu-māt) *verb*

When you **estimate**, you make a best guess about something. I **estimate** that there are 1,500 jelly beans in this jar.

perceive
(pur-**sēv**) *verb*

When you **perceive** something, you notice or become aware of it. The men **perceive** the problem with the bike tire right away.

undertake
(**un**-dur-tāk) *verb*

When you **undertake** something, you begin or attempt it. The man will **undertake** a difficult climb up the mountain.

Talk Together

Make a Vocabulary Example Chart that includes each of the **Key Words**. Compare your chart with a partner's.

Word	Definition	Example from My Life
constant	ongoing	I'm tired of my brother's *constant* questions.

Add words to My Vocabulary Notebook.
NGReach.com

563

Strategic Reading

- Plan and Monitor
- Visualize
- Ask Questions
- Make Connections
- Determine Importance
- Make Inferences
- Synthesize

Use Reading Strategies

Active readers use a variety of reading strategies before, during, and after reading. They think about what they are reading and pause often to check their understanding. Here's how to read actively.

How to Use Reading Strategies

1. Before you read, stop and think: What strategies can help me get ready to read?

2. During reading, think about which strategies can help you better understand what you are reading. Change your reading strategies based on what you need to know and new information in the text.

3. After reading, ask yourself: What strategies can I use to help me think about what I have read?

> Before I read, I _____ .
>
> As I read _____ ,
> I _____ .
>
> After reading, I _____ .

Here's how one student used a reading strategy during reading.

Look Into the Text

One thing surprised and puzzled me. How was I able to look upon that vast sheet of water instead of being in darkness? The landscape before me was lit up like day . But it lacked the brilliance of sunlight. The pale, cold light in this subterranean region was obviously electric, something like the aurora borealis . Only this light was constant and able to light up the entire ocean cavern .

> As I read details about the setting, I can visualize a lake shining under a mysterious light.

Using reading strategies before, during, and after reading helps you better understand and enjoy what you are reading.

Talk Together

Read the literary response and sample notes. Use **Language Frames** and reading strategies as you read. Then talk with a partner about what the strategies helped you understand.

Literary Response

Journey to the Center of the Earth
BY JULES VERNE
Reviewed by Lupe Vela

Journey to the Center of the Earth is one of Jules Verne's most well-known works. In this famous science-fiction novel, Harry, his uncle, and their traveling companion Hans **undertake** a **subterranean** journey beneath the Earth's surface. After reading the book, it's easy to see why the novel is a classic.

Setting is one of the most important elements of any science-fiction novel, and Verne helps the reader visit this imaginary world-within-our-world. Whether it's an enormous **cavern** filled with unusual **formations** or a mysterious **passage**, Verne's vivid descriptions are easy to visualize. He creates a world that is both familiar and strangely unfamiliar. His word choices make the new place seem cold and slightly threatening. ◄

Verne also includes details that help the reader understand and relate to the main characters. Harry is the first-person narrator who describes the events from his own point of view. Through his actions, dialogue, and descriptions, it is easy to see that he feels concerned and wary in this new environment. By contrast, Harry's uncle is delighted by their unusual **circumstances** and, although he **estimates** that they are far below the Earth's surface, he does not **perceive** any danger during their **navigation** of the unfamiliar terrain. By showing these details, Verne succeeds in giving the reader clues about each character's traits and motivations. ◄

While the characters' journey is fantastical fiction, it reminded me of the first time I visited a big city. I was awed by the towering buildings and the **constant** roar of traffic. Like Harry, I felt like I was standing on an unfamiliar shore. I was fascinated and terrified. That's the beauty of Verne's work—he captures both of those feelings perfectly. ◄

Before I read, I will ask: *How does the writer feel about the novel?* I can read on to find the answer.

As I read the writer's response, I look for the main idea in each paragraph to identify her opinions about the novel.

After reading, I will draw a conclusion about the writer's viewpoint based on evidence in the text.

◄ = a good place to use reading strategies to check for understanding

Read Science Fiction

Genre

Science fiction tells about imaginary scientific or technological discoveries and the way they affect people and societies. Science-fiction stories can take place on Earth, in space, or even in different universes.

Sensory Details

Sensory details are words and phrases that connect with one or more of a reader's five senses: sight, smell, hearing, touch, and taste. Fiction writers use sensory details to describe people, places, and events in the story and to help the reader visualize and connect with the text.

> During certain periods, when the wind stopped, **a silence deeper and more terrible than the silence of the desert** fell upon these solitary and arid rocks. **It seemed to hang like a heavy weight** on the ocean waters. I tried to see through the distant fog.

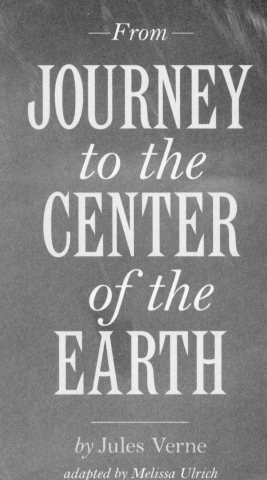

—From—

JOURNEY
to the
CENTER
of the
EARTH

by Jules Verne

adapted by Melissa Ulrich

ILLUSTRATED BY IBRAHEM SWAID

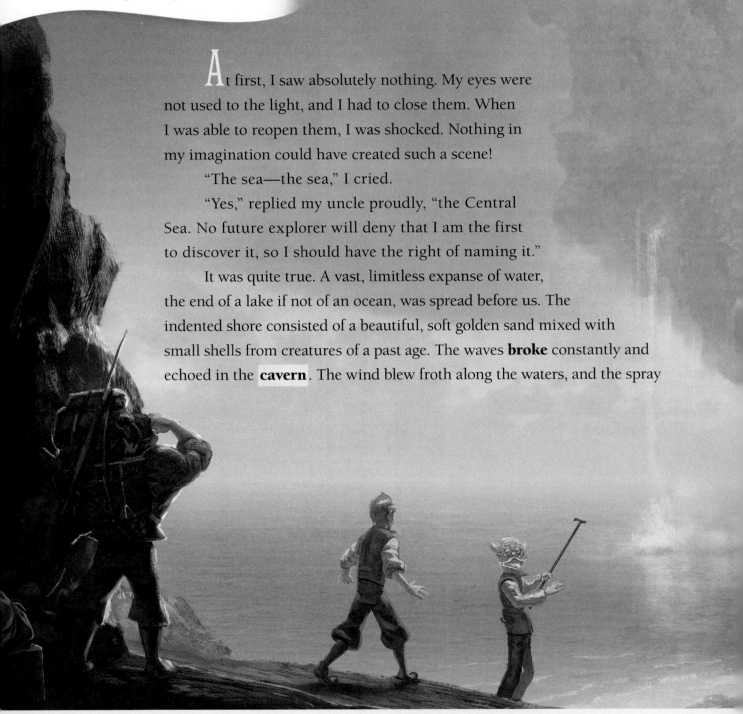

At first, I saw absolutely nothing. My eyes were not used to the light, and I had to close them. When I was able to reopen them, I was shocked. Nothing in my imagination could have created such a scene!

"The sea—the sea," I cried.

"Yes," replied my uncle proudly, "the Central Sea. No future explorer will deny that I am the first to discover it, so I should have the right of naming it."

It was quite true. A vast, limitless expanse of water, the end of a lake if not of an ocean, was spread before us. The indented shore consisted of a beautiful, soft golden sand mixed with small shells from creatures of a past age. The waves **broke** constantly and echoed in the **cavern**. The wind blew froth along the waters, and the spray

In Other Words
broke crashed on the shore

was blown into my face. A mighty **superstructure** of rock rose above to an unimaginable height, leaving only a narrow opening. Where we stood, there was a large area of shore. On all sides were enormous cliffs, partially worn by the eternal breaking of the waves through countless ages. And as I gazed around me, the mighty rocks seemed to disappear into the mist.

One thing surprised and **puzzled** me. How was I able to look upon that vast sheet of water instead of being in darkness? The landscape before me was lit up like day. But it lacked the brilliance of sunlight. The pale, cold light in this **subterranean** region was obviously electric, something like the **aurora borealis**. Only this light was **constant** and able to light up the entire ocean cavern.

The tremendous **vault** above our heads appeared to be made up of a mixture of moving gases. Since we were at the center of the Earth, I wondered how the evaporation of water could take place. Yet there were heavy and dense clouds rolling above, partially hiding the roof. Electric currents lit up the heavier clouds in the distance. It almost looked like lightning. Deep shadows were cast beneath. Suddenly, between two clouds, there would come a ray of unusual beauty and remarkable intensity. And yet it was not like the sun, for it gave no heat.

The effect was sad. Instead of a noble sky of blue, studded with stars, there was above me a heavy roof of granite. It seemed to crush me.

In Other Words

superstructure formation

puzzled confused

aurora borealis northern lights seen from some places on Earth

vault ceiling

569

I cannot describe how impressive it looked. Human language fails to describe its savage beauty. I didn't know if the sudden cooling of the Earth had created this cave long ago. I had read of most wonderful and gigantic caverns or **passages**—but none in any way like this.

"Well," said my uncle, after giving me time to appreciate the wonders of this underground sea, "do you feel strong enough to walk up and down the beach?"

"Nothing would give me greater pleasure."

We began to walk along the shores of this extraordinary place. To our left were rocks piled one upon the other—a gigantic pile. Waterfalls cascaded down the rocks into streams that went into the ocean. **Vapors** rising in **fleecy** clouds from rock to rock indicated hot springs.

My attention was drawn to something unexpected. After we had gone about five hundred yards, we found ourselves close to a **lofty** forest! It consisted of straight trunks with tufted tops that looked like umbrellas. The air seemed to have no effect upon these trees. In spite of a strong breeze, they remained as still and motionless as if they had been frozen.

"It is only a forest of mushrooms," said my uncle.

In Other Words
Vapors Steam and gases
fleecy light and thin
lofty very tall

Looking more closely, I found that he was right. Here were white mushrooms, nearly forty feet high, and with tops of equal size. They grew in countless thousands. The light could not pierce this mushroom forest; beneath them it was dark and gloomy.

The gigantic mushrooms were not the only amazing plants at the center of the Earth. New wonders awaited us at every step. Walking a bit farther, we came upon a mighty group of other trees with discolored leaves. They were the common trees of Mother Earth, only many times larger. There were trees a hundred feet high, ferns as tall as pine trees, and gigantic grasses!

"Astonishing, magnificent, splendid!" cried my uncle. "Behold the humble plants of our gardens, which in the first ages of the world were mighty trees. Look around you, dear Harry. No **botanist** ever before gazed on such a sight!"

"You are right, Uncle," I remarked. "Nature appears to have preserved this vast and mysterious **hothouse** of ancient plants."

"It is indeed a mighty hothouse. But you would also be correct if you called it a large **menagerie**."

In Other Words
botanist scientist who studies plants
hothouse greenhouse
menagerie zoo

▶ **Before You Move On**

1. **Make Connections** How are this forest and beach different from those on Earth? Use details from the text in your answer.

2. **Characters** Why are Harry and his uncle so excited about what they see?

▶ **Predict**

What else will the travelers discover
as they explore the cavern?

I looked around anxiously. If the animals were as large as the plants, this would be a serious matter.

"Look at the dust beneath our feet. The whole soil of the seashore is made of animal bones," said my uncle.

"Bones," I replied, "Yes, certainly, the bones of ancient animals." I stooped down as I spoke and picked up one or two fragments. They were **relics** of a **bygone age**. Some were as big as tree trunks.

"I do not understand how these creatures got here," I said. "If these **prehistoric** animals lived in these caves at the center of the Earth, wouldn't they still be alive here?" As I spoke, I looked around. Nothing alive appeared to exist on these deserted shores.

During certain periods, when the wind stopped, a silence deeper and more terrible than the silence of the desert fell upon these solitary and **arid** rocks. It seemed to hang like a heavy weight on the ocean waters. I tried to see through the distant fog. What was hiding in that mysterious distance? What questions did I wish to ask and did not! Where would this sea end? Where would it lead? Would we ever be able to examine its distant shores?

In Other Words
relics old objects
bygone age time long ago
prehistoric old; ancient
arid dry

My uncle was convinced that we would be successful in our exploration. For my part, I was in a state of painful indecision. I wanted to go on the journey and to succeed, but I feared the result.

I felt so much better when I woke up the next day. After waking up, I went and plunged into the waters of this new ocean. The bath was cool, fresh, and invigorating.

"Now then," he said, "come with me. It is high tide, and I am eager to study **its curious phenomena**."

"What," I cried, rising in astonishment, "did you say the tide, Uncle?"

"Certainly I did."

"How is it possible that the influences of the sun and moon are felt here below?"

"Why not? Why should this vast underground sea **be exempt from** the general law of the universe? Despite the great atmospheric pressure down here, you will notice that this inland sea rises and falls with as much regularity as the Atlantic itself."

As my uncle spoke, we reached the sandy shore. We saw and heard the waves breaking on the beach. The tide was rising.

"This is truly the flood," I said, looking at the water at my feet.

"Yes, my excellent nephew," replied my uncle, rubbing his hands, "and you see by these several streaks of foam that the tide rises at least ten or twelve feet."

"It is indeed marvelous."

"**By no means,**" he responded. "**On the contrary,** it is quite natural."

"This all may appear natural in your eyes, my dear uncle," I said, "but everything here is marvelous. It is almost impossible to believe that what I'm seeing is true. Who in his wildest dreams could have imagined that, beneath the crust of our Earth, there could exist a real ocean, with **ebbing and flowing** tides, with its changes of winds, and even its storms. I, for one, should have laughed at such an idea."

In Other Words
its curious phenomena how this tide works
be exempt from not follow
"By no means," "Not at all,"
On the contrary, Actually,
ebbing and flowing moving

My uncle smiled at my declaration and seemed happy that his expedition to the center of the Earth was so successful.

"Harry, if my **calculations** are correct, we are now 100 miles below the surface of the Earth," said my uncle.

"Are we going back now?" I asked, eager to see the sunlight again and not this strange, cold cave light.

"No, we are not going back. We are going to cross this ocean. Hans is building a raft!"

Hans had made a wonderful raft out of some fossilized wood he had found. When we left the shore, we sailed at a much greater speed than might have been expected from a raft. The dense layers of the atmosphere at that depth had great propelling power and pushed the sail forward with considerable force.

"We are going so fast that we might cross this ocean in 24 hours!" my uncle declared.

Soon, we had sailed so far out that we could not see land. The clouds in the distance turned dark, and there was **an ominous feeling** in the air. A storm was coming upon us, and I looked fearfully at the massing black clouds. Great pieces of seaweed stretched out like snakes on the horizon.

In Other Words
calculations estimates
an ominous feeling a threat of danger

They were thousands of feet long! What natural force could possibly have produced such abnormal and extraordinary plants? What had happened during the Earth's formation that had led to the creation of so many wondrous things?

"There may be many monsters in this ocean," I said, "and I intend to find out. I'm going to try my luck with my fishing line and hook."

Despite having been at sea for many hours, we had not seen any fish. I was about to give up hope for my fishing experiment until Hans pulled in his fishing line. The fish he had caught was small, but it looked strange. I had never seen one like it before.

"This fish went extinct many years ago, and no trace has ever been found except for in fossils!" my uncle said.

Fearfully, I took up the telescope and examined the horizon. If we found a fish that should have been extinct, who knows what else would be swimming in this ocean! Perhaps we would soon see dinosaurs and many other magnificent creatures of ages past.

My uncle grew worried because the sea was much larger than he had thought. We could be at sea for many, many days. I was certain that we would meet some horrible beast before our adventure was over.

▶ **Before You Move On**

1. **Confirm Prediction** What do the men discover in this new world? How does it compare to the world they know?

2. **Mood** What feelings does this scene create? How does the author's word choice support this mood?

Suddenly the raft tilted up **precariously** and dropped again. The waves violently churned beneath us. Nearby, a huge sea lizard rose out of the water. Hans steered the raft in the other direction, only to find a gigantic sea crocodile on the other side. I was horrified to see so many gleaming teeth.

The huge, deadly sea monsters advanced upon us, nearer and nearer. Either we will be eaten by the sea crocodile or the sea serpent, I thought. My uncle informed me that they were an *Ichthyosaurus* and a *Plesiosaurus*. Both had been extinct for a very long time. I was impressed that he could remember facts like that in such a dangerous situation.

We prepared to fight with the weapons we had, but guns would be useless against such terrible creatures. Surprisingly, the two monsters passed right by our raft and lunged at each other in a ferocious attack. They fought for many hours, and we thought that it would never end. Finally, after much **carnage**, they both sank below the surface of the waters.

The wind **died down**, and our raft stopped moving as quickly. A booming and gushing noise filled the air. Hans searched the horizon and saw a huge waterspout in the distance. Perhaps it was another sea creature? My uncle was excited to **perceive** the source of the noise and water, but I was not.

As we sailed closer, we found that it was an island with a huge geyser in the middle! What **volcanic** power could produce such a geyser? The drops of water fell all around us and **assumed** the colors of the rainbow.

I looked at the navigation instruments to chart a map for this island and found that we had already sailed more than 800 miles on this great inland sea.

As we floated past the island, the huge, dark clouds broiled above us. I had never seen a cloud **formation** like that. "I believe we are going to have bad weather. These clouds are falling lower and lower upon the sea, as if to crush it." I said. "We should lower the sail."

In Other Words
precariously dangerously
carnage bloody fighting
died down stopped blowing so hard
volcanic strong; forceful
assumed turned into

"No, keep up the sail, no matter what happens," said my uncle.

Soon, a wild and **raging tempest** came upon us. The raft rose and fell with the storm, and bounded over the waves. My uncle seemed to gaze with pleasure and delight at the **spectacle**.

The sail spread out and looked like a soap bubble about to burst. Fearful claps of thunder and flashes of lightning filled us with awe. The flashes crossed one another, hurled from every side. The thunder **came pealing like an echo**. The mass of vapor **became incandescent**. The waves looked like fire-eating monsters, beneath which burned an intense fire. My eyes were dazzled by the light and my ears were deafened by the roar of the thunder.

geyser

In Other Words

raging tempest powerful storm

spectacle amazing sight

came pealing like an echo crashed loudly

became incandescent glowed

The storm lasted more than three days and three nights, and **our ears were bleeding** with the constant roar of thunder. When our raft finally crashed upon a shoreline, Hans was the one who saved me from the wreckage. I was so tired that I could not even swim. Every trace of the storm had disappeared. My uncle was thrilled.

"We have finally reached the other side of the ocean!" he cried joyfully. Then he took out his compass and frowned. He turned this way and that with his gaze focused on the compass. Whatever position we forced the needle into, it returned to the same unexpected point. It was useless to **conceal** the truth from ourselves.

There could be no doubt that during the storm, a sudden wind had carried us back to the shores **from whence we came**. ❖

In Other Words

our ears were bleeding our ears ached
conceal try to hide
whence we came where we had started

▶ **Before You Move On**

1. **Draw Conclusions** How do Harry and his uncle respond to dangerous **circumstances**? What does this show about the characters?

2. **Mood** How does the description of the storm contribute to the mood of the overall story?

JULES VERNE (1828–1905)

Decades before the first plane took flight, French author Jules Verne wrote about inventions that his readers had never dreamed of, including spaceships, submarines, and televisions. While other authors focused on realistic experiences and settings, Verne brought his imagination to life in stories like *Journey to the Center of the Earth*, *Around the World in 80 Days*, and *20,000 Leagues Under the Sea*. Today, the technology Verne imagined is part of our everyday lives, and Verne is known as the Father of Science Fiction.

Verne wrote *Journey to the Center of the Earth* in French with language that was appropriate for readers in 1864. Although the novel has been translated and adapted into multiple versions since then, the ideas and story all come from the futuristic imagination of Jules Verne.

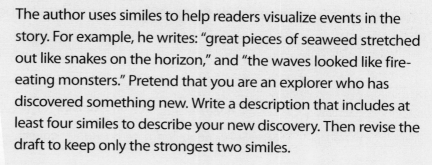

Writer's Craft

The author uses similes to help readers visualize events in the story. For example, he writes: "great pieces of seaweed stretched out like snakes on the horizon," and "the waves looked like fire-eating monsters." Pretend that you are an explorer who has discovered something new. Write a description that includes at least four similes to describe your new discovery. Then revise the draft to keep only the strongest two similes.

Key Words

cavern	navigation
circumstance	passage
constant	perceive
estimate	subterranean
formation	undertake

Talk About It

1. Based on what you know about Earth's geologic **formations**, bodies of water, and life-forms, which details from the story are based on science fiction and which are based on science facts?

2. Compare and contrast the characters of Harry and his uncle. Cite specific examples to support how the characters are similar and different.

3. At the deserted shore, Harry says that the silence "seemed to hang like a heavy weight on the ocean waters." What does this simile show about Harry's response to the journey? Identify another example in the selection in which Harry's word choice conveys a similar mood.

4. Compare the **subterranean cavern** to similar places on Earth. How does your comparison help you understand the setting of the story?

5. How would the story be different if it were told by another character or a third-person narrator? Use specific examples from the text to support your claim.

6. What is an important theme, or message, from the story? Cite evidence about the plot, setting, or characters to support your answer.

Learn test-taking strategies and answer more questions.
NGReach.com

Write About It

Write a brief speech that Harry gives to a group of explorers about his journey. Include **Key Words** and choose words that provide sensory details about the experience.

> I'd like to share with you the **circumstances** of our amazing journey. First, we encountered a remarkable **cavern**.

Word Choice

Use a word choice chart to record examples of the story language in *Journey to the Center of the Earth* and how the words affect the mood of the scenes.

Word Choice Chart

Story Language	What the Words Describe	Mood	Impact on Reader
"vast, limitless expanse of water"	a large body of water	worried, nervous	The description makes me feel nervous about what will happen in the large, unfamiliar place.

Use your word choice chart to share your examples with a partner. Explain how the author's word choice helped you understand and experience the story.

Fluency  Comprehension Coach

Use the Comprehension Coach to practice reading with expression. Rate your reading.

Talk Together

How does an understanding of Earth's features help you understand the setting in this story? In what ways might science fiction inspire exploration? Use **Key Words** as you discuss your ideas with a partner.

Connotations and Word Choice

Sometimes writers choose words that mean exactly what they say. These exact meanings are called literal meanings, or **denotations**. Other times, writers choose words that have a specific feeling, or **connotation**, that is associated with the word. For example, an author might choose to describe someone who saves money as "frugal" or "cheap." Both words have similar denotations, but *frugal* has a more positive connotation than *cheap*.

The chart below shows words with similar denotations but different connotations.

Example	Denotation	Connotation
*I **guess** that our journey will take three days.*	think, predict	**Guess** implies that the speaker is not very sure about the idea.
*I **estimate** that our journey will take three days.*	think, predict	**Estimate** implies that the speaker has thought carefully about the idea.

As you read, consider why the author chooses to include words with certain connotations and how the word choice can affect the mood of the text.

Try It

Answer the questions below.

1. **Read this sentence from *Journey to the Center of the Earth*:**

    *My uncle was excited to **perceive** the source of the noise and water, but I was not.*

    What is the connotation of <u>perceive</u> as it is used in this sentence?

    A feel

    B grasp

    C discover

    D notice

2. **Read this sentence from *Journey to the Center of the Earth*:**

    *The storm lasted more than three days and three nights, and our ears were bleeding with the **constant** roar of thunder.*

    What is the connotation of <u>constant</u> in this sentence?

    A usual

    B same

    C unending

    D long

Connect Across Texts You read a story about a **subterranean** **cavern**. Now read about the mysteries inside of some real-life caves on Earth.

Genre A **science feature** is a short nonfiction text that focuses on a specific scientific topic.

DEEP INTO DARKNESS

by Beth Geiger

A decorated passage in Iron Hoop Cave, Alabama

Darkness surrounds you, the air feels damp, and you hear rushing water. You quickly flip on your headlamp, and its narrow **beam pierces** the darkness to light the inside of a cave.

You reach out to touch a nearby rock wall, but it looks like it oozes a liquid. To your right, a long tunnel snakes its way into the darkness. To your left, a waterfall gushes over a cliff, and you realize that it's the source of the rushing water sound.

You're inside one of Earth's millions of caves. A cave is a natural opening in the ground, and people who enjoy exploring caves, or **caverns**, are called cavers.

Sure, going into a cave is fun, but you're here to learn about this cave. You want to explore and map its twisting tunnels, and you want to study its unique rock **formations** and the animals that scurry across them.

In Other Words
beam light
pierces shines through

MEET A CAVER

Let's **tag along** with Stephen Alvarez, a caver who can give us a tour. He travels the world exploring and photographing caves. Alvarez has **scaled** mountains and has **plunged the depths of** the sea to explore different types of caves. He has also hiked through ice caves and walked through caves formed by flowing lava, which are called lava tubes.

Alvarez has photographed some of Earth's most impressive caves, including the longest cave. It is called Mammoth Cave, and it's located in Kentucky. Mammoth Cave has 580 kilometers (360 miles) of tunnels and **passages**!

Alvarez has also dropped down into one of the deepest known caves. This cave, near the border of Asia and Europe, descends 2.2 kilometers (1.4 miles) underground.

Cavers attach lights to long ropes to help them see as they descend into Mystery Falls, the deepest pit in Tennessee. ▶

In Other Words
tag along travel
scaled climbed
plunged the depths of gone deep into

▶ **Before You Move On**

1. **Visualize** How does the author help you visualize a waterfall on page 584 even though it is not shown in a photo?

2. **Main Idea/Details** There are many different types of caves. List three details from the text that support this main idea.

Ropes and safety gear prevent cavers from falling into river rapids in Ora Cave, New Guinea.

UNDERGROUND DANGER

Cavers don't mind getting scratched or muddy, but staying safe is extremely important. Alvarez never goes into caves by himself. He always goes into caves with other cavers, so that team members can look out for one another.

Serious cavers also need to carry the right equipment. Helmets are **a must**, and kneepads and gloves are helpful, too. Most cavers use headlamps to discern where they are going, and this keeps their hands free to climb and crawl. They also carry **backup** flashlights. Experienced cavers are experts with ropes, and one of Alvarez's favorite things about caving is using rope when exploring.

WATER AT WORK

Water is the key to the formation of many caves, according to Alvarez. Water carves limestone, which is a type of rock made from ancient shells and animal skeletons. Raindrops mix with carbon dioxide in the air and form an acid. This acid can break down, or erode, limestone. Over time, it can create a long maze of tunnels.

In Other Words
a must needed; necessary
backup extra

FROM PEARLS TO POPCORN

When minerals dissolve in dripping cave water, they gradually harden into shapes called decorations. Decorations come in many shapes and sizes. Stalactites hang down from a cave ceiling like fangs, and stalagmites poke up from the cave floor. Over time, a stalactite and a stalagmite can meet, grow together, and form a column.

Some decorations look like wrinkled stone curtains, and others look like freshly popped kernels of popcorn. Some cave decorations have funny names, like "cave pearls" or "bacon strips." Alvarez has seen formations that look like nests of eggs.

Perhaps the most delicate cave formations are called helictites, and you can find them clustered on some cave walls and ceilings. Some clump together like a pile of worms, and others are thicker and look like antlers. One rare type looks like fish tails sticking out of a cave wall! Scientists know a lot about how most cave formations are created, but they still don't know how helictites are formed.

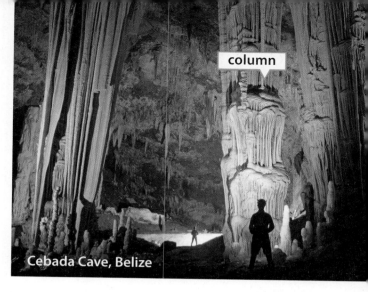

column

Cebada Cave, Belize

Helictites start out as stalactites, but they do not grow straight down. Instead, they twist like a corkscrew or pop out sideways like a hook. Helictites are usually less than half a centimeter wide and five centimeters long (¼-inch wide and two inches long), and they are as delicate—and fragile—as glass.

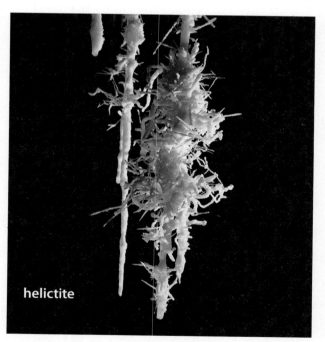

helictite

▶ **Before You Move On**

1. **Cause/Effect** How are some caves formed? Use evidence from the text to support your answer.

2. **Compare/Contrast** Compare helictites and other cave decorations. Draw a conclusion based on the evidence.

CAVE CRITTERS

Beautiful cave decorations are not all that you'll see in caves because many animals live or spend time in caves, too. Some animals only visit caves temporarily, while others make caves their homes.

Cave-dwelling bats **hang out** on the walls of caves during the day and go outside to hunt at night. Raccoons, salamanders, lizards, and snakes all use caves as temporary rest areas. Troglobites are animals that live only inside caves, and some live only in one part of one particular cave. Scientists know of about 7,700 kinds of troglobites.

Troglobites have adapted to life in the dark. Their skin or shells are pale, and most of them are white. Many of these critters have no eyes because eyes are unnecessary when there is no light. Alvarez has seen eyeless fish, shrimps, and spiders. One type of blind crayfish can live for as many as 175 years!

Since they can't see, most troglobites have a **super sharp** sense of hearing, touch, or smell. A troglobite uses these keen senses for **navigation** along winding paths and to tell what's nearby. A troglobite predator can catch its prey without ever seeing the victim!

Cave salamander

Blind crayfish

Snottites

SMALL AND STRANGE

Eyeless animals may be enough to **send goose bumps down your spine**, but they may not be the strangest of all cave dwellers. The weirdest cave creatures may be acid-eating bacteria. These bacteria live only in certain caves, and they can make dangerous, poisonous gas. They ooze and drip from cave ceilings like mucus, and scientists call these slimy blobs "snottites."

In Other Words
hang out spend time
super sharp very good
send goose bumps down your spine scare you

Stephens Gap Cave, Alabama

CAVE THREATS

Explorers like Alvarez know what fragile and wonderful places caves and caverns are, and they also know how important it is to protect them.

Nearly one-third of the drinking water in the United States comes from **subterranean** streams and springs, and these start inside of caves or pass through them. Polluted water from farms or businesses can flow into caves, destroying decorations and killing animals.

Human visitors also can be a threat. A careless caver can destroy in minutes what took thousands of years to form, and that's why responsible cavers try to live by this motto: "Take nothing but pictures. Leave nothing but footprints. Kill nothing but time!" ❖

▶ **Before You Move On**

1. **Compare/Contrast** Use evidence from the text and photos to compare and contrast the three troglobites on page 588.
2. **Paraphrase** Rephrase the caver motto in your own words. Then explain how this attitude is reflected in the text.

589

Key Words	
cavern	navigation
circumstance	passage
constant	perceive
estimate	subterranean
formation	undertake

Compare Fiction and Nonfiction

Both *Journey to the Center of the Earth* and "Deep Into Darkness" feature individuals who explore **subterranean** worlds. Work with a partner to compare and contrast the selections and identify the elements of fiction or nonfiction that make them distinct genres. Then use the information to make a generalization about the way fiction and nonfiction present a similar topic.

Comparison Chart

	Journey to the Center of the Earth	"Deep Into Darkness"
Genre		Nonfiction: Science Feature
Purpose	to entertain	
Structure		
Text Features		

Talk Together

Both science fiction and science articles can describe explorations into unfamiliar worlds. Which genre is more effective at inspiring exploration? Use **Key Words** and text evidence to support your claim.

Combine Sentences

You can combine sentence parts, details, and entire sentences to improve your style and make your writing more interesting.

Grammar Rules Combine Sentences

Combine similar **subjects** with **and** or **or**.	**Stalactites** form in caves. **Stalagmites** also form in caves. **Stalactites** and **stalagmites** form in caves.
Combine **predicates** that tell about the same subject with **and** or **or**.	You **reach out**. You **touch a nearby rock wall**. You **reach out** and **touch a nearby rock wall**.
Combine details from two sentences by using an **adjective clause** that begins with words like *which*, *that*, *who*, *when*, *where*, or *why*.	Water carves limestone. Limestone is a type of rock. Water carves limestone, **which is a type of rock**.
Join neighboring sentences or sentences that have related ideas.	Some animals visit caves. Others live there. Some animals visit caves **while** others live there.

Read Combined Sentences

Writers vary their sentence lengths and connect related ideas by combining sentences. Read this passage from "Deep Into Darkness." Find sentences in which the author has joined related ideas.

> Alvarez has scaled mountains and has plunged the depths of the sea to explore different types of caves. He has also hiked through ice caves and walked through caves formed by flowing lava, which are called lava tubes.

Draft and Combine Sentences

Reread pages 584–586 of "Deep Into Darkness." Write a paragraph that tells what it would be like to explore a cave. Vary your sentences. Then trade sentences with a partner. Find the combined sentences in each other's paragraphs.

Write as a Storyteller

Write Science Fiction

Write a science-fiction story about someone who uses a new invention to explore a geologic feature on Earth or another planet, like Mars. You and your classmates will share your stories during a science-fiction convention.

Study a Model

A science-fiction story tells about the effect of real or imagined developments in science and technology. Read Isabel's science-fiction story about a submarine journey 200 years from now.

Journey to the Bottom of the Sea
by Isabel Shapiro

"Okay, Submarine Commander," Captain Zemo said. "You must descend 36,200 feet into the Pacific to explore a hydrothermal vent. Don't let that new SuperNautilus submarine overheat, and rely on your co-captain."

Carefully, I navigated the SuperNautilus to the ocean floor. **"You found it, Jaxon! There's the vent," co-captain Arva shouted,** pointing excitedly to **the chimney-like structure with rising plumes of black smoke.**

Suddenly, the alarm sounded. The SuperNautilus was overheating! I panicked. Meanwhile, Arva stepped in to steer the sub to cooler waters. The beeping stopped.

"Whew! That was close," I said. "What did Captain Zemo say about cooling down the SuperNautilus?"

"I think it was something about relying on your co-captain," Arva said with a grin.

Isabel uses words that sound like her. The writing has a clear **voice** and **style**.

The beginning introduces the story problem.

Dialogue and **precise words and descriptions** develop the events.

The end tells the solution to the problem.

Prewrite

1. **Choose a Topic** Imagine a new invention that enables you to explore a geologic feature of Earth. What would your invention be like? Talk with a partner to find an idea.

Language Frames	
Tell Your Ideas	**Respond to Ideas**
• My invention might be _____ .	• _____ sounds like a good invention. How would it work?
• I'd like to include some facts about _____ .	• Tell me more about _____ .
• My character will explore _____ .	• What facts can you share about _____ ?

2. **Gather Information** You may need to do research before writing science fiction. Find the details you need to describe the setting and technology accurately.

3. **Get Organized** Use a plot diagram to help you organize your ideas.

Plot Diagram

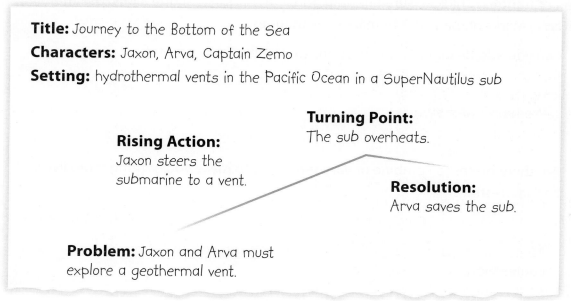

Title: Journey to the Bottom of the Sea

Characters: Jaxon, Arva, Captain Zemo

Setting: hydrothermal vents in the Pacific Ocean in a SuperNautilus sub

Turning Point: The sub overheats.

Rising Action: Jaxon steers the submarine to a vent.

Resolution: Arva saves the sub.

Problem: Jaxon and Arva must explore a geothermal vent.

Draft

Use your plot diagram to write your draft. Use precise words and vary your sentences to keep your writing lively.

Revise

1. **Read, Retell, Respond** Read your draft aloud to a partner. Your partner listens
   and then retells your story. Talk about ways to improve your writing.

Language Frames	
Retell	**Make Suggestions**
• Your story is about _____ . • It takes place _____ . • The main characters are _____ . • The problem is _____ . • The problem is solved when _____ .	• I like what you wrote about _____ . Could you add more details to describe it? • Try developing the characters by _____ . • Maybe you could add dialogue to move events forward, like when _____ . • The order of events isn't clear. Maybe you could use transition words, such as _____ .

2. **Make Changes** Think about your draft and your partner's suggestions. Use the
   Revising Marks on page 617 to mark your changes.

   • Can you add dialogue or descriptions to develop story events?

   > "Whew! That was close," I said.
   > ~~We barely got away.~~

   • Are there places to combine or vary sentences to make your writing more lively
     and interesting?

   > to steer
   > Meanwhile, Arva stepped in. ~~She steered~~ the sub to
   > cooler waters.

Edit and Proofread

Work with a partner to edit and proofread your science-fiction story. Pay special attention to varying and combining sentences. Use the marks on page 618 to show your changes.

Use the marks on page 618 to show your changes.

Grammar Tip

Avoid run-on sentences by using a comma and a conjunction such as *and*, *but*, or *or* to combine two closely related sentences.

Publish

1. **On Your Own** Make a final copy of your story. Practice reading your story aloud before sharing it orally with the class.

Presentation Tips	
If you are the speaker . . .	**If you are the listener . . .**
Before you read, practice saying any scientific or technical terms you may have used.	Connect the story with what you already know about the scientific information.
When you read dialogue, change your expression to reflect the characters and what they are saying.	Listen for details that help you visualize the setting and the story events.

2. **With a Group** Hold a science-fiction convention where you can share your story and listen to others. Practice reading your story several times so that you can read it naturally, with gestures and emotion. Dress in a costume that fits your main character. Present your stories to other classes, or invite younger children to hear them.

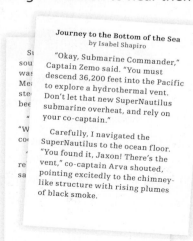

Journey to the Bottom of the Sea
by Isabel Shapiro

Su...
sou...
was...
Mea...
ste...
bee...

"

"W...
co...

re...
sa...

"Okay, Submarine Commander," Captain Zemo said. "You must descend 36,200 feet into the Pacific to explore a hydrothermal vent. Don't let that new SuperNautilus submarine overheat, and rely on your co-captain."

Carefully, I navigated the SuperNautilus to the ocean floor. "You found it, Jaxon! There's the vent," co-captain Arva shouted, pointing excitedly to the chimney-like structure with rising plumes of black smoke.

BIG Question

How does studying Earth tell us about other planets?

In this unit you found many answers to the **Big Question**. Now use your concept map to discuss it with the class. Think about the information that was presented in the selections. What did you learn about the geologic features on Earth? How are those features similar and different on other planets?

Idea Web

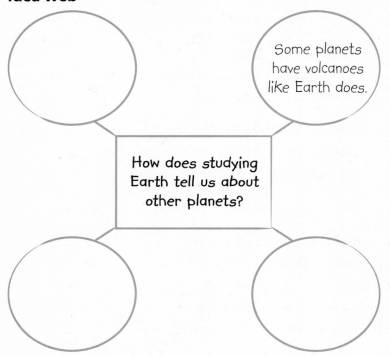

Some planets have volcanoes like Earth does.

How does studying Earth tell us about other planets?

Performance Task: Narrative

Consider what you learned about Earth and other planets, including the ideas in the **Small Group Reading** books. Then imagine that you are an astronaut and can travel to another planet. Write a short story telling about your adventure. Include details about what you might see and do.

Checklist

Does your narrative

- ✓ clearly describe character and setting?
- ✓ clearly develop the sequence of events?
- ✓ include transition words, descriptive details, and sensory language?

596

Share Your Ideas

Choose one of these ways to share your ideas about the **Big Question**.

Write It!

Write an Ode

An ode is a short poem written to praise its subject. Write an ode to one of the planets. The first line should be the most general, so no one knows which planet you are writing about. Each additional line should add more information. Can your classmates guess the planet by the time you finish reading the whole poem aloud?

Talk About It!

Compare and Contrast

With a partner, choose a planet to compare and contrast with Earth. Use presentation software to create a slideshow showing the similarities and differences between the planets. Present your slideshow to the class.

Comparing Planets
Both planets have moons.

Do It!

Create a T.V. Series

Work with a small group to develop an idea for a new science-fiction television series. Choose a planet as your setting, and then agree on the characters and the main storyline for the series. Create a storyboard to show your ideas.

Write It!

Write a Blog Entry

Write a blog entry expressing your opinion about whether you think scientists will eventually find life on Mars. Clearly state your claim and support your opinion with reasons and evidence. If possible, post your blog entry to a class Web site and invite your classmates to share their opinions in the comments section.

Strategies for Learning Language

These strategies can help you learn to use and understand the English language.

1 Listen actively and try out language.

What to Do	Examples
Repeat what you hear.	**You hear:** Way to go, Joe! Fantastic catch! **You say:** Way to go, Joe! Fantastic catch!
Recite songs and poems.	*My Family Tree* *Two grandmas, one brother,* *Two grandpas, one mother,* *One father, and then there's me.* *Eight of us together* *Make up my family tree.* Two grandmas, one brother,...
Listen to others and use their language.	**You hear:** *"When did you know that something was missing?"* **You say:** *"I knew that something was missing when I got to class."*

2 Ask for help.

What to Do	Examples
Ask questions about how to use language.	Did I say that right? Did I use that word in the right way? Which is correct, "bringed" or "brought"?
Use your native language or English to make sure that you understand.	**You say:** *"Wait! Could you say that again more slowly, please?"* **Other options:** *"Does 'violet' mean 'purple'?"* *"Is 'enormous' another way to say 'big'?"*

❸ Use gestures and body language, and watch for them.

What to Do	Examples
Use gestures and movements to help others understand your ideas.	I will hold up five fingers to show that I need five more minutes.
Watch people as they speak. The way they look or move can help you understand the meaning of their words.	Let's give him a hand. / Everyone is clapping. "Give him a hand" must mean to clap for him.

❹ Think about what you are learning.

What to Do	Examples
Ask yourself: Are my language skills getting better? How can I improve?	Was it correct to use "they" when I talked about my grandparents? / Did I add 's to show ownership?
Keep notes about what you've learned. Use your notes to practice using English.	How to Ask Questions • I can start a question with "is," "can," or "do": Do you have my math book? • I can start a question with "who," "what," "where," "when," "how," or "why" to get more information: Where did you put my math book?

Vocabulary Strategies

When you read, you may find a word you don't know. But, don't worry! There are many things you can do to figure out the meaning of an unfamiliar word.

Use What You Know

Ask yourself "Does this new word look like a word I know?" If it does, use what you know about the familiar word to figure out the meaning of the new word. Think about:

- **word families**, or words that look similar and have related meanings. The words *locate*, *location*, and *relocate* are in the same word family.

- **cognates**, or pairs of words that look the same in English and in another language. The English word *problem* and the Spanish word *problema* are cognates.

On the Top of the World

Mount Everest is the highest mountain in the world. It is 29,028 feet (8,848 meters) high. This **magnificent** mountain is covered in permanently frozen snow and ice. But this doesn't stop **adventurous** climbers from trying to reach its peak.

> This English word looks like **magnífico**. That means "beautiful" in Spanish. I think that meaning makes sense here, too.

> I know that **adventure** means "an exciting event" and that an **adventurer** is "someone who takes risks." So, **adventurous** probably means "willing to be a part of risky activities."

Use Context Clues

Sometimes you can figure out a word's meaning by looking at other words and phrases near the word. Those words and phrases are called **context clues.**

There are different kinds of context clues. Look for signal words such as *means, like, but,* or *unlike* to help you find the clues.

Extremely cold temperatures are hazardous to mountain climbers.

Kind of Clue	Signal Words	Example
Definition Gives the word's meaning.	*is, are, was, refers to, means*	Hazardous *refers to* something that causes harm or injury.
Restatement Gives the word's meaning in a different way, usually after a comma.	*or*	Mountain climbing can be hazardous, *or* result in injuries to climbers.
Synonym Gives a word or phrase that means almost the same thing.	*like, also*	Sudden drops in temperature can be hazardous. *Also* dangerous are very high altitudes that make it hard to breathe.
Antonym Gives a word or phrase that means the opposite.	*but, unlike*	The subzero temperatures can be hazardous, *but* special gear keeps the climbers safe.
Examples Gives examples of what the word means.	*such as, for example, including*	Climbers prepare for hazardous situations. *For example*, they carry extra food, equipment for heavy snowfall, and first-aid kits.

Use Word Parts

Many English words are made up of parts. You can use these parts as clues to a word's meaning.

When you don't know a word, look to see if you know any of its parts. Put the meaning of the word parts together to figure out the meaning of the whole word.

Compound Words

A compound word is made up of two or more smaller words. To figure out the meaning of the whole word:

1. Break the long word into parts.

2. Put the meanings of the smaller words together to predict the meaning of the whole word.

keyboard = key + board

key = button
+
board = flat surface

keyboard = flat part of computer with buttons

laptop

keyboard

3. If you can't predict the meaning from the parts, use what you know and the meaning of the other words to figure it out.

lap + top = laptop

laptop means "small portable computer," not "the top of your lap"

Prefixes

A prefix comes at the beginning of a word. It changes the word's meaning. To figure out the meaning of an unfamiliar word, look to see if it has a prefix.

1. Break the word into parts. Think about the meaning of each part.

I need to **rearrange** the files on my computer.

re- + arrange

The prefix *re-* means "again." The word *arrange* means "to put in order."

2. Put the meanings of the word parts together.

The word *rearrange* means "to put in order again."

Some Prefixes and Their Meanings

Prefix	Meaning
anti-	against
dis-	opposite of
In-	not
mis	wrongly
pre-	before
re-	again, back
un-	not

Suffixes

A suffix comes at the end of a word. It changes the word's meaning and part of speech. To figure out the meaning of a new word, look to see if it has a suffix.

1. Break the word into parts. Think about the meaning of each part.

2. Put the meanings of the word parts together.

My **teacher** helps me find online articles.

teach + -er

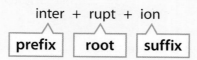

The word *teach* means "to give lessons."
The suffix *-er* means "one who."

A *teacher* is "a person who gives lessons."

noun

Some Suffixes and Their Meanings

Suffix	Meaning
-able	can be done
-al	having characteristics of
-ion	act, process
-er, -or	one who
-ful	full of
-less	without
-ly	in a certain way

Greek and Latin Roots

Many words in English have Greek and Latin roots. A root is a word part that has meaning, but it cannot stand on its own.

1. Break the unfamiliar word into parts.

I won't be done in time if there's one more **interruption**!

inter + rupt + ion

prefix   root   suffix

2. Focus on the root. Do you know other words with the same root?

"I've seen the root **rupt** in the words *erupt* and *rupture*.

'rupt' must have something to do with breaking or destroying something."

3. Put the meanings of all the word parts together.

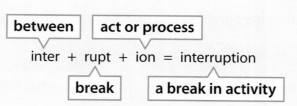

inter + rupt + ion = interruption

605

Look Beyond the Literal Meaning

Writers use colorful language to keep their readers interested. They use words and phrases that mean something different from their usual definitions. Figurative language and idioms are kinds of colorful language.

Figurative Language: Similes

A simile compares two things that are alike in some way. It uses the words *like* or *as* to make the comparison.

Simile	Things Compared	How They're Alike
Cory hiked across the desert **as sluggishly as a snail**.	Cory and a snail	They both move very slowly.
His skin was **like sheets of sandpaper.**	skin and sandpaper	They are both rough and very dry.

Figurative Language: Metaphors

A metaphor compares two things without using the words *like* or *as*.

Metaphor	Things Compared	Meaning
The **sun's rays were a thousand bee stings** on his face.	sun's rays and bee stings	The sun's rays blistered his face.
His only **companion was thirst.**	friend and thirst	His thirst was always there with him.

Figurative Language: Personification

When writers use personification they give human qualities to nonhuman things.

Personification	Object	Human Quality
The **angry sun** kept punishing him.	sun	has feelings
A **cactus reached out to** him.	cactus	is able to be friendly

Idioms

An idiom is a special kind of phrase that means something different from what the words mean by themselves.

What you say:	**What you mean:**
If the topic is Mars, **I'm all ears.**	If the topic is Mars, **I'll listen very carefully.**
Break a leg!	**Good luck!**
Rachel had **to eat her words.**	Rachel had **to say she was wrong.**
Give me a break!	**That's ridiculous!**
Hang on.	**Wait.**
I'm **in a jam.**	I'm **in trouble.**
The joke was so funny, Lisa **laughed her head off.**	The joke was so funny, Lisa **laughed very hard.**
Juan was **steamed** when I lost his video game.	Juan was **very angry** when I lost his video game.
Let's **surf the Net** for ideas for report ideas.	Let's **look around the contents of the Internet** for report ideas.
I'm so tired, I just want to **veg out.**	I'm so tired, I just want to **relax and not think about anything.**
Rob and Zak are together **24-seven.**	Rob and Zak are together **all the time.**
You can say that again.	**I totally agree with you.**
Zip your lips!	**Be quiet!**

Reading Strategies

Good readers use a set of strategies before, during, and after reading. Knowing which strategy to use and when will help you understand and enjoy all kinds of text.

Plan and Monitor

Good readers have clear plans for reading. Remember to:

- **Set a purpose** for reading. Ask yourself: Why am I reading this? What do I hope to get from it?

- **Preview** what you are about to read. Look at the title. Scan the text, pictures, and other visuals.

- **Make predictions**, or thoughtful guesses, about what comes next. Check your predictions as you read. Change them as you learn new information.

Monitor, or keep track of, your reading. Remember to:

- **Clarify ideas and vocabulary** to make sure you understand what the words and passages mean. Stop and ask yourself: Does that make sense?

- **Reread, read on,** or **change your reading speed** if you are confused.

Determine Importance

How can you keep track of all the facts and details as you read? Do what good readers do and focus on the most important ideas.

- Identify the **main idea**. Connect details to the main idea.

- **Summarize** as you read and after you read.

Ask Questions

Asking yourself questions as you read keeps your mind active. You'll ask different types of questions, so you'll need to find the answers in different ways.

- Some questions are connected to answers **right there** in the text.

- Others cover more than one part of the text. So, you'll have to **think and search** to find the answers.

Not all answers are found in the book.

- **On your own** questions can focus on your experiences or on the big ideas of the text.

- **Author and you** questions may be about the author's purpose or point of view.

Visualize

Good readers use the text and their own experiences to picture a writer's words. When you **visualize**, use all your senses to see, hear, smell, feel, and taste what the writer describes.

Make Connections

When you make connections, you put together information from the text with what you know from outside the text. As you read, think about:

- **your own ideas and experiences**
- what you know about the **world** from TV, songs, school, and so on
- **other texts** you've read by the same author, about the same topic, or in the same genre.

Make Inferences

Sometimes an author doesn't tell a reader everything. To figure out what is left unsaid:

- Look for what the author emphasizes.
- Think about what you already know.
- Combine what you read with what you know to figure out what the author means.

Synthesize

When you **synthesize**, you put together information from different places and come up with new understandings. You might:

- **Draw conclusions**, or combine what you know with what you read to decide what to think about a topic.
- **Form generalizations**, or combine ideas from the text with what you know to form an idea that is true in many situations.

Writing and Research

Writing is one of the best ways to express yourself. Sometimes you'll write to share a personal experience. Other times, you'll write to give information about a research topic. Whenever you write, use the following steps to help you say want you want clearly, correctly, and in your own special way.

Prewrite

When you prewrite, you choose a topic and collect all the details and information you need for writing.

1 **Choose a Topic and Make a Plan** Think about your writing prompt assignment or what you want to write about.

- Make a list. Then choose the best idea to use for your topic.

- Think about your writing role, audience, and form. Add those to a RAFT chart.

- Jot down any research questions, too. Those will help you look for the information you need.

> **RAFT Chart**
>
> **R**ole: _scientist_
>
> **A**udience: _my teacher and classmates_
>
> **F**orm: _report_
>
> **T**opic: _honeybees_

2 **Gather Information** Think about your topic and your plan. Jot down ideas. Or, use resources like those on pages 623–627 to find information that answers your questions. Take notes.

Use Information Resources

Books

A book is a good source of information.

Notecard

Where do honeybees live? — research question

The Honey Makers, by Gail Gibbons, page 6 — name of source

—Many honeybees live in dark places like hollow trees. — notes in your own words

—"Honeybees cared for by today's beekeepers live in box-shaped wooden hives." — author's exact words in quotation marks

Read the pages to find the information you need. Take notes.

Many honeybees like to make their homes in dark, enclosed places. Often a colony of wild honeybees builds its hive in a hollow tree. Honeybees cared for by today's beekeepers live in box-shaped wooden hives.

Reference Materials

key words

Tropical Rain Forest

A tropical rain forest is a type of forest that is found near the Equator, in places that are very warm throughout the year and get a lot of rain. It can rain every day in a tropical rain forest. The trees that make up a tropical rain forest can grow very tall. Trees can be so tall, in fact, that their tops grow together into a canopy—a dense network of leaves and branches that makes the ground underneath very, very dark.

A great number of different plants and animals live in tropical rain forests. Some scientists think that half of the world's plant and animal species live in tropical rain forests. Many of these rich forests are currently threatened by logging and farming.

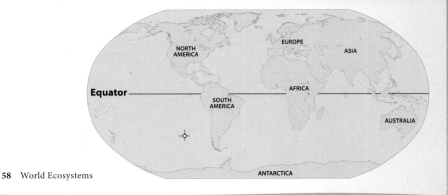

1. Search reference materials, such as atlases, online articles, and encyclopedias, by using **subject area headings** or **key words**.

2. Find the **articles** you want. A good article should contain the most recent information about your topic.

3. **Read** the articles and **take notes**.

Magazines

The **date** tells when the **issue** was published.

This is the **title** of the magazine.

This is the **main topic** of the issue.

These are some of the **topics** in the issue.

. . . and Experts

Arrange a time to talk to an **expert,** or someone who knows a lot about your topic.

- Prepare questions you want to ask about the topic.

- Conduct the interview. Write down the person's answers.

- Choose the notes you'll use for your writing

Internet

The Internet is a connection of computers that share information through the World Wide Web. It is like a giant library. Check with your teacher for how to access the Internet from your school.

1. **Go to a search page.** Type in your key words. Click Search.

2. **Read the list of Web sites, or pages, that have your key words.** The underlined words are links to the Web sites.

3. **Click on a link to go directly to the site, or Web page.** Read the article online. Or print it if it is helpful for your research. Later on, you can use the article to take notes.

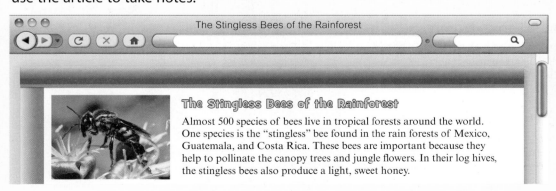

4. **Get Organized** Think about all the details you've gathered about your topic. Use a list, a chart, or other graphic organizer to show what you'll include in your writing. Use the organizer to show the order of your ideas, too.

Cluster

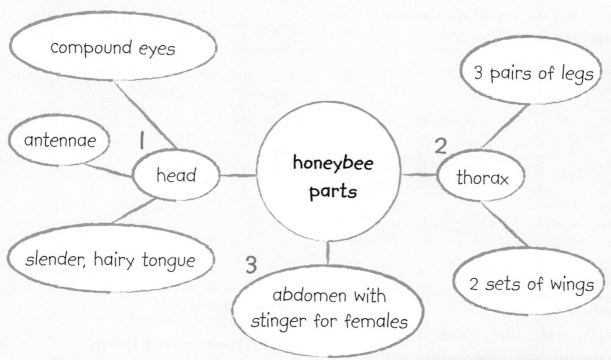

Outline

The Helpful, Sweet Honeybee

I. Important insects

    A. help pollinate plants

        1. flowers and trees

        2. fruits

    B. turn nectar into honey

II. Honeybee homes

    A. around the world

    B. hives

Draft

When you write your first draft, you turn all your ideas into sentences. You write quickly just to get all your ideas down. You can correct mistakes later.

Cluster

Turn your main idea into a topic sentence. Then add the details.

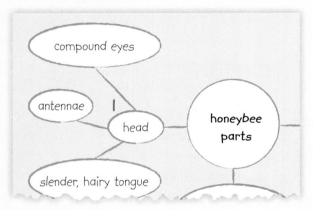

Beginning of a Description

One main part of a honeybee is the head. The bee's head seems to be mostly eyes! They are called compound eyes and have a lot of tiny lenses in them.

Outline

Turn the main idea after each Roman numeral into a topic sentence. Then turn the words next to the letters and numbers into detail sentences that tell more about the main idea.

The Helpful, Sweet Honeybee

I. Important insects
   A. help pollinate plants
      1. flowers and trees
      2. fruits

Beginning of a Report

The Helpful, Sweet Honeybee

You may think that all the honeybee does is make honey. But, believe it or not, this insect is always busy with another important job.

A honeybee helps keep plants growing. It helps to spread the pollen flowers and trees need to start new plants.

Revise

When you revise, you make changes to your writing to make it better and clearer.

1 **Read, Retell, Respond** Read your draft aloud to a partner. Your partner listens and then retells your main points.

You are describing a honeybee's hive. Isn't a bee's nest the same as a hive?

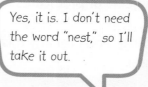
Yes, it is. I don't need the word "nest," so I'll take it out.

Your partner can help you discover what is unclear or what you need to add. Use your partner's suggestions to decide what you can to do to make your writing better.

2 **Make Changes** Think about your draft and what you and your partner discussed. What changes will you make? Use Revising Marks to mark your changes.

In the wild, honeybee scouts look for places to make hives ~~and nests.~~ The opening needs to be high off the ground. (They look for openings in hollow tree trunks.) That way the hive will be safe from ^predators ~~harmful animals.~~ A hive needs to hold thousands of bees and all ^the nectar and pollen they gather.

The best bee's nest will also face south so it stays warm.

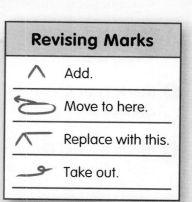

Revising Marks	
∧	Add.
↩	Move to here.
∧	Replace with this.
✐	Take out.

Edit and Proofread

When you edit and proofread, you look for mistakes in capitalization, grammar, and punctuation.

① **Check Your Sentences** Check that your sentences are clear, complete, and correct. Add any missing subjects or predicates.

② **Check Your Spelling** Look for any misspelled words. Check their spelling in a dictionary or a glossary.

③ **Check for Capital Letters, Punctuation, and Grammar** Look especially for correct use of

- capital letters in proper nouns
- apostrophes and quotation marks
- subject-verb agreement
- pronouns
- verb tenses

④ **Mark Your Changes** Use the Editing and Proofreading Marks to show your changes.

⑤ **Make a Final Copy** Make all the corrections you've marked to make a final, clean copy of your writing. If you are using a computer, print out your corrected version.

It is crowded and busy inside a honeybee hive. A hive can have more than 50000 honeybees. Most of them are worker bees. The worker bees create wax from their bodyes to build combs. The combs are layers of Cells, or holes. The cells hold nectar pollen, or larvae.

Editing and Proofreading Marks	
∧	Add.
⸜	Take out.
∧	Replace with this.
⬭	Check spelling.
≡	Capitalize.
/	Make lowercase.
¶	Make new paragraph.

Publish

When you publish your writing, you share it with others.

❶ Add Visuals Visuals can make your writing more interesting and easier to understand. Maybe you will

- import photographs or illustrations
- insert computer clip art
- add graphs, charts, or diagrams

❷ Present Your Writing There are a lot of ways to share your finished work. Here are just a few ideas.

- E-mail it to a friend or family member.
- Send it to your favorite magazine or publication.
- Turn it into a chapter for a group book about the topic.
- Make a video clip of you reading it to add to a group presentation.

A Home for the Honeybee

In the wild, honeybee scouts look for places to make hives. They look for openings in hollow tree trunks. The opening needs to be high off the ground. That way the hive will be safe from predators. A hive also needs to be big enough for thousands of bees and all the nectar and pollen they gather. The best hive will also face south so it stays warm.

Writing Traits

Good writing is clear, interesting, and easy to follow. To make your writing as good as it can be, check your writing to be sure it has the characteristics, or traits, of good writing.

Ideas

Writing is well-developed when the message is clear and interesting to the reader. It is supported by details that show the writer knows the topic well.

	Is the message clear and interesting?	Do the details show the writer knows the topic?
4	❏ All of the writing is clear and focused. ❏ The writing is very interesting.	❏ All the details tell about the topic. The writer knows the topic well.
3	❏ Most of the writing is clear and focused. ❏ Most of the writing is interesting.	❏ Most of the details are about the topic. The writer knows the topic fairly well.
2	❏ Some of the writing is not clear. The writing lacks some focus. ❏ Some of the writing is confusing.	❏ Some details are about the topic. The writer doesn't know the topic well.
1	❏ The writing is not clear or focused. ❏ The writing is confusing.	❏ Many details are not about the topic. The writer does not know the topic.

Organization

Writing is organized when it is easy to follow. All the ideas make sense together and flow from one idea to the next in an order that fits the writer's audience and purpose.

	Is the writing organized? Does it fit the audience and purpose?	Does the writing flow?
4	❏ The writing is very well-organized. ❏ It clearly fits both the writer's audience and purpose.	❏ The writing is smooth and logical. Each sentence flows into the next one.
3	❏ Most of the writing is organized. ❏ It mostly fits the writer's audience and purpose.	❏ Most of the writing is smooth. There are only a few sentences that do not flow logically.
2	❏ The writing is not well-organized. ❏ It fits the writer's audience or the writer's purpose, but not both.	❏ Some of the writing is smooth. Many sentences do not flow smoothly.
1	❏ The writing is not organized at all. ❏ It does not fit the writer's audience or purpose.	❏ The sentences do not flow smoothly or logically.

Organized

Not organized

Voice

Every writer has a special way of saying things, or a voice. The voice should sound genuine, or real, and be unique to that writer.

	Does the writing sound genuine and unique?	Does the tone fit the audience and purpose?
4	❏ The writing is genuine and unique. It shows who the writer is.	❏ The writer's tone, formal or informal, fits the audience and purpose.
3	❏ Most of the writing sounds genuine and unique.	❏ The writer's tone mostly fits the audience and purpose.
2	❏ Some of the writing sounds genuine and unique.	❏ Some of the writing fits the audience and purpose.
1	❏ The writing does not sound genuine or unique.	❏ The writer's tone does not fit the audience or purpose.

Word Choice

Readers can always tell who the writer is by the words the writer uses.

	Do the writer's words fit the message?	Does the language fit the audience? Is it interesting?
4	❏ The writer chose words that really fit the message.	❏ The words and sentences fit the audience and are interesting.
3	❏ Most of the words really fit the writer's message.	❏ Most of the words and sentences fit the audience and are interesting.
2	❏ Some of the words fit the writer's message.	❏ Some of the words and sentences fit the audience and are interesting.
1	❏ Few or no words fit the writer's message.	❏ The language does not fit the audience and loses the readers' attention.

Fluency

Good writers use a variety of sentence types. They also use transitions, or signal words.

	Is there sentence variety? Are there transitions?	Does the writing sound natural and rhythmic?
4	❑ The writer uses lots of different types of sentences. ❑ The writer uses useful transitions.	❑ When I read the writing aloud, it sounds natural and rhythmic.
3	❑ The writer uses many different types of sentences. ❑ Most transition words are useful.	❑ When I read the writing aloud, most of it sounds natural and rhythmic.
2	❑ The writer uses some different kinds of sentences. ❑ Some transition words are useful.	❑ When I read the writing aloud, some of it sounds natural and rhythmic.
1	❑ The writer does not vary sentences. ❑ The writer does not use transitions.	❑ When I read the writing aloud, it sounds unnatural.

Conventions

Good writers always follow the rules of grammar, punctuation, and spelling.

	Is the writing correct?	Are the sentences complete?
4	❑ All the punctuation, capitalization, and spelling is correct.	❑ Every sentence has a subject and a predicate.
3	❑ Most of the punctuation, spelling, and capitalization is correct.	❑ Most of the sentences have a subject and a predicate.
2	❑ Some of the punctuation, spelling, and capitalization is correct.	❑ Some of the sentences are missing subjects or predicates.
1	❑ There are many punctuation, spelling, and capitalization errors.	❑ Several sentences are missing subjects or predicates.

Grammar, Usage, Mechanics, and Spelling

Sentences

A sentence expresses a complete thought.

Kinds of Sentences

There are four kinds of sentences.

A **statement** tells something. It ends with a **period**.	Ned is at the mall now**.** He needs a new shirt**.**
A **question** asks for information. It ends with a **question mark**.	Where can I find the shirts**?**

Kinds of Questions

Some questions ask for "Yes" or "No" answers. They start with words such as **Is**, **Do**, **Can**, **Are**, and **Will**.	**Do** you have a size 10**?**
	     Answer: Yes.
	 Are these shirts on sale**?**
	     Answer: No.

Other questions ask for more information. They start with words such as **Who**, **What**, **Where**, **When**, and **Why**.	**What** colors do you have**?**
	     Answer: We have red and blue.
	 Where can I try this on**?**
	     Answer: You can use this room.

An **exclamation** shows strong feeling. It ends with an **exclamation mark**.	This is such a cool shirt**!** I love it**!**
A **command** tells you what to do or what not to do. It usually begins with a **verb** and ends with a period. If a command shows strong emotion, it ends with an exclamation mark.	**Please** bring me a size 10. **Don't open** the door yet. Wait until I come out!

Negative Sentences

A negative sentence means "no."

A **negative sentence** uses a **negative word** to say "no."	That is **not** a good color for me. I **can't** find the right size.

Complete Sentences

A complete sentence has two parts.

The **subject** tells whom or what the sentence is about.	<u>My friends</u> buy clothes here. <u>The other store</u> has nicer shirts.
The **predicate** tells what the subject is, has, or does.	My friends <u>buy clothes here</u>. The other store <u>has nicer shirts</u>.

Subjects

All the words that tell about a subject is the **complete subject**.	<u>My younger sister</u> loves the toy store.
The **simple subject** is the most important word in the complete subject.	My younger <u>sister</u> loves the toy store.
A **compound subject** has two nouns joined together by the words **and** or **or**.	<u>Terry **and** Brittany</u> never shop at this store. <u>My mom **or** my dad</u> always comes with me.

Predicates

All the words in the predicate is the **complete predicate**.	The stores <u>open today at nine</u>.
The **simple predicate** is the **verb**. It is the most important word in the predicate.	The stores <u>open</u> today at nine.
A **compound predicate** has two or more verbs that tell about the same subject. The verbs are joined by **and** or **or**.	We <u>eat **and** shop</u> at the mall. Sometimes we <u>see a movie **or** just talk with our friends</u>.

Sentences *(continued)*

Compound Sentences

When you join two sentences together, you can make a compound sentence.

Use a comma and the conjunction **and** to combine two similar ideas.	My friends walk to the mall. I go with them. My friends walk to the mall **, and** I go with them.
Use a comma and the conjunction **but** to combine two different ideas.	My friends walk to the mall. I ride my bike. My friends walk to the mall **, but** I ride my bike.
Use a comma and the conjunction **or** to show a choice of ideas.	You can walk to the mall with me. You can ride with Dad. You can walk to the mall with me **, or** you can ride with Dad.

Complex Sentences

When you join independent and dependent clauses, you can make a complex sentence.

An **independent clause** expresses a complete thought. It can stand alone as a sentence.	Mom and her friends walk around the mall for exercise. They walk around the mall.
A **dependent clause** does not express a complete thought. It is not a sentence.	before it gets busy because they want to exercise
To make a **complex sentence**, join an **independent clause** with one or more **dependent clauses**. If the dependent clause comes first, put a **comma** after it.	**Before it gets busy , Mom and her friends walk around the mall for exercise.** **They walk around the mall because they want to exercise.**

Condensing Clauses

Condense clauses to create precise and detailed sentences.

Condense clauses by combining ideas and using complex sentences.	It's a plant. It's green and red. It's found in the tropical rainforest. → It's a green and red plant that is found in the tropical rainforest.

Nouns

Nouns name people, animals, places, or things.

Common Nouns and Proper Nouns

There are two kinds of nouns.

A **common noun** names any person, animal, place, or thing of a certain type.	I know that **girl**. She rides a **horse**. I sometimes see her at the **park**. She walks her **dog** there.
A **proper noun** names a particular person, animal, place, or thing. • Start all the important words with a capital letter. • Start the names of streets, cities, and states with a capital letter. • Also use capital letters when you abbreviate state names.	I know **Marissa**. I sometimes see her at **Hilltop Park**. She walks her dog **Chase** there. Her family is from **Dallas, Texas**. They live on **Crockett Lane**.

Abbreviations for State Names in Mailing Addresses

Alabama	AL	Hawaii	HI	Massachusetts	MA	New Mexico	NM	South Dakota	SD
Alaska	AK	Idaho	ID	Michigan	MI	New York	NY	Tennessee	TN
Arizona	AZ	Illinois	IL	Minnesota	MN	North Carolina	NC	Texas	TX
Arkansas	AR	Indiana	IN	Mississippi	MS	North Dakota	ND	Utah	UT
California	CA	Iowa	IA	Missouri	MO	Ohio	OH	Vermont	VT
Colorado	CO	Kansas	KS	Montana	MT	Oklahoma	OK	Virginia	VA
Connecticut	CT	Kentucky	KY	Nebraska	NE	Oregon	OR	Washington	WA
Delaware	DE	Louisiana	LA	Nevada	NV	Pennsylvania	PA	West Virginia	WV
Florida	FL	Maine	ME	New Hampshire	NH	Rhode Island	RI	Wisconsin	WI
Georgea	GA	Maryland	MD	New Jersey	NJ	South Carolina	SC	Wyoming	WY

Nouns *(continued)*

Singular and Plural Count Nouns

Count nouns name things that you can count. A singular count noun shows "one." A plural count noun shows "more than one."

Add **-s** to most singular count nouns to form the plural count noun.	bicycle ⟶ bicycle**s** club ⟶ club**s**
Add **-es** to count nouns that end in **x**, **ch**, **sh**, **ss**, **z**, and sometimes **o**.	tax ⟶ tax**es** bench ⟶ bench**es** wish ⟶ wish**es** loss ⟶ loss**es** potato ⟶ potato**es**
For count nouns that end in a consonant plus **y**, change the **y** to **i** and then add **-es**. For nouns that end in a vowel plus **y**, just add **-s**.	berry**i** ⟶ berri**es** family**i** ⟶ famili**es** boy ⟶ boy**s** day ⟶ day**s**
For a few count nouns, use special forms to show the plural.	man ⟶ men woman ⟶ women foot ⟶ feet tooth ⟶ teeth child ⟶ children

Noncount Nouns

Noncount nouns name things that you cannot count.
Noncount nouns have one form for "one" and "more than one."

Weather Words	fog heat lightning thunder rain **YES:** **Thunder** and **lightning** scare my dog. **NO:** Thunders and lightnings scare my dog.
Food Words Some food items can be counted by using a measurement word such as **cup, slice, glass,** or **head** plus the word **of**. To show the plural form, make the measurement word plural.	bread corn milk rice soup **YES:** I'm thirsty for **milk**. I want **two glasses of milk.** **NO:** I'm thirsty for milks. I want milks.
Ideas and Feelings	fun help honesty luck work **YES:** I need **help** to finish my homework. **NO:** I need helps to finish my homework.
Category Nouns	clothing equipment mail money time **YES:** My football **equipment** is in the car. **NO:** My football equipments is in the car.
Materials	air gold paper water wood **YES:** Is the **water** in this river clean? **NO:** Is the waters in this river clean?
Activities and Sports	baseball dancing golf singing soccer **YES:** I played **soccer** three times this week. **NO:** I played soccers three times this week.

Grammar, Usage, Mechanics, and Spelling *continued*

Nouns *(continued)*

Words That Signal Nouns

The articles *a*, *an*, *some*, and *the* help identify a noun. They often appear before count nouns.

Use **a, an,** or **some** before a noun to talk about something in general.	**Some jokes** are funny. Do you have **a favorite joke**? I have **an uncle** who knows a lot of jokes.
Use **an** instead of **a** before a word that begins with a vowel sound.	It is **an event** when my uncle comes to visit. He lives about **an hour** away from us.
Do <u>not</u> use **a** or **an** before a noncount noun.	He drives in ~~a~~ snow, ~~a~~ fog, or ~~an~~ ice to get here.
Use **the** to talk about something specific. Do <u>not</u> use **the** before the name of: • a city or state • most countries • a language • a day, month, or most holidays • a sport or activity • most businesses • a person's name	Uncle Raul is **the** uncle I told you about. **The** jokes he tells make me laugh! Uncle Raul lives in **Dallas**. That's a city in **Texas**. He used to live in **Brazil**. He speaks **English** and **Spanish**. Uncle Raul often visits on **Saturday**. In **February**, he comes up for **Presidents' Day**. Sometimes he'll play **soccer** with me. Then we go to **Sal's Café** to eat. He likes to talk to **Sal**, too.

The words *this*, *that*, *these*, and *those* point out nouns. Like other adjectives, they answer the question "Which one?"

Use **this** or **these** to talk about things that are near you.	**This** book has a lot of photographs.
Use **that** or **those** to talk about things that are far from you.	**Those** books on the shelf are all fiction.

	Near	Far
One thing	this	that
More than one thing	these	those

Possessive Nouns

A possessive noun is the name of an owner. An apostrophe (') is used to show ownership.

For one owner, add **'s** to the **singular noun**.	This is Raul**'s** cap. The cap**'s** color is a bright red.
For more than one owner, add just the apostrophe (') to the **plural noun**.	The boys**'** T-shirts are the same. The players**'** equipment is ready.
For plural nouns that have special forms, add **'s** to the **plural noun**.	Do you like the **children's** uniforms? The **men's** scores are the highest.

Pronouns

A pronoun takes the place of a noun or refers to a noun.

Pronoun Agreement

When you use a pronoun, be sure you are talking about the right person.

Use a capital **I** to talk about yourself.	I am Jack. I want to find out about Mars.
Use **you** to speak to another person.	Are **you** interested in Mars, too?
Use **she** for a girl or a woman.	Julia thinks Mars is a good topic. **She** will help write a report about the planet.
Use **he** for a boy or a man.	Jack downloaded some photos. **He** added the pictures to the report.
Use **it** for a thing.	The report is almost done. **It** will be interesting to read.

Pronouns *(continued)*

Pronoun Agreement

Be sure you are talking about the right number of people or things.

Use **you** to talk to two or more people.	
Use **we** for yourself and one or more other people.	*Are **you** prepared for tomorrow?* *Yes. Sam and I are ready. **We** give a report tomorrow.*
Use **they** for other people or things.	Scott and Tyrone set up the video camera. **They** will record each presentation.

Subject Pronouns

Subject pronouns take the place of the subject in the sentence.

Subject pronouns tell who or what does the action.	**Julia** is a good speaker. **She** tells the class about Mars.
	The photos show the surface of Mars. **They** are images from NASA.

Subject Pronouns

Singular	Plural
I	we
you	you
he, she, it	they

Object Pronouns

Object pronouns replace a noun that comes after a verb or a preposition.

An **object pronoun** answers the question "What" or "Whom."	The class asked **Jack and Julia** about Mars.
Object pronouns come after a verb or a preposition such as **to**, **for**, **at**, **of**, or **with**.	The class asked **them** about Mars.
	Jack put **the report** online.
	Jack put **it** online.

Object Pronouns

Singular	Plural
me	us
you	you
him, her, it	them

Reciprocal Pronouns

Reciprocal pronouns replace objects that refer back to the subject.

The subject must be plural. It can be a compound subject.	**Jack and Julia** helped **each other** on the report.
The subject can also be a plural noun.	**The students** followed **one another** outside.

Reciprocal Pronouns

Plural
each other
one another

Possessive Pronouns

Like a possessive noun, a possessive pronoun tells who or what owns something.

To show that you own something, use **mine**.	**I** wrote a report about the sun.
	The report about the sun is **mine**.
Use **ours** to show that you and one or more people own something.	**Meg, Bob, and I** drew diagrams.
	The diagrams are **ours**.
Use **yours** to show that something belongs to one or more people you are talking to.	Have you seen my report, Matt?
	Yes, that report is **yours**.

Possessive Pronouns

Singular	Plural
mine	ours
yours	yours
his, hers	theirs

Use **his** for one boy or man. Use **hers** for one girl or woman.	Here is **Carole's** desk.
	The desk is **hers**.
For two or more people, places, or things, use **theirs**.	**Ross and Clare** made posters.
	The posters are **theirs**.

Grammar, Usage, Mechanics, and Spelling *continued*

Adjectives

An adjective describes, or tells about, a noun.

How Adjectives Work	
Usually, an **adjective** comes <u>before</u> the noun it tells about. But, an **adjective** can also appear <u>after</u> verbs such as *is, are, look, feel, smell,* and *taste.*	You can buy **delicious** fruits at the market. All the fruit looks **fresh**. The shoppers are **happy**.
Adjectives describe • what something is like • the size, color, and shape of something • what something looks, feels, sounds, or smells like	The market is a **busy** place. The **round, brown** baskets are filled with fruits and vegetables. The **shiny** peppers are in one basket. Another basket has **crunchy** cucumbers. The pineapples are **sweet** and **juicy**.
Some **adjectives** tell "how many" or "in what order." When you don't know the exact number of things, use the adjectives in the chart. Possessive adjectives tell who owns something.	The sellers have **two** baskets of beans. The **first** basket is near the limes. When there's **a lot of** sun, the sellers sit in the shade. **I** pick out some oranges. **My** oranges are in the bag. That basket is **Ryan's**. **His** basket is full of apples. **The sellers'** chairs are in the shade. **Their** chairs are under umbrellas.

If you can count what you see, use:		If you can't count what you see, use:	
many	several	much	not much
a lot of	only a few	a lot of	only a littl
few	not any	a little	not any
some	no	some	no

Adjectives That Compare

Adjectives can help you make a comparison, or show how things are alike or different.

To compare two things, add **-er** to the adjective. You will often use the word **than** in your sentence, too.	This is a **small** pineapple. The guava is **smaller than** the pineapple.
To compare three or more things, add **-est** to the adjective. Always use **the** before the adjective.	The lime is **the smallest** fruit of them all.
For some adjectives, change the spelling before you add **-er** or **-est**. • If the adjective ends in silent **e**, drop the final **e** and add **-er** or **-est**.	large larg**er** larg**est** nice nic**er** nic**est**
• If the adjective ends in **y**, change the **y** to **i** and add **-er** or **-est**.	pretty**i** pretti**er** pretti**est** crazy**i** crazi**er** crazi**est**
• If the adjective has one syllable and ends in one vowel plus one consonant, double the final consonant and add **-er** or **-est**.	big **g** bigg**er** bigg**est** sad **d** sadd**er** sadd**est**
A few adjectives have special forms for comparing things.	good bad little better worse less best worst least
For adjectives with three or more syllables, do not use **-er** or **-est** to compare. Use **more**, **most**, **less**, or **least**.	**YES:** Of all the fruit, the guavas are the **most colorful**. **NO:** Of all the fruit, the guavas are the colorfulest. **YES:** The oranges are **more delicious** than the pears. **NO:** The oranges are deliciouser than the pears.
When you make a comparison, use either **-er** or **more;** or **-est** or **most**. Do not use both.	The oranges are the ~~most~~ juiciest of all the fruits.

Verbs

Verbs tell what the subject of a sentence is, has, or does. They show if something happened in the past, is happening now, or will happen in the future.

Action Verbs

An **action verb** tells what someone or something does.	The children **ride** bikes. They **wear** helmets for safety. They **pedal** as fast as they can.

The Verbs *Have* and *Be*

The verb **to have** tells what the subject of a sentence has.	I **have** a bicycle. It **has** twelve gears. My friend Pedro **has** a bicycle, too. Sometimes we **have** races.	**Forms of the Verb *have*** have has had
The verb **to be** does not show action. It tells what the subject of a sentence is (a noun) or what it is like (an adjective).	I **am** a fan of bicycle races. Pedro **is** excited about our next race.	**Forms of the Verb *be*** am, are, is was, were

Linking Verbs

A few other verbs work like the verb **to be**. They do not show action. They just connect, or link, the subject to a word in the predicate. Some of these verbs are **look**, **seem**, **feel**, **smell**, and **taste**.	My bicycle **looks** fantastic! Pedro and I **feel** ready for the race.

Helping Verbs

A **helping verb** works together with an action verb. A helping verb comes before a **main verb**. Some helping verbs have special meanings.

- Use **can** to tell that someone is able to do something.
- Use **could**, **may,** or **might** to tell that something is possible.
- Use **must** to tell that somebody has to do something.
- Use **should** to give an opinion or advice.

Pedro and I **are racing** today.
We **will do** our best.

We **can work** as a team.

We **may reach** the finish line first.

We **must pedal** hard to win!

You **should practice** more.

Contractions with Verbs

You can put a subject and verb together to make a **contraction**. In a contraction, an apostrophe (') shows where one or more letters have been left out.

They are riding fast.
They are riding fast.
They're riding fast.

You can make a contraction with the verbs **am**, **are**, and **is**.

Contractions with *Be*			
I	+ am = **I'm**	she	+ is = **she's**
you	+ are = **you're**	where	+ is = **where's**
we	+ are = **we're**	what	+ is = **what's**

You can make a contraction with the helping verbs **have**, **has**, and **will**.

Contractions with *Have* and *Will*			
I	+ have = **I've**	he	+ has = **he's**
you	+ have = **you've**	I	+ will = **I'll**
they	+ have = **they've**	it	+ will = **it'll**

In contractions with a verb and **not**, the word **not** is shortened to **n't**.

Contractions with *Not*			
do	+ not = **don't**	have	+ not = **haven't**
did	+ not = **didn't**	has	+ not = **hasn't**
are	+ not = **aren't**	could	+ not = **couldn't**
was	+ not = **wasn't**	should	+ not = **shouldn't**

The contraction of the verb **can** plus **not** has a special spelling.

can	+	not	=	**can't**

Verbs, *(continued)*

Actions in the Present

All action verbs show when the action happens. Verbs in the **present tense** show ● that the action happens now. ● that the action happens often.	 Pedro **eats** his breakfast. Then he **takes** his bike out of the garage. Pedro and I **love** to ride our bikes on weekends.
To show the present tense for the subjects **he, she,** or **it**, add -**s** to the end of most action verbs. ● For verbs that end in **x, ch, sh, ss,** or **z**, add -**es.** ● For verbs that end in a consonant plus **y**, change the **y** to **i** and then add -**es**. For verbs that end in a vowel plus **y**, just add -**s**. ● For the subjects **I, you, we,** or **they**, do not add -**s** or -**es**.	**Pedro checks** the tires on his bike. **He finds** a flat tire! Pedro **fixes** the tire. A pump **pushes** air into it. "That should do it," he **says** to himself. He **carries** the pump back into the garage. I **arrive** at Pedro's house. We **coast** down the driveway on our bikes.
The **present progressive** form of a verb tells about an action as it is happening. It uses **am, is,** or **are** and a main verb. The main verb ends in -**ing**.	We **are pedaling** faster. I **am passing** Pedro! He **is following** right behind me.

Actions in the Past

Verbs in the **past tense** show that the action happened in the past.	Yesterday, I **looked** for sports on TV.
The past tense form of a **regular verb** ends with -**ed**. • For most verbs, just add **-ed**. • For verbs that end in silent **e**, drop the final **e** before you add **-ed**. • For one-syllable verbs that end in one vowel plus one consonant, double the final consonant before you add **-ed**. • For verbs that end in **y**, change the **y** to **i** before you add **-ed**. For verbs that end in a vowel plus **y**, just add **-ed**.	I **watched** the race on TV. The bikers **arrived** from all different countries. They **raced** for several hours. People **grabbed** their cameras. They **snapped** pictures of their favorite racer. I **studied** the racer from Italy. I **stayed** close to the TV.
Irregular verbs do not add -**ed** to show the past tense. They have special forms.	The Italian racer **was** fast. He **broke** the speed record!

Some Irregular Verbs

Present Tense	Past Tense
begin	began
do	did
have	had
make	made
take	took
ride	rode
win	won

Verbs, *(continued)*

Actions in the Future

Verbs in the **future tense** tell what will happen later, or in the future.	Tomorrow, Shelley **will clean** her bike.
To show the future tense, you can • add the helping verb **will** before the **main verb**. • use **am going to**, **are going to**, or **is going to** before the **main verb**.	She **will remove** all the dirt. She **is going to remove** all the dirt. I **am going to help** her.
If the **main verb** is a form of the verb **to be**, use **be** to form the future tense.	The bike **will be** spotless. Shelley **is going to be** pleased!
To make negative sentences in the future tense, put the word **not** just after **will**, **am**, **is**, or **are**.	We are **not** going to stop until the bike shines. Pedro is **not** going to believe it. Her bike will **not** be a mess any longer.

Adverbs

An adverb tells more about a verb, an adjective, or another adverb.

How Adverbs Work

An **adverb** can come before or after a **verb** to tell "how," "where," "when," or "how often."	Josh **walks quickly** to the bus stop. (how) He **will travel downtown** on the bus. (where) He **will arrive** at school **soon**. (when) Josh **never misses** a day of school. (how often)
An **adverb** can make an **adjective** or another adverb stronger.	Josh is **really good** at baseball. He plays **very well**.
Some **adverbs** compare actions. Add **-er** to compare two actions. Add **-est** to compare three or more actions.	Josh **runs fast**. Josh runs **faster** than his best friend. Josh runs the **fastest** of all the players.
A few adverbs have special forms for comparing things.	well ⟶ better ⟶ best badly ⟶ worse ⟶ worst
If the adverb ends in **-ly**, use **more**, **most**, **less**, or **least** to compare the actions.	Josh drops a ball *less* frequently than the other players.
When you use **adverbs** to make a comparison with **-er**, **-est**, or with a special form, do not also use **more** or **most**.	Josh jumps ~~more~~ higher than I do. He is ~~more~~ better than I am at catching the ball.
Make sure to use an **adverb** (not an adjective) to tell about a verb.	I do not catch ~~good~~ *well* at all.

Prepositions

A preposition links a noun or pronoun to other words in a sentence. A preposition is the first word in a prepositional phrase.

Prepositions

Some prepositions tell **where** something is.	 above, over — under, below, beneath — beside, next to, by, near — in front of — in back of, behind — between in — out — inside — outside — on — off
Some prepositions show **direction**.	 up — down — through — across — around — into
Some prepositions tell **when something happens**.	**before** lunch **in** 2003 **on** September 16 **during** lunch **in** September **at** four o'clock **after** lunch **in** the afternoon **from** noon **to** 3:30
Other prepositions have many uses.	about among for to against at from with along except of without

Prepositional Phrases

A **prepositional phrase** starts with a **preposition** and ends with a **noun** or a **pronoun**. Use prepositional phrases to add information or details to your writing.	**At our school**, we did many activities **for Earth Day**. We picked up the trash **along the fence**. Then we planted some flowers **next to it**.

Capital Letters

A word that begins with a capital letter is special in some way.

How to Use Capital Letters

A word that begins with a capital letter is special in some way.

Use a **capital letter** at the beginning of a sentence.	**O**ur class is taking an exciting field trip. **W**e are going to an airplane museum.
Always use a capital letter for the pronoun **I**.	My friends and **I** can't wait!
Use a capital letter for a person's • first and last name • initials • title	**Matt J. Kelly and Matt Ross will ride** **with Dr. Bye.** **M**agdalena and I are going with **M**rs. **L**iu.
Use a capital letter for the names of • the days of the week and their abbreviations • the twelve months of the year and their abbreviations	We're going the first **S**aturday in **J**anuary. **Days of the Week** **Months of the Year**

Days of the Week

Sunday	**S**un.
Monday	**M**on.
Tuesday	**T**ue.
Wednesday	**W**ed.
Thursday	**T**hurs.
Friday	**F**ri.
Saturday	**S**at.

Months of the Year

January	**J**an.
February	**F**eb.
March	**M**ar.
April	**A**pr.
May	
June	
July	
August	**A**ug.
September	**S**ep.
October	**O**ct.
November	**N**ov.
December	**D**ec.

> These months are not abbreviated.

Use a capital letter for each important word in the names of special days and holidays.	That will be after **C**hristmas, **K**wanzaa, and **N**ew **Y**ear's **D**ay. **E**arth **D**ay **F**ourth of **J**uly **H**anukkah **T**hanksgiving

Capital Letters, *(continued)*

More Ways to Use Capital Letters

Use a capital letter for each important word in the names of	
• public places, buildings, and organizations	The **W**ilson **A**irplane **M**useum is in the **V**eterans **M**emorial **H**all. It's in the middle of **V**eterans **P**ark, right next to the **P**iney **W**oods **Z**oo.
• streets, cities, and states	The museum is on **F**light **A**venue. It is the biggest airplane museum in **F**lorida. It's the biggest in the whole **U**nited **S**tates!
• landforms and bodies of water, continents, and planets and stars	

Landforms and Bodies of Water	**Continents**	**Planets and Stars**
Rocky **M**ountains	**A**frica	**E**arth
Sahara **D**esert	**A**ntarctica	**M**ars
Grand **C**anyon	**A**sia	the **B**ig **D**ipper
Pacific **O**cean	**A**ustralia	the **M**ilky **W**ay
Colorado **R**iver	**E**urope	
Lake **E**rie	**S**outh **A**merica	
	North **A**merica	

Use a capital letter for the names of countries and adjectives formed from the names of countries.	My friend Magdalena is **C**hilean. She says they don't have a museum like that in **C**hile.
Use a capital letter for each important word in the title of a book, a story, a poem, or a movie.	We are reading ***F**irst **F**light* about the Wright brothers. Magdalena wrote a poem about Amelia Earhart. She called it "**V**anished from the **S**ky." What a great title!

Punctuation Marks

Punctuation marks make words and sentences easier to understand.

period

question mark

exclamation point

comma

quotation marks

apostrophe

Period .

Use a **period** at the end of a statement or a command.	I don't know if I should get a dog or a cat**.** Please help me decide**.**
Also use a **period** when you write a decimal, or to separate dollars from cents.	I saw a cute little dog last week**.** It only weighed 1**.**3 pounds. But it costs $349**.**99!
Use a **period** after an initial in somebody's name, and after most abbreviations. But, don't use a period after state abbreviations.	The salesperson gave me this business card: Kitty B**.** Perry **Downtown Pet Sales** **2456 N. Yale Ave.** **Houston, TX 77074** **TX is the abbreviation for the state of Texas.**

Question Mark ?

Use a **question mark** • at the end of a question • after a question that comes at the end of a statement.	Do you want to go to the pet store with me**?** You can go right now, can't you**?**

Exclamation Point !

Use an **exclamation point** at the end of a sentence to show strong feelings.	I'm glad you decided to come**!** This is going to be fun**!**

Punctuation, *(continued)*

Commas 9	
Use a **comma** • when you write large numbers • to separate three or more things in the same sentence • before the words **and**, **but**, or **or** in a compound sentence.	There are more than 1,300 pets at this store. Should I get a dog, a cat, or a parrot? I came to the store last week, and the salesperson showed me some dogs. She was very helpful, but I couldn't make a decision.
Use a **comma** to set off • short words like **Oh**, **Yes**, and **Well** that begin a sentence • someone's exact words	Oh, what a hard decision! Well, I'd better choose something. The salesperson said, "This little dog wants to go with you." I said, "I like it, but I like those cats, too!"
Use a **comma** between two or more adjectives that tell about the same noun.	Do I get a big, furry puppy? Or do I get a cute, tiny kitten?
Use a **comma** in letters • between the city and state • between the date and the year • after the greeting in a friendly letter • after the closing	177 North Avenue New York, NY 10033 October 3, 2010 Dear Aunt Mia, Can you help me? I want a pet, but don't know which is easier to care for, a cat or a dog? I need your advice. Your niece, Becca

Quotation Marks 〝〟

Use quotation marks	
• to show a speaker's exact words	"Ms. Perry, this is the dog for me!" Becca said.
• to show the exact words from a book or other printed material	The ad said "friendly puppies" for sale.
• the title of a magazine or newspaper article	I saw the idea in the article "Keeping Your Pet Happy."
• the title of a chapter from a book.	Now I'm on the chapter "Working Dogs" in my book.
Use periods and commas inside quotation marks.	"Many dogs are good with people," Ms. Perry said. "You just have to decide if you want to big dog or a little one."

Ms. Perry, this is the dog for me!

Apostrophes ’

Use an **apostrophe** when you write a **possessive noun**.	My **neighbor's** dog is huge. The **Smiths'** yard is just big enough for him.
Use an **apostrophe** to replace the letter or letters left out in a **contraction.**	**Let's** go back to the pet store. **I'll** look some more for the best pet for me.

Dictionary

The definitions are for the words as they are introduced in the selections of this book.

Pronunciation Key

Say the sample word out loud to hear how to say, or pronounce, the symbol.

Symbols for Consonant Sounds			
b	b<u>o</u>x	p	<u>p</u>an
ch	<u>ch</u>ick	r	<u>r</u>ing
d	<u>d</u>og	s	bu<u>s</u>
f	<u>f</u>ish	sh	<u>f</u>ish
g	<u>g</u>irl	t	ha<u>t</u>
h	<u>h</u>at	th	<u>E</u>arth
j	<u>j</u>ar	<u>th</u>	<u>f</u>ather
k	ca<u>k</u>e	v	<u>v</u>ase
ks	bo<u>x</u>	w	<u>w</u>indow
kw	<u>qu</u>een	wh	<u>wh</u>ale
l	be<u>ll</u>	y	<u>y</u>arn
m	<u>m</u>ouse	z	<u>z</u>ipper
n	pa<u>n</u>	zh	trea<u>s</u>ure
ng	ri<u>ng</u>		

Symbols for Short Vowel Sounds

a	h<u>a</u>t
e	b<u>e</u>ll
i	ch<u>i</u>ck
o	b<u>o</u>x
u	b<u>u</u>s

Symbols for Long Vowel Sounds

ā	c<u>a</u>ke
ē	k<u>e</u>y
ī	b<u>i</u>ke
ō	g<u>oa</u>t
yū	m<u>u</u>le

Symbols for R-controlled Sounds

ar	b<u>ar</u>n
air	ch<u>air</u>
ear	<u>ear</u>
ir	f<u>ire</u>
or	c<u>or</u>n
ur	g<u>ir</u>l

Symbols for Variant Vowel Sounds

ah	f<u>a</u>ther
aw	b<u>a</u>ll
oi	b<u>oy</u>
oo	b<u>oo</u>k
ü	fr<u>ui</u>t

Miscellaneous Symbols

shun	frac<u>tion</u>	$\frac{1}{2}$
chun	ques<u>tion</u>	?
zhun	divi<u>sion</u>	$2\overline{)100}^{50}$

Parts of an Entry

part of speech
n. for noun
v. for verb
adj. for adjective
adv. for adverb

The **pronunciation** shows you how to say the word.

The **definition** gives the meaning of the word.

The **sample sentence** uses the word in a way that shows its meaning.

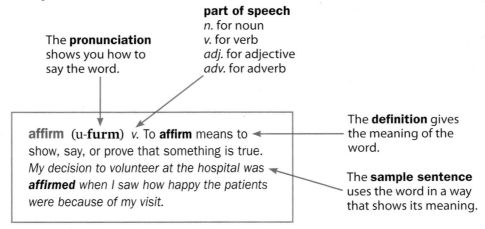

affirm (u-**furm**) *v.* To **affirm** means to show, say, or prove that something is true. *My decision to volunteer at the hospital was affirmed when I saw how happy the patients were because of my visit.*

648

A

advocate (**ad**-vu-kāt) *v.* When you **advocate** something, you support it with words or actions. *The dentist **advocates** brushing your teeth twice a day.*

analogy (u-**na**-lu-jē) *n.* An **analogy** is a comparison. *The **analogy** shows how food is fuel to the body like gas is fuel for a car.*

analytical (a-na-**li**-ti-kul) *adj.* When you study something in an **analytical** way, you break the information into parts so that it is easier to understand. *A scientist does an **analytical** study of the liquid by separating it and studying each part.*

ancestor (**an**-ses-tur) *n.* An **ancestor** is a relative from long ago. *She wanted to learn more about her **ancestors**.*

appeal (u-**pēl**) *n.* An **appeal** is a serious request for help. *The student made an **appeal** to his teacher for help with a project.*

archaeological (ar-kē-u-**lo**-ji-kul) *adj.* An **archaeological** expedition focuses on studying the remains of ancient civilizations in order to understand them. *He found a fragment of an ancient Egyptian jug on his first **archaeological** dig.*

artifact (**ar**-ti-fakt) *n.* An **artifact** is an object, or the remains of one, created by humans during a certain period in history. *The jar was an **artifact** from Hatshepsut's reign.*

aspect (**a**-spekt) *n.* An **aspect** is a part, or feature, of something. *One **aspect** of friendship is comforting your friends if they are sad.*

assemble (u-**sem**-bul) *v.* To **assemble** means to put together. *They use a hammer and nails to **assemble** the birdhouse.*

asset (**a**-set) *n.* An **asset** is something valuable and useful. *When you are hiking, a compass is an **asset** that shows direction.*

associate (u-**sō**-shē-āt) *v.* **Associate** means to keep company with someone. *She **associated** with the new girl in school when she ate lunch with her.*

assumption (u-**sump**-shun) *n.* An **assumption** is something that is believed to be true. *When the dog wagged its tail, the boy made the **assumption** that the dog was friendly.*

authority (u-**thor**-u-tē) *n.* When you have **authority**, you have the power to make decisions and direct other people's actions. *The teacher has the **authority** to make rules in the classroom.*

awareness (u-**wair**-nes) *n.* When you have **awareness** of something, you see or understand it. *They used their **awareness** of traffic and safety rules to cross the street.*

B

boycott (**boi**-kot) *n.* When you **boycott** something, you make a statement by not using or buying certain things. *They started a **boycott** when they refused to ride the buses.*

C

camouflage (**ka**-mu-floj) *n.* **Camouflage** is a color or pattern that helps people or animals hide. *People use **camouflage** to help them hide when they hunt.*

capable (**kā**-pu-bul) *adj.* To be **capable** means to be able to do something without any problems. *Because she studied, she was **capable** of passing her test.*

cavern (**ka**-vurn) *n.* A **cavern** is a deep hole or hollow space. *They explored the **cavern**.*

chamber (**chām**-bur) *n.* A **chamber** is a special room. *The Egyptians had burial **chambers** filled with gold.*

chronological (krah-nu-**lah**-ji-kul) *adj.* When something is in **chronological** order, it is arranged in the order that the events happened. *Historians use a **chronological** time line to chart the events in ancient Egypt.*

circumstance (**sur**-kum-stants) *n.* A **circumstance** is a fact or event that affects something. *Extreme weather **circumstances** prevented us from traveling.*

civilization (si-vu-lu-**zā**-shun) *n.* A **civilization** is the culture of a specific place, time, or group of people. *Greece has a very old **civilization**.*

command (ku-**mand**) *v.* A **command** is an order given from someone in power. *The pharaoh gave the **command** to build a new pyramid.*

commitment (ku-**mit**-munt) *n.* A **commitment** is a promise to do something. *This woman made a **commitment** to volunteer to feed the homeless on weekends.*

composition (kom-pu-**zi**-shun) *n.* The **composition** of something is a list of its general ingredients that make up its whole. *The **composition** of this rock is made from many elements.*

concentrate (**kon**-sun-trāt) *v.* When you **concentrate**, you give all of your attention to something. *He must **concentrate** when he glues the tiny pieces together.*

conform (kun-**form**) *v.* When you **conform**, you follow a rule or way of doing things. *In some schools, all students must **conform** to a dress code by wearing a uniform.*

confront (kun-**frunt**) *v.* To **confront** means to come face to face with something or someone. *He **confronted** his fear of public speaking when he gave the speech in front of the class.*

conquest (**kon**-kwest) *n.* A **conquest** is an act or process of taking over something. *Emperor Qin's **conquest** to unify China was successful.*

consider (kun-**si**-dur) *v.* When you **consider** something, you think about it carefully. *The boy **considers** which snack to choose.*

constant (**kon**-stunt) *adj.* Something **constant** is continuous or happens all the time. *The **constant** rain this week may cause flooding.*

contribute (kun-**tri**-byūt) *v.* To **contribute** means to give an object or an idea to others. *Each student will **contribute** one dollar to help people in need.*

controversy (**kon**-tru-vur-sē) *n.* A **controversy** is a disagreement between groups of people. *Cutting down the trees caused a **controversy**.*

convince (kun-**vints**) *v.* To **convince** means to make someone believe something is true. *The kids will **convince** their mother to agree with their idea.*

crater (**krā**-tur) *n.* A **crater** is a deep hole in the ground caused by an impact from a large object. *The moon is full of **craters**.*

crucial (**kroo**-shul) *adj.* Something that is **crucial** is necessary or very important. *It is **crucial** to drink water when you are hiking.*

D

deception (di-**sep**-shun) *n.* **Deception** is the act of tricking something or someone. *The white moth on the white tree bark caused a visual **deception** so we could not see the moth.*

declaration (de-klu-**rā**-shun) *n.* A **declaration** is an official or public statement made about an issue. *He made a **declaration** against allowing soda machines in schools.*

defensively (di-**fen**-siv-lē) *adv.* To react **defensively** means to defend a viewpoint. *They responded **defensively** during the debate.*

deforestation (dē-for-u-**stā**-shun) *n.* **Deforestation** is the act of cutting down forests. *Uncontrolled **deforestation** almost destroyed the redwoods.*

demonstration (de-mun-**strā**-shun) *n.* A **demonstration** is a public gathering of people to show that they support or oppose something or someone. *They held a **demonstration** against the new law.*

dependent (di-**pen**-dunt) *adj.* When you are **dependent** on something, you need it. *Babies are **dependent** on their parents for everything.*

depict (di-**pikt**) *v.* When you **depict** something, you show it in a picture or with words. *The artist's drawing **depicts** the girl.*

despair (di-**spair**) *v.* When someone feels **despair**, he or she has lost all hope or confidence. *The team **despaired** when they saw that the game had one minute left and they were 20 points behind.*

devote (di-**vōt**) *v.* To **devote** means to give your time or attention to something. *The girl **devotes** her free time to helping at the animal shelter.*

discrimination (dis-kri-mu-**nā**-shun) *n.* **Discrimination** is when someone doesn't have the same rights as others. *Martin Luther King, Jr., spoke out against **discrimination**, because he believed that all people should have equal rights.*

distinct (di-**stinkt**) *adj.* When something is **distinct**, it is easy to notice. *These leaves are two very different, **distinct** colors.*

diverge (du-**vurj**) *v.* When two things or ideas **diverge**, they differ or move away from each other. *This hiking trail has two paths that **diverge** in different directions.*

domain (dō-**mān**) *n.*
A **domain** is the area that is
controlled by a person or a
group of people. *The stage is
the singer's **domain**.*

donate (dō-**nāt**) *v.* To **donate** means to give
something to a good cause or to give something to
people in need. *They **donated** money to help buy new
library books.*

duplicate (dü-pli-kāt) *v.* To **duplicate** means to
copy something. *The fish **duplicated** the movement
of the plant and blended into the background.*

dynasty (**dī**-nu-stē) *n.* A **dynasty** is a sequence
of rulers from the same family or group. *When Rome
took over Egypt, Cleopatra's **dynasty** ended.*

E

ecological (ē-ku-lah-ji-kul) *adj.* When
something is **ecological**, it means that it considers
the relationship between organisms and their
environments. *The new **ecological** plan to preserve
the wetlands would save many animals.*

effective (i-**fek**-tiv) *adj.* Something that is
effective has good results. *An umbrella is **effective**
for keeping dry in the rain.*

eliminate (i-**li**-mu-nāt) *v.* To **eliminate** means to
take out or leave out. *He was **eliminated** from the
spelling contest after he missed a word.*

emerge (i-**murj**) *v.* To **emerge** is to appear from
somewhere hidden. *The sun will soon **emerge** from
behind the cloud.*

empire (**em**-pīur) *n.* An **empire** is a large group
of areas ruled by one person. *The Romans had an
empire that included lands from Europe to Africa.*

encounter (in-**kown**-tur) *v.* An **encounter** is
a meeting. *The photographer took pictures of his
encounter with a bear.*

endangered (in-**dān**-jurd) *adj.* To be
endangered means to be at risk of disappearing
forever. *The ivory-billed woodpecker is an example
of an **endangered** animal.*

endeavor (in-**de**-vur) *n.* An **endeavor** is a serious
effort. *Cleaning the park is a positive **endeavor** for
these volunteers*

ensure (in-**shoor**) *v.* To **ensure** means to make
certain. *This girl uses a watch to **ensure** that she
meets her friend on time.*

envision (in-**vi**-zhun) *v.* To **envision** means to
picture something in your mind. *He can **envision**
winning first place.*

equip (i-**kwip**) *v.* To **equip** means to prepare
oneself for a task. *He was **equipped** with the tools he
needed to plant a new garden.*

erode (i-**rōd**) *v.* To **erode** means to wear away by
the force of wind, water, or another natural force. *The
bank of the pond **eroded** during the recent flood.*

estimate (**es**-tu-mut) *v.* When you **estimate**, you
make a best guess about something. *I **estimate** that
there are 1,500 jelly beans in this jar.*

eventually (i-**ven**-shu-wu-lē) *adv.* When
something happens **eventually**, it happens at a later
time. *The seedling will **eventually** grow into a flower.*

exclude (iks-**klüd**) *v.*
When you **exclude** something,
you leave it out. *I **exclude** nuts
from the recipe because I am
allergic to them.*

exhaust (ig-**zost**) *v.* To **exhaust** means to use
up something. *He **exhausted** his supply of water,
because his water bottle was empty.*

expertise (**ek**-spur-tēz) *n.* **Expertise** is special
knowledge or skill. *A black belt shows a high level of
expertise in karate.*

extinct (ik-**stinkt**) *adj.* Something that is **extinct**
is no longer living. *The dodo bird became **extinct**
because people hunted too many over time.*

F

factor (**fak**-tor) *n.* A **factor** is something that can
lead to a specific result. *Heavy rains were a **factor** in
the terrible flooding.*

figure (**fi**-gyur) *v.* To **figure** means to decide about
something. *She **figured** that if she saved her chore
money, then she could go to the movies.*

formation (for-**mā**-shun) *n.* A **formation** is the
shape of something, or the creation of a structure.
*The rock **formation** almost looked like a dinosaur.*

foundation (fown-**dā**-shun) n. A **foundation** is the base on which something rests. *Many homes are built on concrete foundations.*

G

gene (**jēn**) n. A **gene** is a physical unit that controls what a living cell is like. *The color of your hair depends on your genes.*

geologic (jē-u-**lah**-jik) adj. **Geologic** refers to a specific period of time that is based on geology. *According to geologic data, this rock is very old.*

global (**glō**-bul) adj. When something is **global**, it means that it affects the whole world. *Food shortage is becoming a global issue.*

H

hieroglyphics (hī-ru-**gli**-fiks) n. **Hieroglyophics** were a special form of writing used by the Egyptians. *Hieroglyphics were written all over the walls in the Egyptian tombs.*

humanity (hyü-**ma**-nu-tē) n. **Humanity** is kindness and caring about the suffering of others. *Firefighters show humanity by doing what they must to save others.*

I

impact (**im**-pakt) n. An **impact** is the effect one thing has on another. *The creative science teacher had a positive impact on her students.*

implement (**im**-plu-ment) v. When you **implement** a plan, you make it happen. *The soccer coach will implement new strategies to help his team win more games.*

incentive (in-**sen**-tiv) n. An **incentive** is something that makes you want to take action. *The sale at the store gave customers an incentive to buy more shirts.*

indignation (in-dig-**nā**-shun) n. **Indignation** is anger caused by something unfair or mean. *He showed indignation when he saw the bully take the cupcake away from the little girl.*

infrastructure (**in**-fru-struk-chur) n. **Infrastructure** is the basic foundation or underlying structure of something. *The infrastructure of the skyscraper was made out of metal beams.*

inherent (in-**her**-unt) adj. If something is **inherent**, it comes naturally. *The girl's inherent helpfulness shows when she helps her father with yard work.*

innocence (**i**-nu-sunts) n. Having **innocence** means not to be guilty of doing something wrong. *His innocence was proven when they discovered that the dog was the one who ate the cookies.*

innovative (**i**-nu-vā-tiv) adj. Something **innovative** uses new ideas. *The new glass building has an innovative design.*

inquiry (**in**-kwu-rē) n. An **inquiry** is a question or investigation. *The police will hold an inquiry to ask people how the accident happened.*

inspiration (in-spu-**rā**-shun) n. An **inspiration** is a reason for doing or creating something. *Artists often find their inspiration in the beauty of nature.*

integrate (**in**-tu-grāt) v. When you **integrate** groups, you bring them together. *Martin Luther King, Jr., worked to integrate schools.*

integrity (in-**te**-gru-tē) n. **Integrity** is behaving in a way that is honest, fair, or right. *The girl showed integrity by returning the wallet she found.*

intense (in-**tens**) adj. Something that is **intense** is very strong. *The intense wind made the trees bend over.*

intent (in-**tent**) n. An **intent** is a plan to do something. *The student studies hard with the intent of passing a difficult test.*

intention (in-**ten**-shun) n. An **intention** is an aim or purpose. *The runner practices hard because his intention is to compete in the Olympics in the future.*

interaction (in-tur-**ak**-shun) n. An **interaction** is when people talk or do activities with one another. *This is an interaction between three friends.*

intervene (in-tur-**vēn**) *v.* When you **intervene**, you do something to change an event or a result. *She intervenes when her sons argue.*

invasion (in-**vā**-zhun) *n.* An **invasion** is when a group forces their way into another place. *There was an invasion of ants at the picnic.*

involve (in-**vawlv**) *v.* To **involve** means to include. *Winning a baseball game may involve speed, strength, and teamwork.*

L

landscape (**land**-skāp) *n.* A **landscape** is an area of land that you can see. *She admired the landscape of the mountains in the distance.*

legendary (**le**-jun-dair-ē) *adj.* A **legendary** figure is a famous person who lived long ago. *Many people know about the legendary figure of Mu Lan.*

M

management (**ma**-nij-munt) *n.* **Management** is the conducting or supervising of something. *The lemonade stand was successful under her management.*

mimic (**mi**-mik) *v.* **Mimic** means to imitate closely. *The mockingbird mimics the sounds of other birds.*

modified (**mo**-du-fīd) *adj.* If something is **modified**, a part of it has been changed. *The modified bus has a lift to raise and lower wheelchairs.*

motivation (mō-tu-**vā**-shun) *n.* **Motivation** is the reason for doing something. *My motivation for studying is to get good grades.*

N

navigation (na-vu-**gā**-shun) *n.* **Navigation** is the method of determining position, course, and distance traveled. *They trusted the captain with the navigation of the ship.*

necessity (ni-**se**-su-tē) *n.* A **necessity** is an item that someone needs. *Food and water are the most basic necessities of life.*

nutritious (nü-**tri**-shus) *adj.* When something is **nutritious**, it is good for you to eat. *An apple is a nutritious addition to your lunch.*

O

obligation (o-bli-**gā**-shun) *n.* An **obligation** is something you must do. *It is the boy's obligation to take care of the dog.*

optional (**ahp**-shu-nul) *adj.* Something that is **optional** is not needed or required. *At our school, learning to play an instrument is an optional activity that you can choose.*

organic (or-**ga**-nik) *adj.* **Organic** refers to a type of food that is all natural. *Organic fruits and vegetables are grown without chemicals.*

overcome (ō-vur-**kum**) *v.* To **overcome** something is to succeed at something that is difficult. *If you used to be afraid of dogs but now you like them, you have overcome your fear.*

P

parasite (**pair**-u-sīt) *n.* A **parasite** is an organism that gets food or shelter from living in or on another organism. *The fleas on the dog were parasites.*

participate (par-**ti**-su-pāt) *v.* When you **participate**, you do something with others. *These students participate on a sports team.*

passage (**pa**-sij) *n.* A **passage** is a road, tunnel, or channel that connects one place to another. *He walked down the passage and reached the main lobby.*

peer (**pear**) *v.* To **peer** means to look at something closely. *The archaeologists peered into the tomb to see the treasure.*

perceive (pur-**sēv**) *v.* When you **perceive** something, you notice or become aware of it. *The men perceive the problem with the bike tire right away.*

perspective (pur-**spek**-tiv) *n.* A **perspective** is a point of view. *The students discussed their different perspectives about the issues.*

Dictionary

pharaoh (**fair**-ō) *n.* A **pharaoh** is a ruler of ancient Egypt. *Ramses II is often called the greatest pharaoh of ancient Egypt.*

plunder (**plun**-dur) *v.* To **plunder** means to take something by force. *The robbers plundered the tomb and left nothing but broken jars behind them.*

policy (**po**-lu-sē) *n.* A **policy** is an official guide to how something should be done. *They followed the policy to keep their school clean.*

pose (**pōz**) *v.* To **pose** means to stand still in a certain position. *The boy poses like a superhero.*

position (pu-**zi**-shun) *n.* A **position** is an official rank or job. *The mayor has a high position in a town's government.*

potential (pu-**ten**-shul) *n.* **Potential** is the ability to change or improve in the future. *She has the potential to become a great basketball player.*

poverty (**po**-vur-tē) *n.* **Poverty** is the state or condition of being poor. *People who live in poverty may not have enough food to eat.*

powerful (**pou**-ur-ful) *adj.* A **powerful** person has the ability to control other people or things. *The powerful judge makes decisions in a courtroom.*

practical (**prak**-ti-kul) *adj.* When something is **practical**, it is reasonable. *When he saved up his money to buy a new skateboard, it was a practical thing to do.*

precious (**pre**-shus) *adj.* When something is **precious**, it is very valuable. *Everyone is precious and cannot be replaced.*

prejudice (**pre**-ju-dus) *n.* If you have **prejudice**, you judge things and people before you know about them. *Many people fought to end prejudice.*

preservation (pre-zur-**vā**-shun) *n.* **Preservation** means to keep something from being lost. *The preservation of culture is important, and that is why people celebrate certain holidays.*

presume (pri-**zūm**) *v.* When you **presume**, you think something is true without being certain. *The judge will presume that this prisoner is innocent until he is proven guilty.*

procession (pru-**se**-shun) *n.* A **procession** is when people move forward together during a ceremony or festival. *Ancient Egyptians held funeral processions when important people died.*

production (pru-**duk**-shun) *n.* **Production** is the creation of something for use. *He helped them in the production of cookies for the bake sale.*

promote (pru-**mōt**) *v.* To **promote** means to give someone a higher rank or position. *The colonel will promote the general to a higher rank.*

protection (pru-**tek**-shun) *n.* **Protection** keeps people, animals, and things safe. *Helmets give protection to the bikers' heads.*

R

react (rē-**akt**) *v.* When you **react**, you respond to something. *This grandmother reacts to the flowers by smiling.*

recover (rē-**ku**-vur) *v.* **Recover** means to get something back. *She recovered her health after having the flu.*

regulate (**re**-gyū-lāt) *v.* When something is **regulated**, it is controlled by rules, a law, or an authority figure. *They regulated how many people could enter the zoo so that it wouldn't become overcrowded.*

reinforce (rē-un-**fors**) *v.* When you **reinforce** something, you make it stronger. *The builders can reinforce the floor by adding extra supports.*

reliance (rē-**lī**-unts) *n.* **Reliance** is the condition of needing something or someone else for help or support. *All humans have a reliance on food.*

representation (rep-ri-zen-**tā**-shun) *n.* A **representation** is a picture or other image that stands for a person or thing. *This statue is a representation of an ancient Egyptian king.*

reputation (re-pyū-**tā**-shun) *n.* A **reputation** is an overall quality or characteristic of a person that others notice. *She had the reputation of being the best at math in the class.*

resemblance (ri-**zem**-blunts) *n.* When things share a **resemblance**, they look alike. *The twins share a strong resemblance because their features are very similar.*

resilience (ri-**zil**-yunts) *n.* When you show **resilience**, you can recover from or adapt to difficult situations. *Plants show* ***resilience*** *by growing in places with little or no soil.*

resistance (ri-**zis**-tunts) *n.* **Resistance** is the act of taking a stand against something. *The cat showed* ***resistance*** *when it refused to go outside.*

resolve (ri-**zolv**) *v.* When you **resolve** to do something, you reach a decision about it. *After seeing the litter, they* ***resolve*** *to pick up trash once a week.*

resourceful (ri-**sors**-ful) *adj.* To be **resourceful** means to be creative in finding new materials for your needs. *She was very* ***resourceful*** *when she used the old egg carton for her art project.*

reveal (ri-**vēl**) *v.* When you **reveal** something, you show or explain it to others. *The magician* ***reveals*** *the rabbit that was in his hat.*

revolt (ri-**vōlt**) *v.* To **revolt** means to renounce all allegiance to a government or figure in power. *There are many instances in history when people* ***revolted*** *against bad leaders.*

S

sensitive (**sen**-su-tiv) *adj.* To be **sensitive** means to be aware of the feelings of others. *She had a* ***sensitive*** *nature and didn't like seeing anyone or anything in pain.*

separate (**se**-pu-rut) *adj.* If you are **separate** from other people, you are not with them. *It is not fun to feel* ***separate*** *from the group.*

significant (sig-**ni**-fi-kunt) *adj.* Something **significant** is important. *Finding King Tut's tomb was a* ***significant*** *discovery for archaeologists.*

simulate (**sim**-yū-lāt) *v.* To **simulate** something is to create an imitation of it. *The girl's model* ***simulates*** *what happens during a volcanic eruption.*

structural (**struk**-chu-rul) *adj.* **Structural** relates to the way something is built or put together. *The wooden frame is the* ***structural*** *support of the house.*

subordinate (su-**bor**-du-nut) *n.* Someone who is **subordinate** is under the power of another. *Emperor Qin had many* ***subordinates*** *who obeyed him.*

subterranean (sub-tu-**rā**-nē-un) *adj.* When something is **subterranean**, it means that it is underground. *The cave had many* ***subterranean*** *tunnels.*

supplement (**su**-plu-munt) *n.* A **supplement** is something that is added to meet a need. *A person who needs more vitamins in his or her diet may take a vitamin* ***supplement***.

survey (sur-**vā**) *v.* When you **survey** something, you study it and measure its properties. *They* ***surveyed*** *the land to see if it would make a good location for a house.*

sustain (su-**stān**) *v.* To **sustain** is to continue or keep up an action, event, or thing. *The runner drinks lots of water to* ***sustain*** *her during the race.*

T

terrain (tu-**rān**) *n.* **Terrain** means the physical features of land. *It was a region with many mountains, and it was difficult to hike over the* ***terrain***.

thrive (**thrīv**) *v.* To **thrive** means to grow strong and healthy. *With lots of care, plants can* ***thrive***.

tolerance (**to**-lu-runts) *n.* When you have **tolerance**, you understand and have respect for beliefs that are different from your own. *He showed* ***tolerance*** *when he took off his baseball cap during the ceremony.*

tomb (**tüm**) *n.* A **tomb** is a grave, or a special place for the body of a dead person. *The discovery of King Tut's* ***tomb*** *was very important to historians and archaeologists.*

transform (trans-**form**) *v.* To **transform** something is to change it. *A gardener* ***transformed*** *an old car into a flower planter.*

U

undertake (un-dur-tāk) *v.* When you **undertake** something, you begin or attempt it. *The man will* **undertake** *a difficult climb up the mountain.*

unify (yū-nu-fī) *v.* To **unify** means to bring together as one. *The two railway lines* **unify** *onto a single track.*

utilize (yū-ti-līz) *v.* When you **utilize** something, you use it to do a job. *The gardeners* **utilize** *a shovel to collect leaves.*

V

variation (vair-ē-ā-shun) *n.* **Variation** is the extent to which a thing changes. *The temperature showed extreme* **variation** *when it snowed in the morning and was sunny in the afternoon.*

virus (vī-rus) *n.* A **virus** is something that causes illness. *When you get sick, you have a* **virus**.

W

welfare (wel-fair) *n.* When you care about the **welfare** of others, you care about their happiness, fortune, and well-being. *He was concerned for the abandoned kitten's* **welfare**, *so he adopted it as his own.*

Index

Acknowledgments, continued

Text Credits

10–23 From Facing the Lion: Growing Up Maasai on the African Savanna by Joseph Lemasolai Lekuton (with Herman Viola). Published by National Geographic Society, 2003.

27–33 Aimee Mullins excerpt from The Moth dated August 6, 2013.

IWB Poem Unit 1 The Road Not Taken by Robert Frost, from the book THE POETRY OF ROBERT FROST edited by Edward Connery Lathem. Copyright © 1916, 1969 by Henry Holt and Company, LLC. Copyright © 1944 by Robert Frost. Used by permission of Henry Holt and Company, LLC. All rights reserved.

42–53 The Drummond Agency Pan Macmillan Australia Pty Ltd Orchard Books. Excerpt from Does My Head Look Big in This? Copyright © Randa Abdel-Fattah, 2005. Reproduced by permission of Scholastic Ltd. and Pan Macmilan Australia Pty Ltd. All rights reserved.

57–61 "The Jacket" from The Circuit by Francisco Jiménez. Copyright © 1997 University of New Mexico Press, 1997.

78–91 Deception: Formula for Survival by Robert F. Sisson, National Geographic Magazine, March 1980, Vol. 157, Issue 3, pages 394–415.

95–101 Living Nightmares by Lynn Brunelle, National Geographic Extreme Explorer, October 2013, pages 2–9.

IWB Poem Unit 2 "The Lichen We" and "Lichens" from Ubiquitous: Celebrating Nature's Survivors by Joyce Sidman, illustrated by Beckie Prange. Text copyright © 2010 by Joyce Sidman. Illustrations copyright © by Beckie Prange. Reprinted by permission of Houghton Mifflin Harcourt Publishing Company. All rights reserved.

110–121 Flannery Literary Agency Margaret K. McElderry, Hatchet by Gary Paulsen, Reprinted with the permission of Atheneum Books for Young Readers, an imprint of Simon & Schuster. Children's Publishing Division from HATCHET by Gary Paulsen. Copyright © 1987 Gary Paulsen.

125–131 Title Town Publishing (Beaufort Books), From the book "When I Fell from the Sky" by Juliane Koepcke. Published by The Reader's Digest Association, Inc. ©2014

IWB Explorer Journal Unit 3 Adapted from Hannah Bloch, "Satellite Archaeology," National Geographic, February 2013, pp.60–61.

148–163 Valley of the Kings by Dr. Kent Weeks, Published by National Geographic Magazine, September 1998. Reprinted with permission from the author.

167–171, Animals Everlasting by A.R. Williams, National Geographic, November 2009.

182–197 From Egyptian Diary: The Journal of Nakht. Text copyright © 2005 by Richard Platt. Reproduced by permission of the publisher, Candlewick Press, on behalf of Walker Books, London.

201–207 From Golden Goblet by Eloise Jarvis McGraw, copyright © 1961, renewed © 1989 by Eloise Jarvis McGraw. Used by permission of Puffin Books, a division of Penguin Group (USA) LLC.

IWB History Article Unit 3 "Deciphering Ancient Language" from National Geographic Investigates—Ancient Egypt: Archaeology Unlocks the Secrets of Egypt's Past by Jill Rubalcaba and Janice Kamrin, pages 13–19. Published by National Geographic Society, 2006.

245–249 Mireya Mayor by Mireya Mayor, National Geographic Society, Copyright 2014.

IWB Persuasive Essay Unit 4 What Good Is Diversity? by Phillip Hoose, From The Race to Save the Lord God Bird © 2004 by Phillip Hoose. Reprinted by permission of Farrar, Straus, and Giroux, LLC. All rights reserved.

258–275 Operation Redwood by S. Terrell French Copyright © 2009 by S. Terrell French Used by permission of Amulet Books, an imprint of Harry N. Abrams, Inc., New York. All rights reserved.

279–283 The Super Trees by Joel Bourne, National Geographic Society, October 2009.

279–283 From "The National Parks and Forest Reservations" by John Muir, Published in Sierra Club Bulletin, Vol. No. 7, 1896, pp. 271–284.

IWB Poem Unit 4 "Transplanting Trees" by Joseph Bruchac and Phillip Carroll Morgan from www.josephbruchac.com.

319–325 Puffin Books, "You're Under Arrest", from ROSA PARKS: MY STORY by Rosa Parks with Jim Haskins, copyright © 1992 by Rosa Parks. Used by permission of Dial Books for Young Readers, a division of Penguin Group (USA) LLC.

IWB Biography Unit 5 Russell & Volkening, Inc., Harriet Tubman by Ann Petry, From "Harriet Tubman: Conductor on the Underground Railroad"

334–351 Book Stop Literacy Agency Simon & Schuster, Inc., Iqbal by Francesco D'Adamo, Reprinted with the permission of Atheneum Books for Young Readers, an imprint of Simon & Schuster Children's Publishing Division from IQBAL by Francesco D'Adamo, translated by Ann Leonori. Copyright © 2001 Edizioni El. English translation copyright © 2003 Ann Leonori.

355–365 Puffin Books, From of Thunder, Hear My Cry by Mildred D. Taylor, copyright © 1976 by Mildred D. Taylor. Used by permission of Dial Books for Young Readers, a division of Penguin Group (USA) LLC.

IWB Persuasive Essay Unit 5 A Conflict Close to Home by Aziz Abu Sarah. Reprinted with permission from the author and National Geographic.

382–395 Seedfolks by Paul Fleischman, Text Copyright © 1997 by Paul Fleischman. Used by permission from HarperCollins Publishers and Paul Fleischman.

399–403 American Express Publishing Corporation, Soup for the Soul by Kristin Donnelly, ©2006 Time Inc. Affluent Media Group. All rights reserved. Reprinted/Translated from Food & Wine and published with permission of 2 Time Inc. Affluent Media Group. Reproduction in any manner in any language in whole or in part without written permission is prohibited.

IWB Social Studies Article Unit 6 "Dwaina Brooks" by Phillip Hoose, From It's Our World Too! © 2002 by Phillip Hoose. Reprinted by permission of Farrar, Straus, and Giroux, LLC. All rights reserved.

412–425 From "Feeding the World in National Geographic Investigates: Genetics—From DNA to Designer Dogs", pages 24–25, by Kathleen Simpson. Published by National Geographic Society, Copyright 2008.

412–425 From "Sustainable Earth: Food" by Brian Handwerk from National Geographic News. Published by National Geographic Society.

412–425 "A Five-Step Plan to Feed the World" by Jonathan Foley, from National Geographic Magazine, May 2014, pages 35, 43, 45, and 46. Published by National Geographic Society.

412–425 From Feeding the World, Sustainable Agriculture from the National Geographic online, http://environment.nationalgeographic .com/environment/habitats/ sustainable-agriculture/#close-modal.

429–433 "How Altered" by Jim Richardson and Jennifer Ackerman, National Geographic Magazine (May 2002), pages 33–50.

429–433 From In Favor of Genetically Modified Foods: New technology can help protect against hunger, by Florence Wambugu, From Dr. Florence Wambugu's publication in The Washington Post, August 26, 2001.

429–433 From Against Genetically Modified Foods: Genetically modified food is a risky form of technology, by Michael Bloch.

IWB Persuasive Essay Unit 6 Irrigation Pumps (edit up) by Sandra Postel, From National Geographic online. http://newswatch .nationalgeographic.com/2012/04/18/the-power -of-a-radically-affordable-irrigation-pump/

450–463 From The Emperor's Silent Army by Jane O'Connor, copyright © 2002 by Jane O'Connor. Used by permission of The Viking Press, a division of Penguin Group (USA) LLC.

467–473 "A Silent Army" from Ancient China—Archaeology Unlocks the Secrets of China's Past, by Jacqueline Ball and Richard Levy, pages 26–33. Published by National Geographic Society/National Geographic Children's Books, 2006.

IWB Profile Unit 7 Christine Lee, National Geographic online biography. Published by the National Geographic Society.

IWB Essay Unit 7 Confucius excerpts from The Chinese Classics. Published by Oxford: Clarendon Press, 1893–1895, translated by James Legge.

482–499 From Where the Mountain Meets the Moon, by Grace Lin. Copyright © 2009 by Grace Lin. Used by permission of Little Brown and Company.

566–579 From Journey to the Center of the Earth by Jules Verne, pages 141–193. Published by Tom Doherty Associates, Inc. Copyright 1988.

IWB Science Fiction Unit 8 David Higham Associates, So You're Going to Mars by Arthur Clarke, From The Snows of Olympus: A Garden on Mars by Arthur C. Clarke. Copyright © 1994 by Arthur C. Clarke. Used by permission of Arthur C. Clarke and W.W. Norton & Company, Inc.

IWB Science Fiction Unit 8 From Journey to the Center of the Earth by Jules Verne. Published by Tom Doherty Associates, Inc. Copyright 1988.

583–589 Deep Into Darkness by Beth Geiger, National Geographic Explorer magazine article from May 2010, pages 16–23

Photographic Credits

v (tr) Tom Brakefield/Latitude/Corbis. **vii** (inset) John Foxx/Imagestate Media. (tl) CORDIER Sylvain/Getty Images. (tc) Pete Oxford/Nature Picture Library. **ix** (tc) ©Kenneth Garrett/National Geographic Creative. **xi** (tc) Juniors Bildarchiv/F291/Alamy. **xiii** (tl) Steven Senne/AP Images. **xv** (tl) ALANAH M. TORRALBA/epa/Corbis. **xvii** (tl) ©O. Louis Mazzatenta/National Geographic Creative. **xix** (tc) ESA/K. Horgan/Stone/Getty Images. **xxi** (br) ©MARK THIESSEN/National Geogrpahic Society. **2–3** Francisco Negroni. **4** (tc) ©VINCENT GRAFHORST/FN/MINDEN PICTURES. (c) ©Frans Lanting/National Geographic Creative. **5** (t) Yann Arthus-Bertrand/Encyclopedia/Corbis. (br) Danita Delimont/Gallo Images/Getty Images. **7** (tl) Janine Wiedel Photolibrary/Alamy. (tc) ©James Wheeler/Shutterstock.com. (bc) Ed Bock/Cusp/Corbis. (bl) Blend Images/KidStock/Getty Images. (tr) ©Margaret M Stewart/Shutterstock.com. **9** (tr) ©Linda H. Crumpecker. **10–11** Richard Du Toit/Minden Pictures/Getty Images. **12** (border) Hugh Sitton/Corbis. **12–13** ©ROY TOFT/National Geographic Creative. **14** (bl) ©Anton_Ivanov/Shutterstock.com. **15** (c) Dlillc/Latitude/Corbis. (border) Hugh Sitton/Corbis. **17** (c) Paul Souders/The Image Bank/Getty Images. (border) Hugh Sitton/Corbis. **18** (t) Tom Brakefield/Latitude/Corbis. (border) Hugh Sitton/Corbis. **20** David Cantrille/Alamy. **22–23** Randy Wells/The Image Bank/Getty Images. **23** (border) Hugh Sitton/Corbis. (br) ©Randy Olson/National Geographic Creative. **24** (br) Tom Brakefield/Latitude/Corbis. **27** Photo courtesy of L'Oréal Paris. **28** Catherine MacBride/Moment/Getty Images. **30** (r) Solve Sundsbo/Art and Commerce. **31** (bc) ©Lynn Johnson/National Geographic Creative. **32** (l) ©Terry Richardson/Art Partner Licensing. **33** (tr) Josh Laverty/iStockphoto/Getty Images. **36** (bc) Jim West/Alamy. **37** (c) Diverse Images/Universal Images Group/Getty Images. **39** (bl) Myrleen Pearson/Alamy. (tr) Christine Schneider/Brigitte Sporrer/Alamy. (bc) Tim Clayton/Corbis Sports/

665

666

Reuters/Corbis. **415** ALANAH M. TORRALBA/epa/
Corbis. **418** (b) Bruce Hands/The Image Bank/
Getty Images. **419** (t) W. Wayne Lockwood, M.D./
CORBIS. (inset) Design Pics/Getty Images. **420** (b)
Jim Richardson/CORBIS. **421** (t) Jacek Boczarski/
Corbis News/Corbis. **422** (tl) D. Hurst/Alamy.
422–423 (b) Michel Setboun/Corbis. **425** (b)
Finbarr O'Reilly/Reuters. **426** (br) Jim Richardson/
CORBIS. **429** AgStock Images, Inc./Alamy.
430–431 (b) fSt Images - Patrick Strattner/
Brand X PicturesGetty Images. **432–433** (b) Jim
Richardson/CORBIS. **433** (br) Lynn Johnson/
Aurora Photos. **436** (t) Bloomberg/Getty Images.
439 (b) ©Miaynata/Shutterstock.com. **440** (tc)
©Peter Essick/National Geographic Creative. **441**
©Ben Shannon/National Geographic Learning. (tr)
Eitan Simanor/Alamy. (br) ©Roxana Gonzalez/
Shutterstock.com. **442–443** Suchet
Suwanmongkol/500Px. **444** (t) ©The Metropolitan
Museum of Art/Art Resource, NY. **447** (tl)
Catchlight Visual Services/Alamy. (tc) Comstock
Images/Getty Images. (cr) Caiaimage/Martin
Barraud/Getty Images. (cl) Nicolas McComber/
Getty Images. (bc) ©Lars Hallstrom/Shutterstock.
com. **449** (bc) Corbis Wire/Corbis. **450** (bl) O.
Louis Mazza Tenta/National Geographic Creative.
450–451 Julian Worker/Alamy. (br) Terracotta
Army, Qin Dynasty, 210 BC. horses and carriage, ./
Tomb of Qin shi Huang Di, Xianyang, China/
Bridgeman Images. **452** (br) ©O. Louis
Mazzatenta/National Geographic Creative. **453** (t)
©Narong Jongsirikul/Shutterstock.com. ©XNR
Productions/National Geographic Learning **454** (c)
Emperor Ch'in Wang Ti (221-206 BC) travelling in
a palanquin, from a history of Chinese emperors
(colour on silk) , Chinese School, (17th century)/
Bibliotheque Nationale, Paris, France/Archives
Charmet/Bridgeman Images. **455** (r) ©O. Louis
Mazzatenta/National Geographic Creative. (border)
©Narong Jongsirikul/Shutterstock.com. **456** (t) A
blue-ground embroidered Kesi dragon robe, detail
of dragon (silk) , Chinese School, Qing Dynasty
(1644-1912)/Private Collection/Photo ©Bonhams,
London, UK/Bridgeman Images. **457** (t) Terracotta
Army, Qin Dynasty, 210 BC. horses and carriage/
Tomb of Qin shi Huang Di, Xianyang, China/
Bridgeman Images. (border) ©Narong Jongsirikul/
Shutterstock.com. **458** (border) ©Narong
Jongsirikul/Shutterstock.com. **459** (c) ©O.Louis
Mazzatenta/National Geographic Creative. **460** (tl)
Imaginechina. **461** (tr) Terracotta Army, Qin
Dynasty, 210 BC. warriors (detail)/Tomb of Qin shi
Huang Di, Xianyang, China/Bridgeman Images.
462 (c) ©O. Louis Mazzatenta/National
Geographic Creative. (border) ©Narong
Jongsirikul/Shutterstock.com. **463** (cr) ©O. Louis
Mazzatenta/National Geographic Creative. (border)
©Narong Jongsirikul/Shutterstock.com. **464** (b) A
blue-ground embroidered Kesi dragon robe, detail
of dragon (silk) , Chinese School, Qing Dynasty
(1644-1912)/Private Collection/Photo ©Bonhams,
London, UK/Bridgeman Images. **467** (c) Corbis
Wire/Corbis. **469** (tl) O. Louis Mazzatenta/
National Geographic Creative. (r) ©O.Louis
Mazzatenta/National Geographic Creative. **472** (cl)
ChinaFotress/Getty Images. **473** (tr) ©O. Louis
Mazzatenta/National Geographic Creative. **479** (cr)
Jutta Klee/Canopy/Corbis. (bl) Hill Street Studios/
Blend Images/Corbis. (cl) Jupiterimages/Getty
Images. (c) Pamela Moore/Getty Images. (bc) Win
McNamee/Getty Images. **481** (b) ©Daniana/
Shutterstock.com. **485** (b) stockcam/Getty Images.
499 (cl) ©Alexandre Ferron. **518** (tr) View Stock/
Alamy. **522** (tc) Suchet Suwanmongkol/500Px.
523 (bl) ©O. Louis Mazzatenta/National
Geographic Creative. (tr) Charles & Josette Lenars/
Encyclopedia/Corbis. (bc) ©XNR Productions/
National Geographic Learning. (br) Terracotta
Army, Qin Dynasty, 210 BC. warriors (detail)/
Tomb of Qin shi Huang Di, Xianyang, China/
Bridgeman Images. **524–525** Francisco Negroni.
526 (c) Monashee Frantz/OJO Images Ltd/Alamy.
(c) AP Images/NASA, Jet Propulsion Laboratory's.
(cr) 167/Pete Ryan/Ocean/Corbis. **529** (c) Tim
Gainey/Alamy. (cl) Radius Images/Alamy. (cr) Mark
Sykes/Science Photo Library/Alamy. (cr) Steve
Goodwin/Getty Images. (bc) Oli Scarff/Getty
Images. **531** (cr) ©JPL/NASA. **532–533** Denis
Scott/Motif/Corbis. **534** (br) Science & Society
Picture Library/Getty Images. **535** (l) ©Ira Block/

National Geographic Creative. (bg) Gyro
Photography/Amana images inc/Alamy. **536** (bg)
Gyro Photography/Amana images inc/Alamy. **537**
(bg) Gyro Photography/Amana images inc/Alamy.
538 (b) ©Ralph Lee Hopkins/National Geographic
Creative. **539** (tr) World History Archive/Alamy.
540 (b) ©Peter Essick/Nationa Geographic
Creative. **541** (r) AP Images/NASA/JPL-Caltech/
MSSS/Rex. **542** (bc). (br) Usgs Eros/Nasa. (br) 167/
Pete Ryan/Ocean/Corbis. **543** (b) Gary Crabbe/
Alamy. (cl) Aimin Tang/Getty Images. (bl) Caltech/
Nasa/Jpl. (br) Caltech/Cornell University/Nasa/Jpl.
547 (tl) Wolfgang Bechtold/imageBROKER/Alamy.
548 (br) 167/Pete Ryan/Ocean/Corbis. **551** NASA/
JPL. **552** (tr) ESA/K. Horgan/Stone/Getty Images.
(cr) NASA-JPL-Caltech - Mars Rover/digital version
by Science Faction/Getty Images. **553** (cr)
Bettmann/Corbis. (bl) Scott Tysick/Masterfile. **554**
(bl) Scott Tysick/Masterfile. **555** (tr) Time Life
Pictures/NASA/Getty Images. (tl) InterNetwork
Media/Getty Images. (tl) Science Source. (cl)
Science Source. **556** (br) NASA/World History
Archive & ARPL/Alamy. (tl) Stocktrek Images/
Getty Images. **557** (c) Reuters/Corbis. (tr) World
Perspectives/Getty Images. **560** (c) Mark Andrew
Kirby/Getty images. (b) ©John Eastcott and Yva
Momatiuk/National Geographic Creative. **561** (tr)
Robbie Shone/Aurora Photos (RM)/Corbis. (cl)
©Francois-Xavier De Ruydts. (br) Ken Rygh
Creative Art & Design/Getty Images. (br) Mordolff/
Getty Images. **563** (bl) Joerg Reuther/ImageBroker/
Alamy. (bc) Kennan Harvey/Aurora Open/Aurora
Photos/Alamy. (tl) darryl gill/Alamy. (tr) Vstock FD/
Alamy. **579** (cl) Apic/Getty Images. (bl) Zigy
Kaluzny/Getty Images. **583** (c) ©Stephen Alvarez/
National Geographic Creative. **584** (t) ©Stephen
Alvarez/National Geographic Creative. **585** (tl)
©Stephen Alvarez/National Geographic Creative.
(r) ©Stephen Alvarez/National Geographic
Creative. **586** (tl) ©Stephen Alvarez/National
Geographic Creative. **587** (br) ©Stephen Alvarez/
National Geographic Creative. (tr) ©Stephen
Alvarez/National Geographic Creative. **588** (tr)
©Stephen Alvarez/National Geographic Creative.
(tr) ©Stephen Alvarez/National Geographic
Creative. **589** (tr) ©Stephen Alvarez/National
Geographic Creative. **589** (cr) ©Visual Ulimited/
Nature Picture Library. **592** (tr) Arnold Metzinger/
dieKleinert/Alamy. **596** (tc) ©Francisco Negron.
597 (b) ©Jose Antonio Perez/Shutterstock.com. (tr)
NASA/JPL. **602** (br) Jagdish Agarwal/Corbis
Yellow/Corbis. **603** (tr) Jupiterimages/Getty images.
604 (cl) ©Yuri Arcuri/Shutterstock. **610** (b) Jim
Arbogast/Photodisc/Getty Images. **612** (t) Frans
Lanting/National Geographic Creative; (b) Glove
Turner, LLC/Getty Images. **613** (br) Image Source/
Superstock. **614** (bl) Anthony Bannister/Gallo
Images/Getty Images. **615** (br) ©Andrew
Tichovolsky/Shutterstock.com. **619** (br) Pete
Oxford/Minden Pictures. (t) ©Andrew
Tichovolsky/Shutterstock.com. **621** (tl)
©icyimage/Shutterstock.com. (br) ©icyimage/
Shutterstock.com. **624** (tr) ©Stuart Miles/
Shutterstock.com. (br)©Graça Victoria/
Shutterstock.com. **625** (tr) ©jocicalek/
Shutterstock.com. **628** (tr, tcr) Stockbyte/Getty
Images. (cbr) Comstock/Jupiterimages. (cr)
©Foodcollection/Stockfood America. (b) ©LianeM/
Shutterstock.com. **631** (bc, br) ©Jani Bryson/
iStockphoto.com. (br) Nathan Blaney/Getty images.
632 (cr) Comstock Images/Getty Images. **634** (cr)
Travel Pictures/Alamy. **635** (tr) Medioimages/
Photodisc/Getty images. (tr) Stockbyte Food/Getty
Images. (tr) ©Goodshoot/Jupiterimages. **636** (br)
Myrleen Pearson/Alamy. **638** (cr) ©IIIadam36III/
Shutterstock.com. **639** (b) ©Simone van den Berg/
Shutterstock.com. **640** (b) Dave King/Dorling
Kindersley/Getty Images. **641** (cr) ©Sonya
Etchison/Shutterstock.com. **642** (br) Jim West/
Alamy. **647** (tr) ©Judy Kennamer/iStockphoto.com.
649 (cl) Catchlight Visual Services/Alamy. (tr)
Andersen Ross/Blend Images/Getty Images. **650**
(bl) Aaron McCoy/Photodisc/Getty Images. (cr)
Alistair Flack/Alamy. **651** (tl) Caiaimage/Martin
Barraud/Getty Images. (cr) ©Margaret M Stewart/
Shutterstock.com. **652** (tl) Nicolas McComber/
Getty Images. (br) Christine Schneider/Brigitte
Sporrer/Alamy. **653** (tl) MachineHeadz/Getty
Images. (tr) Blend Images/KidStock/Getty Images.

654 (cl) Ed Bock/Cusp/Corbis. (cr) SW
Productions/Age Fotostock. **655** (tl) Jim Parkin/
Alamy. (cr) Chris McGrath/Getty Images Sport/
Getty Images. **656** (tl) Jim West/Alamy

Illustrator Credits

67 (bl) ©National Geographic Learning. **87**
(b) ©ROBERT E. HYNES/National Geographic
Creative. (c) ©ROBERT E. HYNES/National
Geographic Creative. (t) ©ROBERT E. HYNES/
National Geographic Creative. **239** ©Jenny
Wang/National Geographic Creative. **239** (br)
©Equator Graphics/National Geographic Learning.
257 (c) ©Alexander Ryabintsev/Shutterstock.
com. **416–417** ©Mapping Specialists/National
Geographic learning. **445** (c) Eastphoto/Alamy. **461**
(bl) Bettmann/Corbis. **470–471** ©Hsien-Min Yang/
National Geographic Creative. **536–537** (b) ©SW
Inforgraphics LLC/National Geographic Creative